Dear Maggie and David
Thank you for all
and look forw'd
intellectual adru
Warmest regards
Amrita

rt,
'

£ 80.00

13D
14c

4

# International Trade and Developing Countries

This book provides a much-needed study of the bargaining coalitions of developing countries in the GATT and WTO. It traces, explains and theorises on the formation and achievements of coalitions from 1982 to the present day.

Bargaining together in groups is common practice in international negotiations and the limited bargaining power of developing countries makes coalitions an especially crucial instrument for their effective diplomacy. This book investigates the relevance and workability of coalitions as an instrument of bargaining power for the weak and analyses the coalition strategies of developing countries at the inter-state level.

The book focuses principally on coalitions involving developing countries and international trade. Through the case studies of the Uruguay Round and an analytical overview of more recent coalitions, the book fills a significant gap in the literature of international political economy and international relations.

**Amrita Narlikar** completed her D.Phil. in International Relations at Balliol College in 2000 and is now a research fellow at St John's College, Oxford. Her current research focuses on international economic organisations, trade negotiations and the diplomacy of emerging powers.

# RIPE series in global political economy

Series Editors: Louise Amoore
*University of Newcastle, UK*
Randall Germain
*Carleton University, Canada*
Rorden Wilkinson
*University of Manchester, UK*

Formerly edited by Otto Holman, Marianne Marchand (*Research Centre for International Political Economy, University of Amsterdam*), Henk Overbeek (*Free University, Amsterdam*) and Marianne Franklin (*University of Amsterdam*).

This series, published in association with the *Review of International Political Economy*, provides a forum for current debates in international political economy. The series aims to cover all the central topics in international political economy and to present innovative analyses of emerging topics. The titles in the series seek to transcend a state-centred discourse and focus on three broad themes:

- the nature of the forces driving globalisation forward
- resistance to globalisation
- the transformation of the world order.

The series comprises two strands:

The *RIPE Series in Global Political Economy* aims to address the needs of students and teachers, and the titles will be published in hardback and paperback. Title include:

**Transnational Classes and International Relations**
*Kees van der Pijl*

**Gender and Global Restructuring**
Sightings, sites and resistances
*Edited by Marianne H. Marchand and Anne Sisson Runyan*

**Global Political Economy**
Contemporary theories
*Edited by Ronen Palan*

**Ideologies of Globalization**
Contending visions of New World Order
*Mark Rupert*

**The Clash within Civilisations**
Coming to terms with cultural conflicts
*Dieter Senghaas*

**Global Unions?**
Theory and strategies of organized labour in the
global political economy
*Edited by Jeffrey Harrod and Robert O'Brien*

**Political Economy of a Plural World**
Critical reflections on power, morals and civilizations
*Robert Cox with Michael Schechter*

**A Critical Rewriting of Global Political Economy**
Integrating reproductive, productive and virtual economies
*V. Spike Peterson*

*Routledge/RIPE Studies in Global Political Economy* is a forum for innovative new research intended for a high-level specialist readership, and the titles will be available in hardback only. Titles include:

* Also available in paperback

# International Trade and Developing Countries

## Bargaining coalitions in the GATT & WTO

**Amrita Narlikar**

Routledge
Taylor & Francis Group

LONDON AND NEW YORK

First published 2003
by Routledge
11 New Fetter Lane, London EC4P 4EE

Simultaneously published in the USA and Canada
by Routledge
29 West 35th Street, New York, NY 10001

*Routledge is an imprint of the Taylor & Francis Group*

Typeset in Baskerville by
Newgen Imaging Systems (P) Ltd, Chennai, India
Printed and bound in Great Britain by
Biddles Ltd, Guildford and King's Lynn

*British Library Cataloguing in Publication Data*
A catalogue record for this book is available from the British Library

*Library of Congress Cataloging in Publication Data*
A catalog record for this book has been requested

ISBN 0–415–31859–9

To
**Aruna and Anant**
&
**Batasha**

# Contents

**9   Conclusion**                                                                                      **196**

# Illustrations

**Figure**

**Tables**

# Series preface

The story of international trade regulation in the postwar period is a tale of institutional discrimination. The World Trade Organisation's (WTO) predecessor – the General Agreement on Tariffs and Trade (GATT) – instituted a highly discriminatory process of trade liberalisation wherein the economic preferences of the advanced industrial states prevailed over those of their less able developing counterparts. The creation of the WTO in January 1995 promised the beginning of a new era in international trade wherein developing country access to key markets would no longer be restricted by the limitations of the GATT and all states would be able to participate on an equitable footing.

The promise of a new era was, however, short-lived. The WTO's third ministerial meeting in late 1999 witnessed not only public dissatisfaction on the streets of Seattle, but also a revolt by developing countries. The result was the postponement of the launch of a new round of trade negotiations and the crystallisation of inertia within the Organisation; the response was the instigation of a process of courtship designed, at one and the same time, to nurture public confidence in the WTO and bring developing countries back to the negotiating table. Eventually, assisted to a large degree by the conciliatory international political climate that followed the September 2001 terrorist attacks in New York and Washington, a new trade round was launched at the WTO's fourth ministerial meeting (November 2001) in Doha (officially titled the 'Doha Agenda').

Reflecting the post-Seattle bargain reached between the key protagonists, the new round placed 'development' at its core. However, preliminary reports suggest it has been far from successful. To date negotiations in key areas have stalled or collapsed and, in some cases, failed to get underway. Indeed, it appears that solutions to the disadvantages that the developing countries face in participating in international trade remain as elusive as ever.

Set against this backdrop, Amrita Narlikar's book contributes to understanding the plight of developing countries in international trade and the strategies they have employed to offset the biases with which they have been faced in an important and intellectually challenging way. Narlikar offers a meticulous and critical examination of the relevance and workability of coalitions as instruments to bolster the bargaining power of developing countries in trade negotiations. Drawing upon and contributing to theoretical understandings of coalitions, Narlikar analyses four types of developing country coalitions (bloc, alliance, combination and regionalist) from 1982 to 2001 – precisely the era in which tensions between developed and developing states have been at their highest. In doing so, she seeks answers to five key questions:

1    What are the foundations upon which each coalition has been built and how, if at all, have these changed through time?
2    What are the successes and failures of each type of coalition?
3    What are the strengths and limitations of each coalition and to what extent have these been determined by exogenous and endogenous factors?
4    What strategies have coalitions employed to their advantage?
5    What factors account for the demise or survival of each coalition?

By conducting a comparative analysis, Narlikar is able to generate conclusions that not only contribute greater depth and precision to the study of coalitions but which also have real-world prescriptive value. Given the disadvantages that developing countries continue to face, Narlikar's book is a welcome and timely contribution. It is of equal relevance to students and scholars of international political economy and international relations as it is to those practitioners navigating the turbulent waters of trade politics. It deserves to be read by all.

Louise Amoore, Randall Germain, Rorden Wilkinson
Newcastle, Aberystwyth and Manchester, May 2003

# Acknowledgements

The challenge of writing this book may have been overwhelming, had it not been for the many individuals and institutions who recognised that the bargaining experiences of developing countries in the GATT/WTO must be recounted and analysed. The recognition stemmed not only from an interest in documenting some fascinating and untold histories, but from the fact that many of the experiences of the past affect the present and future negotiating positions and strategies of developing countries. As a result, many diplomats and international bureaucrats were very forthcoming in sharing their experiences. My research draws extensively from their accounts. For obvious reasons, these protagonists requested anonymity and I have not attributed any comments or quotations to them in the text. But this book could not have been written without their generous recollections and insights, and I am extremely grateful to them.

Although I cannot mention the names of my interviewees, I would like to extend my profuse thanks to several people in the diplomatic circles for some very stimulating discussions and their help with access to documents. In particular, my thanks go to Rudolf Adlung, K. G. A. Hill, Mohan Kumar, Mina Mashayekhi, S. Narayanan, S. I. M. Nayyar, Siva Palayathan, S. P. Shukla, Sherry Stephenson, Tran Van Thinh, Chakravarthi Raghavan, Rubens Ricupero, Tokio Yamaoka and B. K. Zutshi. The staff of the UNCTAD and the WTO were very obliging in their assistance with documents and contacts.

While the pages that follow were written at Oxford, my interest in inter-state bargaining, particularly from the perspective of developing countries, goes back to my days as a student at the School of International Studies, Jawaharlal Nehru University. Under the tutelage of many accomplished teachers, especially Kanti Bajpai, Ashok Guha and Pushpesh Pant, I found excitement and challenge in the study of International Relations. A large part of the research for this book was conducted when I was still writing my doctoral thesis at Oxford. I must therefore thank Ngaire Woods for her supervision and useful suggestions.

My work on this manuscript benefited immensely from the close interest, critical comments, and stimulating discussions with Andrew Hurrell, Diana Tussie, and John Odell. I would also like to thank Robert Stern, David Stasavage, Louise Fawcett, Rosemary Foot, and Yuen Foong Kong for their interest and advice. Finally, I may never have completed the journey from the initial draft to this book were it not for Desmond King and Rorden Wilkinson. Desmond King has been the rarest of mentors and I cannot thank him enough for his inspiring guidance and unqualified support throughout. Rorden Wilkinson was the perfect editor and colleague. He was constructive in his criticism, extremely generous with new ideas, and also remarkably patient.

The first part of this work was begun at Balliol College, under the generous support of the Inlaks Foundation and several research grants from the college. Much of it was written at St John's College, Oxford. I am indebted to the college for providing all the necessary financial and institutional support. I would like to extend my gratitude to the very efficient and helpful editorial and production team at Routledge. The manuscript benefited enormously from the comments of three anonymous referees.

I owe much gratitude to my friends for their constant loyalty, but a special note of thanks is due to Linda and Moreton Moore for the many delightful vacations that I spent with them. My greatest debt is to my parents for instilling in me the spirit of intellectual enquiry, for their lively guidance throughout, for their enduring forbearance and for being my inspiration.

# Abbreviations

| | |
|---|---|
| ACP | African, Caribbean, and Pacific |
| ADD | Anti-Dumping Duty |
| AEC | African Economic Community |
| AFTA | Free Trade Area |
| AGC | ASEAN Geneva Committee |
| APEC | Asia–Pacific Economic Cooperation |
| ASEAN | Association of South East Asian Nations |
| BOP | Balance of Payments |
| CAFOD | Catholic Fund for Overseas Development |
| CAP | Common Agricultural Policy (of the EC) |
| CARICOM | Caribbean Community |
| CEAO | Communauté de Etats de l'Afrique de l'Ouest |
| CED | Construction and Engineering Design |
| CRNM | Caribbean Regional Negotiating Machinery |
| CU | Customs union |
| CVD | countervailing duty |
| DSM | Dispute Settlement Mechanism |
| DSU | Dispute Settlement Understanding |
| EC | European Community |
| ECLAC | Economic Commission for Latin America and the Caribbean |
| EEP | Export Enhancement Program |
| ENT | Economic Needs Test |
| EU | European Union |
| f.o.b. | free-on-board |
| FIG | Food Importers Group |
| FTAA | Free Trade Area of the Americas |
| GATS | General Agreement on Trade in Services |
| GATT | General Agreement on Tariffs and Trade |
| GDP | gross domestic product |
| GNS | Group of Negotiations on Services |
| GSP | Generalized System of Preferences |
| HODs | Heads of Delegations |
| ICITO | Interim Commission for the International Trade Organisation |
| IGDC | Informal Group of Developing Countries |

| | |
|---|---|
| IMF | International Monetary Fund |
| IO | International Organisation |
| IPC | Integrated Progamme for Commodities |
| IPR | Intellectual Property Rights |
| IR | International Relations |
| IRS | increasing returns to scale |
| ISI | import-substituted industrialisation |
| ITC | International Trade Centre |
| ITO | International Trade Organisation |
| LAFTA | Latin American Free Trade Area |
| LAIA | Latin American Integration Association |
| LDC | least developed country |
| LMG | Like-Minded Group |
| MERCOSUR | Southern Common Market (Mercado Común del Sur) |
| MFA | Multi-Fibre Agreement |
| MFN | most favoured nation |
| MNC | Multi-National Corporation |
| MTN | Multilateral Trade Negotiation |
| NAFTA | North American Free Trade Agreement |
| NAM | Non-Aligned Movement |
| NGO | non-governmental organization |
| NIC | Newly Industrialising Country |
| NIEO | New International Economic Order |
| NOPEC | Non-Oil Power Exporting Countries |
| NTB | non-tariff barrier |
| NTM | non-tariff measure |
| OAU | Organisation of African Unity |
| OLADE | Latin American Energy Organisation (Organización Latinamericano de Energía) |
| OPEC | Organisation of Petroleum Exporting Countries |
| PT&T | Postal, Telegraph and Telephone |
| RI | regional integration |
| RTA | Regional Trade Agreement |
| S&D | Special and Differential |
| SAARC | South Asian Association for Regional Cooperation |
| SEACEN | The South East Asian Central Banks |
| SELA | Latin American Economic System (Sistema Económica Latinamericano) |
| SSA | Sub-Saharan Africa |
| STABEX | Stabilisation of Export Earnings |
| TNC | Trans-National Corporation |
| TPRM | Trade Policy Review Mechanism |
| TRIPS | Trade-Related Intellectual Property Rights |
| UNCTAD | United Nations Conference on Trade and Development |
| UNDP | United Nations Development Programme |
| VER | Voluntary Export Restraint |
| WTO | World Trade Organization |

# Introduction

Friendship in men is due to mutual deeds of obligation
Among birds and beasts when there is a cause
Among fools when faced with fear or greed
But the wise unite at first sight.

(*Panchatantra*, Book II, Verse 35)

United we stand, divided we fall. The reasoning of the weak in their dealings with the strong is simple and direct. But successful coalition building has proven to be a difficult and expensive process. Allies are often not obvious and need to be carefully identified. Large numbers do not necessarily entail a proportionate increase in influence. And the weak have the choice of balancing against or bandwagoning with the strong. Even after it has been organised, collective action entails costs. This book focuses on the opportunities and constraints that developing countries have faced in the formation and maintenance of coalitions in trade in services. It addresses the question: What does the experience to date tell us about the conditions under which various coalition types are likely to form and to have success in influencing bargaining outcomes?

## The problem: what kinds of coalitions work, and why?

Precisely how various entities – individuals and states – choose their friends is a question that has attracted cross-disciplinary attention. For the discipline of International Relations, the subject has had recognised theoretical and empirical import for two obvious reasons. First, inter-state alignments have a critical impact on the stability or otherwise of the international system. There already exists a vast amount of scholarship devoted to analysing the implications of multi-polar versus bipolar alliance structures for war and peace. Second, inter-state groupings are important not only for systemic reasons but also for the opportunities and constraints that they beget member countries. The importance of these opportunities and constraints is only enhanced if member countries are small and weak. But writings in this area are somewhat limited even in the realm of security studies; in international political economy, and especially with respect to the developing world involved in international trade negotiations, they are minuscule. It is the second reason, that is the importance of coalitions as instruments for gaining advantage in international negotiations, that provides the main impetus for this study. More specifically, the book explores the relevance and workability of coalitions as an instrument of bargaining power for the weak in the General Agreement on Tariffs and Trade (GATT) and the World Trade Organisation (WTO).

Coalitions are obviously not restricted to the area of trade. Developing countries have sought bargaining leeway through coalitions that vary across institutions. Prominent examples include the G-77 in the United Nations Conference on Trade and Development (UNCTAD), the G-24 in the International Monetary Fund, and the Afro-Asian Unity and the Non-Aligned Movement in the General Assembly and other UN bodies. But coalitions in the GATT and the WTO pose a greater challenge. Their record is difficult to trace because they did not enjoy the same institutionalisation in the GATT, which they did in various UN bodies. GATT officials reiterated the operation of 'consensus'-based decision-making procedures, and refused to acknowledge the existence of some well-entrenched coalitions. The limited institutionalisation and lack of recognition, in turn, adversely affected their effectiveness.[1] In other words, coalitions in the GATT present a particularly hard case that demands answers, in terms of secondary empirical writings as well as theoretical insights into their formation and maintenance. Further, it may be hoped that any theories that work for a hard case are also likely to have some applicability in other cases where institutional conditions are less adverse for coalition formation.

An analysis of coalitions in the GATT/WTO is not only intellectually challenging, but also has immense topical significance. The increasing encroachments of the WTO into areas traditionally seen as lying within domestic economic jurisdiction place new imperatives upon developing countries. However, they also allow developing countries more bargaining chips and a possibility of placing their own agenda onto the negotiating table. Coalitions provide developing countries with a means of capitalising on the new opportunities. Services present one such critical issue area where stakes for countries – developed and developing – are very high. But the issue area of services is of special relevance to this work (as a work on coalitions involving developing countries in the GATT/WTO) for a different reason. The entry of services into GATT discussions provided the critical turning point where traditional patterns of coalition diplomacy of developing countries collapsed. In their place emerged several new coalition experiments. This new phase of coalitions, characterised by a very rapid turnover and divided loyalties, entailed considerable costs for developing countries. Stability of allies is a crucial asset for the weak. A lack of such allies results in renewed transaction costs every time a new negotiation begins or a new sub-sector comes up for discussion. The resulting instability and its adverse impact on the already limited bargaining power of developing countries make the need for a study such as this one even more pressing.

The aim of this book is to analyse the coalition strategies of developing countries at the inter-state level, particularly in the context of international trade. A two-pronged methodology is used to approach this question. First, I present an empirical account of coalitions involving developing countries, from 1982 to 2001, with a focus on the issue area of services. Second, I engage with some key theoretical issues and suggest an alternative theoretical framework with which to approach inter-state coalitions. The process of doing this involves an investigation into possible and viable bases to coalition formation, the ways in which states choose their allies, the intra-coalition deals that are made to sustain the coalition, and the relationship of the coalition with states and institutions outside. By answering these questions, the book provides a framework of conditions that enable effective coalition formation, offers a typology of coalitions, assesses the relevance of each method of coalition formation and maintenance with reference to country profiles, and also identifies strategies that can be used to bolster intra-coalition cohesion and increase external influence. What emerges in the end is a theory of inter-state bargaining coalitions with some definite policy implications.

## Methodology

Given the nature of the enquiry, the book uses theoretical and empirical methods to complement each other. The theoretical approach is used as a first cut and draws hints from a plethora of writings: formal theories of clubs and coalitions, theories of domestic political economy and theories of international relations. It is found that these theories offer some critical insights into the various kinds of cements that can bind a coalition together and also highlight some of the problems of coalition building. But they still do not answer the key question: given all the methods suggested by these theories, on what basis do states, particularly weak states, choose their allies? Chapter 1 attempts to overcome this shortcoming by aggregating and systematising the insights of these theories. Such an aggregation is not entirely fruitless as it facilitates the development of a typology of coalitions based on the different methods that various theoretical approaches suggest for their construction and maintenance. But the exercise in aggregation also proves useful in identifying issues that these theoretical approaches miss, and without which no theory of coalitions – at least at the level of inter-state relations – can be complete. How states choose their allies cannot be understood without taking the context into account. 'Context' here includes the institution in which the coalition operates, the nature of state interests, the particular issue, the stage in the negotiation, support and opposition outside, the nature of the agenda, and the range of strategies available. At this point, an empirical analysis of comparable coalitions becomes necessary to assist in theorising. The empirical content of the book provides illustrations of which method of coalition formation has worked and which has not, and in what circumstances.

Chapters 2–8 deal directly with the empirical record. Chapter 2 examines the institutional opportunities and constraints that the GATT and the WTO have presented to developing countries and the importance that coalition-building has in this context. Reasons for focusing mainly (though not exclusively) on the services sector are explained. Chapters 3–8 focus on the coalitions. Within the nearly two decades covered in the book, it is possible to see two phases of coalition formation. The first phase extends from 1982 to 1998. Even while straddling two institutions, these years present the pre-negotiation, negotiation, and implementation of the Uruguay Round. They also provide the stage on which a variety of coalition experiments were played out. Chapters 3–7 present case studies of coalition types that we find in this phase, with each chapter analysing one coalition type. The run-up to the Seattle Ministerial in 1998 inaugurated the second phase with preparations to launch a new round (later materialising in the Doha Development agenda). The coalitions from 1998 onwards build significantly on the lessons of the Uruguay Round, resulting not in entirely new coalition types but in interesting permutations of the old types with some new effects. Chapter 8 analyses some of these permutations in the build-up to the Ministerials at Seattle and Doha. As the post-1998 coalitions represent combinations of the coalitions already discussed in the four preceding chapters, the eighth chapter is more of an overview of recent coalitions rather than one presenting a fifth category of coalitions. Through the case studies of the Uruguay Round (Chapters 3–7) and an analytical overview of more recent coalitions (Chapter 8), the book fills a gap in the literature of international political economy and international relations where most GATT/WTO-based coalitions have eluded record.

The close relationship that the empirical analysis bears with theory building makes it more than just an interesting historical account of a story still largely untold. To utilise the empirical research to its maximum advantage, a comparative method is used. The book presents studies of different coalition types involving developing countries in the issue area of trade in services. Each case study is subject to a similar set of questions such as: On what basis was the coalition structured and did this change over time? What was its record of successes and failures? What were the conditions that proved necessary and sufficient for the successes of the coalition? What were the strengths and limitations of the coalition, and to what extent were these determined by internal or external factors? What strategies did the coalition employ to its advantage? Finally, what were the reasons for the survival or collapse of the coalition? The end result of employing a comparative method is that the case studies yield more than simply the specifics of each coalition type. Rather, some general rules that apply across coalition types emerge with respect to corresponding country profiles. These rules, which promise generalisability and some policy-prescriptive value, pertain to both the structure of the coalition and processes that can be used to buttress it.

Questions that the book chooses not to answer also affect the choice of methods employed. For instance, the book addresses the question of coalitions at the inter-state level and hence operates only minimally at the domestic level. There are four reasons for this, which are elaborated in the next chapter while discussing the usefulness of theories of domestic political economy for the study, but are worth highlighting here. First, as the book addresses the question of inter-state coalition formation rather than the formation of state interests, interests of states are assumed as given and are found most easily in national statistics. Second, in the case of developing countries, domestic lobbies have played a much smaller role in determining foreign economic policy than in the developed democracies.

Third, the abstruse Green Room consultative process that underlies GATT/WTO negotiations, even until recently, remained relatively impervious to direct domestic pressures. Hence the 'national interest' of the black box of the state is more easily represented in the GATT/WTO than in most other institutions. Finally, there are several theories and case studies that deal with domestic trade coalitions and their agenda (e.g. protectionist versus free trade), but very few that examine the question of inter-state trade coalitions. As a result, the enquiry in this book is conducted mainly at the inter-state level, though some attempt has been made to incorporate the role of domestic lobbies in situations where they have been particularly active. Similarly, by addressing the subjects of coalitions in a GATT/WTO context, it is recognised that the theoretical implications of the book will have the most direct relevance for coalitions operating in the same institutional context. While at least some of the theoretical lessons of the study will be of use for developing countries in other institutions as well, it is worth emphasising that all theoretical insights that emerge in the book are limited to bargaining coalitions working *within* multilateral institutions. Such coalitions are to be distinguished from groups of countries that promote cooperation within themselves in that there is a clear outside (e.g. non-group members participating in the institution) towards which the joint bargaining is directed.

A note on the sources is relevant at this point. Documenting the cases was a difficult task and encountered many of the problems faced by writers of contemporary history. Secondary writing on the elusive coalitions of developing countries in the GATT and the WTO is extremely limited, and hence primary sources were crucial. The main problem here was the selective institutional recognition of GATT coalitions, which means that there were very few direct references to group activity in GATT and WTO documents (especially until the end of the Uruguay Round). Nonetheless, coalition behaviour is traceable when certain groups of countries operate jointly in preparatory committees and produce joint proposals. The consistency with which the group operates provides some indication as to the coherence that the group enjoys, and is hence also one of the indicators of its survival and sustainability. Documents from the WTO proved vital in tracing this behaviour, even if they did not refer to it as 'coalition' activity. Many of the coalitions in the GATT, especially some bloc-type ones, worked in association with UNCTAD-led research initiatives, and hence UNCTAD documents provided a useful record. The personal accounts of some of the key diplomats – found as records of their speeches and written accounts, and further procured through interviews – shed interesting light on the undocumented 'Green Room diplomacy' of the GATT. But given the political and often polemical character of coalition diplomacy, it was necessary to conduct interviews not just with insiders but also with outsiders of a group. Overall, interviews have been used only to assist in the interpretation of a wide selection of documents. An analysis of the actual interests of the states, as demonstrated in trade shares, helped sift the rhetorical aspects of diplomacy from the 'real', or explain the interplay between the two in certain coalition types. Having this eclectic mix of sources proved enormously useful in piecing together a story that has so far largely remained a puzzle.

## The argument

On the basis of its theoretical and empirical findings, the book argues that coalitions reveal effectiveness and longevity only under certain conditions. This, however, does not mean that every coalition is a shot in the dark, completely dependent on external conditions or random context with no rules to ensure success. Rather, conditions conducive to the coalition are not just external to it but also internal, and depend on the nature of its membership. Only some kinds of coalitions work for certain countries. Coalition types that match with country types are specified, as are the various methods of coalition construction and maintenance that work best in specified circumstances. The end product is a theoretical framework that takes into consideration both the inside and the outside of the coalition under construction. It addresses the contributions and deficiencies of existing theories by providing some answers as to how states can choose optimally between the different methods of coalition formation, suggested by the existing theoretical approaches, and adding new methods and strategies where the old theories are silent. The framework provides guidelines as to when it will be most useful for a country to bandwagon or balance; how interests, ideas, and identity balance out in various situations; whether the coalition should operate across issues or focus at the level of the sub-sector; the point at which defection becomes likely; and how the nature of the coalition itself evolves with progress in the negotiations. While no one size fits all, the book allows us to determine on a practical level, to a relatively more accurate degree than ever before, exactly which kinds of coalitions work, when, and for which country types.

The historical account and comparative analysis of coalitions presented in the book also allow the formulation of rules of strategy. Once a coalition is formed, the book advances strategies that the coalition can best employ to reinforce itself and its influence. Depending on the potential weaknesses of the coalition and the stage of the negotiation, different mixes of strategies can be productively devised. For instance, certain strategies have proven especially useful in enhancing the legitimacy of the coalition, while others are more relevant for reducing the potential for divisions within it.

Beneath the theoretical analysis and policy prescriptions of the book, there pervades a realisation that comes from most historical accounts, namely that no coalition functions in a vacuum, and favourable external conditions can prove crucial in contributing to its successes. However, the comparative analysis also reveals that even when faced with the same set of conditions, coalitions reveal very different levels of effectiveness and results. For instance, Chapter 6 studies the example of the Cairns Group, a coalition that owed a significant part of its successes to the rift between the European Community (EC) and the US. However, the chapter also presents a study of the Food Importers' Group, and finds that the coalition was unable to make much use of the same circumstances that the Cairns Group utilised so effectively. The contrast reinforces an initial assumption that underlies the work: effective bargaining is at least as internal to the coalition as external to it. With the appropriate coalition type and strategy set, developing countries can go a long way in enhancing their bargaining leeway in trade negotiations.

## Plan of the book

The organisation of the book is as follows. Following this introduction, the first chapter elaborates on the key theoretical issues of bargaining in coalitions, particularly as they apply to developing countries. First, it clarifies and expands upon the principal assumption that underlies this study, namely that coalitions provide developing countries with a critical instrument for expanding their bargaining power. To this end, it identifies the weaknesses of developing countries and then explains how coalitions assist in overcoming some of these weaknesses. Second, the chapter engages with theorising on coalitions from various disciplines and levels of analysis to derive any insights that assist in understanding what kinds of coalitions work at the inter-state level. The limitations of these theories – independently and as an aggregate – assist greatly in defining the agenda of enquiry for the book. The book tries to answer questions for which these theories have no answers. Examples of these questions are: On what basis do states choose their allies in the international political economy? Under what circumstances do they balance or bandwagon? What are the various ways that states employ successfully to sustain the coalitions they form? These questions are presented up front in Chapter 1.

Having established the importance of coalitions for developing countries and identified some of the reasons as to why they are not easy to construct, Chapter 2 identifies precisely why coalitions of the weak have been especially elusive in the GATT and the WTO. It also explains why the introduction of services into the pre-negotiation phase of the Uruguay Round marked a new phase in the participation and group activity of developing countries in the GATT. With the stage thus set, subsequent chapters analyse specific attempts at coalition formation. Chapters 3–7 encompass case studies, which are organised in cumulative fashion on a time scale, where coalitions described in each succeeding chapter draw on the example and lessons of the preceding ones.

Chapter 3 studies the first coalition of developing countries that arose to meet the challenge of services – the G-10. However, the G-10 had a long history in a well-entrenched albeit weak coalition of developing countries in the GATT, that is the Informal Group of developing countries. A part of the chapter is hence devoted to examining the Informal Group. The G-10 epitomised what may be seen as the traditional, bloc-type diplomacy of developing countries. In spite of its subsequent collapse, replacement by an alternative type, and limited obvious successes of its agenda, the G-10 is important in demonstrating the costs and benefits of the traditional diplomacy. The rise and fall of the G-10 are inseparable from the advent of an alternative type of diplomacy of developing countries that is discussed in Chapter 4.

Chapter 4 analyses the rise of the challenger to the G-10 and the type of diplomacy that it represented. The new diplomacy began as the 'Jaramillo process,' which gradually evolved into a coalition of the G-20, and then the Café au Lait and the G-48. In its more advanced avatars of the Café au Lait and the G-48, the group exemplified a new style of coalition diplomacy that is termed an alliance type in the typology provided in the book. The hallmark of the Café au Lait was that it was a crossover coalition, that is one that combined developed and developing countries. It focused on a particular issue area over which countries coalesced, presented itself as a positive negotiating coalition rather than a blocking one, sought recourse in extensive research and discussion rather than ideology, and had middle and small powers rather than the big powers at its helm. The chapter highlights its successes while at the same time identifying specific conditions that facilitated the achievements of the group but also limited its applicability as a model.

The G-10 and the G-20 serve as the archetypal bloc and alliance respectively. In their aftermath, two trends are discernible. The first combined strategies of the G-10 and the G-20 in varying proportions resulting in coalitions of different types. These are discussed in Chapter 5 under the title of 'combination diplomacy'. The chapter investigates why several coalitions within this type have had very short life spans, and specifies the conditions and countries for which combination diplomacy is especially relevant. The second trend involved attempts to follow the path exactly as was shown by the G-20. Chapter 6 studies this trend and presents a comparative study of the Cairns Group on agriculture, the Food Importers' Group and the Friends of Services Group. There are two reasons why the Cairns Group forms a part of a study whose central focus is coalitions in services. First, the Cairns Group borrowed from, and epitomised, the G-20 issue-based and Café au Lait crossover diplomacy, demonstrating their viability and limitations. Second, the Cairns in turn became a 'model' for other coalitions – the Food Importers' Group, the Friends of Services, and several other later coalitions drew succour from the example that it was seen to set. The extremely high profile of the Cairns Group, however, presents a striking contrast to the low visibility of the Friends' Group and limited achievements of the Food Importers' Group. The chapter analyses the extent to which strategies of the Cairns Group were successfully reproduced in alternative conditions, and with what results. All coalitions studied in Chapter 6 are categorised as developed or evolved alliances, which arose in the aftermath of the G-10/G-20 episode and took the methods of the Café au Lait further.

Chapter 7 investigates the fourth and final coalition type, which has utilised regionalism as a springboard for bargaining. It finds that regional integration arrangements are not the sole or even the best path to the formation of regional bargaining coalitions among developing countries. A comparative study of regionalism in Latin America and East Asia yields an alternative basis to coalition formation in the GATT/WTO.

Chapter 8 examines the coalitions that emerged with the pre-negotiation phase of the new Doha Development agenda, that is from 1998 in the lead-up to Seattle and subsequently the Doha Ministerial. Note that the coalitions in this chapter cover diverse issue areas and not just services or even primarily services. The reason for this is, in good measure, the change at the ground level, that is several other new issues have emerged in relation to the new Round, and coalitions too have acquired several new foci. The central finding of this chapter is that while most of the recent coalitions are but permutations of the old, the lessons of the Uruguay Round have not gone unlearnt. However, present-day coalitions have to be understood not only in terms of their antecedents but also in terms of how previous types have been adapted to a rapidly evolving context. The chapter highlights the continuities and changes in coalition strategies used by developing countries. It also takes into account the role that non-state actors have come to play in the WTO and analyses the extent to which these changes have affected the actual coalitions and also coalition possibilities available to developing countries.

Chapter 9 presents the conclusions of the study. It summarises the empirical findings through an analytical framework for conceptualising and classifying coalitions. This analytical framework adds to the typology of coalitions that is provided in Chapter 2. By bringing together the theoretical implications of the case studies, the chapter also provides a theory of inter-state bargaining coalitions. The theory offers explanations and policy prescriptions to diplomats and analysts on the structure and strategies that coalitions of developing countries may employ for effective bargaining in the WTO.

# 1 Bargaining together: why and how?

Acting as a united group, these birds are flying away with my snare
But without doubt, they will fall as soon as they quarrel among themselves.
(*Panchatantra*, Book II, Verse 9)

Bargaining together in groups is common to both developed and developing countries. The limited bargaining power of developing countries makes coalitions an especially crucial instrument for their effective diplomacy in international negotiations. This chapter examines the bargaining weaknesses of the developing world and explains how inter-state coalitions enable developing countries to overcome some of their weaknesses. However, effective coalitions are not easy to construct or sustain. The chapter presents a brief overview of methods available for coalition construction and maintenance, as provided for by a cross-disciplinary set of theories on coalitions. The study provides us with some useful insights into the problems of cooperation and collective action among independent actors. Unfortunately, many of these insights are often contradictory and context dependent. Taken individually or as an aggregate, none of these theories answers the key question: which method of coalition formation is likely to prove the most sustainable, and under what circumstances? Keeping in view the gaps in the literature, the penultimate section aggregates and distils the insights of various levels of theorising to propose a typology of coalitions. The concluding section summarises the findings of the theoretical exercise conducted in the chapter and also highlights the gaps in the theories that the remainder of the book addresses.

## 1.1 Bargaining constraints of developing countries

Attempts to strengthen their bargaining positions by forming coalitions are not limited to the powerless: witness the joint positions adopted by Canada, the European Union (EU), Japan, and the US as the 'Quad' in the GATT/WTO, or the G-8 in the conduct of international economic management. The difference between the developing and developed worlds, however, lies in the fact that for the former coalitions form one of the few instruments in their bargaining repertoire. To borrow a concept from security studies, the weak have few sources of 'internal balancing' and hence must rely on 'external balancing' arrangements.[1] An analysis of the sources of the bargaining weaknesses of developing countries and their effects follows below.

The concept of bargaining power varies according to the context in which it is applied. In industrial relations for instance, bargaining power is conceptualised in terms of results: 'the success of one group in obtaining compliance with its wishes regardless of the opposition of others'.[2] Many theorists of international relations, however, view the concept in structural terms.[3] Bargaining power is seen as the ability to bring the opposing party to the negotiating table and exchange concessions that are the least unacceptable to both parties. It derives from a threat of violence, rather than an actual use of violence. Thomas Schelling's definition, while formally referring to the arena of military strategy, is applicable to most issue areas: 'The power to hurt is bargaining power. To exploit it is diplomacy – vicious diplomacy, but diplomacy nonetheless.'[4] The deficiency of bargaining power adversely affects the negotiating position of developing countries in most international deals.

The vulnerabilities of the developing world have diverse sources. The small island economies of the Caribbean with their proximity to the US face very different opportunities and threats from the smaller African economies. Brazil and India, despite their comparable economic size, differ significantly in their historical legacies and threats from within the neighbourhood (and hence have different opportunities for regional cooperative endeavours). The contrasts across regions and development levels are wider still. Developing countries vary widely in the size of their markets, resource availability and competitive advantages, colonial legacies, domestic instability, and internal and external security threats. It is, however, possible to find three levels of weaknesses with similar implications for international bargaining, which are common to all developing countries.

The first level of weakness that reduces the bargaining capacity of developing countries is the domestic one. Developing countries, even after half a century since the first wave of decolonisation, continue to face problems of 'quasi-statehood'.[5] Ayoob argues that developing countries are still caught up in the early stages of state making. In itself a tumultuous process, its disruptive effects have been exacerbated by the nature of decolonisation, the telescoping of a 400-year-long evolutionary Westphalian process into a few years, and the entry of developing countries into a state system where the developed countries are accomplished players.[6] States that are rife with internal divisions are unlikely to be able to pursue efficient policies at home, or present an effective front abroad. It is noteworthy that these domestic problems run deeper than simply the governmental one with its associated lack of legitimacy. The deep-rooted character of these problems has led some scholars to suggest that Third World countries can be classified only in a separate class of state, with little connection to the established Western concept.[7] While Mohammed Ayoob's argument is political in its focus, its analogue may be found in the economic development of these countries. Missing or partially evolved states are accompanied by missing or partially evolved markets. Problems of resource scarcity, limited economies of scale due to small market size, minimal demand or supply power, and inadequate infrastructural networks appear in varying degrees across the developed world. The different compositions of political and economic weaknesses, nonetheless, produce a similar effect that is common to most developing countries, that is the power of manoeuvre of the emergent state is greatly circumscribed.

The second and third levels, that is the regional and international, interact with the domestic, to increase further the vulnerabilities of developing countries. Arbitrarily drawn political borders by the colonial powers only partially explain regional conflict. Rather, construction of regional balances becomes especially important as it is seen as 'a necessary component of state-building strategy because it facilitates state-making on the part of the stronger state at the expense of its weaker neighbours'.[8] Regional conflicts, however, increase the instability of the state and preclude attempts at overcoming problems of economies of scale through regional cooperation. The late entry of developing countries onto a pre-existing international system makes them rule takers rather than agenda setters. Unfavourable and even unfair rules for the newer entrants find expression not merely in time and norm constraints upon domestic processes of state evolution but also in international organisations such as the International Monetary Fund (IMF) and the World Bank (in rules such as weighted voting), in the qualified egalitarianism of the United Nations through the institution of the P-5 in the Security Council, and in attempts at global economic management through the G-8 that exclude the developing world.

The implications of weaknesses that operate at the three levels mentioned above are twofold. First, and irrespective of the dominance of a particular level of weakness and its interplay with the others, developing countries are characterised by 'peripherality'.[9] While dependency theory offered some important insights into the developing world based on this notion, the concept of peripherality can be taken further. The concept does not refer only to the peripheralisation from the core in terms of production patterns. It has also been pointed out that production patterns based on dependency do not necessarily create poverty.[10] The notion of peripheralisation and its importance need to be linked with the three levels of weakness and the inability of developing countries to emerge as full players in the international system despite the post-war egalitarianism. The industrial economies designed the system and continue to be the agenda setters in international institutions that regulate and restructure the international economic system. A lack of adequate time necessary for effective state-building; the near-impossibility of alienating juridical sovereignty once it had been achieved;[11] domestic constraints in the form of demands for political participation, economic redistribution, and social justice at a very early stage in the state-making process; the highly disruptive colonial inheritance and so forth, all placed the newly independent at an initial disadvantage which persists today. Peripheralisation of developing countries is as true of the least developed among them and the poorest, as it is for the rich oil-exporting economies. Its most obvious result is a reduced 'skill' component in the bargaining power of developing countries.[12]

The recognition of this peripheralisation was the chief force that underlay the creation of the 'Third World'. But it also created and reinforced a second feature common to developing countries, which has been succinctly termed 'Third World Schizophrenia'.[13] As the intruder majority in a system of states that was not built to suit their advantage, developing countries have sought to divest the developed world of its control and power in international institutions. The call for systemic change derives from their experience with exploitation and is facilitated by their joint majority in international forums. But the vulnerabilities of these states give them a vested interest in the preservation of predictable norms of state behaviour. Systemic change would destabilise their own weak state structures and possibly undermine their newly achieved international recognition. This schizophrenia manifests itself in several ways. As the intruder majority in international forums, developing countries raised the call for the New International Economic Order (NIEO), based on assumptions of distributive justice that differed from those of the existing economic system. Simultaneously and paradoxically, they emerged as the most enthusiastic supporters of existing international structures, reinforcing the legitimacy of international institutions and deriving their own legitimacy through enthusiastic participation. The dependence of the developing countries on the existing system for their legitimacy and survival further reduced their bargaining power. The schizophrenia has undermined the value of developing countries as either credible threats or credible allies, and also detracted from one of the few bargaining counters that the weak possess, that is resolve in negotiations.[14] If peripherality adversely affects the bargaining skill of developing countries, schizophrenia impairs their will.

Irrespective of the domestic particularities and the nature of interaction between the three levels of weakness, the results of peripherality and schizophrenia are similar for developing countries. The fact that diverse weaknesses translate into two similar phenomena at the international level has led developing countries to pursue international remedies to correct international imbalances of power. The effort is understandable, given especially that the international constraints operate in close interaction with the domestic to diminish the bargaining power of developing countries. Hence, the international weaknesses of developing countries are not merely a symptom of deep-rooted domestic maladies; rather, they are as much a cause of them. It is true that domestic remedies would correct some of the weaknesses that derive from the same level and also have international ramifications. Internal balancing offers the additional advantage of greater reliability, which contrasts with the uncertainty that comes from a dependence on allies through external balancing. In many cases however, internal balancing is at best a hypothetical possibility for developing countries. Little reliability is to be gained through internal reliance on war-prone quasi-states or price-taking economies with small markets and absent economies of scale. At least in the short run, and through international change that they might hope to effect in the long run, coalitions offer a way out of the politico-economic predicament of developing countries.

## 1.2 Why bargain together?

When power differentials are high, efforts at internal balancing are likely to yield minimal successes. In contrast, external balancing in the international political economy promises certainty of allies and joint strength with which to posit an alternative agenda. Recognition of the potential benefits of external balancing provided the chief motivation behind the vigorous coalition diplomacy of developing countries, which dates back to the wave of decolonisation of the 1940s and 1950s. Joint action in organisations such as the General Assembly had clear and demonstrable efficacy due to rules of majority voting. A large, visible presence and association with coalitions further helped the newly independent countries define their international identities, as well as refurbish the legitimacy of their emergent states. But the gains from coalition activity went deeper, in many ways addressing some of the weaknesses that were analysed in the previous section. This section examines the benefits that developing countries derive from bargaining in coalitions. It finds that behind the intuitive reliance of the weak on safety in numbers, there is a powerful and persuasive logic.

The most important benefit of joint bargaining is the pooling of bargaining resources to allow greater negotiating weight to the weak. It is possible to conceptualise such a pooling in the most obvious terms of material resources (as in the case of commodity suppliers that attempt cartels) to overcome small market size, limited resource endowment, and even absent economies of scale. Combined bargaining power based on greater economic weight might resemble the 'coercive power of trade unions'. When power is thus aggregated and achieves a critical mass, the weak too acquire a capacity to say 'no' and affect the outcome of international decision-making through their participation or otherwise.[15] The absence of such a large collective from the negotiating table would render any agreement reached without them meaningless. Small European economies have enjoyed a visible presence in the GATT since the 1960s, by virtue of their joint market power through the EC. In extreme cases, such coalitions that amass a critical collective weight might operate as cartels and exercise their coercive diplomacy by restricting supply, raising prices, and holding non-members to ransom.

The bargaining power of developing countries is not constrained by limited supply and demand power alone. Many of the least developed countries (LDCs) do not have the resources to invest in research in new issues and develop a coherent articulation of their goals and demands. It is true that these limitations are located in domestic factors, but coalitions present an external strategy of at least alleviating some of the effects of these domestic deficiencies. Coalitions allow a pooling of organisational resources, and enable countries with ill-defined interests to avail themselves of the research efforts of allies and a possible country-wise division of research and labour across issue areas. The importance of this pooling, particularly to the weakest of developing countries, cannot be overemphasised, especially in GATT/WTO-type 'member-driven organisations'. The small secretariat of such organisations means that the greater part of the analysis of issues for agenda-setting and negotiating purposes has to be done by the members themselves. Even without getting into qualitative assessments of research expertise, it is possible to see the urgent problems that many developing countries face due to the smallness of their delegations. As recently as 2000, twenty-four developing countries had no permanent representation in Geneva. The average size of developed country delegations in Geneva in 2000 was 7.38, whereas developing country delegations averaged 3.51. These averages conceal vast differences: for instance, Bangladesh has only one person responsible for the WTO, whereas India has six members on its mission to the WTO.[16] These data on membership further disguise the fact that several of these countries are formally 'inactive' for not having paid their dues for more than three years. At the beginning of 1997, twenty-three developing countries were included in this category. At that time, this implied that they were not able to receive technical assistance from the organisation, although a subsequent WTO Council decision changed this rule. But members in financial arrears are still not allowed to chair WTO bodies.[17] Similarly, a presence in Geneva is almost a necessary condition for appointment, although 'Non-residents may be appointed in exceptional circumstances where the necessary expertise can only be found in capitals.'[18] Coalitions, hence, become important for developing countries, not only because they facilitate a sharing of resources like markets, but also because of other kinds of resources like representatives, research, and lobbying skills.

The benefits of organisational cost-sharing and joint markets are not limited to the obvious aggregation of resources. A coalition represents institutionalisation of external balancing, thereby offering certainty to weak states that is often elusive to them through internal balancing. This institutionalisation also reduces the trans-action costs of finding new bargaining chips and building new diplomatic link-ages, every time a new set of negotiations begins. For countries that are highly vulnerable to the vagaries of external markets and commodity prices as well as internal political/economic instability, even minimal international certainty deriv-ing from coalition memberships and associated burden-sharing is no small asset.

Coalitions often produce cross-institutional effects. Advantages of membership of a multilateral coalition spill over into other multilateral and bilateral dealings. The identification of India and Brazil as the leaders of the G-77 in the UNCTAD (along with Argentina, Egypt, and the former Yugoslavia), for instance, gave them greater bargaining leeway at the bilateral level and also a place in international forums like the GATT.

Cross-institutional spillover effects and influence within the operating institu-tion are both magnified by norms of international democracy and ideas of the legitimacy of large numbers. Even when the coalition does not enhance the strength of the members sufficiently to hold the strong at ransom, large member-ship enhances the credibility of demands. The legitimacy attached to large num-bers is most obviously found in institutions that espouse the norm of international democracy through rules of majority voting. The General Assembly with its one-nation-one-vote rules exemplified how the weak could control the agenda through 'the tyranny of the majority'.[19] The 1960s and 1970s provide several examples of this power, and hence the naming of the 1960s as the development decade and the call for the NIEO. But even in other international organisations that practise weighted rather than majority voting or GATT-type club behaviour,[20] demands presented by coalitions enjoy greater legitimacy than those presented by lone countries.

While the advantages of bargaining in coalitions in terms of the international position of developing countries are obvious enough, the double-edged sword of joint bargaining also cuts into the domestic level. The vociferous participation of the newly independent developing countries in the UN, particularly through groupings such as Afro-Asian unity and the Non-Aligned Movement (NAM) is an example of how national governments have sought international recognition as well as domestic credibility through this international identity. Between the 'third way' that developing countries sought in international forums and the domestic legitimacy that their governments commanded, there was often a close correlation.[21] These considerations further explain why some of the bigger members of the coalition are often willing to bear the costs of free-riding by smaller members. The bigger members bring in a greater resource base to the pool, and enjoy the returns of prestige deriving from their leadership status. The Big Five of the GATT, discussed in detail in Chapter 3, provide one example of such trade-offs. The smaller countries are able to handle the practicalities of everyday negotiation better, due to the sharing of organisational and agenda-setting costs by the coalition. Sometimes, the benefits go deeper: the smaller countries find that research conducted for the collective by the bigger countries assists in the interest identification of all members. Depending on the size and nature of membership, the smaller powers can enjoy considerable bargaining leeway with their allies and ensure that their particular interests are logrolled onto the group's agenda. Especially when the coalition comes equipped with an ideology, it reinforces and even moulds the national identities of participants (large or small). Given all these advantages, it is hardly surprising that the weak prefer to travel international pathways in groups. But the benefits of joint action are also accompanied by costs.

To each of the advantages discussed above, there is a flip side of qualifications and limitations. While resource aggregation has a sound logic behind it, it does not follow that the bigger the coalition, the more effective it is likely to be. Coalitions that base themselves simply on the premise of larger numbers and bigger markets soon find themselves facing incompatible interests and unsustainable costs of reconciling them. It was precisely such problems of contradictory and numerous aggregations that resulted in the failure of the 'South coalition' across institutions.[22] Similarly, while sharing of organisational resources is an asset for the weak, it is accompanied by the risk that the powerful in the group will use their organisational skills and resources to dominate the agenda and perhaps even structure the interests of the weak. Coalitions increase certainty in international affairs through reliability of allies, but also reduce the policy flexibility of countries and thereby eat into the already limited negotiating space of the weakest of developing countries. Irrespective of the extent of vulnerability and limitations of internal balancing, bargaining together is fruitful only in certain contexts, after questions such as bargaining with whom, against whom, over what, and for how long have been duly considered. In other words, coalitions – seldom easy to form or sustain – are perhaps even more difficult for the developing world whose quasi-states are particularly jealous guardians of their limited sovereignty and find cooperative action even more difficult. The paucity of successful alliances involving the Third World has not gone unnoticed.[23] The next section explores existing scholarship on the problems of coalition formation and solutions to them.

## 1.3 Methods of coalition formation: a theoretical overview

The problem of achieving collective action has attracted cross-disciplinary attention. By extending and applying different theories to the question of inter-state bargaining coalitions, it is possible to trace three essential methods of coalition formation. First, one group of rationalist theories (which includes formal theories of coalitions, most theories of domestic political economy, and Realist theories of International Relations (IR)) highlights the importance of interests – collective or aggregated – in fostering collective action among states. Second, neo-liberal theories of IR emphasise that coalition creation and maintenance are not simply products of initial structural conditions or interests. Rather, various types of processes can be used to promote cooperation among states. Finally, constructivist theories concentrate on the role of ideas and identity in coalitions. The three levels together take us far in understanding why coalitions are difficult to construct and maintain. But in advancing positive measures for coalition building, these theories prescribe diverse and often contradictory methods. The vast body of theorising on coalitions and bargaining notwithstanding, there is no grand theory of coalitions to be found that could guide states in the choice of their allies. A brief overview of the contribution of these theories follows below, along with a tabular summary on theories and their applications at the end of this section.

### 1.3.1 Theories highlighting interest-based methods of coalition-building

Formal theories of clubs and coalitions, theories of the domestic political economy, and Realist theories of alliances operate at very different levels of analyses and employ a diverse range of methodologies, but they have one theme in common. All these theories emphasise the role of common interests in promoting coalition formation and maintenance, while also providing us with different and useful insights into the problems underlying collective action.

*Formal theories of clubs and coalitions*

Formal theories of clubs and coalitions, irrespective of different methodologies adopted, share a common research agenda of finding out 'who will join with whom and how they will divide the rewards'.[24] These theories are particularly useful in conceptualising some of the fundamental problems of collective action among independent actors.[25] In this brand of theorising, a club is defined as 'a voluntary group deriving mutual benefit from sharing one or more of the following: production costs, the members' characteristics, or a good characterised by excludable benefit'.[26] Club goods can be distinguished from public goods by their excludability. Occasionally, the former set of goods also displays partial rivalry, that is when one person's consumption of a unit of the good detracts from the consumption opportunities of another person. As such, club goods represent 'impure' public goods.[27] The main problem that renders the provision of public goods difficult is that of free-riding because pure public goods are non-rival and inclusive. As access to the good cannot be restricted to the providers, actors prefer not to join the collective effort to provide the group and instead enjoy the benefits from the outside. But the problems of producing club goods go further. Between the constraint of partial rivalry of the good of joint action and the opportunity of excluding non-members from the benefits, the coalition must find the optimal combination of members. To grapple with the problem of determining the optimal combination – in terms of coalition size as well as compatibility of members – several formal theories have been proposed.

A prominent and widely discussed example of a formal theory of coalitions is William Riker's concept of the 'size principle' and 'minimum winning coalitions': 'In social situations similar to n-person, zero-sum games with side-payments, participants create coalitions just as large as they believe will ensure winning and no larger.'[28] Theoretical qualifications and counter-arguments to Riker's principle include William Gamson's theory about cheapest minimum winning coalition,[29] and Norman Frohlich *et al.*'s coalitions that are larger than minimum coalitions as insurance against blackmail or defection.[30] The biggest advantage of Riker's size principle and other related theories is that they focus a diverse and confusing range of questions into one very precise question with claims to universal applicability. But in its attempt to suggest an explanation to coalition formation that is sufficiently generalisable, formal theory misses out on some crucial issues.

Aggregated or separately, formal theories (game-theoretic, socio-psychological, or experimental in approach) ask the question: what is the efficiency principle that underlies coalition formation, and how are pay-offs distributed once the efficient coalition is formed? The resulting cost–benefit analysis is crucial in illustrating the importance of material resources/commonalty of interests as the first source of cohesion that independent actors use to form a coalition. But the question addressed in this book – what kinds of coalitions work and why – is not simply one of efficiency, although it is true that a coalition is unlikely to survive if it is an inefficient one. Rather, to answer the question, several other issues besides efficiency need to be addressed. For instance, how are allies chosen in the first place, particularly when they seem similarly balanced in terms of resource position? What bargains are negotiated within the coalition to assure against the defection of allies? Pay-offs, as Eric Browne points out, are not predetermined according to contribution of individual members.[31] Logs are rolled to ensure loyalty and the pay-offs distributed according to the dependence of the 'coalition' (often referring not to a reified coalition, but to its agenda-setting, dominant members) on each member. To ensure that it is a 'winning' coalition, what strategies can the coalition adopt, and thereby improve its negotiating weight through other means besides initial resource distribution? Formal theories of clubs and coalitions leave these key questions unanswered.

When applied to international relations, the limitations of formal theorising become even more obvious. Unlike a count of seats won by parties to build political coalitions in government and further effect a proportional distribution of positions in the coalition government, the 'weight' of individual states and their contribution to the coalition is difficult to assess. One way out of this difficulty would be to calculate the weight of potential allies in terms of market/resource power. But sometimes even small allies can have a big influence within coalitions. The critical leadership of smaller developing countries in the creation and main- tenance of certain coalition types is illustrated later in the book. At this juncture, suffice it to note that coalition partners bring other attributes besides quantifiable economic power to the coalition, and hence they are not seen as free-riders. This links up with the second problem in the application of such theories to interna- tional relations. Unlike the distribution of cabinet positions among political allies in proportion to their contribution in terms of seats won, the distribution of pay-offs in international relations is often not proportional to the contribution of partners. Finally, especially in the context of the Third World where very weak states seek the maximum possible insurance against the more powerful and also potential defections, coalitions are likely to err on the side of excess. Many Third World coalitions have indeed combined incompatible interests and have shown scant regard for the principle of minimum winning coalitions or variations of the type.

### *Trade policy coalitions in the domestic political economy*

In answer to some of the issues raised above, it may be useful to examine the con- tribution of theorising on coalitions that is not at the purely abstract level. There exists a well-developed corpus of writing on interest groups in the domestic polit- ical economy, which addresses two central questions. First, and of direct relevance to us, is the question: Who aligns with whom and why? Second, do the interest groups thus formed have a protectionist or a liberalising trade agenda, that is how are these domestic groupings aligned in their attitude to international trade? A note of caution in adapting these theories to the subject of inter-state bargaining is important, as domestic lobbies have different interests and work under a differ- ent set of opportunities and constraints from states. But in spite of these differ- ences, theories of coalitions in the domestic political economy offer some critical insights into the motivations and methods of alignment that may be applied at the international level.

Theories of domestic interest groups may be utilised in two ways. First, it is possible to conceptualise international trade negotiations as a two-level game, wherein domestic bargaining affects the positions that states adopt internationally. The reverse is also true, that is the international level has often been put to effective use to curtail the pressure of domestic lobbies at home. An extreme ver- sion of this approach would be to see international coalitions as a reflection of the domestic (e.g. a strong pro-trade agricultural lobby at home would necessarily imply membership of the Cairns Group). But there are three reasons why such an approach has only limited relevance for trade coalitions in the GATT/WTO involving developing countries and were touched upon in the Introduction. They are discussed below before tracing the lessons that theories of coalitions at the domestic level have for inter-state coalitions.

First, the question of trade coalitions as addressed in this book does not go back to investigating interest formation. Interests of states are taken as given and are found most easily in national statistics. For instance, the fact that agriculture contributes to over 60 per cent of Argentina's export income explains the country's enthusiastic membership of the Cairns Group. Of course domestic lobbies influence the position that each sector occupies in the national policy and its voice in the international trade policy of the country. But how some domestic voices are filtered out and others thrive in the making of international trade policy is not the central question of this book. Second, particularly in the case of developing countries, lobbies have traditionally played a much smaller role than in developed democracies. Third, and most important, the abstruse 'Geneva process' has been traditionally likened to a 'club'. The reasons and implications of this are discussed in greater detail in the next chapter. But the 'almost English Club atmosphere ... the codified language',[32] has made the Green Room consultative process relatively impervious to direct domestic pressures. The absence of protectionist lobbies in Geneva and the minimal indirect pressures on the ambassadors have been noted elsewhere with accompanying explanations.[33] The links between Geneva and capitals often also become more tenuous as the negotiations themselves and their technical content advance, even as formal links continue. One diplomat writes, ' ...it became our pattern to acknowledge receipt of instructions, study them carefully, and then, following discussions with key negotiators of other countries, communicate back to Washington our view of what alternate instructions might follow that could be negotiated.... To my recollection, we never received a countermanding set of instructions but were permitted to move ahead with the negotiations on a pragmatic basis.'[34] In other words, the 'national interest' is more easily represented at the GATT/WTO than in other institutions, irrespective of how the national interest was first constructed. Theories of domestic coalitions hence bear only little direct relevance to the question of inter-state bargaining coalitions, though an attempt has been made to incorporate the role of these domestic lobbies in the analysis for cases where lobbies were particularly active.

The second way in which theories of coalitions in the domestic political economy offer insights into inter-state bargaining coalitions is through analogy. The composition and character of domestic coalitions offer some important insights by analogy into the motivations and methods of international alignments. The two traditional theories of trade policy coalitions link their formation and agenda with factor specificity. Two different economic models provide the basis for their divergent conclusions. The first, as proposed by Ronald Rogowski, uses the Heckscher–Ohlin model in which factor specificity is assumed to be so low that a costless movement of factors across industries is possible.[35] According to the Heckscher–Ohlin model, countries export manufactures that utilise the abundant factor, and import goods that are intensive in the scarce factor. As a result, trade benefits owners of abundant factors, and harms owners of scarce factors. Coalitions will hence form along factor or class lines, with owners of abundant factors favouring coalescing with a free trade agenda, and owners of scarce factors developing a common platform of protectionism. For instance, landowners are likely to be less protectionist if land is abundant and labour is scarce.

Extending the theory to the inter-state level, we find that the theory offers possibly an important insight for inter-state coalitions. The first consideration that guides coalition formation among states in the international political economy would seem to be a similar resource/factor endowment. Note that this corresponds with the stress laid on a sharing of resources and a cost–benefit analysis advanced by formal theories of clubs and coalitions. States that share similar interests as commodity exporters are likely to form a common platform. The most obvious attempts at such coalescing include the Organisation of Petroleum Exporting Countries (OPEC), various attempts at commodity cartels like that of coffee-producers, and the call for the Integrated Programme for Commodities (IPC) in the UNCTAD. The first coalitions that sprang up on the services issue were those of the capital and technology abundant countries that foresaw a common comparative advantage as services exporters. Developing countries, too, as largely capital and technology poor economies, came together with a protectionist agenda that sought to exclude services from the GATT purview. These coalitions are examined in greater detail in the first half of Chapter 5.

The second theory on trade coalitions is based on the Ricardo–Viner model. This line of reasoning assumes that factor specificity is very high, that is some factors cannot move at all across industries.[36] In other words, 'the fortunes of the specific factors in an industry then rise and fall together, whether they are the same type of factor or not'.[37] Steel-workers, for instance, are workers and in that capacity find their interests similar to those of other workers. But as they work in the steel industry, they find interests in common with those of managers and shareholders in the steel industry, at least in the short run.

The theory provides us with two concepts that are useful for inter-state bargaining coalitions. The first is the idea that disaggregated, rather than just factor-level, interests are important. In trade negotiations, issues such as services have proved especially prone to disaggregation along lines of sectors and sub-sectors. The reasons for these disaggregative tendencies are explained in detail in Chapter 5. Second, the theory reinforces the concept of the short versus the long run. The concept is important because even when states have similar resource endowments, different patterns of development often give them an immediate or potential advantage in certain sectors. Chapter 5 uses this concept to explain the splits within the broad coalition of developing countries on services. Though the direct applicability of this theory to the question of inter-state bargaining is limited, the two concepts provide crucial reminders on why interests often do not aggregate along the lines of resource/factor endowments.

In addition to the two theories described above, which link trade policy coalitions with factor specificity, there is a third economic model – the increasing returns to scale (IRS) model – with implications for coalition formation.[38] North–North intra-industry trade is best explained by product differentiation and IRS. The benefits of intra-industry trade are higher than those obtained from comparative advantage, because intra-industry trade allows countries to benefit from larger markets. Intra-industry trade also has a beneficial effect on income distribution and, thereby, coalition formation. This effect is a product of the fact that as intra-industry trade takes place among differentiated products, there is no direct substitution of one product by another, or no sectoral reallocation.

Most scholars have directed their attention to the implications of IRS-led intra-industry trade for softer distributional effects and hence lesser conflict in terms of opposing coalitions. But the theory also has important implications for inter-state relations. States with intra-industry trade are likely to find cooperative endeavours among themselves easier to sustain. Developing countries that lack such trade patterns and where trade is based more on comparative advantage than product differentiation would, in contrast, find cooperation difficult with both developing and developed counterparts. Diana Tussie uses the IRS model to explain the minimal successes of regionalism in the developing world.[39] It can be further extended to understand the successes of some coalitions that have utilised regionalism as a springboard for joint bargaining in the GATT/WTO. Chapter 7 conducts an enquiry along these lines.

All the economic models just described explain preference formation in the domestic political economy. They reinforce and hone the understanding that we derived from formal theories on the possible preferences that may underlie inter-state coalition formation. Similar to formal theories, these theories recognise the importance of resource-based similarities in determining alignment loyalties. But there is no obvious method of arbitrating between the contradictory explanations that the different theories of domestic political economy provide. Moreover, most of the hints that they give us into inter-state coalition building are indirect and involve a considerable extension of the original theories. This is unsurprising, given that the theories just applied are really concerned with domestic coalitions. It may also then be hoped that theories of IR will succeed where theories of domestic political economy falter. Realist theories of IR are examined below.

### *Realist theories of international relations*

Realist theories of IR resemble theories of domestic political economy and formal theories of coalitions in their emphasis on interests as the primary determinant of coalition loyalty. Rather than take cooperative action among independent state actors as a given, Realism introduces assumptions of anarchy, power maximisation, national interests, and relative gains to demonstrate that permanent, stable coalitions are not an inevitability. Realist and Neo-Realist theories further highlight that while alliances are based on a degree of cooperative action among states, this cooperation may well be directed towards aggressive and conflictual ends.

The Realist conceptualisation of cooperative action among states is a minimalist one. Lord Palmerston was not far from most Realist accounts that can be found in IR theory even today, when he stated that England 'has no permanent friends; she has only permanent interests'.[40] An alliance is guided mainly by interest and the international configuration of relative capabilities. States need to keep their alliance options open because they are as uncertain about the intentions of their allies as their adversaries. Uncertainties deriving from the anarchical nature of the international system lead states to be concerned about cheating and relative (not absolute) gains.[41] States often deal with these uncertainties by forming balances or bandwagons, and Realism gives us extensive explanation as to the motivations behind either strategy.

That states balance against increases in power is seen as almost axiomatic by Realist scholars of international relations. Kenneth Waltz argues that 'If there is any distinctively political theory of international politics, balance-of-power theory is it.'[42] Balancing behaviour predominates because the first concern of states is not power maximisation but survival.[43] Hence instead of bandwagoning with the stronger side, states often choose to deter rising hegemony by balancing. While traditional balance of power theory has been associated with Great Powers, Waltz also applies it to smaller states. 'Secondary states', he argues, flock to the weaker side, where 'they are both more appreciated and safer'.[44] While bandwagons and hegemony may allow the small the benefits of free-riding, they also pose considerable risks in a world where the big fish eat the little fish. Developing countries are likely to be even more wary of such bandwagons for fear that their newfound statehood be undermined by their 'Big Brother' ally. George Liska supports this point: the weaker state fears that its identity will be undermined by the more powerful ally. The strong state will also be reluctant to ally with the weak for fear of overextending its commitments and resources.[45] In international political economy, this would translate into a simple balancing by developing countries against the developed countries. Groupings such as the G-77 in the UNCTAD and various avatars of the South/Third World in other organisations exemplify such behaviour. But theoretical counter-argument and historical example both reveal that states sometimes prefer the bandwagon option.

Bandwagoning, in its broadest usage, may be defined as 'joining the stronger coalition'.[46] Stephen Walt argues that the likelihood of bandwagoning is directly proportional to the weakness of the state, that is the weaker the state, the more likely it is to bandwagon. This happens because 'weak states add little to the strength of the defensive coalition, but incur the wrath of the more threatening states nonetheless'.[47] Walt further argues that bandwagoning becomes more likely as aggregate capability, geographical proximity, offensive capabilities, and perceived intentions of the threatening state increase. While weak states may choose balancing when threatened by other similarly positioned states, they are inclined to bandwagon when threatened by a Great Power. Given the extremely high power differentials between most developed and developing countries in the international political economy, the theory would suggest that developing countries would bandwagon with coalitions like the Quad in the GATT or the Group of Ten in the IMF. The willingness of the Café au Lait Group even to discuss services was seen by the G-10 as a bandwagoning with the developed countries.

Balancing and bandwagoning posit two opposing alignment strategies. To adjudicate between their applicability, most scholars have taken the step of determining which type of behaviour is more common empirically. Randall Schweller argues, however, that such a line of enquiry is misleading. The motivation for bandwagoning is fundamentally different from balancing and can only be understood by introducing the concept of the revisionist state.[48] States satisfied with the status quo show balancing behaviour aimed at loss minimisation and preservation of systemic stability. But maintaining status quo is not the primary goal of revisionist states. Motivated more by profit than by merely survival or security, revisionist states bandwagon with the ascending revisionist power. Schweller contextualises theories that stress the importance of power and threat in balancing or bandwagoning by factoring in the intentions of the state as they relate to the international system.

Revisionist bandwagoning suggests that developing countries will not necessarily ally with the state with the largest market. Rather, the weak would ally with others that seek revision of the international system. Such bandwagons are certainly evident in special arrangements between some developed countries and groups of developing countries. The Nordic Group of Like-Minded countries, for instance, had worked in close association with developing countries in seeking greater equitable arrangements in the international system.

Between theories of balancing, bandwagoning, or revisionist bandwagoning, no clear winner emerges in the context of developing countries. Developing countries have attempted all the strategies that emerge from these theories – sometimes simultaneously – choosing to bandwagon with some powers, balance against other powers, seek the preservation of the system, and also lobby for systemic change. The reason for these contradictory trends is twofold. First developing countries are driven by a schizophrenia in their international relations, which was discussed in Section 1.1. As a result, they reveal tendencies to both bandwagon and balance in their revisionist and status quo capacities. Second, especially if the Realist assumption of interest-driven minimalist alliances is accepted, it is important to remember that interests in the international political economy often differ across issue areas. Whether a state will pursue a liberalising agenda or a protectionist one, whether it will seek trade-offs through issue linkages or not, and if military and political considerations will enter to determine economic alliances are determined by the place that the particular issue occupies in the state economy and the stakes of other parties in it. The institutional structure and its voting rules in which alignment strategies operate also go far to determine how far the weak choose to balance by forming a South-type coalition or bandwagon, and also how long-lasting the coalition will be. Coalition strategies of the developing countries in various UN bodies with majority voting have been distinctive in their formalisation, stability, and coalescing of the developing world. In contrast, coalitions in the GATT have been less institutionalised and more elusive. Raw interests, at least in international political economy, are considerably modified through issue specificities, processes, and institutions.

### 1.3.2   Theories emphasising processes and institutions

To all the domestic political economic models that were discussed in Section 1.3.1, James Alt and Michael Gilligan attach an important qualification, namely that domestic political institutions act closely with the various preference formations to determine whether a coalition will actually result.[49] Certain political institutions, for instance, reward small sectoral groups, which would render the costs of organising large inter-sectoral collective action particularly high. In contrast, if the political system rewards mass movements, sectoral groupings will merge to derive benefits. For either of the two types of coalitions based on theories of Heckscher–Ohlin or Ricardo–Viner to emerge, accompanying political conditions are critical. For instance, coalitions suggested by Rogowski require not only low factor specificity, but also low collective action costs and political institutions that reward mass movements. For the other extreme of coalition type to emerge, besides factor specificity, collective action costs must be high, and institutions must be less majoritarian. Coalitions also thrive on inertia, that is often coalitions continue to outlive their purpose and successes and reveal a similarity with institutional lags. The explanation lies in the high start-up costs of organisation; established groupings come with evolved coordinating agencies and institutions and hence find survival easier.

Some important analogies may be found between the effect of the domestic political context on interest groupings, and the international institutional context on inter-state bargaining coalitions. Some institutions like the UN and UNCTAD have proved particularly conducive to the operation of large bloc-type coalitions. In the GATT, by contrast, coalitions were difficult to sustain. The difference has been attributed in part to the contractual obligations that are negotiated in the GATT, as opposed to the declaratory documents that are approved in the UN.[50] Further, the persistence of certain coalitions, despite their failures, links up with the fixed costs invested in their creation, and the high costs of building new ones. This is a powerful explanation which helps us understand, in Chapter 3, why some coalitions, such as the Informal Group and its later G-10 version, remained unchallenged in spite of some visible failures and the availability of an alternative path of coalition formation.

The neo-liberal institutionalist stream of IR theorising places a similar emphasis on processes, regimes, and institutions to explain cooperation among states in the anarchical international system.[51] Coalitions in this perspective are not simply an incidental by-product of collective interests or short-term collaborative and coordinating mechanisms. Rather, they can be consciously created by altering strategies, changing the duration of interaction, altering pay-off patterns and introducing side-payments. Coalition-building is quite simply taking advantage of a mixed-motive situation by emphasising its cooperative elements and underplaying or overcoming its conflictual elements. Consequently, various inter-state cooperative endeavours (including alliances) are seen as less precarious, longer lasting, and driven by considerations other than immediate narrow interests and relative gains. A less deterministic account of coalitions results.

Interests continue to be important, as in Realism. Robert Axelrod and Robert Keohane accept Realist assumptions that in world politics, 'there is no common government to enforce rules, and by the standards of domestic society, international institutions are weak'.[52] Nonetheless, new instruments are introduced by different variants of the neo-liberal institutionalism to highlight the cooperative elements of several inter-state relationships. States may pursue a strategy of tit for tat and cooperate on a reciprocal basis. Conditional cooperation based on reciprocity is more likely if the game is iterated. The length of the game can be extended through a decomposition of pay-offs and long shadows of the future, which make states more willing to consider long-term gains and sustain cooperation. Issue linkages and side-deals can be used to give vested interests to different states in the cooperative endeavour. Cooperation is also more likely if the costs of verifying the compliance of partners and sanctioning cheaters are low. Herein lies the importance of institutions, for they reduce verification costs, increase iterativeness, and make threats of retaliation against defectors more credible. Verification and sanctioning can also be made easier if smaller numbers are involved.[53] Coordination problems among large numbers can be reduced through leadership and hierarchies.

How does this translate into the realm of developing countries in the international political economy? Neo-liberal institutionalism suggests how, once partners in a mixed-motive game are selected, cooperation can be sustained. Instances of logrolling and issue linkage can be found in most coalitions of developing countries. Developing countries also attempted to resolve the large-n problem in most of their coalitions by establishing informal hierarchies. In the Informal Group of developing countries in the GATT, for instance, Argentina, Brazil, Egypt, India, and the former Yugoslavia assumed the responsibilities of leadership. As the Big Five of the Informal Group, these countries bore the costs of research, agenda-setting, logrolling to incorporate the interests of smaller members, and free-riding particularly by those LDCs that were unable to invest research or representation in trade matters. The institutionalisation of South coalitions in other organisations such as the UNCTAD was used to reinforce the Informal Group through sharing of research and memberships, and enhancing iterativeness of the interaction cross-institutionally. All these processes proved critical in cementing a host of contradictory interests into a long-lasting coalition of developing countries in the GATT. These processes are examined in detail in Chapter 3.

Neo-liberal institutionalism leaves several questions on coalitions unanswered. First, as it does not offer a direct theory on alliance formation, it does not tell us how coalition partners are identified in the first place, before strategies for cooperation can be employed. Especially when large numbers are involved, as in the GATT, how do states decide on their potential coalition partners? Do they ally with the most 'like-*minded*' states, or do they work on the principle of greatest similarity of interests and proceed from there? Second, intricacies of the relative versus absolute gains debate notwithstanding,[54] it is not clear how far states are actually capable of assessing these gains, particularly when multiple partners are involved. In the absence of a clear cost–benefit analysis, what other factors determine the choice of alliance partner? Third, all the prescribed strategies given by neo-liberal institutionalism can also yield the opposite effect. Reciprocity can also yield an 'echo effect' of retaliation and defection.[55] Issue linkages, particularly when considered in terms of aggregate power resources and security matters, can exacerbate mutual distrust and increase reluctance to cooperate even in 'soft' areas due to their spillovers into critical issues. Finally, whether process can achieve anything at all without conducive conditions (i.e. interests) to start with and if it can emerge as an independent factor once launched are questions that can be effectively answered empirically. The case studies conducted in the rest of this book provide us with concrete instances of the role that structures play in cementing coalitions versus the role played by strategies. A comparative overview of these case studies further enables us to establish an ordering of the methods that can be employed for coalition formation.

### 1.3.3   *Constructivist theories: ideational and identity-based methods of coalition formation*

Constructivist or reflectivist theories facilitate a maximalist conceptualisation of coalitions by going beyond the 'rationalist' approach. Instead of taking state actors and interests as exogenously given, reflectivist theories treat interests as endogenous to interaction. Hence, this genre of theorising contrasts with all the theories discussed hitherto in the chapter, which assumed actors and their interests as given, and then considered instruments of achieving cooperation. By posing the rival claim that interaction redefines and changes the identities and interests of actors, reflectivist theories offer answers to some of the problems that were raised above. Most important, they suggest explanations regarding the basis on which states choose who to ally with in the first place, before the complicated machinations and coordination and collaboration actually begin. They also provide an explanation to the survival of some coalitions after external conditions or state interests have changed substantively, and the original rationale for the coalitions has disappeared.[56] It is possible to delineate various theories within this genre into weak and strong versions. The first emphasises the importance of ideas in conditioning, changing, and cementing interests.[57] The second is even more far-reaching and constructivist in the true sense of the word: it stresses the socially constructed identities of states.[58] For both versions, however, the identification of like-minded states with each other underlies coalition formation.

The idea that political ideas often underlie alliances is not new. Its logic is simple: states sharing similar internal features are likely to bear greater trust mutually, as they find it harder to anticipate aggressive intentions towards them from an inherently 'good', that is similar, state. The clearest enunciation of this logic is to be found in Democratic Peace Theory, but it was also visible in the alliance system of the Cold War. Alignment based on ideology is one way of defending one's ideological principles. Ideology-based alliances further enhance the legitimacy of a weak regime by demonstrating that it is a part of a large and popular movement.[59] But in most rationalist arguments, there is only a small place that ideological factors can occupy. For instance, even Walt, while incorporating ideology, treats it as a secondary, rather than a primary, factor in alliance formation. He argues that states follow ideological preference only if they are already fairly secure. 'When faced by great danger, however, they will take whatever allies they can get.'[60] Internally weak regimes are likely to seek ideology-based alliances to enhance their legitimacy. Finally, he notes that ideological affinity between allies is often claimed subsequent to the formation of alliances. In other words, ideology under rationalism is but a handmaiden in the service of pre-existing structural interests.

Presenting a striking contrast with rationalism, even weak versions of constructivism accord central importance to the role of ideas. Rather than a camouflage for structural interests, ideas determine, in a big way, what those interests might be. Drawing on the work of Geertz, Ngaire Woods highlights four roles that ideas can perform,[61] which may be suitably applied with respect to coalition construction. First, ideas provide an important explanatory factor in coalition construction and maintenance and thereby provide a method of coalition formation. Particularly in situations of uncertainty, in the absence of well-defined preference structures and in the initial choice of alliance partners from numerous alternatives, ideas can play a key role. Second, the cathartic function of ideas facilitates the identification of the 'other', thereby reinforcing the boundaries between the inside and the outside of the group. By creating morale, they can assist in the resolution of the conflict between short-term costs and long-term gains. Third, ideas reinforce group solidarity and facilitate coalition maintenance. Fourth, ideas assist in defining interests through their advocatory function and can also impact on the outside by placing the re-created, shared interests onto the international agenda. It could be argued that the diversity of developing countries was united as a group by precisely such a set of ideas. The idea of the 'South' offered developing countries a shared reading of history in terms of their exploitation. It posited them as a collective against the North, that is their exploiters, boosted their morale by promising them greater equality in the international system, offered them a way to achieve this aim, that is through group solidarity, and provided them some simple rules of thumb that they could apply to new situations for which they were individually ill prepared. Chapter 3 examines the role of some of these ideas in the maintenance of the Informal Group.

The second version of constructivism goes even further. In this stronger version, ideas, along with other factors such as interdependence and iterated cooperative behaviour, trigger off the reformulation of national state identities with a collective. Even symbolic actions help reinforce the collective identity thus formed. Hence, Alexander Wendt writes, '…when Third World states develop an ideology of "nonalignment" … states are engaging in discursive practices designed to express and/or to change ideas about who "the self" of self-interested collective action is'.[62] Further, collective identities persist even after the original rationale for them, in terms of structural interests or ideas, has disappeared.

The implications of collective identity formation for coalition creation and maintenance are far-reaching. If states belong to a coalition because of their mutual and collective identification with it, problems of relative gains, coordination, verification, and sanctions atrophy away. It is noteworthy that coalitions based on collective identity wherein certain states show a willingness to undergo relative losses do not rely on altruism. Rather, like the two prisoners who may identify with each other due to their being placed in a similar situation and may find a way out of the Prisoners' Dilemma, '"We" may be the natural unit of the first person decision.'[63] In other words, collective identities do not violate assumptions of the pursuit of self-interest; instead, they involve a redefinition of the self in terms of not the individual but the collective.

Theories of ideas and identity help explain how certain alliance partners are chosen in the first place, how costs of collective organisation and problems of relative gains and compensatory deals may be overcome, and why some coalitions persist even after the original motivation for them is gone. In incorporating processes in traditionally structural explanations, and showing the importance of non-material factors in state behaviour, the impact of these theories has been huge. But the extent to which coalition loyalty is determined by the structural interests of individual members versus a shared idea or identity remains debatable and is likely to vary across coalitions. The key question for us is: under what conditions, if at all, can ideas and identities provide the chief composition of the cement that can bind a coalition together? In attempting to answer this question, it is also important to consider Realist caution that sees non-rationalist factors as a *post facto* justification for the pursuit of interests that are determined by relative power distributions rather than in terms of ideas. If a pre-existing host of well-entrenched interests underlie the umbrella of ideas or identity uniting the coalition, it is important to establish a ranking of the three factors. The role of structural conditions and evolving processes and their interplay and evolution are recurring themes in this book. All the case studies help identify the conditions in which the rankings might change, and further facilitate some generalisations on the subject of ideas versus interests and their interplay, through a comparative approach.

In sum, what we have so far are three methods of coalition formation as derived from theories of coalitions drawn from diverse disciplines. However, when presented with the menu of methods just described, which one would developing countries be best off choosing? The lessons of the theories, resulting methods of coalition formation, and questions that remain unanswered are summarised in Table 1.1.

## 1.4   Definitions and typologies

Even if the theories examined in the previous section yield contradictory methods of coalition formation, they can be usefully employed to formulate a classification of coalitions based on the method that the coalition uses for bonding. This section proposes such a typology derived from the analyses presented in the previous section. But before presenting this typology, some definitional issues are clarified.

'Everyone knows what an alliance is; but no two scholars or editors can agree on a definition.'[64] Given the disagreement on definitional issues, it is not surprising that terms such as alliances, coalitions, and alignments are often used interchangeably. This book uses the term 'coalition' as an umbrella term that encompasses different types of alignment categories. A coalition refers to 'any group of decision-makers participating in … a negotiation and who agree to act in concert to achieve a common end'.[65] Such a definition includes all concerted activity involving cooperation among actors, which is aimed at achieving a well-defined, shared interest, that is the pursuit of 'a common end'. It also excludes certain types of cooperation. For instance, *ad hoc*, incidental policy convergence among

*Table 1.1* Theories of coalitions, lessons for inter-state bargaining, and resulting methods of coalition formation and maintenance

| Theories | Lessons | Resulting methods of coalition formation |
|---|---|---|
| Formal theories of bargaining | Importance of efficiency, trade-off between large numbers and viability | Interest-based methods |
| Theories of domestic political economy<br>(a) Rogowski | By extension through analogy<br>(a) Coalitions form on the basis of comparative advantage | |
| (b) Ricardo–Viner | (b) Considerations of comparative advantage disaggregate into interests at the level of the sector and sub-sector | |
| (c) Increasing returns to scale | (c) Nature of intra-industry trade determines regional formations | |
| Realist theories of IR | Importance of interests in determining coalition formation – coalition dissipates once interests change or goal fulfilled | |
| Institutionalist version of theories of domestic political economy:<br>Alt and Gilligan | Some institutions especially conducive to massive coalition formations such as the UN and others where coalitions are difficult, such as the GATT | Process-based methods |
| Neo-liberal institutionalist theories of IR | Coalitions cemented not by initial structures but through processes that promote the cooperative dimensions of interaction and minimise conflictual ones | |
| Constructivist theories of IR | Ideas and identity internal to the interaction as opposedand help define interests in terms of mutual and collective gain | Ideational and identity-based methods |

*What remains unanswered even after aggregation of theories*

Given all the methods suggested by existing theories, on what basis do states, particularly weak states, choose their allies? Some of the insights from the theories are mutually contradictory. For instance, the prescription that emerges by extending the Rogowski model is in direct opposition to that which emerges by extending the Ricardo–Viner model; the basis that Realism suggests to coalition formation discounts that suggested by Neo-Liberal Institutionalism and Constructivism; the internal contradictions of game theoretic approaches are too many to elaborate here. It could be argued that the insights from each of these theories are relevant at different times, but then we need to know precisely when this is so. Finally, under what conditions and with which strategies can particular coalition types ensure effective influence and durability? In other words, what are the various coalition possibilities that exist for developing countries, and when, how, and why do they work best?

state actors or a long-term harmonic game does not equal a coalition. To be classified in the category of coalitions, group behaviour must involve conscious coordination: a coalition exists only when its members are aware of acting in such a collectivity.

On the basis of the discussion of the rationalist and constructivist theories in the previous section, it is possible to delineate coalitions in terms of two ends of a spectrum: alliance type and bloc type. This typology is put forth with caution, and in recognition of the fact that most coalitions encompass elements of both types in varying degrees and can often be found in the middle of the spectrum rather than the two ends. Nonetheless, this somewhat purist categorisation is conceptually necessary to recognise that, depending on the method employed at construction and maintenance, different results ensue.

The distinguishing characteristic of the first type is that the coalitions therein are concrete manifestations of the very specific give and take that is envisaged by most rationalist theories. Relative power considerations, trade-offs through logrolling and resulting collective weight are all factored in the construction of this type. While such coalitions may combine interests across sectors, they are easiest to construct when they are issue-based. This is because assessment of deals and complementary logrolling are most feasible within a restricted issue area. This would also suggest that these coalitions are likely to persist as long as the original cause for coalition creation persists and intra-coalition deals continue to yield expected pay-offs to members. The stability of alliance-type coalitions, in other words, rests on the fulfilment of the self-interest of members, and their inability to dislodge members from other alliances to form a more beneficial coalition.[66]

It is noteworthy that the term alliance is usually associated with security matters. Walt, for instance, includes informal and formal arrangements in this category, but identifies their defining features as 'a commitment for mutual military support against some external actor(s) in some specified set of circumstances'.[67] Nonetheless, the term bears considerable relevance to us as the type of interaction entailed in alliances minus the security dimension is easily found in focused coalitions engaged in compensatory trade-offs among members. Wendt gets to the heart of the matter when he defines alliances as 'temporary coalitions of self-interested states who come together for instrumental reasons in response to a specific threat. Once the threat is gone, the coalition loses its rationale and should disband'.[68] Three features may be extrapolated to alliance-type coalitions in the international political economy: (1) self-interested actors as opposed to collective identities; (2) instrumental reasons for coming together as opposed to ideational reasons; and (3) directed towards specific threats rather than forming an identity that makes an ideological point and hopes to be relevant in all situations. Issue-based coalitions that combined developed and developing countries over particular sub-sectors in services exemplify this type and are discussed in Chapter 5.

Blocs form the second coalition type. Blocs are characterised by the fact that they combine only 'like-minded' states and utilise the constructivist method for cementing members into a coalition. It is possible that a coalition may begin as an alliance type and then develop a collective identity among its members to form a bloc. Alternatively, bloc-type coalitions may utilise pre-existing similarities with other states. The noteworthy characteristic is the conscious restriction of membership to states sharing the same set of ideas or identity, once these states have been identified. Blocs, in general, need not be issue-specific, and can outlive any original issue that brought the states together. As such, blocs reveal great durability, adapting themselves to new issues, even after the original issue for their creation has been resolved and irrespective of the successes or failures of the group in achieving that resolution. Examples of bloc-type coalitions include developing countries operating together as the Third World, or the group of Islamic countries taking a common stance on population issues.

Alliance-type coalitions versus blocs offer different advantages. One is likely to work better in some situations than the other. Agenda-setting and negotiating require intra-coalition flexibility and reworked deals, and hence are likely to thrive with alliance-type coalitions which fulfil the separate interests of individual members. Alliance-type coalitions offer the advantage of being able to include new members without concerning themselves about whether the potential entrant is sufficiently like-minded or not, and can also include new deals and issue linkages without fearing that this might compromise the ideology of the group. Blocs, in contrast, are likely to be best at proposal-making and blocking, that is processes which do not challenge the collective idea or identity of the group through carrots offered to individual members.[69] The G-77 in the UNCTAD presents one example of such a bloc. Of course, in the real world today, states do not usually consciously identify a priori that they would like to build coalitions with agenda-setting versus proposal-making versus negotiating versus blocking aims. Interviews with diplomats indicate that few coalitions involving developing countries limit themselves to purely proposal-making rhetoric of UNCTAD-style diplomacy, while even alliance-type issue-based coalitions hope to exercise sufficient influence to be able to block the negotiations, if necessary. Also, depending on the interests of states with respect to particular issue areas, countries decide on their preferences for alliances versus blocs, or which type will form the large component of the coalition.

Finally, it is important to remember that the definitions given above also exclude some multilateral collective activity. Collusion, that is agreement between firms to cooperate by raising prices, dividing markets or otherwise restraining competition,[70] for instance, forms the basis of cartels; but cartels are deviant cousins of coalitions. They may choose to bargain but, on account of their production monopoly, are not under pressures of necessity to do so. The empirical experience of developing countries with cartels has shown OPEC successes in the 1970s to be more the exception than the rule. Cartelisation also invited retaliation through the search for substitutes, and further undermined whatever minimal advantage developing countries had enjoyed as suppliers of commodities. Hence while all coalitions hope to have the collective resource-based weight of cartels, they have a chosen alternative, more positive ways of bargaining as well as other sources of influence. Similarly, as the chapter on regionalism argues, coalitions based on regionalism are different from regional trade arrangements. Unless regional trade arrangements are utilised as a common bargaining platform, they are not included in the set of coalitions that form the subject of this book.

## 1.5   Conclusion

This chapter has demonstrated ways in which bargaining in coalitions may assist developing countries in overcoming some of their weaknesses. Recognising that coalitions are difficult to construct and maintain, it tapped into different types of theories that are directly (theories of International Relations) or indirectly (formal theories of coalitions and theories of coalitions in the domestic political economy) applicable to inter-state bargaining coalitions. The theories offer different viewpoints into the methods that states can employ to provide cohesion to the coalition as well as the source of bargaining influence that they chiefly draw on. Most rationalist theories stress the importance of structural interests in uniting the coalition, and hint at resource-based structural weight for exercising influence. But even the most hard-core Realists recognise that this bargaining power is contextual, and is dependent on other factors such as cohesion of the opposing bloc. Neo-liberals go further in emphasising context and institutions to explain the big influence of small allies. Unity among allies, divisions among opponents, information access, an 'epistemic consensus', voting patterns in international organisations, and relative costs of coalition formation all determine the strength that may accrue to the weak. Constructivist interpretations are the most far reaching in emphasising that certain ideas (even when propagated by small and weak coalitions) are likely to gain widespread acceptance. They also suggest the importance of shared identities in overcoming the internal costs of collective organisation and allowing greater relative weight to the coalition irrespective of a smaller aggregated resource base. Each of these theories explains a different part of reality. Precisely when a Realist, neo-liberal institutionalist or constructivist strategy would be adopted, and when a coalition would be a minimalist alliance or a maximalist bloc are determined by context. Here, context refers to potential countries involved, the nature of state interests, the short versus the long term in the realisation of those interests, the issue under consideration, support and opposition outside, the range of strategies available, and so forth. States differ on their aims and hence opt for functional, alliance-type coalitions in some cases or wide-ranging blocs restricted to like-minded states in others, or combine both types in varying degrees. In other words, it is almost irrelevant to speak of the methods and types of coalition formation without specifying who employs these methods and what they seek to achieve. Such an enquiry is conducted in the following chapters.

# 2 Coalitions in the GATT and the entry of services

> Power, place and time facilitate each other.
> (*Arthashastra*, 9.1.33)

While the problems and possibilities of forming coalitions are many, certain institutions and contexts exacerbate the original problem of choosing allies and cementing coalitions. This chapter analyses the structures and processes that underlie the functioning of the GATT and the WTO and examines how they have affected coalition formation among developing countries. It also provides reasons for choosing trade in services as the central focus of enquiry. The entry of services into the GATT pre-negotiation and negotiation phases is shown to be critical for developing countries in two ways. First, the services sector precipitated unprecedented challenges as well as potential opportunities for developing countries and thereby necessitated innovative attempts at viable coalition formation, hence the much more active participation of developing countries in the GATT since the 1980s. Second, the services issue delivered a deathblow to the old type of coalition diplomacy of developing countries in the GATT but also spawned new coalition types. The chapter also assesses the implications of heightened developing country participation and new coalition patterns since the 1980s, and locates these implications in the context of the WTO.

## 2.1 Participation and coalitions: developing countries in the GATT

The WTO may be a young institution, but it has a long history of evolution in the GATT and continues with many of the structures and decision-making procedures of its predecessor. Immediately after the Second World War, policy-makers recognised that there was a strong correlation between a stable and prosperous economic system and international peace. The memory of the adverse consequences of the beggar-thy-neighbour policies of the 1930s was still vivid and generated an unprecedented support for multilateralism by most countries, including the US. As part of the effort to build a stable economic system based on multilateral institutions, tariff negotiations were opened up among twenty-three countries in 1946 that were aimed at building the International Trade Organisation (ITO).

The tariff concessions and rules that emerged from these negotiations became known as the GATT, which was accepted on a provisional basis and entered into force on January 1948. The Havana Charter establishing the ITO was agreed to by 53 of the 56 countries that had attended the meeting in the same year. But ratification of the Charter proved difficult in many national legislatures. The US government's announcement in 1950 that it would not seek Congressional ratification of the Charter effectively rendered the ITO a non-starter. And the 'provisional' GATT continued to provide the rules for the multilateral trading system for the next forty-seven years.[1]

Even at the formation of the GATT, 11 of the 23 original signatories were developing countries. However, despite their fairly large proportion of the total membership, which soon grew to a majority position, developing countries maintained a low profile in the GATT. Any attempts that they made to influence the agenda of the GATT were usually through indirect channels. For instance, external pressure was occasionally wielded on the GATT through the G-77 in the UNCTAD and through majoritarian activities in the General Assembly. But the activity of developing countries in other institutions contrasted with their limited participation in the GATT. The Informal Group of Developing Countries (IGDC) in the GATT was traditionally dominated by the big five – Argentina, Brazil, Egypt, India, and the former Yugoslavia, and included Chile, Jamaica, Pakistan, Peru, and Uruguay as the other active members. But informality took its toll in ambiguous stances and membership: Israel and Turkey, and Spain and Greece (until their accession to Europe), were also a part of the group. The group offered a weak and poorly visible comparison against the more well-institutionalised groupings like the NAM and Afro-Asian Unity in the UN General Assembly and the G-77 in the GATT. Academic analysis reflected this reality, and hence while there is an abundance of writing on traditional North–South debates associated especially with the NIEO or international debt bargaining,[2] writings on coalitions in the GATT are scarce.

The minimal collective organisation of developing countries in the GATT also compared poorly with the well-entrenched coalition patterns of the developed countries in the same institution. This point is of considerable importance as it illustrates that the GATT *per se* was not universally conducive to coalition formation. Of course, the participation of developed countries was partly spurred by individual member initiatives, that is by economies large enough to exercise considerable bargaining power on their own. But the importance of collective action in furthering the active involvement and influence of the developed countries was obvious in the effort they spent in operating through coalitions. These coalitions included the Quad,[3] the Nordic group of like-minded countries, and the EC.

The reluctance of developing countries to participate actively in the GATT merits some surprise at first glance. The GATT entitled every country to one vote; this provision has been retained in the WTO through Article IX:1 of the Agreement Establishing the WTO and allows developing countries the possibility of commanding a wide majority in GATT decision-making processes, irrespective of their small share in world trade. This egalitarian voting structure presents a striking contrast to the weighted voting system prevalent in other international organisations like the IMF. Yet, not even the temptation of this potential voting power and resulting bargaining leeway could jolt developing countries into an enthusiastic, UN-type, bloc-based participation in the GATT.

Several reasons may explain this seemingly recalcitrant behaviour. Unwillingness to participate in the institution did play a partial role. The unwillingness of developing countries to participate in the GATT derived from the free trade ethos espoused by the GATT, which often contradicted the policies of greater protectionism and interventionism in the developing world, especially in the late 1950s and 1960s. Additionally, the GATT was seen as a poor substitute for the stillborn ITO. Unlike the ITO, the original Articles of Agreement made no mention of economic development. The GATT also avoided distinctions between stronger and weaker parties, and was thereby seen to expose developing countries to unfair competition. But a good measure of the unwillingness of developing countries to make use of the power of their large numbers in the GATT was a product of their belief that its institutional structures and procedures were unfavourable to their participation.

There were three main characteristics of the GATT that rendered participation in the organisation difficult. Although formally a democratic, one-member-one-vote institution, most decisions in the GATT were taken by consensus. More of a de facto norm in the GATT, consensus-based decision-making was institutionalised in the WTO through Article IX:1, which states: 'The WTO shall continue the practice of decision-making by consensus followed under GATT 1947.' Consensus is arrived at 'if no Member, present at the meeting at which the decision is taken, formally objects to the proposed decision'. There were four key problems with consensus decision-making, all of which persist even today. First, the key assumption in consensus decision-making procedures is presence, and many developing countries lacked permanent presence in Geneva and therefore have simply not been able to object to the 'consensus'. Second, consensus was arrived at through an open show of hands as opposed to a secret ballot. Many developing countries feared an open display of dissent and therefore resorted to the alternative of remaining silent. However, silence too was interpreted as a lack of objection and therefore equalling consensus. Third, the goal of consensus was used by the developed countries as an excuse to hold small group exclusionary meetings. Fourth, any insistence on majority voting would simply have resulted in the bypassing of the GATT by the developed countries, and recourse to bilateral and regional arrangements. Such threats were indeed put to use by developed countries in the Uruguay Round, as is discussed in Chapter 3. Given the norm of consensus decision-making, there was little question of making use of the power of the large numbers that developing countries enjoyed as GATT members.

Second, the provisional nature of the GATT meant that it had a very small secretariat. In 1951, in recognition of the fact that the decision-making sessions of the Contracting Parties were not enough, an inter-sessional committee was formed. This was replaced in 1960 by a Council of Representatives – also a body of national delegates – with greater powers for the everyday management of the GATT. The Secretariat that was eventually established was known as the Interim Commission for the International Trade Organisation (ICITO), with its name indicating its provisional nature.[4] As a result, the onus of negotiating and implementing the agreements fell on the members themselves. Not only did they have to be present to participate in the consensus-building process, but they were also required to have an informed presence to participate knowledgeably and actively in some of the technical issues that were negotiated. It was the members of the GATT themselves who took the decisions and enforced them, leaving the Secretariat to provide technical and administrative support. Contrasting power balances between the developed versus the developing worlds were hence translated into the GATT in contrasting resource availability and diplomatic expertise. It is not surprising that the GATT was seen as a 'Rich Man's Club' where only the most powerful were able to represent their interests.

Third, consensus decision-making and member-driven character necessitated considerable reliance on a network of informal processes to facilitate the working of the institution. This behind-the-scenes activity that is key to negotiating consensus took place in a variety of small group meetings and informal meetings of Heads of Delegations (HODs). Its greatest drawback was that it diminished the benefits of certainty that derived from belonging to an institution and were crucial for developing countries that have traditionally sought an 'authoritative allocation of values' as per Stephen Krasner.[5] Particularly in the days of the GATT and even the pre-Seattle days of the WTO, developing countries were often not even informed of key informal meetings that were called to beat the consensus into shape, and hence were left out of this crucial stage of consensus building. In the absence of strict rules about the agenda, membership, and frequency of the meetings, the informal protocols of interaction and culture of the institution acquired overwhelming importance. The 'almost English Club atmosphere ... the codified language'[6] made the Green Room consultative process even more inaccessible for developing countries.

In addition to all the procedural constraints highlighted above, the GATT operated on the Principal Supplier Principle and hence negotiations directly reflected the strengths of the parties. As per this de facto principle, negotiations took place between principal suppliers and consumers, and were then extended to other members on the basis of Article 1 (granting most favoured nation (MFN) status to all members).[7] In fact, developed countries often packed the negotiating agenda with issues of interest to themselves, disregarding or excluding issues where the comparative advantage of developing countries lay (e.g. classically, agriculture, and textiles through exceptions). Not only did developing countries usually lack principal supplier status for most products that were brought within the GATT agenda, but they were also poorly informed to contribute to the expanding agenda of the WTO. Their inability to participate in complex new issues was further exacerbated by the fact that they encountered the new issues only after the developed countries had agreed upon an essential complete version. Given these built-in procedural and structural constraints, developing countries refused to engage in reciprocal negotiations and instead insisted on Special and Differential (S&D) treatment and free rode on whatever they could through MFN.

All the institutional constraints highlighted above affected not only the individual participation of developing countries but also their coalition formation.

Identifying possible allies with common interests was not an easy task, especially when negotiations in the GATT involved precise concessions, in contrast to rhetorical enunciation of principles and declarations as in the General Assembly and the UNCTAD. This was an even bigger problem given the demands that the informal diplomacy and member-driven character of the institution placed upon member countries. Delegations from developing countries often lacked the expertise and coverage that were easily wielded by the developed world. The difference in resource availability is clear from the numbers of delegates: at the December 1990 Brussels GATT summit, the US delegation consisted of over 400 delegates, which was more than the combined total of the staffs of the sub-Saharan African and Latin American trade missions.

Also of direct relevance to coalition formation was the fact that the GATT apparatus had taken pride in not allowing group-dominated diplomacy, hence the relentless emphasis on the consensus-based approach, despite the elaborate network of informal coalitions that actually beat the 'consensus' into shape. Cleavages along North–South lines were pronounced, but GATT officials refused to recognise them as such.[8] The non-recognition of coalitions, while extending to coalitions of developed countries as well, had a much deeper and more adverse impact upon the participation of developing countries in the GATT, as explained below.

For developed countries, shares in international markets were sufficiently high to allow them a voice as agenda-setters and hard-bargain drivers in GATT negotiations. The need for coalitions was not quite as urgent because even a small set of developed-country partners could form a dominating coalition in the GATT (e.g. the Quad). High stakes and small numbers meant that coalition creation and maintenance were possible, even without institutionalisation. This presented a striking contrast to developing countries for whom higher numbers were necessary to allow the critical weight necessary for agenda-setting, while the absence of recognition and institutionalisation rendered this construct even more difficult to build and maintain. It is not surprising that developing countries saw the GATT as an especially unfavourable arena for their diplomacy and preferred to direct their precious diplomatic resources and effort elsewhere.

The adverse structural features of the GATT reinforced some initial reservations of developing countries regarding the new institution. The mandate of the GATT had been seen as severely limited and a poor sop for the provisions of the stillborn ITO. Unlike the ITO for instance, the original Articles of Agreement made no mention of economic development, and the GATT made little attempt in its initial years to change this. The GATT also avoided distinctions between weaker and stronger parties, and was thereby seen to expose developing countries to unfair competition. Ideologically, the free-trade ethos espoused by the GATT often contradicted the preferred economic policies, especially after the late 1950s and 1960s, of greater protectionism and interventionism championed by a large proportion of the developing world. Trade was still seen, at best, as only one and not necessarily the most efficient engine for growth; aid, protection, and self-sufficiency provided alternative paths whose potential had still not been negated by experience.[9]

There inevitably existed a close interplay between GATT structures and the nature of international trade outside. Given that North–South trade was small compared with North–North trade, developing countries assumed that, at least in the GATT institutional context, minimal North–South trade would considerably reduce their negotiating leverage. The de facto weighted voting that resulted from Green Room diplomacy (from which most developing countries were excluded) was seen as confirmation of the suspicion that, irrespective of one-member-one-vote rules, the influence of developing countries in the GATT would be minimal. Limited North–South trade also undermined their willingness to participate in an institution in which their stakes were not high anyway. At least some developing countries in the post-colonial era chose to rely on the unilateral benevolence of the developed world to look after their trade interests, which further promoted a passive negotiating approach.[10]

All of the above meant that the sullen recalcitrance of developing countries in refusing to participate actively in the GATT was more a product of their inability to do so rather than unwillingness. Their interests in the GATT were few, given limitations on their participatory and agenda-setting powers. In contrast, the costs of active participation were high, given the limited research resources and constraints on institutionalised coalition-building. Most preferred to expend diplomatic resources and efforts in alternative forums like the UNCTAD, where their coalitions were allowed more lasting impact through institutional recognition, and they were more likely to get issues of their own interest onto the negotiating table. As a result, the proverbial GATT bicycle began moving, while developing countries got left behind.

## 2.2   Introducing services in the GATT

Services entered the GATT with a bang. The first result of that explosion was to shake developing countries out of their passivity. It brought the realisation that the challenges and opportunities presented by the new issues could be dealt with only through active participation in the GATT. The services sector also opened up an alternative path to achieve such a proactive role, namely that of participation through different types of coalitions.

The introduction of the services issue at the 1982 Ministerial began by catalysing the Informal Group into an unprecedented and formalised version, the G-10. The pre-launch phase of the Uruguay Round also precipitated the involvement of developing countries into a new coalition experiment of the Café au Lait Group on services, that is the G-20 that grew into the G-48. It is noteworthy that the group was unprecedented to the GATT as well as to other international institutions in combining developed and developing countries into what is termed in this book as a 'crossover' coalition. It was also unique in its issue-area focus and in bringing some of the smaller, less powerful developing countries to the fore. The successes and failures of these two distinct coalitions sparked off a riot of alternative coalition attempts. Section 2.3 provides a description and classification of these new coalition types and further analyses the implications of this new pattern of coalition activity. The jump from indirect participation in the 'Rich Man's Club' for over three decades to a mayhem of multiple, cross-cutting, and overlapping coalitions was dramatic. This section traces the cause for this jump.

Most market-oriented approaches have ascribed the shift in developing countries' behaviour, from minimal coalitions and involvement to their prolific growth and active engagement, to an enlightened acceptance of more liberal trade policies and a rejection of models of state-led growth. This line of explanation accords considerable importance to the adverse conditions of the 1980s that increased the vulnerabilities of developing countries. There is some truth in such interpretations for adversity necessitated a reaction of some sort. But the critical turning point came with the introduction of services in GATT discussions. The services issue provided the immediate cause and catalyst to the reaction and also determined the form that such a reaction would take, that is through coalitions facilitating an active involvement of developing countries to meet the unprecedented challenges and opportunities that forays into the new issues posed. As such, even a preliminary discussion of services in a GATT context represented a crisis situation for the developing-country members and generated a corresponding response. The greater part of this section studies why the entry of services onto the pre-negotiation GATT agenda provided the turning point for active coalition formation among developing countries, after taking more conventional explanations into account.

It is true and unsurprising that the general economic slowdown of the 1980s drove developing countries to the negotiating table. The deceleration of world growth had several causes, such as the oil crises and deflationary policies that were employed by the developed countries to deal with their deficits. But its impact on developing countries was particularly adverse. The shares of developing countries in world exports stood at 31 per cent in 1950 but had declined to 23.8 per cent by 1985.[11] The UNCTAD estimates the resultant cumulative loss at $93.1 billion, during the period 1981–1986 for the developing world. Declining aid flows from the North and unsustainable commercial borrowings by developing countries heightened their vulnerabilities further. In 1981 alone, the non-oil developing countries had borrowed over $70 million to finance their overall current account deficit.[12] In such circumstances, developing countries were forced to consider the East Asian model of export-oriented growth, and seek an expansion of their world trade to counter their widening deficits. This path, however, also proved difficult to follow, due to the rising grey-area measures of protectionism and increasing resort to bilateralism that had further marred the workings of an already skewed multilateral trade system. Developing countries could no longer afford to stand on the sidelines of GATT negotiations. The free ride on the principal supplier principle was over, and non-tariff measures (NTMs) were likely to increase unless a proactive stance was taken against them.[13]

The intensity of participation of developing countries in the GATT since the pre-launch phase of the Uruguay Round is historic. But why developing countries chose the institution of the GATT to deal with the adverse scenario is not obvious. In many ways, the GATT was seen as a failing institution due to its inability to counter NTMs. The failure of the 1982 Ministerial did little to assure members of the efficacy of the GATT. Developing countries could have simply persisted in their old habit of expressing their agenda through UNCTAD diplomacy. At another extreme, they could have chosen the path of unilateral liberalisation. The choice of vociferous participation in the GATT instead, and through active coalitions, was determined most immediately by the entry of services.

The possibility of an inclusion of the services sector in GATT negotiations greatly increased the stakes in participation. Recognition of these high stakes was prevalent among developed and developing countries alike, despite initial ambiguities about definition and composition of the issue. The effort expended by developed countries, and particularly by the US, to bring trade in services within the purview of the GATT had various motivations. The initial momentum came from a perceived shift in their comparative advantage by the developed countries. Lobbying by a small group of financial services firms to maintain or improve rights of establishment abroad was another factor. The momentum was reinforced by the recognition by some policy-makers of the importance of securing the support of these lobbies to counter anti-GATT sentiment in the US.[14] Developing countries, which had hitherto been essentially indifferent to GATT proceedings, became vigilant when the services issue was considered at the Ministerial. While they were still uncertain about the competitiveness of their services sector, it was clear that their participation was essential, whether to slow down the juggernaut of services liberalisation or to bandwagon with it.

The push for an inclusion of services within the GATT differed from all previous agenda-setting episodes by the developed countries. The proposed agenda was fraught with greater hurdles and opportunities for developing countries than ever before. First, an international agreement on services threatened unprecedented encroachments on domestic economic legislation. While affecting both developed and developing economies, any reduction in domestic authority was seen as especially detrimental to the quasi-states of the Third World. Second, services represented a qualitatively 'new' set of issues. Developing countries feared that services would engage the attention and resources of the GATT with a corresponding disregard of the old issues that were of major concern to them. Third, despite inadequate theorising on the subject, it was clear that services represented the key to the health of national economies. This was as true of developing countries as the developed countries. The importance of the sector can be gauged from the fact that the services sector was the largest economic sector in both developed and developing countries, contributing to a higher percentage of gross domestic product (GDP) than either the extractive or manufacturing sector (see Table 2.1). Given its importance, concessions on the sector as a whole or any of its sub-sectors without a complete understanding of their implications could seriously endanger other sectors of the economy. Fourth, it was recognised that services as an extremely influential and important sector gave developing countries a new opportunity. By withholding or offering their support, they could utilise services as a bargaining chip. Underlying all these dangers and opportunities was the uncertainty associated with the new sector, which rendered developing

*Table 2.1* Percentage of GDP and employment by economic sector: 1981

| Economic sector | Development category | | | |
|---|---|---|---|---|
| | Lower income | Middle income | Upper middle income | Industrialised |
| GDP | | | | |
| Extractive sector | 42 | 27 | 15 | 7 |
| Manufacturing | 10 | 16 | 21 | 27 |
| Services | 48 | 57 | 64 | 66 |
| Employment | | | | |
| Extractive | 72 | 53 | 25 | 9 |
| Manufacturing | 10 | 14 | 22 | 24 |
| Services | 18 | 33 | 53 | 67 |

Source: Riddle (1986), p. 6.

countries even more ill prepared than usual to carefully analyse and contribute to the proposed agenda.

The attempt to include services in the GATT immediately galvanised developing countries into a blocking coalition. Over sixty-one developing countries expressed resistance to endorsing the new round. Reservations of developing countries were shaped by arguments of exceptionality of the services sector, the inapplicability of conventional theories of trade in goods to services, and the oxymoron of 'trade in services' given that services were regarded as non-tradables. Most of these arguments were gradually invalidated. It was emphasised that services could indeed be traded, particularly after the distinction between embodied and disembodied services was recognised and suitable modes of supply to facilitate their delivery incorporated.[15] Theoretical and empirical work concluded that 'conventional trade theory applies not only to goods but also services'.[16] While recognising that developed countries enjoyed a comparative advantage in services owing to their physical and skilled human capital abundance, it was also pointed out that developing countries could also develop their comparative advantage either through an accumulation of physical and human capital or through a concentration in labour-intensive services. It was suggested that even an increase in their services imports would accrue large gains to developing countries, especially in view of their role as intermediate inputs in most other activities.[17] Developing countries realised that the only way of minimising the difficulties and availing themselves of the opportunities was through the process of concerted action in groups.

Even after some of the initial concerns of developing countries were resolved, reasons for caution continued. Certain characteristics intrinsic to the services sector had impeded developing countries from cultivating a comparative advantage therein. For instance, the importance of pervasive asymmetries of information meant that services markets rely on reputation rather than price competition to signal quality. Not only is this asset enjoyed by companies with longer histories in the services market, that is companies from industrialised countries, but as a sunk cost, reputation creates barriers to entry. The fact that tradability of goods is dependent upon efficient provision of services, and the services market represents the most rapidly growing sectoral market today, renders the sector a specially sensitive one. The inclusion of 'trade in services' – first less directly through the dual track and subsequently more obviously through the Single Undertaking – opened up a Pandora's box of issues that necessitated international encroachments into the realm of domestic policy. Even developed countries, let alone the developing countries, were ill prepared for the spillovers into areas of domestic legislation and unconventional trade issues (including investment measures and even immigration policies). The criticality of the services sector, its great potential for expansion, and the immediate lack of developing country advantage in the sector all led to the search for a bargaining strength that could be collectively obtained through coalition maintenance.

The need of developing countries to operate collectively in the GATT was further exacerbated by the scarcely disguised play of power politics in the services sector. While considerations of power operate in all areas of economic diplomacy, the newness of the services sector increased the scope of power manipulation manifold. From the inclusion of services within GATT auspices to matters of definition and promotion of particular modes of supply, the incorporation of the agenda of developed countries, particularly the US agenda, was evident.[18] It is noteworthy that developing countries had started out with the hard-liners' stance of resisting any discussion on the new issues. The 'compromise' reached at the Ministerial in 1982 accommodated the US proposal for a work programme on services, which would allow the GATT to prepare a technical base for negotiations in the area. Slipping from the initial hard line, developing countries agreed to the work programme. But they also pointed out the difficulties involved in trade in non-tradables as well as an inadequacy of theoretical and empirical work on services to allow any negotiations at all. Another 'compromise', this time at Punta del Este, initiated negotiations on 'trade in services'. Developing countries now merely asserted the need to avoid cross-sectoral linkages through the preservation of the dual-track mechanism. Yet another 'compromise' subsequently, and the dual track mechanism was abandoned with the incorporation of the General Agreement on Trade in Services (GATS) within WTO institutions. Still hoping to bargain competitively in future services negotiations, several developing countries had argued that the mode of supply through direct presence, that is Foreign Direct Investment (FDI) (which would benefit the Northern Multi-National Corporations (MNCs) without allowing any gains to the developing countries) be restricted; in fact, this mode of supply received the greatest attention in GATS schedules. Finally, recognising that the negative blocking strategies of the G-10 had yielded few successes, even the erstwhile hard-liners adopted a positive agenda of lobbying for supply of services through the factor movement of labour (to counter the greater freedom of movement that was accorded to capital). The annex on professional services, however, is replete with legitimisation of non-tariff barriers (NTBs) such as the Economic Needs Test (ENT), and little has been done to facilitate the liberalisation of embodied labour intensive services in which developing countries have a comparative advantage. These 'compromises' that developing countries were compelled to make reinforced the need for coalitions and their maintenance.

The attempt to optimise the opportunities against the losses caused by an inclusion of services in the GATT resulted in the series of coalition experiments analysed in this book. The next section provides a brief description of these experiments and analyses the costs and benefits of their very rapid turnover.

## 2.3   'Shifting coalitions' in the GATT and WTO

The response of developing countries to the new threats and opportunities posed by the international trade scenario in general, and the services issue in particular, was to participate actively in the GATT through joint platforms. In the aftermath of the successes and failures of the G-10 and the G-20, developing countries began their experiments with various combinations of coalition types. The new experimental coalitions were characterised by a very rapid turnover and short lives. A brief account of these coalitions is provided below. Table 2.2 provides a summary of the dates, membership and agenda of some of the coalitions that are studied in this book. Particularly in the Uruguay Round phase, the coalitions covered in this book are those that pertain especially to services. However, with reference to the new Doha Development Agenda, the book also covers coalitions in other issue areas. Note also that this is because by 1999, services already formed a part of the built-in agenda, and there were several other issues that began to occupy developing countries. It is also worth noting that many of the coalitions have ambiguous dates and periods of operation. This is because of the informality that surrounds coalitions in the GATT and WTO. As a result, many coalitions (e.g. the Informal Group of Developing Countries and as its name indicates) had existed in the past but only swung into action in response to the services issue. There are others that came up as intermittent chat groups and dissipated after the production of one joint proposal. Note also that this is by no means an exhaustive list of developing country coalitions, or even developing country coalitions on services, especially when coalitions belong to the occasional chat-group variety. Rather, it provides illustrations of the prominent coalitions of each type that emerged and left important lessons for future coalitions involving developing countries.

For analytical purposes, this book classifies the chaos of coalitions in services into four types. Variants of all the four types have continued into the present. First, combining the features of the two archetypal coalitions of the bloc-type G-10 and the alliance-type G-20/Café au Lait, some coalitions were constructed within the bloc of developing countries but acquired a services focus. Other coalitions in different issue areas were built in more recent years using the same principle of adhering to a bloc of developing countries. The second category drew on the lessons of the previous category and moved closer to the Café au Lait in forming small, crossover alliance-type groups but with a sub-sectoral focus. Note that the term 'crossover' is used in this book to refer to coalitions that combine both developed and developing countries. However, we also see some variants of the sub-sector alliance that were limited to developing countries. The third type epitomised the Café au Lait and also incorporated the lessons of the Cairns Group on agriculture. These were the crossover alliances that operated at the level of the issue area or sector level rather than the sub-sector level. The Friends of Services Group exemplified this type of alliance diplomacy in services. This type also

Table 2.2 Prominent coalitions of developing countries in GATT and WTO

| Coalition type | Name of coalition | Dates of operation | Membership (At the time of formation) | Agenda |
|---|---|---|---|---|
| Archetype bloc | IGDC – institutionalised as the G-10 (Chapter 3) | Institutionalised as G-10 in 1982; dissipated as G-10 in 1986 though survives even today as the IGDC | In pre-Uruguay phase, led by Argentina, Brazil, Egypt, India, and the former Yugoslavia, but was inclusive of all developing countries (ambiguously defined) | Very broad with traditional, Third Worldist stance; catalysed as G-10 particularly by opposition to inclusion of services in GATT in the early 1980s; functions today more for information exchange and issue identification |
| Archetype alliance | Café au Lait – G-20 comprising developing countries liased with G-9 developed countries; eventually constituted the G-48 (Chapter 4) | Formed in 1983 and continued until 1986; continued in new incarnations like Friends of Services in the Uruguay Round | G-20 = Bangladesh, Chile, Colombia, Hong Kong, Indonesia, Ivory Coast, Jamaica, Malaysia, Mexico, Pakistan, Philippines, Romania, Singapore, Sri Lanka, South Korea, Thailand, Turkey, Uruguay, Zambia, and Zaire; G-9 = Australia, Austria, Canada, Finland, Iceland, New Zealand, Norway, Sweden, and Switzerland | Began as an informal information exchange on services led by Colombia and Switzerland and crystallised into a 'negotiating' coalition between the G-10 hardliners and the Quad |
| | Developing Countries on Services (Chapter 5) | Attempted bloc immediately after 1986 | The broad group of developing countries | Limit GATT negotiations on services and emphasis on development issues |

(Continued)

Table 2.2 (Continued)

| Coalition type | Name of coalition | Dates of operation | Membership (At the time of formation) | Agenda |
|---|---|---|---|---|
| Type I – Bloc of developing countries (issue-based focus and cross-issue) | Like-Minded Group (Chapter 8) | Formed in 1996 – continues to date | Cuba, Egypt, India, Indonesia, Malaysia, Pakistan, Tanzania, and Uganda | Initially formed in opposition to the 'Singapore issues' but then evolved focus on issues of implementation; now also conducts research and organises joint positions on other issues such as Trade Related Intellectual property rights (TRIPs), that is, may be seen as a return to the archetype bloc |
| | Small and Vulnerable Economies (Chapter 8) | Since 1996, in preparation for Singapore Ministerial | Barbados, Dominica, Fiji, Grenada, Jamaica, Lesotho, Mauritius, Papua New Guinea, Solomon Islands, St Lucia, Trinidad and Tobago | Preferential treatment for the group, technical assistance |
| | LDC Group | Since 1999 in WTO context | Angola, Bangladesh, Benin, Burkina Faso, Burundi, Central African Republic, Chad, Congo, Djibouti, Gambia, Guinea, Guinea Bissau, Haiti, Lesotho, Madagascar, Malawi, Maldives, Mali, Mauritania, Mozambique, Myanmar, Niger, Rwanda, Senegal, Sierra Leone, Solomon Islands, Tanzania, Togo, Uganda, Zambia, and 13 observers to WTO | Support for general developing country issues, for example, implementation, TRIPS and Public Health; focus on problems specific to LDCs including accession issues, problems of representation and research, technology transfer; technical assistance, and capacity-building |

| | | | |
|---|---|---|---|
| Type II – Alliances with sub-sector focus (crossover and those with developing-country membership) | | | |
| Air Transport Services (Chapter 5) (crossover) | Early part of Uruguay Round | Malaysia, Singapore, Australia, New Zealand, and Nordic countries | Caution on liberalisation; emphasis on regular reviews |
| Like-minded developing countries on Mode 4 (Chapter 5) | Uruguay Round | Argentina, Colombia, Cuba, Egypt, India, Mexico, Pakistan, and Peru | Labour mode – annex on Movement of Natural Persons |
| Friends of Geographical Indications (developing country) (Chapter 8) | Seattle and Doha | Dominican Republic, Egypt, Honduras, India, Jamaica, Kenya, Pakistan, Sri Lanka, and Thailand | Protection of geographical indications be extended to products beyond wines and spirits |
| Type III – Evolved, issue-based alliance (crossover and those with developing-country membership) | | | |
| Cairns Group (Chapter 6) (crossover) | Formed in 1986 – continues to date | Argentina, Australia, Brazil, Canada, Chile, Colombia, Fiji, Hungary, Indonesia, Malaysia, New Zealand, Philippines, Thailand, and Uruguay | Inclusion of agriculture within GATT purview and subsequently greater liberalisation of agriculture |
| Friends of Services (crossover) (Chapter 6) | Continuation of Café au Lait after 1986; new incarnation of G-24 on services today | More of a chat group with a fluid membership with core membership of preceding coalition retained | Exchange of views on services liberalisation |
| Food Importers' Group (developing-country membership) (Chapter 6) | Uruguay Round | Jamaica, Egypt, Mexico, Morocco, and Peru (with backing of India, Nigeria, and South Korea) | Counter to Cairns Group to highlight costs of agricultural liberalisation to food-importing countries |

(Continued)

Table 2.2 (Continued)

| Coalition type | Name of coalition | Dates of operation | Membership (At the time of formation) | Agenda |
|---|---|---|---|---|
| | Friends of the Development Box (developing-country membership) (Chapter 8) | Preparatory process for Seattle; coalition continues today | Cuba, Dominican Republic, Honduras, El Salvador, Haiti, Honduras, Kenya, Nicaragua, Nigeria, Pakistan, Peru, Senegal, Sri Lanka, Uganda, and Zimbabwe | S&D treatment for developing countries and LDCs in agriculture through a 'Development Box'; Development Box provisions would not extend to developed countries |
| | G-24 on services (developing-country membership) (Chapter 8) | Formed in 1999 on Guidelines and Negotiating Procedures in Services Negotiations | Argentina, Bolivia, Brazil, Colombia, Cuba, Dominican Republic, Ecuador, El Salvador, Honduras, India, Indonesia, Malaysia, Mexico, Nicaragua, Pakistan, Panama, Paraguay, Peru, Philippines, Sri Lanka, Thailand, Uruguay, and Venezuela | Formed to address Guidelines and Negotiating Procedures; also maintains positions on assessment and credit for autonomous liberalisation |
| | Friends of Fish (crossover) (Chapter 8) | Since run-up to Seattle Ministerial | Australia, Iceland, New Zealand, Norway, Peru, Philippines, and US | Elimination of fish subsidies |
| Type IV – Bloc, regional basis (usually RTA-related) | ASEAN (Chapter 7, 8) | ASEAN Geneva Committee constituted in 1973, active especially over the Uruguay Round | Hong Kong, Indonesia, Malaysia, Thailand, Singapore, Philippines, and Brunei | Coordination and delegation of issues within membership across issues; has founded it harder to maintain coordinate position in recent years |
| | Latin American Group (Chapter 7) | A few, occasional documents over Uruguay Round | Fluid membership under auspices of different regional arrangements such as the Latin American Free Trade Area (LAFTA) and the Latin American Economic System (SELA) | Diverse issues but infrequently produced joint documents |

| Mercado Común del Sur (MERCOSUR) (Chapters 7, 8) | Regional Trade Arrangements (RTA) formed in 1991 with coordination efforts in WTO | Argentina, Brazil, Uruguay, and Paraguay | Claim coordination across issues; outsiders point to consistent position mainly over agriculture |
|---|---|---|---|
| African Group (Chapter 8) | Active particularly in run-up to Seattle and Doha ministerials | Membership of the Organisation of African Unity (OAU) – Angola, Benin, Botswana, Burkina Faso, Burundi, Cameroon, Central African Republic, Chad, Congo, Ivory Coast, Democratic Republic of Congo, Djibouti, Egypt, Gabon, Gambia, Ghana, Guinea, Guinea Bissau, Kenya, Lesotho, Madagascar, Malawi, Mali, Mauritania, Mauritius, Mozambique, Namibia, Niger, Nigeria, Rwanda, Senegal, Sierra Leone, South Africa, Swaziland, Tanzania, Togo, Tunisia, Uganda, Zambia, Zimbabwe, and 7 observers to WTO | Research and coordination of positions across issues of concern to developing countries, for example, TRIPS, technical assistance |
| African, Caribbean, and Pacific (ACP) Group (Chapter 8) | Active in run-up to Doha after signing of the Cotonou Agreement on 23 June 2000 | Angola, Antigua and Barbuda, Barbados, Belize, Benin, Botswana, Burkina Faso, Burundi, Cameroon, Central African Republic, Chad, Congo, Ivory Coast, Democratic Republic of Congo, Djibouti, Dominica, Dominican Republic, | Coordination with African Group but central focus was the waiver necessary for the Cotonou Agreement |

(Continued)

Table 2.2 (Continued)

| Coalition type | Name of coalition | Dates of operation | Membership (At the time of formation) | Agenda |
|---|---|---|---|---|
| | | | Fiji, Gabon, Gambia, Ghana, Grenada, Guinea, Guinea Bissau, Guyana, Haiti, Jamaica, Kenya, Lesotho, Madagascar, Malawi, Mali, Mauritania, Mauritius, Mozambique, Namibia, Niger, Nigeria, Papua New Guinea, Rwanda, St Kitts and Nevis, St Lucia, St Vincent and the Grenadines, Senegal, Sierra Leone, Solomon Islands, Suriname, Tanzania, Togo, Trinidad and Tobago, Uganda, Zambia, Zimbabwe, and 9 observers in WTO | |
| | Caribbean Community (CARICOM) (Chapter 8) | Since 1997 with establishment of the Caricom Regional Negotiating Machinery | Antigua and Barbuda, Barbados, Belize, Dominica, Grenada, Guyana, Jamaica, St Kitts and Nevis, St Lucia, St Vincent and the Grenadines, Trinidad and Tobago, and Suriname | Pursued S&D, greater market access, greater liberalisation to allow easier access to imports, and S&D for small economies |
| | Paradisus Group (Chapter 8) | Formed in run-up to the Doha Ministerial but not sustained thereafter | Dominican Republic, El Salador, Guatemala, Honduras, Nicaragua, and Panama | Mainly procedural issues of institutional reform |

evolved to include permutations that continued to operate at the sector level but were restricted to a developing country membership. The fourth type focused more on the failures of the archetype coalitions, that is the G-10 and the Café au Lait, to then evolve independent and previously untried coalition patterns. The approach was based on an attempt to utilise regionalism as a springboard for bargaining, for example, the Association of South East Asian Nations (ASEAN). Each of these four reveals some successes. But none of them has provided a model coalition that could be adapted to other situations within the services sector or outside it. In good measure, this is because of the lack of a comparative analysis of these coalition types and the identification and reproducibility of conditions that facilitated their successes. Uncertainty about the conditions in which one type will prove effective has resulted in the spreading of risk by most developing countries through simultaneous membership of different coalitions. Also, varying degrees of longevity of each group have produced cross-cutting, overlapping networks across space and time. The only pattern that has emerged so far is that of 'shifting coalitions',[19] that is a pattern defined best by its lack of pattern and a multiplicity of *ad hoc* coalitions that is particularly dominant in the services sector. An assessment of the net effect of this pattern on the bargaining power of developing countries follows below.

Most observers have greeted the new pattern of shifting coalitions with enthusiasm. Given that the participation of developing countries in diverse coalition experiments has enhanced their GATT/WTO participation to an unprecedented level, it is unsurprising that those long dismayed by the North–South stalemate would greet the new activism with optimism. Open-ended coalitions are also seen as favourable to the bargaining power of the developing country involved, hence writings like '…from the point of view of the proverbial hard-nosed trade negotiator, promotion of national or group interests – is best conducted in the context of shifting and eclectic coalitions of countries and/or interests'.[20] Other practitioners of trade diplomacy in the WTO, noting the conversion of developing countries to liberalisation, have questioned the purpose of building coalitions at all today. Both reasons for optimism are disputable for the reasons outlined below.

Dealing with the second viewpoint first, the willingness of developing countries to agree to unilateral liberalisation is frequently an attempt by the weak to make a virtue of necessity. In the absence of any bargaining alternatives, and in the face of bilateral and organisational pressures (such as from the Bretton Woods institutions on structural adjustment), developing countries have frequently opened up certain sectors to international competition at a pace that even free traders would caution against. For example, the opening up of the financial sector in South Korea was seen as a major factor in precipitating the East Asian Financial Crisis of the late 1990s. This 'willingness' to unilateral and competitive liberalisation is as much a product of the absence of viable coalition possibilities as a cause of them. In the absence of the bargaining power derived from collective action, developing countries are compelled to make unilateral concessions, which, in turn, further deters the operation of joint platforms.[21]

The utility of the 'shifting coalitions' model is also questionable. From a systemic point of view, it is true that the absence of a North–South stalemate is most conducive to the rapid progress of the Multilateral Trade Negotiation (MTN). Such progress finds favour with the dominant powers, which are the agenda-setters.

From the viewpoint of developing countries, however, continuously shifting *ad hoc* coalitions imply significant costs. For the former leaders of the South who also played a dominant role in the Informal Group, for instance, these costs have involved a dramatic reduction of their domestic and international credibility, besides the costs of striking favourable bargains on critical issue areas. For smaller countries, the costs come in the form of greater uncertainty. Unfruitful attempts to establish certainty through short-term bandwagoning with the developed countries on a sub-sectoral basis have undermined their bargaining power further. Balances with their more developed counterparts have generated additional costs of reducing the credibility of their coalitions with other developing countries. In general, the effect has been to undermine whatever little unified market power that developing countries might have had, and also detract from their ability to exchange sub-sectoral concessions and achieve superior package deals.

For most developing countries, shifting coalitions mean increasing transaction costs. These costs derive from the continuous search for new allies and defections from old allies: costs that most developing countries are ill equipped to meet. The co-existence of divided loyalties further detracts from commitment to any single negotiating platform and hence also its credibility. For the weak in international relations, stability of allies is an enormous source of strength. That strength is significantly marginalised with the emergence of the shifting coalitions model. The resulting increase in the vulnerability of developing countries is evident in both traditional and new issues. In fact, in some ways, the creation of the WTO has exacerbated these problems.

The formation of the WTO has marked an unprecedented institutionalisation of coalitions. The newly found recognition of trade-related alliances is far removed from the studied oversight of such patterns by the GATT. It is interesting to note that even the Director General of the WTO participates in some informal coalition activity. For instance, the so-called 'Invisible Group' involved the Director General and officials from the trade ministries of the 'major trading countries' (including the members of the Quad group and developing countries like Brazil, India, and South Korea). As an attempt to involve capital-level officials, it met about twice a year to discuss, usually in general terms, upcoming issues of importance to the WTO.[22] Recent diplomatic sources point out that the group still re-emerges before ministerials. More recently, the Doha Development Agenda made explicit references to groups such as Small and Vulnerable Economies group and the LDC group. References to coalitions such as the Cairns Group and the ASEAN can be easily found on the WTO website. While the fact of institutional recognition of coalitions by the WTO is an important step in itself, it still tends to be rather selective and biased in favour of certain types of coalitions. Many developing country delegations complain that some of their coalitions continue to face adverse odds in terms of selective recognition from the WTO and constraints deriving from necessary infrastructural backup that their scarce resources disallow. These coalitions of developing countries are more prone to dissipation, as opposed to those that gain institutional recognition from the WTO. Expectedly, the turnover of these unrecognised coalitions is high, as their members lurch from one issue-area coalition to another, in search of one that will give them the highest and most long-lasting results.

Developing countries continue to encounter problems of coalition building and maintenance in the WTO as they did in the GATT, especially as the WTO retains many of the structural and procedural features of its predecessor's. But effective participation in the WTO has acquired unprecedented urgency. In contrast to the GATT, the WTO goes behind borders through far-reaching rules on NTMs, and unlike the voluntary codes of the Tokyo Round, all members are bound to these rules. GATT, TRIPS, and GATS all fall within its purview through the Single Undertaking. The WTO is able to monitor the policies of members through the Trade Policy Review Mechanism (TPRM) and also has a much stronger Dispute Settlement Mechanism (DSM) in comparison to the GATT's. A stronger DSM and the Single Undertaking together can allow cross-sectoral retaliation, that is the WTO can allow aggrieved parties to retaliate in issue areas where it hurts the offending party the most. Finally, unlike the IMF and the World Bank, which lose their enforcement powers on a country once its debts are repaid, the WTO's members are bound by the international trade rules negotiated in the organisation.[23] Hence, developing countries find themselves members of an organisation with procedures and infrastructure very similar to the GATT's, but whose mandate goes far deeper. The only hope that developing countries have in working this elaborate network of rules is through effective participation. As the onus of participation in the organisation falls on the members themselves, coalitions provide one of the few and critical instruments whereby developing countries can exercise a voice in the WTO. The quest for effective and sustainable coalitions has hence acquired even greater relevance and urgency.

## 2.4   Conclusion

The pre-launch phase of the Uruguay Round represented a break with the past. This chapter has explained why the participation of developing countries in the GATT in former years was minimal, despite the theoretical equality promised to them by a one-member-one-vote system. It has demonstrated that the entry of services into GATT discussions acted as the trigger that launched developing countries as active members of the GATT. Increased activity was manifested in a variety of coalition types, which tried to increase the bargaining leeway of developing countries.

Increased participation, however, is a necessary and not sufficient condition, for effective influence. Enhanced participation of developing countries has taken the form of 'shifting coalitions'; the costs of this model have reduced the bargaining efficacy of the countries involved. To translate the increased participation of developing countries into actual influence, a study of coalitions is vital. Subsequent chapters conduct case studies of the different coalition types to derive and analyse the lessons of past experience of developing countries with coalition formation in the GATT/WTO. On the basis of these lessons, both theoretical and prescriptive conclusions will be drawn.

# 3  Bloc diplomacy: the Informal Group and the G-10

Friendship exists between those of like habits and temperament.
(*Panchatantra*, Book I, Verse 285)

The first concrete coalition that arose in response to the entry of services in GATT discussions was the Group of Ten developing countries in the GATT, that is the G-10. The G-10 coalition is of particular interest to this study in two ways. First, the high profile adopted by the G-10 represented a qualitative break from the limited activity of developing countries in the GATT in the past. Second, the G-10 embodied bloc diplomacy at its most pronounced in the GATT. The performance of the group precipitated a chain reaction of similar and counter-coalitions, thereby radically transforming the coalition diplomacy of developing countries in GATT negotiations. This chapter examines the historical roots of the G-10 by tracing the activities of the Informal Group of Less Developed Countries in some detail. It then investigates the conditions that proved conducive to the formation of the G-10. It identifies the chief characteristics and strategies of the group and examines the extent to which they were influenced by the roots of the coalition in the Informal Group. The relative successes and failures of the G-10 are also analysed. The concluding section outlines the theoretical and empirical lessons of the case. The case is crucial in arbitrating between the various methods of coalition formation that were analysed in Chapter 1. It illustrates various combinations of interests that can be used to sustain the coalition, where ideas and identity fit in to reinforce this reality, and what kinds of costs different combinations entail.

## 3.1  Roots of the G-10: the Informal Group

In the high drama and controversy generated by the activity of the G-10, the parentage of the coalition is often forgotten. In many ways, the G-10 was a direct derivative of the Informal Group. The omission of this link from the accounts of diplomats and academics may be attributed to the fact that the Informal Group was a weak coalition. Its informality, shifting agenda, choice of alternative forums, and indirect methods to influence GATT activity together impart an elusive character to the group. In spite of its weaknesses, however, the Informal Group affected future coalition activity in two critical ways. First, it provided developing countries with a pre-existing framework for action. Through its membership, agenda, and negotiating strategies, the Informal Group served as an institutional springboard for the emergence of the G-10. Second, the legacy of the Informal Group was a double-edged sword. The G-10, by adopting and formalising the model of the Informal Group, also inherited its weaknesses. This section examines the agenda and limitations of the Informal Group and finds that the coalition was weakly bound. It also addresses the question: What method was used to construct the coalition that ensured its survival, in spite of its weaknesses? These issues are of immediate relevance here because of the direct influence that the agenda and the nature of the Informal Group exercised on the formation, working and eventual collapse of the G-10.

### 3.1.1 *Establishing precedents: tracing the Informal Group*

The Informal Group of less developed contracting parties formed a part of the elaborate diplomatic network that underlay GATT negotiations. By the time of the Uruguay Round, the group had become associated with the leadership of the Big Five, that is, Argentina, Brazil, Egypt, India, and the former Yugoslavia. It also included Chile, Jamaica, Pakistan, Peru, and Uruguay as other active members. Irrespective of its informality and in spite of the vacillations of its agenda, the group displayed a consistency of membership. This consistency of membership and a broad bloc-based approach to development issues were maintained in liaison with other trade-related institutions.

The attempt by developing countries to wield a collective influence in GATT negotiations goes back to the days of preparation of the Havana Charter. From the beginning, the common platform shared by developing countries was used to voice several contradictory positions. For instance, developing countries were vociferous in their condemnation of the GATT for its failure to practise the philosophy of free trade that it preached. Simultaneously, they propagated the view that developing countries deserved special concessions and exceptions because 'equality of treatment is equitable only among equals. A weakling cannot carry the burden of a giant'.[1] Incompatibilities of the evolving agenda were a product of the very different requirements of countries of very diverse historical experience, geographical imperatives, political regimes, economic character, and ideological inclinations. They also meant that the group would be beleaguered by uncertainty of agenda through much of its life. The surprising follow-up, however, was that the group continued to thrive and exists even today.

Subsequent years saw an increasing dissatisfaction of developing countries with the GATT, which brought them closer together. The agreement had excluded the development provisions and commodity framework of the Havana Charter, which had been of particular interest to developing countries. Only one Balance of Payments (BOP) provision existed through Article XII. Article XVIII, entitled 'Adjustment in Connection with Economic Development', was included, but its limited applicability provided another unifying element for the developing countries. Many developing countries found that the low tariffs (that had already been negotiated by the developed countries) demanded on entry into the GATT would prove detrimental to their infant industries. The coalescing of the developing countries into the Informal Group was accompanied by their self-identification as outsiders in the 'Rich Man's Club'.

The Informal Group left a trail of its activity, not only through its criticism of the club character of the GATT but also through a positive agenda. Analysts, emphasising the defensive and passive character of the participation of the LDCs in the GATT, often overlook this. The reasons for the oversight may be attributed to the decreasing relevance of this agenda over time due to the minimal successes that it generated. Both the existence of the positive agenda in early years and its subsequent attrition are important as they provide us an insight into the blocking strategies that were later adopted by the G-10, partly in emulation of the Informal Group.

The demands of the Informal Group as part of the positive agenda were several. These demands were well matched by failures. Developing countries had supported an inclusion of agriculture into the GATT, but agriculture in the GATT came to be treated differently from industrial products by allowing the imposition of quotas under special conditions. The original exception was granted so that the Congress could continue its price-support programme. In 1955, the US was granted a waiver enabling it to legalise import controls on agriculture. With the creation of the European Common Agricultural Policy, agriculture became the most striking departure from general GATT principles of MFN and reciprocity. It was also a defeat for the Informal Group's attempt at establishing free access to export markets in agriculture. Similarly, the group's attempts to free international trade in textiles through universal rules were frustrated. With the accession of Japan to the GATT in 1955, some members were allowed to impose import controls on Japanese goods, especially textiles. The Multi-Fibre Agreement (MFA) of 1974 represented the crystallisation of restrictions that had appeared through the Short Term Arrangement of 1961 (directed against the competitive advantage of the textile and clothing industry of Hong Kong, India, Pakistan, and other members of the Informal Group), and the Long Term Arrangement of 1962. Of some 20,000 tariff concessions reached by the Dillon Round (Geneva, 1960–1961), only 160 bindings on the reductions of duties were on items of interest to developing countries.[2] These results validated developing countries' initial suspicions that the GATT was an institution unfavourable to their interests. Irrespective of their participatory efforts at constructive contributions, the GATT process of liberalisation and tariff reduction had only focused on areas where the competitive advantage of developed countries lay.

The Informal Group found that while demands for greater liberalism had yielded only limited successes, the strategy of demanding exceptional treatment for developing countries bore some fruit. This strategy was often pursued through alternative institutions where developing countries had an organisational advantage and could exercise indirect pressures on the GATT. It emphasised the exceptionalism of the Informal Group, posited against developed world groupings like the Quad. Frequently, a blocking agenda was pursued, with demands for exceptions from the liberal trade in selective sectors that was being pursued in the GATT. As a result of such demands by the Informal Group, Article XVIII was modified in 1954–1955 to include XVIII*b* that allowed the use of Quantitative Restrictions for BOP purposes whenever foreign exchange reserves were below the level considered necessary for development. Effectively, on account of its vagueness, the provision came to authorise easier recourse to infant industry protection. The Haberler Report of 1958 recognised that 'prospects for exports of non-industrial countries are very sensitive to internal policies in industrial countries, and on balance their development will probably fall short of the increase in world trade as a whole'.[3]

The strategy of emphasising developing country exceptionalism had cross-institutional motivations and successes. The designation of the 1960s as the UN Decade for Development by the General Assembly was one of the examples of these successes. The formation of the UNCTAD in 1964 was another. The creation of an institution to cater specifically to the needs of the developing countries as an organ of the General Assembly, accompanied by the formation of the G-77 within it, had two implications for the Informal Group. First, it provided the Informal Group with an allied institutional structure in the UN. Second, it represented a recognition that the GATT had failed to address the concerns and interests of developing countries, and hence the creation of an alternative institution. This challenge of the UNCTAD precipitated conscious policy changes in the GATT that were directed towards increasing the involvement of developing countries. A committee for Trade and Development was established to address issues of development. The International Trade Centre was charged with assisting developing countries in export promotion. The addition of a new chapter entitled Trade and Development (Part IV) in the GATT, in 1965, was another change induced by the activities of the Informal Group within the GATT, in alliance with the UNCTAD.

Though Part IV recognised the principle of non-reciprocity, it still did not imply a Generalised System of Preferences (GSP). By 1968, the UNCTAD was able to pass a resolution that recognised 'unanimous agreement' in favour of the early establishment of non-reciprocal and non-discriminatory preferences. In 1971, as a result of coalition pressure from within and outside, the GATT was compelled to surrender its MFN principle in favour of the GSP for developing countries, for a ten-year period. The 'Enabling Clause' passed during the Tokyo Round created the permanent legal basis for operation of the GSP, and provided departures from MFN and other GATT rules.

The 1970s were marked by the articulation of the demand for a New International Economic Order (NIEO), which included trade reform on its agenda. The set of demands for international commodity agreements (a common fund to support these agreements, non-reciprocal reductions in developed country barriers to developing country exports, expanded GSP, better financed domestic adjustments) provides an example of the specific trade agenda rather than just the rhetorical call for distributive justice.[4] The call for economic reform was emitted in organisations parallel to the UNCTAD such as the GATT and the General Assembly, and in various groupings of the Third World. Irrespective of the assertions of GATT officials to the contrary, the North–South dimension had pervaded all aspects and institutions concerned with trade negotiations. The increasing consistency and coherence of the articulation of demands by developing countries across institutions was matched by increasing activity of the Informal Group in the GATT. From the eleven developing countries that had come together at the time of the signing of the GATT, seventy-eight developing countries officially declared their participation in the Tokyo Round. The Tokyo Round made an explicit commitment to secure additional benefits and improve the participation of developing countries in international trade.

A recognisable caucus of developing countries can hence be traced in the GATT, through the trail of its activity, agenda, and characteristic strategies. The consistency of its activity and membership further allow us to characterise this Informal Group as a coalition. However, the successes of the alternative agenda that acquired prominence in the Group were matched by a blazing trail of failures. The survival of the group, in spite of the original contradictions and failures (described briefly in this section), requires explanation. The next section highlights some of the failures of the group, and finds that the Informal Group, though a coalition of sorts, was a very weak coalition.

### 3.1.2   Qualifying the achievements of the Informal Group: a weak coalition

That the Informal Group pursued its activity seriously and consistently was discovered in the previous section. A set of countries jointly formulating and lobbying for an agenda formed this coalition activity. However, the group was afflicted by several weaknesses. Some of these weaknesses were implicit in the fact that the group needed to resort to alternative forums such as the UNCTAD and the General Assembly, and work in liaison with the G-77 to influence the GATT. The group also encountered a range of concrete failures of its agenda. The GATT did nothing to implement Part IV, the Graduation Principle introduced in the Tokyo Round undermined even the minimal gains that had been derived from S&D, Trans-National Corporations (TNCs) continued to be uncontrolled, and issues critical to developing countries such as agriculture and textiles remained exceptions to GATT MFN principles.[5] Repeated failures usually render the maintenance of a coalition difficult. The limitations of the Informal Group become even more obvious once its collective economic and political bases are examined. This section examines these precarious bases.

Except at the very broadest level, a unity of structural interests of a large group of very disparate countries is difficult to imagine. Roger Hansen writes that, with the exception of demands for an automatic resource transfers and greater access to Northern markets, differences of interests among the countries of the South were greater than the commonalties.[6] This was as true of the Informal Group as the other coalitions representing the South, such as the G-77 in the UNCTAD, and the G-24 in the IMF. The highly liquid OPEC countries did not share Southern views on monetary reform. The rapidly industrialising countries did not share the official Southern view on debt relief. The GSP yielded minimal and declining benefits for a few developing countries while imposing actual costs on others. The exercise of oil power had very substantive costs for the greater part of the South. Commodity exporters had a very different perspective on the IPC and the Common Fund than commodity importers. A closer inspection reveals that the collective agenda professed by the group did not benefit all members equally. The problem was not merely one of relative gains (not an easy problem in itself) that impedes cooperation among states, but also of losses which accrued to some members from the collective agenda. For this reason, the Informal Group was a weak coalition, and an unusual one at that.[7]

Among the consistent and successful campaigns of the Informal Group, the GSP is notable. The call for the GSP in the GATT was linked with similar demands raised by developing-country coalitions elsewhere. It formalised the broad theoretical idea of special treatment for some countries on account of their international and domestic weaknesses. The UNCTAD resolution in favour of non-reciprocal, discriminatory preferences was passed in 1968. The idea entered into trade practice with the adoption of the GSP in 1971 in the GATT. The GSP provides an example of the diverse and apparently irreconcilable interests that were brought within the fold of the Informal Group. The case begs the question that may also be raised with most other campaigns of the Informal Group: How did the group sustain a collective economic agenda when interests of members underlying the agenda were so disparate?

The GSP had repercussions on all members of the Informal Group; the beneficial aspect of these repercussions was limited. The system was a serious derogation from GATT principles of a rule-based multilateral trade regime. It induced a greater dependence of the South on the North, as each developed country set its own rules for eligibility and extent of GSP treatment. In fact, some authors have even argued that had developing countries been more active in reducing trade barriers in previous MTN and through full-fledged reciprocity, more significant reductions might have been made in barriers on products of interest to them.[8] Martin Wolf interprets it as a system that was offered as bait to divide the South: it resulted in selectivity of benefits for the advanced developing exporters and prevented the others from developing their potential in the areas under GSP.[9] Principal benefits of the GSP accrued in the form of better export opportunities for the Newly Industrialising Countries (NICs). For latecomers, it involved actual material losses because the arbitrarily granted quotas were already occupied by the more advanced developing countries.[10] The GSP was limited to a very specific set of products; many have argued that it excluded most products in which developing countries had an active or potential comparative advantage.[11] The scheme induced a further marginalisation of developing countries from the GATT; issues of importance to developing countries such as agriculture or textiles were either excluded from the GATT or granted protectionist treatment on an *ad hoc* basis. Even for the chief beneficiaries, the system had decreasing marginal utility: the value of preferences declined as tariffs were progressively lowered among the industrialised countries through normal GATT processes.[12]

Despite these limitations, the Informal Group maintained its 'unanimous' position on the GSP. Unequal benefits accruing to the more developed economies were endured, arbitrary benefactions in violation of GATT rules were accepted, olive branches such as regional or selective preferences from the North could not break the collective support for the GSP, and the principle of Graduation was jointly resisted. Given that few collective benefits were to be had from the scheme, the common front of the Informal Group requires explanation.

The persistence of the Informal Group, even in the absence of any collective benefits that were jointly pursued by the members, may yet be explained if a collective political agenda that subsumed the diverse economic aims of the individual members can be found. Stephen Krasner perceives such a collective political agenda of the South. Internal and external vulnerabilities unite developing countries and precipitate their common pursuit as a group, of 'principles and norms that would legitimate more authoritative as opposed to more market-oriented modes of allocation'.[13] In other words, structural political imperatives of weakness draw even economically diverse countries onto a common platform, which rests on the demand for authoritative regimes.

A part of Krasner's analysis is simple and convincing. Developing countries are more vulnerable to international pressures. Vulnerabilities to external shocks are heightened by their limited slack resources and adjustment capabilities caused by domestic weaknesses. In contrast to Krasner's interpretation, however, vulnerabilities of developing countries do not translate into a consistent demand for more predictable and hence authoritative international regimes. The Informal Group demonstrates the limitations of this analysis amply.

The Informal Group did not display a consistent pursuit of international stability and predictability. It is true that in the late 1940s and early 1950s, developing countries participated together in the GATT with the call for rule-based regimes in areas of interest to them, such as agriculture and textiles. Hence also the regret enunciated by developing countries that lasted well into the 1980s about the failure to establish the ITO and the inadequacies of the GATT as a poor substitute for the original. But even in the early phase, an alternative was present: a strategic alternative that was exercised with caution but also increasing frequency.

The alternative to authoritative, rule-based regimes was described in the previous sub-section. It included demands such as the call for S&D treatment, non-reciprocal concessions from the North, and the GSP. Initially these strategies, which exposed developing countries to greater arbitrariness, were pursued with caution. But as the failures of the Informal Group to persuade the North to accept universal regimes in agriculture, textiles, and commodities became clear, the switch to the alternative strategies became much more pronounced. Even after the entrenchment of the demand for non-reciprocity in the agenda of the Informal Group, the dalliance with the call for rule-based regimes continued. Hence, while seeking stabilisation of commodity prices under the IPC, developing countries also included a demand for greater competitiveness in products where their comparative advantage lay. The contradiction has invited interpretations far different from the Krasnerian one. Paraphrasing Hudec, for instance, Wolf writes of the desire of the Third World to establish a situation where one group of countries has the most obligations and another most of the rights.[14]

The Informal Group was hence characterised by a vacillation in positions, of which the Krasner-type demand for rule-based systems represented one extreme. It is noteworthy that this set of contradictions and vacillations was maintained *en bloc.* For example, in the 1980s, the group sought a Krasnerian removal of arbitrary NTBs, a need for standstill and rollback, the inclusion of agriculture, tropical products and textiles, and other issues of interest into the GATT agenda. But simultaneously, the group resisted the inclusion of services and intellectual property into a rule-based schedule in the Uruguay Round. This resistance is especially surprising in the light of Krasner's theory and the fact that rules in Intellectual Property Rights (IPRs) and services would have allowed developing countries a stability in sectors where they were particularly vulnerable. In a similar fashion, the pursuit of a code for MNCs and the establishment of the Centre for Transnational Corporations, à la Krasner, were accompanied by a determined resistance to the inclusion of Trade-Related Investment Measures (TRIMs) in the Uruguay Round.

That the members of the Informal Group spoke from a collective platform in the GATT and related forums is clear, but the foundations of the platform did not lie in shared economic aims. The professed collective economic agenda concealed the incompatible demands of member countries. The conflicting stance adopted by the group, when examined from Krasner's perspective, confirms that the foundations did not lie in a consistent collective political aim either. The absence of a collective economic or political aim that was jointly pursued by the members of the Informal Group has two implications. First, at least in the light of negotiation theory and Realist/Neo-Realist theories of IR, a 'coalition' wherein members have no economic or collective interests in common will be extremely difficult to maintain. Second, the fact that such a group (a group characterised by considerable longevity, a collective agenda, and a consistent membership) exists requires explanation. The method that bound the Informal Group, in spite of the structural odds against it, is examined in the next sub-section. The peculiarities of this method also exercised a critical impact on the workings of the G-10, the successor of the Informal Group.

### 3.1.3 *Explaining the cohesion*

The existence of the Informal Group, in spite of its weaknesses, can be understood by examining the method that was used to bind the members together. This section finds that the coalition was a precariously maintained artifice, held together by three critical elements. The first and principal reason for preserving the coalition with the collective agenda that it professed was the direct benefits that it offered to the members. Note that the gains were not those that resulted from the collective agenda (which the previous paragraphs have shown to be inconsistent within itself in terms of its various goals, as well as congruent with the aims of only some members). Rather, the different gains were accrued through trade-offs and side deals, which occurred within the group. This patch-work of individual gains was obtained under the cover of the inchoate collective agenda described in the previous section. Second, the bilateral and minilateral deals that formed the substance of the Informal Group were sustained through an intra-coalition hierarchy. The third method that was used to bind developing countries into a coalition was that of ideology. Even the three factors of group cohesion together, however, were a poor substitute for a collective agenda of com-mon interests of all members. This concoction of methods for maintaining the coalition had a price: a price that was paid for by the Informal Group by develop-ing into a weak coalition. Its more institutionalised successor, the G-10, adopted similar methods and collapsed on their account. The three components of the method that was used to forge the Informal Group together are discussed below.

*Ingredient 1: logrolled interests*

Unlike two prisoners facing a common dilemma, members of the Informal Group were caught up in different games. Varying individual motivations as opposed to collective motivations helped sustain the group. Robert Rothstein points out that the greater part of the agenda of the South was set by the advanced developing countries. Even when certain programmes entailed losses for these countries, many of the higher-ranking developing countries were assured market access with their coalition partners.[15] The members of the Informal Group pursued a similar strategy; the coalition was used to bring different things to different members.

Political gains were immense from the leadership of the Group and its cousins in other forums. These gains provided the motivation for the advanced develop-ing countries to accept the costs of leadership and the losses incurred by the col-lective agenda. A Brazilian delegate observed that even though the G-77 is not formally constituted in the GATT, the weight of the group behind it makes it a voice that cannot be ignored by the developed countries.[16] Even when stakes were low, these countries saw the returns in terms of international influence, high enough to merit active participation and leadership. India in the Uruguay Round hence opposed the inclusion of services vociferously, not because of its own competitive advantage but because of its continued enactment of the role of spokesperson for developing countries: 'India responded as a coalition player and as part of its objective of retaining the leadership role, rather than acting on its own self-perceived or even attributable national concerns.'[17]

Other members had their own axes to grind through profession of support for the collective agenda. Linkages and trade-offs were common. Political and diplo-matic support was expressed by some countries for an objective cherished by another member where their own interests were not substantially involved, and a quid pro quo was sought in areas of equal importance.[18] The Informal Group was thus the end product of long processes of logrolling, as opposed to jointly pursued aims. India acquiesced to the GSP in return for the status that it gained as leader of the group and the Third World. Argentina was willing to support traditional demands of the Informal Group based on protection of the domestic market, but it defected from the group as soon as the prospect of agricultural liberalisation emerged with the launch of the new round (agriculture being an issue of paramount importance for the country). The support of smaller countries for the group derived from their lack of expertise in terms of representation at Geneva, as well as technical expertise. For many, the absence of well-defined interests was accompanied by a dearth of alternative coalition possibilities. As members of the Informal Group, they could use their voice and vote to lend legitimacy to the coalition and were granted a free ride onto its agenda. In some cases, their interests could be defined by the agenda of the coalition; in cases where interests were well defined, they could be logrolled onto the collective agenda. A small minority of developing countries utilised their membership of the Informal Group to drive much harder bargains elsewhere. The ACP countries were granted significant concessions from the EC through the Lomé conventions, including the Stabilisation of Export Earnings (STABEX) scheme along the lines of the IPC. The fact that the Informal Group had demanded and supported such preferential treatment for developing countries in the GATT is not entirely coincidental.

It is also noteworthy that some members of the Informal Group and its allied groupings signalled their willingness to negotiate with the North through their moderate positions within the groupings. Jamaica provides a classic example of such diplomacy later: while still a member of the Informal Group in the 1980s, it presented itself not so much as an exporter of services, but as an exporter of reason and bridge-building efforts. Particularly when coalitions are weak, members may prefer to spread their risks by simultaneously joining other coalitions. Note however, that the pursuit of alternative agendas contributes to a further weakening of the original coalition, as happened with the Informal Group.

Smaller cliques within the group were also not uncommon. These included the occasionally coordinated positions among the SELA and the ASEAN. Often, these groupings conformed more to the interests of individual members.

The Informal Group was hence a basket of individual aspirations: side deals, intra-member bilateral trade-offs, minilateral makeshift arrangements, and linkages were woven together to create much of the wickerwork. These intra-coalition deals and logrolling formed the substance of the coalition. Devoid of any collective aims, the coalition was hence weak.

*Ingredient 2: Intra-coalition hierarchies*

The bungled set of bilateral deals and small group trade-offs was converted into a long-lasting coalition, through the presence of hierarchies within the group. As discussed in Chapter 1, hierarchies constitute one of the methods prescribed by Neo-liberal Institutionalists for achieving collective action, particularly when large numbers are involved. Leadership of the Big Five – Argentina, Brazil, Egypt, India, and the former Yugoslavia – played a critical role in cementing the coalition, but the stratification within the Informal Group as a result of this leadership also generated costs. The peculiarities of the leadership of the Informal Group, and the costs that it generated, are examined here.

While the potential for stratification within the Informal Group was considerable, there was no obvious hegemon that could don the mantle of leadership. The
Big Five, and other larger members of the developing world,[19] shared many
weaknesses with their counterpart members. Like other members of the coalition,
these countries were afflicted by problems of poverty, international weakness, and
quasi-statehood.[20] Sources of leadership were diverse: economic size in the case
of Brazil and India; occasionally clearer political objectives which depended on
the extent of state development and colonial history, and worked more favourably
for the states of Latin America and South Asia; political status accruing from
importance in other forums like the NAM in the case of Egypt, India, and the former Yugoslavia; or simply the practical ability to maintain a permanent delegation at Geneva. Of course, some power differentials were stark, such as Nigeria
versus Guinea, India versus Maldives, or Brazil and Argentina versus the Central
American economies. But power differentials were seldom high enough to allow
even obvious regional hegemonies. Witness, for instance, South Asia, where
regional integration has been repeatedly curbed to prevent Indian hegemony, and
Latin America, where Brazil and Argentina balanced each other. The diverse
sources of power made comparisons of leadership potential difficult, while the
mood of majoritarianism and consensus-based approach of the GATT meant
that there was little that was unconditional, unqualified, or collectively accepted
about the leadership status of members who claimed it.

Any advantages that the core members, that is the Big Five, of the Informal
Group enjoyed merely gave them the status of aspirants to greater importance in
international affairs. This status had to be wooed from other members, in forums
that were dominated by an atmosphere of 'egalitarianism and pluralism'.[21] While
this was generally true of most leadership attempts in coalitions of developing
countries, it was particularly true of the Informal Group. Members of the group
had come together to counter the Rich Man's club character of the GATT, and
could not have reconciled the creation of internal clubs and hierarchies within
their own coalition akin to those prevalent outside it in the forum. Aspirant
leaders of the coalition needed followers, as much as potential followers needed
leaders to provide them with a voice in international negotiations. This mutual
need and the absence of any clear, emergent hegemonic leadership significantly
moulded the erratic, internally inconsistent agenda of the Informal Group, deri-
sively referred to as a 'shopping list'. No dominant agenda through hegemonic
imposition could emerge. Rather, the interests of all the members were logrolled
and aggregated into an inconsistent and expansive agenda.

To create and sustain their international leadership, the Big Five were willing
to make significant trade-offs in agenda formation. Brazil provides one example.
Brazilian interests were clearly unfavourably affected by the continuation of preferential arrangements such as the Lomé Convention and the Caribbean Basin
Initiative. But 'to press for the elimination of this unknown economic cost would
involve large political costs as it would undermine the much-battered coalition of
developing countries...'[22] This, in turn, would undermine the international status
of Brazil, which was closely linked to its leadership of the coalition. In later years,

Brazil professed support for the dismantling of the MFA, despite its competitive disadvantage in relation to other developing countries including India and South Korea, in cotton and yarn production. Compensatory moves from India, the Philippines and others came with their support for the elimination of the new protectionism, that is, Anti-Dumping Duties (ADDs), counterveiling duties (CVDs) and Voluntary Export Restraints (VERs).[23] Tariff graduation under GSP schemes, introduced in the Tokyo Round, entailed some costs for Brazil, but was almost never an issue of overwhelming importance as trade gains entailed by the GSP are estimated at about 1 per cent of total exports.[24] Yet if there was one running thread to the Brazilian position in the MTN, it was the adamant backing provided to S&D – a support that infiltrated Brazil's position even in alternative coalitions (such as the Cairns, which is acclaimed by some analysts as being based not on political factors but on 'solid economic interest'[25]) and threatened to deter agreement in areas of critical importance to the country. Any regional hostilities that arose between Latin America and Africa over special treatment of European Economic Community (EEC) associates and Commonwealth members were countered through conscious logrolling. Commodity agreements and the IPC offer another example where the economic interests of Brazil (as well as Colombia and other commodity producers of the region which were already in a strong position) dictated at least some ambivalence in support for the 'collective' Southern position. The entrance of several African countries into coffee and tea markets aroused fear of new competitors for Brazil in its current exports, as well as the danger of exclusion from markets as in iron ore which it had hoped to enter in strength, and yet these entrances were not resisted.[26] In fact, the proliferation of attempts at establishing commodity agreements continued, propelled by UNC-TAD–ITC-led prescriptions, and through 'special' treatment that was meted out to them under the GATT. The coffee agreement was significantly facilitated by the willingness of Brazil to limit its production and even burn its own coffee, thereby allowing not only higher prices but also new entrants.

Brazilian willingness to incorporate the diverse and numerous demands of all its potential coalition partners did produce some economic returns, such as the inclusion of a call to abolish NTBs in the 1980s or, in certain cases, the willingness to accept the links between trade and debt and monetary reform. But no primacy was accorded to the Brazilian demands, even though a large proportion of the costs of research and collective bargaining was borne by Brazil. Demands for GSP, resource transfers, easier terms of aid, stabilisation and increase in commodity prices, and support for OPEC policies were all fitted in.

Indian participation in the trade coalition of developing countries in the GATT, and in the G-77 as a leader, was similarly characterised by a few national demands that were put on agenda but which existed in a flotsam of incompatible demands that were readily accepted. Indian involvement in the world economy was consistently lower than that of Brazil's, and stakes in the GATT were few. Some direct economic interests did indeed prompt Indian participation in the GATT. The government's reliance on Quantitative Restrictions (QRs) to conserve foreign exchange led it to push the GATT to sanction the use of quotas for development. Some benefits were derived from the inclusion of Article XVIII*b*. But Indian involvement in the GATT went far beyond what the export constitution of its GDP dictated. In the call for the GSP (from which it could derive only limited gains because of the low level of its exports), in its opposition to the Graduation Principle (which would have had little negative effect on India, and perhaps only positive spin-offs by eliminating the benefits enjoyed by its competitors like South Korea and by depriving the developed countries of an excuse to exercise arbitrary concessions and even more NTBs against all developing countries), in its staunch opposition to the inclusion of the new issues in the Uruguay Round (even when there was little clarity about where its comparative advantage/disadvantage in services lay), India remained at the forefront.

For some of the other leaders, economic motivations appeared more prominently, though here too, politics played a critical part. Argentina's biggest source of economic gain – agriculture – was not included in the GATT until the Uruguay Round. Nevertheless, Argentina devoted considerable bargaining effort over issues such as the protection of its domestic markets through the use of Article XVIII*b* and emerged as a core member of the group. At least a part of the Argentine activism in the GATT may be explained by the rivalry between Argentina and Brazil, and the attempts to share the international prestige that Brazil already enjoyed in the G-77 through greater involvement in an alternative forum where stratification was not as formalised or entrenched.

The cases of Egypt and the former Yugoslavia provide similar examples of economic and political motives driving their willingness to bear the costs of organisation of the group, include multiple agendas, and allow free rides to smaller members. The former Yugoslavia was exceptional in the political alternative that it sought to the two power blocs; GATT politics was, to a large extent, a continuation of that search. Egypt had continued with the practice of playing many more than two pianos, that is joining several types of alliances and coalitions simultaneously and sometimes over time. Participation in the Informal Group in trade gave it another alternative, which could be used as a stick in its dealings with other coalitions.

Irrespective of where their economic interests lay and sometimes through avid logrolling, the core of the Informal Group in the GATT in liaison with the G-77 was formed. It is perhaps not a coincidence that the Big Five were large and considerably diversified economies, that is countries for which stakes did not lie in one critical issue area but were distributed across several. Such diversified stakes rendered identification of their 'real interests' difficult; it also made it easier for them to exchange trade-offs and establish linkages to create an agenda which satisfied at least a part of the diffused needs that individually afflicted each of them. Argentina was an exception in having had a clearly identified interest in agriculture, but until the inclusion of that issue within the MTN, it resembled the other core group members in a multi-pronged, interest-based approach.

Obvious economic pay-offs were few and provide insufficient reason to explain the organisational efforts of the leaders. Nor were these efforts a product of an ideological commitment precipitating the national sacrifices of the leaders in favour of the collective. The more important pay-off was the international prestige that came with the leadership. Political mileage was to be had by incorporating the demands of other members, amassed at bilateral, minilateral, or international levels. In the case of Indian support for OPEC-induced price rises, for instance, political support over Kashmir, besides the benefit derived from a collective unanimous position, was sought in exchange. Regional arrangements were mutually tolerated, as were differential preferences. The Informal Group was a coalition worth preserving for its leaders only occasionally for the material benefits of having an identifiably significant issue incorporated onto the collective agenda, but consistently so for the political gains that such leadership yielded.

This leadership, however, was maintained at a heavy price, which affected the efficacy of the coalition. It included costs incurred by the leaders themselves in organising collective action. The many inconsistent demands that had to be incorporated within the collective agenda represented another cost. Through the acceptance of the disparate demands of large and small developing countries, a coalition had been formed, and its leadership had emerged, but both processes had entailed compromises. These compromises had their costs, the greatest being the emergence of a weak coalition with an inconsistent agenda. The same compromises were adopted by the G-10, giving the group an original fault that would contribute to its collapse.

*Ingredient 3: the construct of ideology*

Uniting the diversity of members, inconsistent demands, and ambiguous leaders into the Informal Group was an ideology. The role of ideology in providing cohesion to groupings of developing countries elsewhere has invited the comment of several scholars. Robert Rothstein, for instance, writes '…the real glue that has kept unity from disintegrating, and that at least delays or dilutes immediate preoccupations with self-interest, may well be an emotional commitment to the idea of a Third World – not so much shared interests, but shared problems, a common interpretation of past and present exploitation, a sense of shared fate in the future, and consequently a strong desire to stand together and not apart.'[27] In the case of developing countries in the GATT, ideology provided the cover for the many side-deals that took place within the group and prevented the dissipation of the coalition into the short-term bilateral and minilateral trade-offs that actually constituted it. The leaders played a significant role in the construction and maintenance of this ideology. The main tenets of the ideology are described in the remainder of this sub-section.

Two core, constitutive ideas formed the basis of this ideology and pervaded different versions of 'the South' in the GATT, UNCTAD, the General Assembly, and elsewhere.[28] First, the countries of the South were united by a shared perception of powerlessness of members. This powerlessness was rooted in the positioning of developing countries in the international system, and from varying degrees and types of exploitation that they had been subject to from the powerful states. Second, many developing countries shared the conviction that powerlessness of individual states could be overcome through group solidarity to improve relative bargaining positions. These core beliefs, in some ways, seemed to substitute for the lack of a collective political and economic aim, and redefined individual aims in terms of the collective. They provided rules of membership and reinforced these rules through a shared interpretation of history, an explanation of current problems, and a vision for the future. The shared reading of history can be summarised in what has been called the 'psychology of decolonisation'.[29] From this perception of history, also emerged an account of the present. Domestic problems of weak government regimes, and international problems of minimal influence, were ascribed to the legacy of suffering, exploitation, imposed patterns of underdevelopment, and poverty. Yet, developing countries were not condemned to this position of weakness in the international system. By promoting solidarity, these weak countries could exercise a great influence on the international system. The basis of this strength was moral. They would derive better results from international negotiations by appealing to the guilt-ridden conscience of the West and draw succour from the broad base of their platform.

This broad set of beliefs, however, still left the course open for various types of strategies for the Informal Group. The demand for free trade and universal rules versus the demand for exceptional treatment of developing countries and greater protectionism represented the two ends of the strategic spectrum. The gradual adoption of the latter type of strategy over the former was described in some detail in Section 3.1.1.

Consistent association of the Informal Group with demands of distributive justice and special treatment yielded some unexpected benefits. This set of strategies emphasised the difference or the 'otherness' of the group in multilateral diplomacy. As mutual give and take would imply a symbolic acceptance of the unfairness of the system, demands were made for unilateral concessions from the North. Not even the severe losses incurred by the non-oil developing countries during the OPEC crisis could prompt defections. These instrumental beliefs reinforced the solidarity of the group, strengthened the core beliefs of unfairness in the system, and reinforced the coalition by emphasising the difference between the North and the South. By proving themselves useful in strengthening the core, the instrumental beliefs became entrenched in it. The long term over which these strategic beliefs were maintained resulted in their becoming inseparable from the collective identity that various versions of the South (including the Informal Group) claimed to possess.

Perhaps even more important, these ideologies became embedded in the individual agendas of the leading members of the coalition. Particularly in the case of Brazil and India, the vigorous espousal of the ideational element was accompanied by the conformity of these international ideas with their domestic policies of ISI. These linkages made domestic and international withdrawal from the advocated principles very difficult.

In other words, the Informal Group was, first and foremost, a weak coalition of logrolled interests. Leadership by some members and a common ideology united these diverse interests within one coalition. The importance of ideology, however, for both the identity of the leaders and the identity of the coalition greatly reduced the flexibility of the coalition and its ability to modify strategies to adapt to new circumstances. The Informal Group was a weak, precariously maintained, brittle coalition, that would snap at even a strategic challenge to its existence. The G-10, which adopted most of the strategies and workings of the Informal Group, fully demonstrated the strains and weaknesses of its precedent.

## 3.2 Factors and events: mobilising the coalition and evolving an agenda

The Informal Group lumbered along for over thirty years, exercising a quiet influence on the GATT in liaison with other groupings elsewhere. Its transformation into a coalition with a precise agenda and a dramatic and visible presence in the GATT was a product of several new circumstances. Building on the pre-existing base of the Informal Group, developing countries responded decisively to the new circumstances. The mobilisation occurred in two phases. The first phase saw the increasing and vocal participation of the unity of developing countries through the Informal Group. The second phase witnessed fractures within the Informal Group, and the simultaneous reinforcement of the agenda of the Informal Group through the G-10.

The first and perhaps most important factor which forced developing countries into serious mobilisation as a coalition was that of necessity. The possibility of inclusion of services within GATT auspices threatened to take the GATT well beyond its traditional mandate of trade and border issues. Inclusion of services was seen as a move with potential for cross-sectoral retaliatory trade that would impede the growth of both the goods and services sectors of developing countries. The US call for the ministerial meeting of 1982 began by catalysing the Informal Group into action.

Merely the call for a Ministerial to discuss the launch of a new round was enough to alert the developing countries. Misgivings about a new round were a product of suspicion of the US agenda. American aims had already found expression in other forums. In 1981, William Brock (the US Trade Representative) had put forth the idea of a new round; in January 1982 at the Davos Symposium of the European Management Forum, Brock called for a Ministerial meeting to launch a new round to deal with the new issues of investment, services, technology, and agriculture, and also to facilitate an improvement of the rules and methods to deal with non-market activities and ensure greater participation of the Third World in the world trading system.[30] The new agenda foreshadowed encroachments by the GATT into the domestic realm, and in critical areas (such as services) in which interests of developing countries were still underdeveloped and ill defined.

Developing countries were unanimous in opposing the launch of the new round. The arguments were simple: the voluminous backlog of pending issues (liberalisation in agriculture, textiles, tropical products, removal of NTBs such as VERs, ADDs, and CVDs) had to be dealt with first. Paraphrasing the arguments of developing countries Rubens Ricupero writes, 'What purpose would it have served …to add more floors (i.e. new issues) to a building whose foundations were likely to collapse at any moment?'[31]

It was also clear that the push for an inclusion of the services issue from the US was a product of the shift in the American competitive advantage. The US was losing its competitive edge in manufacturing, and felt increasingly threatened by the EC's emergence as a leading producer of agriculture. The strength of the US in services industries led it to push for the opening of services markets through the GATT. Developing countries noted that there already existed some regimes among the Organisation for Economic Cooperation and Development (OECD) countries guiding services activity. The attempt to extend the agenda of the GATT, therefore, was seen as an attempt to capture the markets of developing countries.[32] Inclusion of services within the GATT would allow developed countries easy bargains with their poorer counterparts, through linkages with conventional areas that were of interest to the latter. Developing countries were determined to resist such linkages, particularly as former promises of standstill and rollback had not been fulfilled in the past, and would now be used to demand additional concessions from them. Issues of interest to them had been sidelined before; developing countries were unwilling to allow another expansion of the GATT agenda that would deflect attention from former promises that had been made to them.

Second, catalysing developing countries into a coalitional coherence of the G-10 was the ambiguity and newness associated with the services sector. Some of the conceptual difficulties highlighted by developing countries with respect to services were described in the previous chapter. Debates and controversies were a result of two conceptual ambiguities.[33] First, in the early 1980s, there was no accepted theoretical basis, which could provide an accurate account of the services economy and its role in economic development. Contrary to traditional product cycle models, developing countries feared that services complemented and reinforced traditional manufacturing sectors. The critical position that services might occupy even in developing economies necessitated great caution. Second, existing statistics on services were scarce, making it even more difficult to assess the impact of a services liberalisation. Developing countries, which were even more uncertain about the configuration of their services sector, realised that much caution was needed in making commitments that they had not understood. There was considerable epistemic disagreement on whether measures pertaining to the new issues would reduce developing countries to the status of perennial primary producers and compromise their sovereignty. Theoretical ambiguities necessitated caution and also allowed developing countries a negotiating space that was based on a demand for more research on the sector.

The third factor conducive to the mobilisation of coalition activity in the GATT was the context of a transatlantic rift that opened up opportunities for developing countries to bargain with either side. This attempt by the G-10 to optimise its negotiating space by utilising differences within the Quad has been largely ignored from most accounts. The tactics of the G-10 are often contrasted with those of the Cairns Group, which is usually cited as the epitome of a bridge-building coalition that exploited the transatlantic divide on agriculture. The omission may be explained by the fact that the hard-line tactics of the G-10 have deflected attention from any signs of diplomatic subtlety that were displayed by the group.

The reason why the group was able to adopt such a hard-line position, both in the preliminary discussions of 1982 and subsequently when the group fractured producing the first organisational divide among developing countries, lay in the external condition of a potential divide between the EC and the US. The push for a round on services came from the US, with some support from Canada (discussions on barriers in banking and computer services between the two had begun in 1983), but the initial response of Europe (with the exception of the UK) and Japan, was one of hesitation. Michael Hart notes two principal objectives which guided the EC position in the GATT – to keep new GATT rules from impeding greater European integration and to develop rules that would constrain American unilateralism under Super 301 and other measures. Neither was a wholly negative stance.[34] But the initial European position was one of scepticism, given the limited work that had been done on the implications of a liberalisation of the services sector.[35] Particularly in the early 1980s, when theoretical understanding on the services sector was minimal, the EC was still uncertain about the implications of a services liberalisation. Concern was directed particularly towards effects on the French audio-visual media and fear of an American cultural invasion, state-run monopolies of Postal, Telegraph and Telephone (PT&T), relative strengths in the fields of civil aviation, and financial services. The EC also anticipated that the new round would entail unprecedented pressures directed against the CAP and in favour of agricultural liberalisation and was, in all, ambivalent about the launch.

As a result, India and Brazil had succeeded in developing a degree of understanding with the EEC on issues of mutual concern. The reinforced Informal Group and the G-10 saw a possibility of securing EC support and were hence able to develop and maintain their 'hard line'.[36] The ambivalence of the EC and sympathy towards the G-10 continued until the eventual 'defection' of the EC to the 'Dirty Dozen'.[37]

The fourth factor that facilitated the rise of the G-10 was the pre-existing Informal Group. The existence of the Informal Group allowed the G-10 to exploit ready-made links with the UNCTAD to its advantage. The G-10 was able to utilise the agenda of the Informal Group as a springboard to develop its own agenda. The services issue was located within the broader context of North–South diplomacy in the GATT. The attempt at inclusion of services into the GATT agenda was seen as a part of the series of events wherein developed countries included issues of interest to themselves within GATT negotiations and disregarded the needs of developing countries. Utilising and building on institutional inertia, the G-10 was able to draw on the membership, agenda and strategies of the Informal Group to deal with a new set of challenges.

### 3.2.1   Phase I: increasing activism of the Informal Group

The first reaction of developing countries to the four new factors described above was to remobilise the Informal Group. Led by the original Group of Ten (i.e. the Big Five accompanied by Chile, Jamaica, Pakistan, Peru, and Uruguay), which had traditionally included the most vocal members of the Informal Group, developing countries voiced their unanimous opposition to the launch of a new round. Until the unfinished business from the Tokyo Round was completed and existing derogations from the GATT were addressed, their opposition to the new round would continue. In conformity with former practice, the Group worked in association with developing country groupings in other forums. At the UNCTAD, the foreign ministers of the G-77 expressed collective opposition to the US moves in the GATT to bring issues relating to services, investment and technology within the GATT framework.[38] Member countries of the SELA expressed doubts about the desirability of initiating negotiations on services and on the legal competence of the GATT in the field.[39] That this opposition of developing countries was taken seriously is illustrated by the desperate moves by the US to introduce proposals of weighted voting on the basis of trade shares in the GATT.[40]

As a result of this active resistance to the US sponsored agenda, the 1982 Ministerial was a compromise. The US was successful in establishing a work programme on services, which would allow the GATT to prepare a technical base for multilateral negotiations in this area. But it was agreed that the contracting parties could undertake national studies on trade problems in this sector and exchange relevant information through international organisations 'such as GATT' (rather than specifically under GATT, which would have allowed the linkages that developing countries saw as potentially deleterious to their interests). The results of these examinations were to be reviewed at the Fortieth GATT Session in 1984. The decision also empowered the contracting parties to consider any action that seemed appropriate or desirable.[41] The US appeared to have given up the investment issue. Trade in counterfeit products was included but as a part of the work programme. Admittedly, the Ministerial resulted in a big compromise for developing countries, that is discussion on the services issue. The issues of standstill and rollback had still not been attended to. But the Informal Group, with the active participation of its ten core members (and other, newly active members such as Colombia) had succeeded in its primary goal of stalling the initiation of a new round.

Developing countries had assumed that the decision on the work programme, reached at the Ministerial, was to work as a process independent of the GATT. But the US and other developed countries interpreted this as a 'kind of preparation for the new round'.[42] Various attempts were made by the US to rally support for this interpretation, for instance, at the 'secret talks at Lausanne' involving Brock and ministers from the UK, FRG, and Japan, as well as Brazil, Mexico, Singapore, Indonesia, the former Yugoslavia, and the Philippines. Trade ministers from India, Malaysia, South Korea, Colombia, and Peru were among those who had been invited, but who boycotted the meeting. Failing their participation, the former set of countries were invited.[43] The attempt by the US to take the discussions outside the GATT is noteworthy. Even at these conferences outside the GATT, developing countries reportedly continued to maintain their common stance of resisting US moves to include services, investments, and trade in high-technology goods. At informal consultations held in Geneva (summoned at the instance of the

US and Canada), Indonesia, Philippines, Singapore, Jamaica, Tunisia, Brazil, Colombia, Chile, and Hong Kong were reported to have been present but did not modify their positions or negotiate on the matter.[44] The unified position of the South was presented at the GATT consultative group of 18 (cg-18), still arguing that old issues of standstill and rollback be addressed first, before the launch of any new round.[45] The joint Third World paper tabled by Uruguay reiterated this stance.[46]

Despite the unified position of the Third World, by the beginning of 1985, the new round seemed inevitable. The US had renewed its pressure and was now supported by the EC at informal gatherings like the Davos Symposium. Two factors eventually tilted the EC balance from scepticism to a cautious support for the US position. First, studies revealed that the EC was a 'services superpower', and hence interest in services liberalisation grew. Second, services was an issue that promised to consume much attention in the new Round and could therefore divert attention away from, or at least facilitate trade-offs on agriculture.[47] President Reagan, on 6 February, in his 'state of the union' message to a joint meeting of the US house and senate, asked the trading partners of the US to join it in a new round of trade negotiations to expand trade and competition, and strengthen the world economy.[48] The position of the EC and Japan both seemed to be tending towards the US.[49] The EC now emphasised a step-by-step approach, with a high-level meeting in mid-1985 for 'consultation and reflection' and perhaps launching of the preparatory process to a new round, if not launching the round itself in 1986.[50] At a high-level meeting in Ludwigsburg, the West German economic minister was quoted as saying that there had been 'unanimous agreement' on beginning a new round the next year. He acknowledged that Third World countries had had 'some reservations' but that the industrial countries should hold bilateral talks with them.[51] Besides the use of bilateral pressures, the US had indicated that the services issue was 'the linchpin' of the consultations on the work programme and the US contribution to the GATT budget. The US delegate launched a diatribe against an analogue to the G-77 in the GATT ('if you want to ruin GATT, the best way to do it is to speak in blocs').[52] Attempts were made to highlight the differences between the members of the Informal Group. The variety of carrots offered and sticks brandished to break the opposition of the Informal Group indicates that the resistance of developing countries was taken seriously.

Not all the strategies, described above, were unsuccessful. Signs of rifts within the Informal Group were emerging, even though every attempt was made by developing countries to demonstrate that any reformulation of their stance was consistent with their initial position. Hence, Ambassador Shukla (coordinator of the Informal Group) stated that the 'agreed conclusions' on services at the annual session of the contracting parties did not go beyond the ministerial declaration of 1982. Kazimir Vidas of the former Yugoslavia, Paul Nogueria Batista of Brazil, Osvaldo Lopez Noguerol of Argentina, and Mahmoud Abdel-Bari Hamza of Egypt endorsed this position. Regarding services, developing countries had agreed to authorise the Chairman of the GATT contracting parties to organise formal meetings to exchange information on national studies. In June 1985, India presented another joint paper entitled 'Improvement of World Trade relations'.

The paper was issued on behalf of twenty-two developing countries and revealed a hardening of their position against US moves for a new round and its efforts to promote 'new themes alien to the GATT'. Brazil proposed a draft in which its position for separate negotiations on services and goods (to prevent trade-offs between the two) was endorsed by India, Argentina, Egypt, the former Yugoslavia, Pakistan, Colombia, Nigeria, Zaire, Trinidad and Tobago, Peru, and Venezuela. The draft tried to recreate the myth of constancy to the agenda, and so referred to the decisions taken by developing countries in 1982 and 1984 in asserting that the issue of services was not within the competence of the GATT. But note that these statements did not refer to the sources of dissonance, which were already in the offing and working in parallel to the supposedly 'unanimous' position.

### 3.2.2   *Phase II: the 'hard-liners' emerge – the rise of the G-10*

Signs of questioning of the 'unanimous' position of developing countries came from different members of the Informal Group. Most of the potential dissidents were smaller members, more willing to make a compromise with the progressively convergent positions of the developed world. These dissidents would soon coalesce along the Jaramillo track, and subsequently into the Café au Lait Group (or the G-20), discussed in detail in Chapter 4. At this juncture, suffice it to note that there was a serious threat to the unanimity of the Informal Group.

The differences within the Informal Group came to the fore in 1985. At a rare postal ballot that was called by the US, two-thirds of the contracting parties supported the convening of a special session.[53] This was in consonance with the view being propagated by the US and Western media that, except for the opposition of four or five countries, about sixty-five countries had voted for the convening of a special session in support of the US position (and in opposition to the view propagated by the Big Five of the Informal Group that any extension of the GATT treaty to 'other specie outside its framework' could be done only through a plenipotentiary action or unanimous agreement of GATT contracting parties, and that services was too vital a sector to be opened up to international negotiation). These statistics demonstrate that despite the attempt by the core of the Informal Group to maintain a façade of unity of the South, almost half of its members had moved away from the group position.

In complete disregard of any dissidence, the core of the Informal Group constituted by the Big Five plus a new set of adherents, Cuba, Nigeria, Nicaragua, Tanzania, and Peru, held fast to their earlier stance. By 1985, at the November session of the contracting parties, an agreement to launch the new round was reached. The agenda of the Informal Group and the G-10 had been hugely compromised. But the new incarnation of the G-10 had a very specific agenda, namely to pursue the initial stance adopted by the Informal Group regarding the issues of standstill and rollback and the refusal to allow the inclusion of the new issues in the new round. Any possibility of finding a middle ground with the other developing countries was ignored.

The G-10 further proceeded to prepare a draft declaration for the launch of the new round. Notably, this task was undertaken outside the Informal Group led by Colombia, and in omission of parallel deliberations among other developing countries. The draft appeared as a response to the US paper presented to the Prepcom and a G-9 proposal. The US paper aimed to make international trade in services 'as open as possible' through a multilateral agreement that would establish disciplines governing services trade, taking into account 'legitimate objectives of national laws and regulations applying to services' and addressing 'specific trade barriers and unfair trade practices' encountered by particular service sectors.[54] The G-9 'non-paper' (so called because it was not a formal proposal), tabled by Australia, New Zealand, Canada, Austria, Finland, Iceland, Norway, Sweden, and Switzerland, gave some recognition to the problems of developing countries that required S&D treatment. But it also emphasised the need to have a 'multilateral framework of principles and rules for the conduct of trade in services'. The paper retained the American emphasis on the introduction of services, investment issues, and intellectual property rights in the new round.[55] Seeking no compromise with these proposals or with potential ones among other developing countries, the G-10 draft was presented as a fait accompli to the prepcom on 23 June 1986.[56] The promised support that it had from the EC was one of the factors contributing to the formalisation of the proposal.[57] The draft called for a new round on goods and other traditional GATT matters, and contained no reference to trade in services or the other new issues.

The G-10 move did not provoke immediate, cohesive, retaliatory action from the 'Enthusiasts'.[58] The G-10 coalition, in turn, was anxious to deny any rumours about its isolation from the Informal Group; thus, Batista spoke about the wrong impression that had been created to the effect that the position of the G-10 on trade liberalisation did not have much support.[59] The G-10 also tried to present itself as a responsive coalition, rather than an intransigent bloc, and submitted a revised version of their draft (W/41/rev.1) to the Prepcom, dated 10 July.[60] The original draft had envisaged government commitments at the highest level; now, however, in view of possible difficulties and delays involved, the group proposed that the commitments be entered into through two protocols, to be signed by ministers at Punta del Este and ratified in the normal GATT way. The second draft also extended the rollback commitments to include both developed and developing countries, rather than just developed countries in favour of the developing countries. Some linkages were sought between the trade liberalisation process in GATT and parallel actions on commodity stabilisation and between trade, money and finance issues, but the hard line on services was retained.

All members of the Informal Group, excluding the G-10, objected to the draft and proposed that it be discussed more fully in the Informal Group. Yet, the G-10 displayed no inclination for compromise, arguing that debate would serve no purpose as the submission was not on behalf of all developing countries but only the draft signatories. This position of the G-10 was an unprecedented and overt violation of 'the discipline of conventions and practices that had until then guided and tempered the working of developing country delegations in the GATT'.[61] Ambassador Jaramillo made a statement regretting the unprecedented nature of the G-10 action. In view of the intransigence of the G-10, and the pursuit of alternative priorities by the Colombia-led group, the process of drafting an alternative draft proposal formally began. The rupture within the Informal Group represented the decisive break in the coalition of developing countries in the GATT and all the peculiarities of its diplomacy.

## 3.3   Evaluating the G-10

The blow to the Informal Group and eventual collapse of the G-10 hint at the first obvious sign of the failure of this coalition type. Closer inspection reveals that the dissipation of a coalition need not reflect its limitations: some coalitions are formed for specific purposes and may disappear once the purpose is met. The G-10 had both successes and failures to its credit, which make an assessment of its achievements less clear cut than some diplomatic accounts suggest.[62] The section below provides such an assessment. The second part of this section investigates the conditions that promoted the successes of the group and also analyses operative constraints.

### 3.3.1   *An account of successes and failures*

At a minimal level, the resistance of the G-10 against the inclusion of services generated attempts at more rigorous definitions and understanding by all the parties involved. The demand by the coalition that talks proceed only after definitional clarity had been achieved necessitated counter-action in the form of more research by both the developed countries and the 'Enthusiasts'. A developed country official is hence quoted as saying, 'Although it is clear that the G-10 were operating in a vacuum of reality, they did contribute to clarity and progress in the Round.'[63] The participation of developing countries was unprecedented in the Uruguay Round, as was the attention that their participation commanded from the developed countries. In large measure, this attention was a product of the politicisation of the services issue by the G-10.

There were some procedural victories with the promise of substantive implications. The two-track negotiating strategy was adopted at Punta del Este. Some attention was given to allowing provisions of interest to developing countries, such as the commitment to strengthen the development process in them.

The agenda that eventually became the GATS was a direct product of the challenging group's proposal, but it incorporated several qualifiers that were proposed by the G-10, often initially in allegiance with the EC. It is noteworthy that the GATS has been described as a 'soft' agreement.[64] This was because the original preference of the EC and developing countries prevailed (i.e. the initial position of the Informal Group in an informal alliance with the EC). The GATS had only one generally binding obligation – MFN – and it allows countries to list exemptions from it. The positive list approach is another feature of the 'soft' agreement. Article XIX allows developing countries to offer fewer specific commitments. The language of Article XIX comes from the Montreal declaration, which in turn 'was the result of the initial negotiating stances taken by the major developing countries'.[65]

The successes of the G-10 can be best judged in terms of an exercise in damage limitation within operative constraints. The consistent position of the G-10 had been that an inclusion of services into the GATT would prove detrimental to developing countries. While unable to completely prevent such an inclusion, the G-10 was able to insert brakes in the process of services liberalisation. The GATS that eventually resulted remains, to this day, a weak agreement.[66] Many of the so-called weaknesses of the GATS are the safeguards that the G-10 had built in.[67]

In many ways, the G-10 represented the epitome of the Informal Group in the GATT. It presented the agenda of the Informal Group in its most precise and concrete version, and successfully politicised North–South rifts to a level that was unprecedented in the GATT. This politicisation was important in two ways. First, it necessitated an appropriate response from the countries that had an alternative agenda, and hence the research expended in understanding the services issue by the developed and some smaller developing countries. Second, developing countries became protagonists who could not be ignored in the new round.

Despite these successes, the G-10 coalition is seen as a bargaining debacle by both developed and developing countries. In some ways, the failures of the G-10 are obvious. First, its 'evolving' agenda may well be seen as simply a series of defeats and failures of the initial agenda of developing countries. The slide of the group from its resistance to even allowing a new round to the new two-track negotiating approach was dramatic. Second, in the longer term, the eventual inclusion of the GATS within the WTO rendered cross-retaliation possible after all. This left the concept of the two-track approach meaningless. And little has been done to include areas of advantage to developing countries in return.

It is possible to counter the above two failures of the group by pointing out that sliding from an initial hard line may represents good bargaining strategy. Further, the G-10 cannot be blamed for the longer-term failures of its agenda. Rather, the responsibility of eventual failures lies with successor coalitions of the G-10. The G-10 had limited aims that went up to Punta del Este, and in this respect, its successes were many. The issue of successor coalitions, however, takes us to the greatest failing of the G-10.

The most adverse aftermath of the rise of the G-10 was the rift that it produced in the traditional coalition of the Informal Group (representative of the South) in the GATT. The initial challenge to the G-10 was minimal. It came in the form of the 'Enthusiasts' who chose to follow the Jaramillo track. The transformation of that minimal challenge into a deathblow to a whole pattern of North–South diplomacy is described in detail in the next chapter. At this point, it is important to note that the dogged resistance of the group to compromise on the agenda through reconciliation, as suggested by the Café au Lait group, resulted in the formal, organisational rift in the Informal Group. It was a rift from which the over-thirty-year-old grouping never quite recovered. While the group continues to meet today, it is a coalition in little else but name.[68] Most members agree that its impact on the members themselves as well as a coalition outside is minimal. As the next chapter argues, a change in the old type of diplomacy was perhaps inevitable, and this would have affected the workings and composition of the Informal Group. The nature and timing of the fissure, however, were largely a product of the recalcitrance of the G-10. The G-10 episode deprived developing countries of their old coalition pattern; the search for a substitute continues to this day.

### 3.3.2   *Conditions conducive to success and operative constraints*

Some of the conditions that had facilitated the remobilisation of the Informal Group and the rise of the G-10 persisted to further assist in the working of the coalition. The first of these was the conceptual ambiguity of the services issue. The G-10 successfully utilised this ambiguity, initially to curtail the launch of a new round, and later in terms of definition. On account of the issues raised by the G-10 regarding lack of epistemic consensus on services, the question of definition and coverage was kept open. The hope behind this was that labour-intensive services and the labour mode of supply would be included to balance the developed country bias in favour of capital-intensive and technology-intensive services.[69] The role of the G-10 in promoting definitional clarity has already been mentioned.

Second, until the eve of the launch, the G-10 successfully utilised the EC–US differences as a bargaining opportunity, hence the 'soft' agreement that prevailed in the end as a result of the allied efforts of the G-10 and the EC.

Third, and more important, the G-10 built upon the base provided by the Informal Group to produce a much more specific agenda and membership. As such, the G-10 represented a crystallisation of the more amorphous Informal Group. Two characteristics of the Informal Group proved particularly useful to the G-10. The G-10 built upon the North–South confrontation that had formed a part of the ideational component of the method used to bind the Informal Group, and further politicised it in an unprecedented way. The coalition also utilised and further built on the hierarchies of the Informal Group, initially to provide leadership to all developing countries, and later to focus on the agenda of the ten. Both legacies of the coalition and their contribution to its successes are described below.

Previous attempts by the Informal Group to present most GATT debates in North–South terms proved useful to the G-10 in two ways. First, when the G-10 chose a dramatic and visible involvement in the GATT, the platform of the South allowed the required politicisation to command such a presence in the GATT. Recalling the ideational component of the method used to bind the Informal Group, the G-10 utilised and expanded on this ingredient, hence the refusal to allow even a preliminary discussion of the new round until old promises to developing countries had been met. For the same ideational reasons, a mere exploration of the new issues by the 'Enthusiasts' was seen as a sign of defection. The ideational component lent considerable moral fervour and provided the base of a pre-existing agenda to the G-10.

Second, the G-10 also adopted the pre-existing hierarchies of the Informal Group to attempt to set the agenda. The role of the Big Five was critical to the

G-10, and it derived directly from their role in the Informal Group. In taking the initiative of leadership of the G-10, however, the Big Five took their role much further. The possibility of inclusion of the services issue represented a crisis point in some ways for developing countries. The G-10 offered a response by building on existing leadership patterns, and also underplaying the role of the smaller powers.

It is ironic to note that the legacy of the Informal Group to the G-10 was as much a reason for the collapse of its successor as its achievements. The Janus-like face of its legacy impaired the G-10's ability to utilise bargaining opportunities to their fullest. Further, external conditions were not consistently favourable, and the G-10 was unable to deal with their adverse implications due to its structural limitations. An account of the operation of the various sets of constraints that contributed to the failings of the group follows.

The ambiguity of the services sector opened a new negotiating space for developing countries. The G-10, while raising issues of definition and clarification, did not exploit this negotiating space further. In contrast to the Café au Lait (case study in Chapter 4), the G-10 made no attempt to engage in discussion on services, clarify issues, or present alternative ways of conceptualisation. In the absence of this constructive role, the G-10 lost its opportunity to set the agenda.

The absence of a constructive agenda of the G-10 brings us to the second critical flaw in the coalition, that is that the G-10 was a blocking coalition. A part of the reason for the limited successes of the Informal Group in the past had been the use of blocking strategies that fitted well in the North versus South paradigm. The G-10 adopted the same strategies, and thereby also inherited their weaknesses. A high-level UNCTAD official provided an important critique of G-10 blocking strategies, which is pertinent here, that is the blocking strategies went against the 'culture of liberalisation' of the GATT.[70] The self-exclusion of the G-10 from the agenda formation process meant that all developed country demands were incorporated. The resulting agenda was not only too ambitious but also too overloaded to later include and implement the demands of the developing countries and particularly the G-10.

Third, the G-10 had made the strategic move of getting a foot in the negotiations when potential differences existed between the US and the EC. Compare, however, these differences with the transatlantic rift in agriculture,[71] and the minimal nature of the former becomes obvious. Scepticism of the EC over the inclusion of services, and the consequent research endeavours, did not amount to an opposition to the US. The eventual support of the EC for the Café au Lait draft should have come as little surprise, keeping in mind the aggregate advantage of the EC in services. Given the nature of the transatlantic divide as well as its own strategy, the G-10 could not, and chose not to, present itself as a bridge-building coalition. It could not, therefore, command the legitimacy that the Cairns Group would later acquire by emphasising its mediatory role.

The most decisive deterrent to the successes of the G-10 was its legacy from the Informal Group. The same factors that had assisted in the mobilisation of the coalition paradoxically proved detrimental to its maintenance. The detrimental effects of the legacy had two sources. First, and as was described earlier, the Informal Group was a weak coalition. Many of the intrinsic weaknesses of the Informal Group were exacerbated and exposed as a result of the formalisation of the agenda and the strategies of the group by the G-10. Second, unprecedented challenges and new circumstances rendered the weak cementing strategies of the Informal Group even more dysfunctional. The rise of the alternative coalition G-20 formed a part of these new conditions, which are analysed in depth in the Chapter 4. The remainder of this section focuses on the first source.

Section 3.1 offered an insight into how the Informal Group was a precariously maintained coalition. The carefully constructed common platform was preserved by the unique balance of logrolled interests, intra-group hierarchy, and ideology. Critical to this balance was an ambiguity of agenda that allowed sufficient possibility of logrolling and aggregating conflicting demands to fulfil the discrete interests of members. By replacing this ambiguous agenda with a very specific one, the Informal Group reduced the scope of such logrolling and exposed its own key weakness, the lack of a collective agenda. The reduced logrolling, further, came at a time when alternatives available to smaller countries were greatly expanded. This expanded menu is examined in the Chapter 4.

Second, the mix of ideology and intra-group hierarchies, which had been used in the past to maintain the multiple deals within a weak coalition, also imparted great inflexibility to the group. Even the smallest challenge to the norms of the group would threaten its survival. The G-10 inherited this brittle and frayed mantle in circumstances that were much harder than those faced by the Informal Group.

Developing on the strategy employed by the Informal Group, the G-10 was initially successful in highlighting the North–South divide. However, owing to the high stakes of the leaders in this ideational component of the coalition, the G-10 was unable to abandon the North–South terms of the debate, even when they had become a hindrance to negotiating ability. These difficulties had already been visible in the case of the Informal Group; the entrenchment of one version of the agenda in the identity of the group and its largest members was described earlier. The G-10 heightened these difficulties by politicising the issue of services dramatically in North–South terms, thereby rendering withdrawal from its position especially difficult.

The political costs of a withdrawal from the hard line were especially high for the leaders of the former Informal Group and then the G-10. The domestic and international status of these countries rested on an adherence to the hard line. Hence, the G-10 disallowed a compromise with the second offspring of the Informal Group, the Jaramillo Group. The leadership clung with even greater desperation to old ideas when challenged by a new set of harsher external conditions and alternative approaches. The principal and immediate challenge was the G-20. The new conditions, the G-20, and their impact on the fall of the G-10 are analysed in Chapter 4.

## 3.4   Preliminary theoretical findings and conclusion

Definitive conclusions on the G-10 can be drawn only after a comparative analysis with its challenging coalition, the G-20 or Café au Lait. But even when examined in its own right, the G-10 leaves us with some important lessons, empirical and theoretical.

Empirically, the importance of the G-10 lies in its dramatic mobilisation of developing countries into a coalition with a booming voice. In the attention that it secured for developing countries and the counter-coalitions that it triggered, the G-10 presents a landmark. The politicisation of the services issue on North–South lines, however, was achieved by the G-10 through a piggybacking on the agenda of the Informal Group. As such, it inherited the deficiencies of a weak coalition. It further exposed the limitations of this weak coalition by putting its strategies to much more formalised and specific uses – uses that the strategy and its underlying set of deals were never made to deal with. By inheriting the characteristics of the Informal Group and bringing them into sharper focus, the G-10 doomed itself and a whole pattern of diplomacy to failure. The failings of the G-10 were a direct product of the weak foundations of the group, rather than a poor strategy. If anything, the structure imposed limitations on the strategic manoeuvre of the group, and thereby reinforced the fixed adherence of the group to its hard line.

Some theoretical lessons of the G-10 experience are obvious, even without the benefit of the comparative light of the G-20 example. The G-10 revealed the dangers of basing a coalition in aggregated and logrolled interests at the expense of an internally coherent and mutually compatible, shared agenda among members. Without internal coherence, a coalition is difficult to maintain. A combination of multiple deals, intra-group hierarchies, and ideology may somehow plaster over differences when the coalition engages mainly in rhetorical diplomacy (e.g. the G-77 demanding the New International Economic Order, NIEO). But they do not substitute for the lack of a collective economic interest when it is engaged in the actual details of agenda-setting and trade negotiation. The example of the G-10 is also useful in arbitrating between the three methods of coalition formation that were discussed in Chapter 1. The G-10 example reveals that co-operative, neo-liberal processes (e.g. logrolling, creation of hierarchies) and even the introduction of ideas and identity can prove inadequate in cementing bargaining coalitions. Structures and interests are necessary preliminary conditions for successful coalition formation, even if they might not be sufficient conditions.

The G-10 also hints at the importance of external conditions on the eventual successes that the coalition will have in influencing the agenda or negotiating outcomes. This is especially the case when coalitions of the weak are concerned. A wide range of factors may be included in the category of external conditions: the degree of conceptual ambiguity surrounding the issue, the nature and extent of divisions within the Quad that might allow the prevalence of a 'third way', the possibility of harnessing the support of one of the Quad members, and so forth. Whether these external conditions turn out to be simply influencing/facilitating conditions or determining conditions, however, can be determined only through a comparative analysis with other coalitions responding to the same set of conditions. The case study of the G-20, presented in Chapter 4, facilitates such an analysis.

It was noted even in the mid-1980s that the G-10 experiment marked the culmination of the old style of rhetorical, North–South diplomacy that had been omnipresent in the GATT in former years.[72] Its theoretical implications were also finding some implicit recognition. For instance, the failings of the G-10 triggered the new fad with issue-based coalitions among developing countries, thereby inaugurating new patterns of coalition formation. Note that issue-based coalitions laid a primary emphasis on common interests, and thereby adopted quite a different approach to the combination of methods that was used by the G-10. The G-10 (along with the Informal Group) had demonstrated the dangers of basing a coalition in aggregated and logrolled interests that were united by intra-group hierarchies and ideology. Issue-based coalitions that brought together collective material interests were seen as the obvious, if somewhat simplistic, answer.

The reaction to the G-10 style of diplomacy was pronounced. Veritable shudders by UNCTAD officials well into the late 1990s, when asked about the G-10, indicate how deep the lessons of the G-10 had sunk in. But the attention that developing countries received as a result of its activity in its early phases was unsurpassed. The G-10 displayed several successes, as outlined in Section 3.3. It thereby offers some constructive lessons for coalition diplomacy, which are being recognised in some developing country circles as progressive disillusionment with issue-based diplomacy has set in. This mixed bag of lessons along with parallel and related lessons of the Café au Lait are critical in allowing us an understanding of the particular circumstances in which certain coalition types emerge and survive effectively. Further, the efficacy of coalition types depends on which countries adopt them. The next chapter throws further light on the subject by examining the counter-coalition that provided the alternative to the G-10. Before launching into the next coalition type, it is worth remembering that the bloc-based diplomacy examined in this chapter and the alliance diplomacy studied in the next chapter were a product of successive and mutual reactions and counter-reactions. The study of alliance diplomacy in the next chapter also illuminates how the G-20 challenged the weak base of the G-10 and eventually became the archetypal alliance-type coalition of the Café au Lait.

# 4   Alliance diplomacy

## The issue-based, crossover coalitions of G-20 and Café au Lait

We will unite the white rose and the red:
Smile, heaven, upon this fair conjunction,
That long hath frown'd upon this enmity!
(William Shakespeare,
*Richard III*, Act V, Scene 5)

The new alliance diplomacy that emerged in the mid-1980s had humble origins. It began as an informal process of information exchange with few claims to grand coalition building. The G-20 and the Café au Lait were de facto products of this informal process. However, in spite of their spontaneous, informal and unplanned nature, the G-20 and the Café au Lait paved the way for a new pattern of coalition diplomacy in the GATT. Its chief characteristics were an issue-based focus, crossover links, that is combined developed and developing countries, flexibility of agenda, and simplicity of coalition structure. Further, the new alliance diplomacy was not simply an alternative that could co-exist easily with the bloc-type coalitions that developing countries had traditionally known. Rather, the emergence of the G-20 came to represent the first formal rift within the Informal Group. By presenting the immediate challenge to the G-10, the G-20 exposed some of the critical weaknesses of bloc-type diplomacy. The rejection of North versus South bloc diplomacy by many negotiators and academics alike was a consequence of this exposure. As an independent coalition type (however de facto and spontaneous), through its direct links with the collapse of the G-10, and for the sharp policy reversals in GATT diplomacy of developing countries that it catalysed, the G-20 represents a landmark in the history of coalition formations involving developing countries. The far-reaching implications of the new alliance diplomacy, in spite of its modest beginnings, can be estimated from the fact that, at least in certain quarters, the new round that was launched in 1986 came to be known as the Café au Lait Round.[1]

This chapter traces the origins, evolution, successes, limitations, and lessons of the new diplomacy. It analyses the factors and events that led to the formation of the grouping. It discovers that the Jaramillo Group started out with limited aims. Precisely how an investigative forum became the G-20/Café au Lait and subsequently the G-48 that brought down the G-10 is examined in the Section 4.2.

It is found that the transformation of a mainly investigative process into a well-entrenched coalition was as much a product of the insecurities of the G-10 as a result of the strengths of the new type of diplomacy. The chapter also highlights the successes and limitations of the G-20. It discusses the particular features and external conditions that were critical to the successes of the group, whether they can be reproduced under similar conditions, and any theoretical lessons that the coalition offers. The concluding section outlines the lessons of the new alliance diplomacy and its aftermath. The entire analysis is presented in a comparative light of the G-10, drawing on the insights of the previous chapter.

## 4.1   First steps: formation of the Jaramillo Group

In many ways, the G-20 arose in response to the same set of factors that had catalysed the Informal Group and subsequently the G-10. As these factors have been analysed in some detail in the previous chapter, only a brief recapitulation is necessary here. The first and foremost issue was that of including services within the purview of the GATT. The vital role of services in national development necessitated great vigilance and voice in any international negotiations that touched this critical sector. Second, theoretical ambiguities and limited data on services transactions reinforced the need for caution. Conceptual uncertainties increased the possibility of developing countries getting cornered into agreeing to definitions and agenda that were set by the developed countries and excluded the interests of the weak. But the same uncertainties also presented developing countries with the opportunity of finding a niche in the negotiations through alternative conceptualisations while setting the agenda. Third, at least in the initial stages, there was a transatlantic fissure that developing countries could exploit. Fourth, the existence of the Informal Group provided an institution where developing countries could organise an appropriate response. However, the response of developing countries to these factors was not uniform. While one set of countries went along the traditional path of the Informal Group and became crystallised into the G-10, another set chose different strategies to respond to the same conditions and evolved as the Jaramillo Group, the Café au Lait/G-20 and the G-48. The Jaramillo Group represented this alternative group at its most informal, while the G-48 formed the final version of the competing coalition that challenged the G-10. The evolution of this alternative path is analysed later.

The origins of the alternative coalition of the G-20 lay in an informal process that came to be dubbed the Jaramillo track. The track was the result of the decision in 1982, which urged interested countries to undertake national studies and exchange information among themselves. In the absence of an official GATT programme to facilitate such an exchange, some developing and developed countries came together in 1983. They met in a series of informal meetings to explore the issue. Colombia's ambassador to the GATT, Felipe Jaramillo, was selected to chair the meetings, and it was after his leadership that the group acquired its name. It is noteworthy that Jaramillo's position as the Chairman of the contracting parties established a de facto linkage of the group with the GATT. This association, however informal, imparted greater legitimacy and presence to the group. The institutional linkage was formally acknowledged and ratified at the autumn session of the GATT in 1985. At the session, GATT members issued a statement inviting the Jaramillo Group to continue its work and prepare recommendations for consideration at the next session of the contracting parties.

The Jaramillo Group was a product of the ambiguity that surrounded the new issues and the need for more research and exchange of information before the implications of the US-led programme move for services liberalisation in the GATT could be fully understood. It was also a result of the incipient differences within the developing world. These differences had expressed themselves in various statements, often predating and unassociated with the Jaramillo Group. For instance, the East Asians – as the ASEAN and in other combinations and countries – were openly critical of the position of the Informal Group. Besides the position of the Informal Group, there were other sources of dissatisfaction. The South Koreans had begun to talk of their large share in international trade in relation to other developing countries and demanded due weight to their views in the Informal Group and outside. The Andean group had also become more active and wanted a greater say in the Informal Group.[2] The services issue brought all these latent dissatisfactions to the fore. The postal ballot of 1985 has already been mentioned in the previous chapter. The ballot had indicated that almost half the members of the Informal Group had moved away from the hard line. Deliberations within the Jaramillo Group provided the dissidents and sceptics of the Informal Group with a rallying point.

From the launch of the Jaramillo process, two sets of developing countries nurtured a reluctance to be associated with the hard line of the Informal Group. It is possible to classify these two sets in terms of gain-enhancing and loss-minimising. The first group of countries, later known as the 'Enthusiasts', saw the potential of possible and direct gains from an inclusion of services within the GATT process. The Enthusiasts also included countries that had little to gain or lose on services but recognised that the issue was a valuable bargaining counter with which trade-offs in other issue areas could be obtained. At least for some of the smaller members of the Informal Group, membership of the coalition was a product of lack of alternatives. Now for the first time, alternatives were emergent, and the Enthusiasts were keen to exploit them.

The Enthusiasts in the Jaramillo process included the East Asian countries, Colombia, Jamaica, Chile, and Zaire. As members of the Informal Group, the East Asian tigers had traditionally maintained a passive position. But now, a dissociation from the position of the Informal Group (at least in its hard-line version) promised significant gains, while even passive adherence to the traditional position threatened losses. The East Asians saw a definite advantage in participating in the potential negotiations, rather than stalling them through blocking and boycott. Singapore, on behalf of the ASEAN countries, presented a draft alternative to India's June draft, in which it committed itself neither to the US position nor to the developing countries' 'common' position. The ASEAN indicated its willingness to explore the new issues for a possible inclusion in the new round and provided issues of interest and concern to ASEAN and other Third World countries were given priority.[3] Unsurprisingly, the ASEAN countries and South Korea found natural allies in countries that claimed a similar openness to exploration of the new issues and had come together under Jaramillo's leadership.

The East Asians were among the first of the 'Enthusiasts', that is those willing to discuss the new issues. The reasons for this willingness were simple. Even conventional GATT issues relating to manufactured exports had acquired considerable importance for the East Asians. A large proportion of their manufactured exports were subject to VERs and CVDs, for example, nearly 50 per cent in the case of South Korea. As they moved within the product cycle model, the complaint that the GATT did not cover issues of interest to developing countries found diminishing appeal with them. The Informal Group's strategy of stalling the negotiations threatened exclusion that they could not afford. In addition, with respect to the services sector, there was considerable ambiguity. Korea provides an instance of those countries where national interests in the new area were not clearly defined.[4] Nevertheless, recognising possible trade-offs in the manufactured goods sector, Korea led the East Asian group into accepting a linkage between trade in goods and services.[5] At least some of the East Asian countries were at a stage of development where they could hope to derive benefits from a liberalisation of the services sector. Finally, compared with bilateral arm-twisting over NTBs and arbitrary formulae of graduation, a multilateral round was certainly the preferred option for economies so heavily involved in world trade. Hence, the East Asian tigers were among the earliest and the most enthusiastic members of the Jaramillo track. Their participation in the Jaramillo deliberations had the symbolic value of dissociating themselves from the hard-line blocking strategies of the Informal Group and indicating their support for a new round, as suggested by the developed countries. It also served the concrete purpose of discovering where their national interest lay in services through the Jaramillo research initiative, thereby to derive maximum gain from agenda-setting and subsequent negotiations.

Other Enthusiasts were guided by a similar set of motivations to join the Jaramillo Group. Though guarded in their dissent from the hard-line Group, they were vociferous in suggesting a positive approach to the new round. Underlying their willingness to even consider discussion of the new issues was the prospect of potential benefits. Towing the G-10 hard line would have negated the possibility of realising these gains. Colombian leadership stemmed from the possibility of including tropical products within the MTN. Concessions on services were a small price to pay for such an inclusion, given the high stakes involved in the tropical goods sector. Jamaica, another Enthusiast, suggested a compromise on the new issues, while simultaneously stressing its support for the Informal Group.[6] As a small country that has always been big in its participation in GATT affairs and whose interests were well defined, Jamaica's participation in the Jaramillo track stemmed from an anticipation of considerable gain. The services inclusion suggested a reduction in the huge transportation costs that Jamaica incurred from its export activity. These costs had been raised substantively during the oil crises and had adversely affected Jamaica's export potential. Like other small, island economies in the Caribbean, it was obvious even in the preliminary pre-negotiation stage that the competitive advantage of these economies lay in tourism services. Pakistan was willing to trade concessions on services in return for a liberalisation of textiles. Some of the African economies were more interested in a few subjects related to their limited foreign trade, such as tropical products and fear of the erosion of preferences under the Lomé Convention.[7] In other words, the Enthusiasts saw potential gains in the new round, either directly through the services sector (e.g. Jamaica), more often indirectly through linkages (e.g. Colombia, Chile, Uruguay), and occasionally through both sources (e.g. the East Asians). These gains outweighed any benefits such as prestige through membership of the Informal Group. They also outweighed any potential compensation from the G-10 in return for pursuing the hard line. Still without committing themselves to the new round and the new issues, the Enthusiasts met regularly to develop a better understanding of the suggested services liberalisation and to indicate an openness to explore the new issues.

The second set of developing countries that participated in the Jaramillo process was led by considerations of loss minimising. Some in this group included small countries that were driven by the uncertainty of their own interests and fears of the costs of exclusion. If the G-10 hard line was strictly adhered to, and American threats were anything to go by, such exclusion was not improbable. Hence, Zaire, for instance, ended up openly supporting negotiations on services, fearing that without an international code on wider market access in the services area for developed-country suppliers, its own economy would become dominated by relatively inefficient producers from the developing world.[8] Some other LDCs were still undecided and would support the position of developing countries, whichever way it swung. The Jaramillo track allowed them an exploration of their interests without committing them to a hard-line position that they might regret later. The Jaramillo process was, for these countries, a learning process in the true sense where interests were defined and a conceptual understanding of the new issues was honed. The benefits of research sharing were important in the face of the limited abilities and resources of LDCs to deal with conceptual and practical ambiguities surrounding the new issues. Even those participants that had been initially sceptical found that their support for the Jaramillo process increased as the deliberations progressed. The deliberations clarified the interests of these countries, thereby increasing their commitment to the group and the liberalisation agenda. Even for the less enthusiastic, it became more obvious that the G-10 hard line was unlikely to yield results. In contrast, the Jaramillo process had given them a hearing that they were usually denied. It also commanded at least institutional approval from the GATT and some developed countries, and also perhaps could yield favourable trade-offs and linkages. All in all, the path shown by Jaramillo offered a safer bet.

The institutionalisation and evolution of the Jaramillo process was hence a product of interests of the smaller developing countries which feared that the hard line of the G-10 would deprive them of potential benefits and possibly impose costs. However, it is important to note that, up to this point, the Jaramillo Group did not represent a challenge to the Informal Group or the G-10. Until as late as early-1986, South Korea articulated support for Brazil's position in the prepcom by asserting that, unless there were firm commitments on standstill, rollback, and safeguards, 'there is nothing in the new round' for developing countries.[9] Jamaica, later seen as the 'bad guy' by the G-10 for its key role in the Jaramillo Group, emphasised the need for reaching a decision by consensus.[10] Even as a group, participants of the Jaramillo track laid no claims to an alternative consensus or agenda to challenge the G-10.

In September 1986, Jaramillo summarised the conclusions of the seven formal meetings that were held under the GATT mandate since November 1985. His claims were modest: '...in the absence of national examinations from developing contracting parties, and perhaps some other elements of information on specific subjects which might be thought desirable, the documentation at present could not be said to be exhaustive. Therefore, it would be wise at this stage to leave open the possibility of examining any new information which could be made available. Moreover, while the exchange of information had been useful, I did not find any consensus on which to base recommendations to the *contracting parties* on the question of the appropriateness and desirability of multilateral action on services.'[11] Precisely how this moderate investigative forum was catalysed into a fully fledged contending coalition of the G-20/Café au Lait and the G-48 is explored in the next section.

## 4.2   From Jaramillo process to Café au Lait coalition

The transformation of an open, investigative forum into the G-20/Café au Lait coalition that eventually challenged the G-10 and precipitated the decisive collapse of a whole style of diplomacy was sudden and dramatic. The G-10 initially participated in the Jaramillo process but with suspicion and few positive inputs or attempts to reach compromises. While the developed countries offered national studies on the basis of which information could be exchanged, the hard-liners merely pointed to the inadequacies of these studies. For example, 'The representative of Brazil...commented that, as in other studies, there was a lack of precision in the Norwegian examination on the identification of barriers to services transactions; the barriers referred to often amounted to rules governing the right of establishment of foreign enterprises, and only in limited cases did they appear to have trade implications.'[12] Similarly, the Egyptian delegate indicated similar reservations including the use of the terminology 'trade in services' at all.[13] Constructive suggestions to accompany these critical interventions, particularly by the Big Five, were few and far between. This blocking role of the Big Five provoked considerable annoyance, especially as it stood out in contrast to the constructive participation of the smaller developed and developing countries that were working towards breaking the GATT stalemate. For instance, Pakistan tried to incorporate the interests of developing countries onto the services agenda, rather than block the negotiations. Hence, it pushed for the inclusion of labour as an integral component of some services sectors, such as construction or restaurant business and suggested a discussion of immigration restrictions relevant to such situations.[14] But the G-10 continued with their negative inputs and soon after chose to part ways from the Jaramillo Group.

The parting of ways represented the transformation of the G-10's initial suspicion into an actively adversarial strategy. The response of the G-10 to the Jaramillo process was extreme, almost as if a hammer was used to swat a fly. The decision of the G-10 to engage in independent deliberations was described in Chapter 3. It is noteworthy that the G-10 chose to hold deliberations outside the Informal Group that was led by Colombia (i.e. Jaramillo). There was a conscious exclusion of the 'Enthusiasts' from this process. A few of the uncommitted developing country delegations were invited. These delegations, however, dropped out after attending a few meetings, as it became clear that the G-10 required them to adopt an openly negative stand on services. The G-10 draft, prepared on the basis of the limited papers available, was presented as a *fait accompli* to the Informal Group in June 1986. Even while making the presentation, the G-10 were well aware that the draft would be unacceptable to many of the Jaramillo Group, and particularly the Enthusiasts, as it made no mention of services. Suggestions by the Jaramillo track participants for a fuller discussion of the draft were dismissed. An explicit dissociation from the Jaramillo Group was evident in the G-10's argument that their submission was not on behalf of all developing countries and represented only the signatories of the draft. It was in reaction to these events that the countries of the Jaramillo process came together in a Group of Twenty, to finally became the real challenge that the G-10 had conjured it up to be.

This section explores the emergence of the powerful challenge of the G-20/Café au Lait from its weak parent, the Jaramillo Group. Section 4.2.1 investigates reasons as to why the G-10 refused to accommodate a relatively moderate process of questioning within its agenda. It discovers that the roots of this refusal lay in the inability of the G-10 to reconcile itself to even minor strategic changes. The inflexibility of the G-10 in turn had its roots in the combination and nature of the methods that were used to bound the coalition together, and the weaknesses that it had inherited and exacerbated from its precedent, the Informal Group (which were described in detail in Chapter 3). Inflexible strategic moves of the G-10 finally catalysed the reaction of the Jaramillo Group. This reaction is analysed in Section 4.2.2. The bugbear of the Jaramillo Group finally became an actual challenge to the G-10, first through the formation of the G-20/Café au Lait and subsequently through the emergence of the G-48.

### 4.2.1   *The reaction of the G-10: insecurities and weaknesses*

Chapter 3 demonstrated that the G-10, resting on the foundations of the Informal Group, was a precariously maintained coalition. The coalition rested on the threefold interplay between logrolled interests, intra-coalition hierarchy, and ideology. In terms of institutionalising the weak foundations of the Informal Group and an adverse international scenario, the G-10 was at its most vulnerable and, hence, also most resistant to change. The mere existence of a parallel process, that is the Jaramillo Group, threatened to disrupt the precarious balance that the G-10 upheld. The threat of the Jaramillo process to all three sources of cohesion of the G-10 is examined in this sub-section.

Chapter 3 discovered that the Informal Group was, first and foremost, a product of diverse, individual aspirations that were logrolled together into an ambiguous, self-contradictory collective agenda. As such, it was at best a weak coalition. The G-10 exacerbated these weaknesses by employing the same strategies of logrolling to serve a much more specific agenda. Its claim to a collective position on services was unprecedented and also incompatible with the diverse set of interests that underlay it. The emergence of the Jaramillo track parallel to the G-10 came at a time when the G-10 was especially vulnerable and unable to indulge in any more logrolling.

Declining world growth of the 1980s (dubbed as the 'lost decade' for developing countries) and an international context of hardship for developing countries had several effects. One of these was a decline in international goodwill, and a diminishing of aid flows from North to South. Increasing competition among developing countries for international assistance as well as markets (rendered more inaccessible due to the rise of NTBs) made the preservation of the collective façade more difficult. Increasing differentiation within the developing world, located partly in a differential response to the international context, presented new challenges to the logrolling strategy of the Informal Group.[15] Members of the Informal Group were at their most diverse, and the G-10 was faced with the unenviable task of logrolling their different interests when they were qualitatively incompatible. Further while the Informal Group was becoming more differentiated (split on both conventional and new issues, as well as the differential importance attached to both), the new issues offered some common cause to the developed world. Accompanying the internal differentiation within the Informal Group was the external crackdown as a result of bilateral pressures, particularly from the US.[16]

The new pressures of this difficult external environment had two effects on the coalition dynamic typified by the Informal Group and the G-10. First, vulnerabilities of the smaller countries made them more receptive to carrots that developed countries offered them. Such carrots included a wider menu in the GATT agenda and concessions on critical issues through trade-offs on services. Second, the bigger developing countries were less able to bear the costs of compensatory deals with which to woo the smaller defectors. The collective stance claimed by the Informal Group and the G-10 was at its weakest, rendering the G-10 insecure and particularly resistant to change. Further, the Jaramillo process was based on potential interests of the smaller countries that lay directly in the services sector and/or indirectly through linkages. These interests were described in Section 4.1. The mere exploration of these interests exacerbated the insecurities of the G-10, partly from the recognition that they would not be able to logroll these interests onto their own agenda. Linkages and reciprocal concessions explored by the Enthusiasts aggravated the G-10's fear of cross-sectoral retaliation between goods and services.

Note, however, that the threat of the Jaramillo Group was a potential threat that could have been mitigated if not averted. Members of the Jaramillo Group had not presented an alternative set of demands, even though the exploratory exercise had hinted at them. Until as late as 1986, the agenda of the Jaramillo Group was minimal, that is a preliminary and tentative suggestion at further discussion of the services issue before any conclusive positions were adopted. The Jaramillo Group had further indicated willingness to compromise, even after the G-10 had come up with its alternative and extreme draft. The decision of the G-10 to take the negotiations outside of the Colombia-led Informal Group, the conscious exclusion of the Enthusiasts from the deliberations, and the refusal even to consider the views of the Jaramillo Group once the draft had been presented all suggest pre-emptive overreaction. The sources of this reaction were located in the direct and immediate challenges that the Jaramillo Group posed to the intra-coalition hierarchy and ideology of the G-10. These challenges were more by default than design. Given, however, that intra-coalition hierarchies and ideology were really what had given a collective dimension to the logrolled interests that made up the G-10, these challenges proved to be crucial.

Chapter 3 discussed, in some detail, the importance of ideology as one basis that lent cohesion to the Informal Group and the G-10. The Informal Group shared core constitutive beliefs with its cousins in other organisations (i.e. variants of the South). These core beliefs of powerlessness and importance of group solidarity had initially allowed considerable instrumental leeway to the Informal Group. The group experimented with the instrumental ideology that stressed the active participation of developing countries in a universal, rule-based system. However, through processes of trial and error and in response to the reactions of the North, the Informal Group adopted the alternative strategy increasingly and with greater consistency. This strategy emphasised the importance of special treatment of developing countries, due to the exceptionality of their historical and current circumstances. It resulted in minimal reciprocity, a demand for unilateral concessions from the developed world, and a refusal to play the GATT game as that would impart greater legitimacy to what was seen as an unfair system. These beliefs were important in providing the collective façade to the aggregated, logrolled deals that formed the basis of membership. The G-10, drawing on its legacy from the Informal Group, adopted the same strategy as a springboard for bargaining on services.

There were several reasons why the strategy became inseparably and unchangeably linked with the coalition. First, and most important, the aggregated agenda meant that the coalition relied considerably on the cohesion that was provided to it by its ideology. As was argued previously, the coalition was weak and precariously maintained. This precarious balance reduced even the strategic flexibility of the coalition. Second, the strategy had been adopted after enthusiastic attempts by developing countries to support free trade in textiles, agriculture, and other areas of interest to them had failed. The strategy of exceptionality that was eventually adopted contradicted the initial strategy of pursuing a universally applicable, rule-based system. Its proponents, hence, went to extremes to pledge their adherence to the strategy of demanding unilateral concessions for developing countries, and stressing its benefits. After such visible attempts to profess allegiance to one path, withdrawal from it became very difficult. Third, by emphasising the importance of special treatment of developing countries, the strategy reinforced the cohesion of the group by highlighting its political and economic difference from the developed world. As internal differentiation within the developing world increased, the strategy became even more important in building common interests and suggesting a continued solidarity. It was hence seized upon with great gusto by the G-10, and manifested itself in their refusal to consider linkages between services and other areas (thereby denying reciprocity).

The Jaramillo Group had unintentionally threatened the G-10, simply by showing a willingness to consider the services question and discuss possible trade-offs across issues. The hints at issue-based negotiations implied by the services focus of the Jaramillo track would preclude the cross-sectoral aggregation of interests that had characterised the bloc-type diplomacy of the G-10. The suggestion of reciprocal concessions implied a willingness to engage in give-and-take deals with the developed world. Such willingness was seen not only as a violation of the instrumental beliefs of the G-10 but also as a questioning of its core principles. It implied an acceptance of a system that was inherently unjust. Further, it meant a rejection of the demand for unilateral concessions and the common platform that had emerged from it. In the absence of collectively pursued interests, ideology was critical to the preservation of the G-10. By suggesting alternatives to the strategic and core ideology, the Jaramillo Group effectively threatened the very existence of the G-10.

While the innocuous strategic questioning by the Jaramillo Group threatened the ideological premises of the G-10, the most serious implication of the potential alternative to the old way was the challenge that it posed to the leaders of the Group. Chapter 3 illustrated the importance of the Big Five in allowing free rides to smaller countries, and in aggregating the conflicting demands of the diverse group into a collective platform of ideology. By posing as a potential threat to the leadership of the G-10, the Jaramillo Group shook the third pillar that had preserved the Informal Group and the G-10, namely that of intra-coalition hierarchy.

Before analysing how the Jaramillo Group shook the leadership of the G-10 to its core, recall the weak base of the latter as discussed in Chapter 3. The Big Five, that is Argentina, Brazil, Egypt, India, and the former Yugoslavia did not enjoy an unqualified supremacy in the G-10. The base of their leadership lay in a process of compensations to other members of the group. In return for the preservation of a medley of irreconcilable contradictions as part of the agenda, the Big Five were accepted as leaders of the Group.

The resulting leadership had three key weaknesses. First, the leaders were faced with the task of managing an impossible agenda, which was so widespread and internally inconsistent that it greatly limited the power of manoeuvre of the group. It also further weakened the leadership by making it responsible for the maintenance of this complex agenda. Second, to lend coherence and workability to the many conflicting demands on its agenda, and to provide some rules of the thumb for smaller powers that could not afford individual research and diplomatic enterprise, the leaders laid great stress on the strategies described above. From this emerged the third and highest cost of leadership. This cost came in the form of the very visible and close association of the leadership with the ideology of the coalition. The impact of the Jaramillo collective thought process on the instrumental component of ideology, that is the second cost of leadership, has been described above. However, the Jaramillo Group threatened the Big Five in three additional ways.

First, the hard-won and laboriously maintained leadership of the Big Five was at its most vulnerable in the 1980s. The discrepancy between the political prestige of these powers and their limited economic achievement was becoming obvious particularly in the light of the East Asian successes. The Jaramillo track incorporated the voices of the malcontents who aspired to greater importance in the GATT, particularly the East Asians. It also included sceptics who had followed the strategies advocated by the leaders in the past, incorporating also their domestic dimensions (e.g. Import Substituted Industrialisation, the search for self-sufficiency at best, or alternatively South–South reliance) but with little result. Partly keen of their own accord to adopt alternative models of growth, and partly as a result of bilateral and Fund pressures to reform after the debt crises, these countries threatened to provide the aspiring leadership (e.g. of the NICs), with a following. The potential challenge made the already insecure Big Five particularly averse to change.

Second, the services focus of the Jaramillo Group threatened to undo the cross-sectoral aggregation of deals that the Big Five had guarded as leaders of the Informal Group and the G-10. While the members of the Jaramillo Group certainly attempted linkages with other areas, the trade-offs were much more restrained because they had the common factor of services. This method of intra-group diplomacy differed significantly from the intra-coalition deals that were described in Chapter 3, and was also incompatible with it.

Third, and most important, by suggesting a change in strategy, the Jaramillo track was seen as rejecting the path of leadership that the Big Five had shown. A strategic withdrawal was no longer possible, nationally or internationally. The Big Five had played a prominent role in devising the instruments of S&D, GSP, and demands of unilateral concessions from the developed world. To admit failure of these strategies was to admit failure of their international leadership. Any issue-specific, economic gains that might accrue to these highly diversified economies through instrumental change would be a poor sop for the political loss of their international prestige. The only exception was Argentina, which had very high stakes in the single issue of agriculture and hence defected once agriculture was placed on the agenda. The commitment of the Big Five to the strategic component of the group's ideology contrasted with that of the smaller countries. For the smaller countries that had become active in the Jaramillo track, a change in strategy was easy, given the clearly identifiable gains that could be derived. But for the leaders, the old strategy was critical to their assumption of leadership and hence could not be abandoned. A threat to the leadership was not merely one against the interests of the leaders themselves. It was also a threat to the coalition of the G-10 and its style of diplomacy, due to the reliance of both on a leadership that had constructed the collective ideology to facilitate interest aggregation of large and small members.

On closer inspection, therefore, the pre-emptive attempt by the G-10 to strike the Jaramillo threat in its bud was not so much of an overreaction after all. The

Jaramillo process had ignited and exacerbated some of the latent and explicit insecurities of the G-10. These insecurities could be traced back to the Informal Group and were located in the flawed composition of the cement that was used to hold the coalition together. The G-10 was founded on the same base and type of deals as the Informal Group and was unprepared to deal with the new set of challenges, temptations to defect, and strategic imperatives that came with the 1980s and the new issues. Inflexibility was inevitable, given these insecurities. The precarious construct of aggregated interests, ideology, and leadership was not prone to adaptability, even in 'normal' times; it was especially endangered and hence inflexible in the new context. The immediate danger came from the minor changes hinted at by the Jaramillo Group. The G-10's pre-emptive self-defence was rooted in its heightened weaknesses and insecurities. The impact of the self-defence too was far-reaching. Even the developed countries saw the potential rift that was emerging within the Informal Group and were quick to adopt a policy of 'divide and conquer'.[17] Hence the adoption of terms such as radicals/hard-liners (G-10) versus the moderate majority (the Jaramillo Group) by the US and its allies to reinforce differences. Such policies only deepened a rift that was already inevitable.

### 4.2.2   The rise of the G-20/Café au Lait

The intransigent refusal of the G-10 to reconsider its June draft, and its explicit dissociation from the Informal Group, finally provoked a reaction from the Jaramillo track. A few days later in the meeting of the preparatory committee, Jaramillo made a statement regretting the unprecedented and regrettable nature of the G-10's decision to work independently of the Informal Group. In view of these developments, amendments that would have normally been discussed in the Informal Group would be presented directly to the preparatory committee. Under Jaramillo's leadership, the process of drafting an alternative proposal was begun.[18] A group of twenty countries came together to discuss a draft that had been prepared by Ambassador Hill of Jamaica. From the Jaramillo process had emerged the G-20: a coalition now explicitly challenging the G-10.

The G-20 included Bangladesh, Chile, Colombia, Hong Kong, Indonesia, Ivory Coast, Jamaica, Malaysia, Mexico, Pakistan, Philippines, Romania, Singapore, Sri Lanka, South Korea, Thailand, Turkey, Uruguay, Zambia, and Zaire. Quite explicitly a negotiating coalition, the G-20 realised that there was little point in repeating the G-10 exercise, that is arriving at an independent draft and presenting it as fait accompli to the preparatory committee. If stalemate was to be avoided, negotiation with the developed countries was necessary.

Recognition of the above led the G-20 to liase with the G-9 (Australia, Austria, Canada, Finland, Iceland, New Zealand, Norway, Sweden, and Switzerland). Switzerland, under Ambassador Pierre Louis Girard, was particularly active in the consultations. Under the joint leadership of Colombia and Switzerland, and combining the majority of developing and middle and smaller developed countries, the Café au Lait group had emerged. The group was so called after its co-chairmen. Even the nomenclature suggested a challenge to the G-10 that had been called the Tea Party Group, as it was started when the US delegation invited the 'more important' delegations to a tea party.[19] After two preliminary meetings between the two groups, it is reported that Ambassador Kun Park of Korea hosted a dinner for senior officials from capitals and Geneva ambassadors.[20] G-10 countries were not invited. Support for the alliance between the two groups was clearly expressed. The cooperation between the G-20 and the G-9 signified the full emergence of the Café au Lait and involved the shift in venue for the meetings to the European Free Trade Association (EFTA) building. By the end of June, Jaramillo was coordinating regular informal meetings between the G-9 and the G-20, under the label of 'friends of the new negotiations'.[21]

The Café au Lait members were aware of the need for support from the Quad for any agenda to go through the GATT process. Cross-cutting links and loops provided the background for possible cooperation. Canadian involvement in the G-9 brought the Quad into consultation with the G-9. Together, this group of developed countries had come to be known as the 'Dirty Dozen'. Ambassador Tran van Thinh's support for the G-10 was now uncertain with the EC's involvement in consultations between the Quad, the G-9, and the G-20. The role of the US, EC, and Japan in the process of consultation has been described as active but not dominating.[22] On 17 July, on the basis of these deliberations, a draft was submitted on behalf of Colombia and Switzerland to the preparatory committee.[23] Further discussions indicated that the Café au Lait draft had come to command the explicit support of nearly fifty members. In this stage, when it commanded support of the majority of GATT members, and explicit support of some forty-eight countries, the Café au Lait group is referred to as the G-48 in some diplomatic accounts.[24]

The second revision of the Colombia-Swiss draft (W/47/Rev.2, 30 July 1986) could legitimately make the claim 'This document represents the culmination of intensive consultations among a large number of participants in the Preparatory Committee. We believe it has broad support to be the basis for discussion by ministers at Punta del Este.' Despite the backing that it enjoyed, the Café au Lait group revealed an openness for further consultation. In contrast to the G-10 strategy of placing drafts as fait accompli, the Café au Lait saw its draft formulation as a 'dynamic process which could be perfected in the consultations of the prepcom'. The investigative forum led by Jaramillo had thus evolved into the G-20, the Café au Lait, and the G-48. The draft declaration of 30 July, as proposed by Colombia and Switzerland with the explicit support of the G-48, provided the basis for the Punta del Este declaration for the launch of the Uruguay Round.

There were several noteworthy features of the Café au Lait draft that won it the support of almost all GATT members except the G-10. It was lauded by contemporary observers for making 'all the right noises' about the need to halt protectionism, and strengthen and extend the open trading system and the GATT.[25] It incorporated the concerns of developing countries, without overplaying the importance of S&D. Hence, the draft stated, 'The developed countries do not expect reciprocity for commitments made by them in trade negotiations to reduce or remove tariffs and other barriers to the trade of developing countries... .'[26] But it won the support of developed countries by stating, 'Less-developed contracting parties expect that their capacity to make contributions or negotiated concessions or take other mutually agreed action under the provisions and procedures of the General Agreement would improve with the progressive development of their economies and improvement in their trade situation and they would accordingly expect to participate more fully in the framework of rights and obligations under the General Agreement.'[27] It included provisions for standstill and rollback. The draft also incorporated those issues as subjects for negotiation, which had initially led some of the smaller developing countries to participate in the Jaramillo process (e.g. tropical products, natural resource-based products, textiles and clothing, and agriculture). Unlike the ostrich-like policy of the G-10 of avoiding any reference to the new issues, the Café au Lait addressed all the three issues of TRIPS, TRIMs, and services. On services, its position was driven by the recognition of the dangers of an absence of multilateral rules in this critical sector. Though still a bracketed clause, its proposal on services stated that 'Negotiations in this area shall aim to establish a multilateral framework of principles and rules for trade in services with a view to increasing transparency and liberalizing trade, having regard to the growth and development concerns of developing countries.' Regarding the choice of forum and the single undertaking, the draft revealed openness to negotiation: 'When the framework of principles and rules ... has been established, the *contracting parties* shall take a decision regarding its incorporation into the GATT system.'[28] Given the wide support that it enjoyed, it is not surprising that the Punta del Este declaration based itself extensively on this draft.

## 4.3   Successes and limitations

The greatest testament to the successes of the Café au Lait is the series of imitative attempts that it generated. The emphasis on 'issue-based coalitions' with the launch of the Uruguay Round was unprecedented and emerged directly from the example of the Café au Lait group. The first part of this section provides an account of the successes of the group and investigates their sources. Section 4.3.2 analyses the constraints to determine, on balance, the extent to which the Café au Lait may be seen as a 'model' coalition.

### 4.3.1   Achievements and their sources

The Jaramillo process and, subsequently, the G-20, the Café au Lait, and the G-48 had several successes to their credit. First, they served as a forum of expression for the smaller developing countries. But in its second achievement, the group, in all its incarnations, went further. Its draft provided the blueprint for the Punta del Este declaration. By helping resolve the impasse on services, the group had prevented the GATT bicycle from toppling over, saved the multilateral system, and had also successfully expressed the voice of smaller developing countries in agenda-setting. Compare these achievements with the procedural and limited victories of the G-10, and the contrast is obvious.[29] The contrast also points to the need to analyse how and why the coalition succeeded.

The greatest comparative advantage of the Café au Lait group was that in none of its incarnations was it shackled by the institutional legacy of the Informal Group. It is worth recalling that Ambassador Jaramillo was the Chairperson of both the Informal Group and the Jaramillo process, when the G-10 decided to take deliberations outside the Informal Group. Despite this move, the G-10 retained the precariously maintained structure of the Informal Group and attempted to apply it to unprecedented circumstances. In contrast, the Jaramillo process, irrespective of its institutional linkages with the Informal Group, began as an open process to explore the services issue. As such, it transcended previous North–South boundaries as well as the ideological and hierarchical rigidities of the G-10.

The ability of the Jaramillo process to transcend pre-existing coalition frameworks derived from a new source of unity for its potential members. The G-20 and the Café au Lait groups that eventually resulted were united by a base whose composition was simpler than that which had united the Informal Group and the G-10. The new groups had an issue-based focus and brought together countries with interests in services. Admittedly, there was some logrolling here, akin to the Informal Group, for example, countries that derived direct benefits from a services inclusion (most developed countries and some developing countries) and others that saw potential linkages in key areas by using services as a bargaining counter. Services, however, provided the hub of this logrolling, which meant that the group was much more focused in comparison with the deals governing the Informal Group.

The convergence of interests around one issue area gave the coalition a simple structure, in contrast to the complicated and random logrolling of the G-10. The simple, issue-based structure of the G-20 and Café au Lait ensured flexibility of agenda and negotiating strategy. The previous chapter argued that the G-10 was a coalition precariously maintained through the interplay of three diverse factors, so that a rigidity of strategy and resistance to change became inevitable and essential for the survival of the group. That the G-10 was a blocking coalition before anything else is hence unsurprising. The contrasting structure of the G-20 makes it equally clear why the coalition could be included in the genre of 'negotiating coalitions'.[30]

The fourth source of strength for the G-20 was its origins in the investigative process led by Jaramillo. The emphasis on research accompanied by common interests that were maintained through an issue-based-focus fed a virtuous cycle that strengthened intra-group coherence and also won it external legitimacy. The mechanism of operation of this virtuous cycle was simple. Members of the Jaramillo process could afford to undertake an open research-based enquiry because they were not bound into the same institutional rigidities and complicated logrolling as the G-10. The process of research, in turn, helped to identify interests. Members with obvious differences of interests dropped out. The original research orientation left a deep imprint in the evolution of the coalition and the new diplomacy that it represented and requires some elaboration.

In terms of promotion of intra-group solidarity, the information exchange and consultation along the Jaramillo track were critical in winning the loyalty of smaller developing countries for the subsequent coalitions that emerged. The Jaramillo meetings gave smaller countries an opportunity to voice their doubts and examine where their own interests lay. The emphasis on research was especially important to many LDCs, which lacked the individual expertise and resources to carry out such an exercise on their own. It also gave them a collective legitimate weight that was based on 'knowledge' against subsequent G-10 attempts to present their refusal to discuss services as the joint decision of all developing countries. If the G-10 'identity' lay in its balance of interests, ideology, and hierarchy, the G-20's developed into an 'otherness' that opposed the G-10's rigidities and reluctance to further information and its exchange. Besides the provocation issued by the G-10 in the summer of 1986, the shared investigation had heightened the suspicion of some LDCs that India and Brazil were really pursuing their own regional spheres of influence in services under the guise of Third World solidarity.[31]

The openness of the Jaramillo Group and the G-20 to research also won it adherents from the developed world. In the context of conceptual and empirical ambiguities surrounding the new issues, the Jaramillo-led search for an evidence-based expertise from which the negotiations could be conducted was valued by both developed and developing countries. The national studies of developed economies exchanged in the Jaramillo meetings and further discussion between developed and developing countries helped in the creation of a technical consensus.[32] Perhaps even greater importance of the research initiative lay in the legitimacy that it won for the group. More countries and groupings were willing to support draft formulations by a group that had arrived at them through rigorous technical discussion and showed a willingness to discuss these formulations further. The positive approach conveyed by the importance accorded to research was accompanied by a greater willingness to accept reciprocity than the G-10. In adopting such an approach, developing countries had indicated an unprecedented conformity to GATT principles. Hence, the Jaramillo process attracted implicit institutional support from the GATT that the G-10 never did.

The expansion of the G-20 into the Café au Lait, that is a group that combined developed and developing countries, was a result of the realisation of common interests described above as well as the research orientation of the group and its openness to negotiation. In overcoming the North–South divide, the Café au Lait group was unprecedented. It was also a particularly appropriate style of diplomacy for the GATT whose 'consensus-based culture' had rendered it a difficult forum to practise bloc diplomacy. The Café au Lait group further presented itself as a 'bridge-building' coalition, engaged in mediatory diplomacy in the space provided by the EC–US rift as well as the extremes of the US position versus the G-10. Its alternative name – Friends of the New Negotiations – was indicative of this positive, mediatory stance. In its willingness to conduct discussions within the GATT fold (i.e. the Jaramillo track meetings on services) and subsequently to present its discussions to the Prepcom, the group had signalled its commitment to the GATT. Smaller countries and middle powers, and even GATT officials valued this commitment, especially as it came at a time when both the US and the hard-liners had repeatedly threatened or asked to take the negotiations outside the GATT. By emphasising all the above features and strategies, the G-20 and the Café au Lait were seen, above all, as a legitimate and constructive experiment that an increasing number of countries became willing to join.

### 4.3.2 External conditions and qualifications

Conscious strategies to increase intra-group coherence and external legitimacy of the G-20 notwithstanding, the coalition was one which had greatness thrust upon it rather than achieved it of its own accord. There were three external conditions that were uniquely favourable to the operation of the coalition and which transformed it from an ambiguous investigative process into an issue-based coalition with a very specific agenda.

The first of these external conditions was described in detail in Section 4.2.1. The Jaramillo process was a research-oriented process with little ambition in the power politics of the GATT. Its transformation into the G-20 was a reaction to the repeated provocations from the G-10. The limited agenda of the Jaramillo process and its constructive approach were not a challenge to the extant practices of developing country diplomacy at the time. The reason why a limited investigative forum was catapulted to the status of challenger of a well-entrenched coalition style (rooted in the institution of the Informal Group and the G-10) had more to do with the weaknesses of the G-10 than the strengths of the G-20. The use of a counterfactual is revealing here. Without the pre-existing condition of a frayed G-10 and its flawed coalition base, minor reforms suggested by the Jaramillo process would have simply been incorporated within the old coalition. It is likely then that the Jaramillo process would simply have dissipated rather than transformed into an opposing, independent coalition of the G-20.

Second, the services issue had just emerged onto the world economic stage and was at a very nascent stage of conceptualisation. The features of research and flexibility were appreciated far more than any other 'normal' time. The preliminary stage of negotiations on services was also, in some ways, the easiest. As countries have become involved in the actual exchange of concessions (rather than broad issues of definition and agenda-setting) in sub-sectors with their encroachments into the domestic economy, reproduction of the coalition type that began with the Jaramillo process has become far more difficult.

Third, the fact that the pro-liberalisation stance eventually adopted by the Café au Lait fitted within the broad US agenda cannot be easily dismissed. The Café au Lait draft certainly tempered the much more extreme liberalisation measures that the US had advocated. But the broad conformity of a coalition's agenda with the hegemonic one introduces some important qualifications in its achievements. The whole point of coalition-building by developing countries is to give them bargaining power against the already powerful. Even if the Jaramillo process revealed that there was no such opposition of interests between most developing countries and the developed countries, the successes of the Café au

Lait group are less impressive given that they conformed with the agenda of the Big Three. The utility of the model is also suspect if it is assumed that such interest conformity with the US is not necessarily reproducible in other negotiations.

In other words, the successes of the Café au Lait were a product of a unique set of external conditions rather than intrinsic to the group and its strategies. The strategies described in the previous section acquired relevance only after the initial facilitating conditions were in place. The G-20 was successful, but only within the boundaries of these conditions.

Some critics of the Café au Lait Group have even questioned the successes attributed to the coalition. In particular, those who had supported the G-10 point out that the agenda of the G-20/Café au Lait remained unfulfilled.[33] On trade-offs and linkages in tropical products, agriculture, and natural resource products, the GATT remained slow. In the services sector, in contrast, developing countries have been under increasing pressure to increase the pace of liberalisation. The legitimacy of such a criticism, however, is questionable. The fact that the G-20 and the Café au Lait were unable to follow up the agenda that they had successfully negotiated and placed on the GATT table does not discredit the achievement of having placed that agenda in the first place. Note, however, that members of the Café au Lait had attempted to continue with the group after the final draft declaration and the launch of the Uruguay Round. The failure to preserve the group was real and takes us to a critical flaw in the new diplomacy that the group had inaugurated.

One common theme to the Jaramillo Group and its subsequent coalitions was that of issue-based diplomacy. This issue-based diplomacy provided the pivot around which the focus on services, openness to research and discussion, and middle power mediatory diplomacy revolved, but it also had unanticipated costs. The most important of these was the absence of alternative links and institutions, which would preserve the coalition once the issues changed or evolved. While the previous chapter had demonstrated that institutional 'baggage' deters negotiating flexibility, the aftermath of the Café au Lait points to the costs of a lack of cross-issue links and minimal institutionalisation. As soon as the issue of services in its pre-negotiating phase was dealt with and initial determining conditions were altered, the coalition would lose its relevance. This is precisely what happened, despite attempts to preserve the Café au Lait grouping in the form of the Hotel de la Paix group and the Friends of Services group. The limitations of the Friends of Services group, even though it emerged directly from the Café au Lait group and was modelled along the same lines, are analysed in Chapter 6.

## 4.4   Theoretical implications

While in its unqualified, unadapted version, the Café au Lait experience has little utility as a model, it offers some important lessons, many of which complement the lessons of the G-10 experience that were discussed in Chapter 3. First, the relative successes of the G-20/Café au Lait reinforce a crucial lesson that the failures of the G-10 have already hinted at, namely that of the importance of structures and interests in providing the basis for coalition formation. The

G-20/Café au Lait visibly demonstrated the advantage of having a simple interest-oriented issue-specific coalition base that allowed flexibility and also fulfilled the interests of members. The reproducibility of such an issue-specific focus is suspect at this stage and in the light of the discussion in Section 4.3.2 with respect to the specificity of external conditions in which the new issue arose. However, irrespective of the reproducibility or otherwise of the G-20 experiment, simply the comparison between the G-10 and the G-20/Café au Lait is revealing for both academics and practitioners. In contrast to the specific interest-oriented Café au Lait stood the G-10 with its complicated adherence to randomly logrolled interests, intra-coalition hierarchies, and ideology. The inability of the G-10 to rise to the challenge of the new issues was rooted in this complicated structure. In arbitrating between the various methods of coalition construction and maintenance, the failures of the G-10 and the successes of the G-20 both demonstrate that considerable stress must be laid on shared interests and the collective structure that results. Once a compatible, coherent structure of shared interests has been established, however, the G-20 adds a second theoretical lesson, which lies in the realm of process-based methods that can be used to preserve intra-coalition cohesion and influence.

The G-20 presented a striking demonstration of the impact that processes can have, once the base of the coalition has been constructed on collectively shared interests. The reliance of the Café au Lait on research and information exchange for reinforcing internal cohesion and external legitimacy provides one example of the effective use of process and has been discussed in some detail earlier. The process was important not only in the end products that it generated, that is a better conceptual understanding of the services issue generally and interest identification by the countries involved in particular, but also in its importance to the coalition in three ways. First, the willingness of the Jaramillo track to exchange and discuss issues allowed an unprecedented participation to the smaller developing countries and also allowed them to assist themselves in identifying their own interests through the joint research effort. This ensured the loyalty of the smaller members to the group in a way that the G-10 simply could not command through its appeals to rhetoric and insistence on an explicitly negative position by all members irrespective of their needs. Second, as the Jaramillo group based its recommendations on research, discussion, and a willingness to negotiate, it received recognition and legitimacy from outside, by both non-members and the GATT as an institution. Finally, the research initiative was crucial in allowing the group to come up with constructive proposals, which reinforced the positive approach of the group and its ability to present itself as a mediating, negotiating coalition.

The roots of the Café au Lait in an informal, de facto process of information exchange indicate that it is possible for a coalition to have an impact, even if it lacks formal structures. At first glance, this may seem somewhat paradoxical, given that one of the problems of developing countries in the GATT had been that their coalitions lacked institutional recognition in contrast to the G-77 in the UNCTAD or the (NAM) in the General Assembly. However, recall the case of the G-10 whose well-developed, institutionalised agenda meant that the group found itself locked into rigid and intractable positions in the pre-negotiation phase. The formality of the G-10 presents a striking contrast against the informal nature of the Jaramillo process. The initial informality of the Jaramillo meetings was an asset in itself in that it allowed greater negotiating flexibility to the group and also allowed participants to maintain an open, investigative position rather than commit in the way that the G-10 demanded. It is noteworthy that the Jaramillo process, after some time, did gradually come to enjoy an institutionalisation in the form of recognition from the GATT. This recognition was unprecedented and imparted a legitimacy to the activities of the group that the G-10 or the Informal Group had never enjoyed.

The fourth lesson that the diplomacy of the Café au Lait offers is in the realpolitik of coalition-building. Bargaining influence is not simply a direct product of aggregated resources; rather, the external legitimacy that it enjoyed gave the Café au Lait a much louder voice than could be justified simply in terms of economic or political weight. The sources of this external legitimacy were identified in the previous section as research, positive approach, bridge-building stance, reciprocity, and adherence to GATT ideology and institutions. The G-10's behaviour revealed the converse of this lesson, that is the damage that a lack of legitimacy could do. It also reinforced the legitimacy of the Jaramillo process by its refusal to discuss the issue, blocking strategies, extreme 'hard-line' position, demands for unilateral concessions, and preference for other institutions besides the GATT as well as the decision to take its deliberations outside the Informal Group. The comparison drives the lesson home: a group of the weak and poor could win over a majority of developed and developing countries due to the openness of its approach and willingness to negotiate.

Finally, the G-10 case study had hinted at the importance of external conditions in determining coalition effectiveness. The analysis of the G-20/ Café au Lait in the previous section confirms that external conditions prove crucial in the making and breaking of coalitions. However, it is worth bearing in mind that the Jaramillo group faced at least some conditions that were similar to those encountered by the G-10. The fact that the Jaramillo group successfully carved out a niche for itself in the conceptual ambiguity that surrounded the services issue through its extensive research process provides a striking instance of how the G-20 utilised external conditions to far better advantage than the G-10. Similarly, the G-20 couched its agenda in terms such that it continued to command the support of the US and also gradually won over the support of the EC (thereby shattering the G-10's hopes of playing off the EC against the US). The G-10 responded to the same set of conditions in very different ways. Instead of using research to carve out a niche of reason in conceptual ambiguity, the G-10 adopted a negative agenda of blocking. Instead of indicating a willingness to exchange information, it presented a recalcitrant refusal to discuss the new issues. Instead of proactively pursuing trade-offs with the EC to ensure its support, it adopted a policy of disengagement. Of course, it worked to the further advantage of the G-20 that its evolving agenda was a pro-liberalisation one in conformity with the 'culture' of the GATT and the US, as opposed to the blocking, negative agenda of the G-10. The frailties of the G-10 also provided a background in which the G-20 seemed like a particularly attractive option. Hence, the G-10 directed scarce effort at optimisation of its external environment to its advantage, while the G-20 successfully utilised some of the constraints (such as the lack of an epistemic consensus on including trade in services within GATT auspices) as opportunities. The contrast between the two coalitions that worked in the same external environment and issue area reinforces an initial assumption that underlies this study, namely that effective bargaining is, at least to some degree, as internal to the coalition (in terms of its structure and strategies) as external to it.

## 4.5 Aftermath and conclusion

The G-20/Café au Lait episode was dramatic. It had catapulted small developing countries into an unprecedented position of leadership and, for the first time, transformed them into players that even developed countries desired to ally with. It had also discredited and permanently shattered a well-established coalition of developing countries and exposed the inadequacies of a whole pattern of coalition-building and maintenance as typified by the G-10. Not only was the process of coalition-building under the G-20 important, but it also yielded substantive successes. That the immediate response to the new coalition type in diplomatic and scholarly circles was over-enthusiastic is not entirely surprising.

The aftermath of the G-20/Café au Lait episode on coalition formations in the GATT was cataclysmic. It delivered the deathblow to the G-10. The first to defect from the already isolated G-10 was Argentina, after which the group unravelled rapidly. The successes of the G-20/Café au Lait were seen as discrediting not only the G-10, but the whole style of North versus South bloc diplomacy that it had represented. The episode heralded a new euphoria among the smaller developing countries, as well as the developed countries, about their role in multilateral diplomacy. The Café au Lait was cited as an example of issue-based diplomacy, where even smaller countries could exercise bargaining power. The sources of this bargaining power were simple. A focus on particular issues meant that power was no longer fungible, and even small countries with large interests and determination could exercise influence within a coalition that focused on the relevant issue area.[34] The fact that the G-20 had been led by the smaller countries, which were not traditionally leaders of the South, and had further combined with the middle powers of the developed countries led observers to jump to some over-optimistic conclusions. For instance, it was believed that the age of the bullying Gang of Five and the Quad was over and that the era of mediating middle powers had begun. Stand-offs and showdowns were out; bridge-building and reconciliation were in. Complicated structures that necessitated rigid ideologies were to be replaced by simpler coalition structures based on interests in the issue area. The Cairns Group was the most visible offspring of this euphoria.

In the euphoria following the successes of the Café au Lait, the new coalition type was adopted as a model coalition with little attention to the qualifications highlighted in the previous section. The Café au Lait was directly responsible for the subsequent series of imitative issue-based coalitions. Various types of these coalitions are studied in Chapters 5 and 6. Suffice it to note here that several of these attempts proved unsuccessful because the Café au Lait model was taken out of its context and facilitating conditions. The new phase of experimentation was typified by a flurry of short-lived, overlapping, and cross-cutting loyalties. Its result was uncertainty of allies and new and expensive transaction costs for developing countries, every time a new issue area was introduced or the negotiations entered a new phase. And now, there was no institutionalised bloc (however weak) to fall back on. In the light of these subsequent experiments and its own collapse, the consequences of the formation of the Café au Lait were destructive. The coalition had destroyed an old style of diplomacy, without providing developing countries with a viable alternative. Given the dependence of the coalition on external conditions before its strategies could have any effect, the Café au Lait provided an interesting pathway but not a model. This point is developed in Chapter 6 through a study of the successes and failures of coalitions that epitomised the strategies of the G-20 and the Café au Lait in different issues and contexts.

This chapter has argued that while the successes of the G-20/Café au Lait were significant, they were rooted in the particular context of an already frayed G-10, ambiguity surrounding the new issues, and conformity with the agenda of the developed world. By introducing a new pattern of issue-based diplomacy, the group also imposed new costs of coalition formation on developing countries. The specificity of its circumstances has meant that the group has not yielded an alternative coalition model to replace the Informal Group coalition type that it destroyed. While not quite providing a whole base for new coalition types, the G-20/Café au Lait events have offered some important and universal lessons of strategy. The pertinence of intra-group coherence, less random logrolling of interests, flexibility, and external legitimacy derive from the teachings of the G-20/Café au Lait. Precisely how developing countries have interpreted these and other lessons from the G-10 and G-20 examples and employed them with alternative bases is explored in the remainder of this book.

# 5 Combination diplomacy

## Issue-based blocs and sub-sectoral crossover alliances

> One has no constant friend or enemy.
> *(Panchatantra*, Book II, Verse 116)

With the launch of the Uruguay Round, two coalition trends emerged on the wrecks and remains of the Informal Group and the path paved by the G-20. One trend involved an attempt to combine the mixed lessons of the G-10 and the G-20 and construct a coalition that adopted the best strategies of both groups. The other parallel trend sought to institutionalise the G-20/Café au Lait with minimal change, on the assumption that the successes of the new coalition represented the way forward. Two features common to both trends are noteworthy. First, the rift between the former hard-liners and the 'Enthusiasts' did not disappear. Many of the prominent members of the Informal Group, for instance, backed the first coalition type that tried to draw on the positive lessons of the G-10. The Enthusiasts were particularly active in the attempt to sustain and reproduce the Café au Lait. Second, both attempts were pursued simultaneously and warily, at least at the time of the launch of the Uruguay Round. This chapter examines the basis and successes of the first trend, that is combination diplomacy that sought to fuse the best strategies of the G-10 and the G-20. The second trend of building coalitions on the blueprint of the Café au Lait is examined in detail in the Chapter 6.

In many ways, the new trend at cautious balancing of two extreme coalition types was almost an expected and natural one. It manifested itself in a new coalition type that was issue-based in its focus on services but bloc-type in drawing on the Southern or Third World identity of developing countries and restricting membership to them. The first section of this chapter finds that in terms of both historical experience and analytical content, the bloc-type coalition with an issue-based focus was founded on careful reasoning. Contrary to expectation, however, the attempt barely materialised into a fully fledged coalition. The second section explains this somewhat counter-intuitive result. It finds that an issue-based coalition focusing on services was particularly difficult to sustain because higher and contradictory stakes of members were involved in sub-sectors, especially as the members were in the actual negotiation phase of the Round, and many diverse categories existed within the broad category of services. The section explores the various patterns of disaggregation and corresponding interest alignment.

Sub-sector, crossover coalitions are the result of such disaggregation. Section 5.3 examines the role of external conditions, particularly cohesiveness within the developed world in facilitating such alignment. Section 5.4 studies the limitations that affect coalitions with a sub-sector focus and highlights the conditions under which the type is likely to be most successful. The sub-sector coalition type is found to be a useful bargaining platform for a specified sub-set of developing countries. Reasons for this are provided in the light of theoretical reasoning as well as empirical analysis of the previous sections. Section 5.5 concludes.

## 5.1   Issue-based bloc on services

The attempt by some developing countries to revive their formal bloc, but with a focus on services, was not simply a remnant of an institutional inertia of the Informal Group and the hard-liners. The first and major part of this section discusses why such a coalition was an expected and rational one. The latter part examines the materialisation of this effort and finds that the end product was a coalition barely in name. This requires explaining, given the apparent logic and soundness of the attempt. The rest of the chapter searches for the relevant answers and also iden-tifies conditions under which such attempts might be successful.

A coalition directed specifically towards addressing interests in the services issue, but which restricted its membership to developing countries, was an expected product of three conditions. First, such a bloc-type coalition of deve-loping countries represented a response to the lessons of the G-10 and the G-20 and combined both strategies. Second, a careful analysis of the services issue sug-gested that developing countries shared several common interests in the sector. Third, developing countries had existed as a bloc in the past. Admittedly, the bloc had taken a beating with the G-10/G-20 episode, but learning from their mis-takes and further drawing on their cultural and ideational links, developing coun-tries could harness their former affinities according to the issue-based strategies of the G-20. All three elements of this rationale promised a firm base to the new South-sector coalition and are examined below.

First, the constraints faced by the G-10 and the successes of the G-20 yielded some inescapable lessons. A simple coalition structure such as that of the G-20, which catered to the similar interests of all its members, was the more sustainable coalition. The G-10, with the multiplicity of logrolled interests across issue areas and its complicated and inflexible structure of ideology and hierarchy to unite them, provided a dramatic contrast. From these lessons, developing countries recognised that their next successful coalition would have to restrict logrolling within a particular issue. This also meant that the coalition would be constituted by similar members sharing similar interests. The impact that the G-10 had had in catapulting developing countries to a position of unprecedented prominence was also not forgotten. One of the biggest strengths of the bloc-type diplomacy of the Informal Group and the G-10 had further been certainty of alliance partners for some of the smallest and the weakest. The next coalition hence attempted to combine certainty of alliance partners with a simpler, issue-based structure.

Second, learning from the Jaramillo-led coalitions and drawing on the UNCTAD, developing countries including the former hard-liners began a rigorous research initiative. Such an initiative indicated that at least at the broad aggregated level, it is possible to speak of developing countries as a group sharing a common set of interests in services negotiations. A resulting coalition comprising primarily developing countries and focusing on the services issue seemed a definite possibility. Large amounts of data to substantiate this position were generated by the UNCTAD and in UNCTAD-assisted national studies.

Third, there were several interests in services that developing countries held in common. As a group, developing countries run deficits in trade in services (with the exception of tourism and services delivered through the movement of labour, though the latter are often categorised as 'labour remittances' rather than 'other services'). In traded services, nine of the top ten exporters and importers in 1982 were found to be developed countries. This dominance had been increasing, as over the previous decade, and developed countries had succeeded in converting their $1.3 billion deficit in 1970 to a $9.8 billion surplus in 1980. In contrast, developing countries had gone from a moderate deficit of $3.8 billion in 1970 to a substantial deficit of $57.3 billion.[1] This position worsened once factor services,[2] particularly FDI, were included, while the US emerged as overwhelmingly dominant.

At the disaggregated level, too, some similarities among developing countries were, and continue to be, obvious. For instance, most developing countries reveal a deficit in 'other services'. Trade deficits in a particular sector may not be a problem, *per se*, but they certainly become problematic when generated in critical sectors such as producer services. Producer services are a key component in the category of 'other services'. The term refers to key services 'linked with production functions, which ensure the design and optimisation of production and trade conditions, or are associated with the downstream phases of production which determine the use of goods and services produced.'[3] They have been found to have the highest growth potential. They are also a source of developing-country deficits.

There are also some qualitative similarities in the services component of the domestic economies of developing countries. First, in many developing countries, the services economy is critically influenced by colonial links – railways, for instance, in the case of India. Pre- and post-colonial political considerations have been especially important in Africa. Inadequate intra-South networks in transport services have been a major deterrent to South–South trade.

Second, contrary to predictions of the product-cycle model or the historical experience of the North, an important segment of labour has moved directly from the primary sector into services (without the intermediate manufacturing stage) in developing countries. This employment in the services sector, however, has usually not been in those jobs demanding a skilled output, largely due to the absence of supportive infrastructure or education.

Third, in developed countries, producer services occupy close to 20 per cent of GDP. This figure is limited to 5 per cent in low-income developing countries, 7.5 per cent in the middle-income developing countries, and 10.5 per cent in the upper-income developing countries.[4] The high tradability of these services, linkages that they generate, and their contribution to value-added, all imply that the weakness of the sector in most developing countries is a deterrent to their international competitiveness in other sectors as well. In the services trade, most developing countries show deficits, with the tourism sector providing the notable exception. Only a few show surplus positions outside this sub-sector.

It is true that contrary to assertions of the hard-liners, the services sector is not minor in developing economies. Table 2.1 illustrated that services contribute substantially to output and employment in developing countries as in developed countries. However, in developing countries, the dominant sub-sectors such as wholesale and retail can offer no substitute for key sectors like producer services. The dominant sub-sectors usually fail to satisfy the demand for specialised knowledge that arises from other sectors, as the services content in production and trade steadily increases. This has led to the reliance of developing countries on services imports through trade and FDI. Irrespective of the position occupied by services in the domestic economy, services imports in many cases have considerably aggravated the burden of debt servicing in developing countries. The position of services in the current account transactions of developing countries region-wise is illustrated in Table 5.1.

*Table 5.1* Current account transactions of developing countries, by region, 1980–1986
(A) Percentage; (B) billions of dollars

|  | West Asia | Other Asia | Latin America | Africa | Total developing countries |
|---|---|---|---|---|---|
| *Transaction* (A) | | | | | |
| Exports | 19.5 | 43.9 | 22.8 | 13.8 | 100.0 |
| Merchandise | 16.3 | 46.7 | 23.0 | 14.1 | 100.0 |
| Interest income | 57.3 | 19.3 | 21.3 | 2.1 | 100.0 |
| Property income | 66.7 | 8.3 | 16.7 | 8.3 | 100.0 |
| Labour income | 13.8 | 43.6 | 13.8 | 28.9 | 100.0 |
| Transport | 7.4 | 48.4 | 25.4 | 18.8 | 100.0 |
| Travel | 5.4 | 47.1 | 35.4 | 12.1 | 100.0 |
| 'Other' services | 33.6 | 36.8 | 16.6 | 13.0 | 100.0 |
| Imports | 17.9 | 41.6 | 25.6 | 14.9 | 100.0 |
| Merchandise | 16.0 | 48.3 | 21.1 | 14.5 | 100.0 |
| Interest payments | 2.9 | 24.9 | 59.2 | 13.0 | 100.0 |
| Property payments | 11.3 | 30.2 | 36.8 | 21.7 | 100.0 |
| Labour payments | 71.9 | 3.0 | 5.4 | 19.8 | 100.0 |
| Transport | 18.6 | 39.1 | 24.7 | 17.5 | 100.0 |
| Travel | 14.0 | 44.4 | 30.4 | 11.2 | 100.0 |
| 'Other' services | 39.9 | 29.5 | 13.7 | 17.0 | 100.0 |
| *Balance* (B) | | | | | |
| Merchandise | 9.0 | 16.9 | 18.2 | 5.3 | 49.4 |
| Interest | 23.0 | −8.7 | −31.3 | −8.0 | −25.0 |
| Property | −0.4 | −3.1 | −3.7 | −2.2 | −9.4 |
| Labour | −9.0 | 9.0 | 2.1 | 3.0 | 5.1 |
| Transport | −6.9 | −6.1 | −5.2 | −3.5 | −21.7 |
| Travel | −1.6 | 2.6 | 2.6 | 0.7 | 4.3 |
| 'Other' services | −6.6 | −1.2 | −0.7 | −3.2 | −11.7 |

Source: UNCTAD, Trade and Development Report, 1988, p. 288.

The services sector affects the balance of payments through other means besides imports and debts. The reduction of potential export earnings of developing country producers due to the loss of value-added revenues can only be estimated by comparing the free-on-board (f.o.b.) prices with those obtained in the domestic market of importing countries. There is also an opportunity cost involved as export of goods may be hindered due to the absence of services or appropriate services (such as transport networks). A close inspection revealed that there existed common interests among developing countries in services that could be tapped into to build a new coalition base.

The fact that this new potential base was founded on researched interests but conformed to the membership of the Informal Group (i.e. a greater majority of developing countries) was a useful coincidence. Admittedly, the old pattern of bloc-based diplomacy had received a battering as a result of the events of the G-10 and the G-20. But there was no reason why developing countries could not harness the more successful strategies of their historic alliance to new-found interests and a new style of diplomacy. Particularly in the light of the sector similarities of services in developing country quantitative and qualitative current account profiles, it is not surprising that one of the first coalition attempts after the G-10/ G-20 episode utilised a bloc-type issue-based approach.

In association with the UNCTAD, and on the basis of the historical experience and research described above, an attempt was made to develop a joint platform among developing countries. But the attempt never went far enough to create a solid coalition. It found its initial expression in an attempt to revive the Informal Group of developing countries, soon after the Punta del Este declaration. According to various diplomatic sources, both the former Hard-liners and Enthusiasts pledged allegiance to their common grouping. It persisted in UNCTAD documents, which continued to stress the differences in the position of developed and developing countries. Observers commented on the similar positions that were individually expressed by developing countries.[5] It was also possible to speak of a joint developing country approach with a common agenda. As a part of this agenda, developing countries emphasised that the discussions should first focus on statistical issues, definitions, and identification of sectors covered by the multi-lateral framework. They laid stress on the mandate of the Ministerial Declaration and the stated objective therein of 'promoting economic growth of all trading partners and development of the developing countries.'[6] Once again, Brazil and India took the lead, though individual submissions were also made (e.g. by Mexico, Argentina, Brazil, and Peru) emphasising an approach broadly similar to the joint one.[7] But once this point was reached, the attempt never went much further.

Having declared their support for these joint positions, developing countries parted ways. A plethora of coalitions along narrower interests was attempted. Coalitions emerged, demanding greater importance be accorded to the labour mode; others were formed on even narrower issues such as air transport. Some attempted to ground themselves in a regional base. The pursuit of these alternative coalition experiments provides an important indication that the bloc-type, issue-focused approach had not provided a solution to the bargaining difficulties of developing countries. Except for the occasional UNCTAD official's suggestion of a renewed attempt, or similar suggestions from some of the former 'hard-liners', the approach only had minimal impact in the Uruguay Round.

Why did the bloc-type coalition that included the G-20's issue-based focus prove so difficult to sustain? To answer this question, the next section examines the lines along which shared interests tended to disaggregate. The first fissure occurred at the sector level, where certain countries revealed a positive position on services. This commonality of position further had a regional basis and is examined in detail in Chapter 7. The second fissure operated at the sub-sectoral level and thereby undermined attempts to create a broad coalition that operated for the sector as a whole. The next section studies this network of sub-sectoral interest alignments.

## 5.2   Disaggregating services: sub-sector coalitions

The tendency of the services sector to disaggregate into sub-sectors was partly a product of the stage that the negotiations had entered with the launch of the Uruguay Round. Once services were on the two-track agenda, grandiloquent statements that swept away sub-sector differences were no longer adequate. Concrete give-and-take necessarily devolved to the level of the sub-sector. Focus on individual sub-sectors yielded a very different configuration and grouping of interests from that which had been assumed by the bloc-type coalition of developing countries. The result was the obvious unsustainability of the bloc but also the emergence of an alternative coalition type. The alternative type had an even narrower focus than the Café au Lait or the issue-based bloc type and was eclectic in the mix of members that it brought together.

Although developing countries shared some overall interest in the broad area of services, deep differences underpinned this apparent commonality. These differences dominated the apparent shared interest among developing countries that was described in the previous section. The first source of division of interests was resource-based. Developing countries discovered that their competitive advantage lies in services that can be labour-intensive, technology-intensive, or based on geographic/strategic/cultural advantage. The relevant sub-sector accordingly dominated their coalition loyalties. The second source of division was located in the actual versus potential advantage that the country saw for itself in the services sector. This, in turn, depended on factors such as the size and nature of the domestic market, fixed costs already invested in services, and the infrastructural context. Third, developing countries found their interests in services differentiated according to the extent of specialisation in one sector versus diversification of the economy (disallowing a concentration of diplomatic resources in one sub-sector category in the case of diversified economies). This tripartite division and its role in the emergence of a complex pattern of sub-sector coalitions are elaborated next.

### 5.2.1  *Different resource endowments*

Different resource endowments and infrastructure levels allow countries to develop a competitive advantage in some sub-sectors, as opposed to others. Coalition alignments are often related to commonalty of competitive advantage and the resulting shared interest in particular sub-sectors. Sources of this shared competitive advantage are explored below.

One explanation to sources of comparative advantage, particularly with reference to technology-based services, is offered by Sanjaya Lall. He uses the example of shipping to point out that a simple Hekscher-Ohlin type of analysis based on national capital–labour endowments does not explain ground realities ('The USA … is presumably better endowed with physical capital per head than Norway, Japan, or the UK, and yet seems to have a much weaker competitive position … '). The main reason for this discrepancy may be found in the highly specific nature of skills, information, and contacts that is a requirement for the shipping industry. If only general skills were needed in the production of shipping services, capital-intensive economies with a well-educated labour force would have been dominant in the industry in exact conformity to traditional comparative advantage models.[8]

The fact that many services, like shipping, require specificity of knowledge has allowed developing countries to cultivate a competitive advantage in several unlikely sub-sectors. It is noteworthy that this specific knowledge can be drawn from diverse national sources, on the basis of historical, institutional, social, cultural, and strategic peculiarities, and is not simply dependent on capital investment in knowledge. 'Certain skills, for instance, are best learnt with low labour endowments, low levels of human capital, small R&D investments and relatively restricted markets.'[9] The East Asian tigers cultivated this type of competitive advantage through small technological innovations in the inventions of the industrialised world. Lall cites India as another example. India's position of leading exporter of technological services to other developing countries may be located in its high skill- (though not innovation-) based technologies to a certain level below the international standard. Three sources of a competitive edge for developing countries in technology-based services have been suggested. First, developing countries may be more competitive in producing technology adapted to local needs of other developing countries. Second, they may be able to provide technologies complementary to the developed countries as franchised subcontractors/partners, particularly when taking on simpler (though highly skilled) tasks of detailed engineering, construction, and so forth. Third, non-overlapping with developed countries, there are some services that are specific to developing countries (such as charcoal-based steel manufacture or 'gasohol' in Brazil) and where developed countries are not competitors at all. Often, these advantages are culture-, education-, language-, or location-specific, giving some developing countries competitive sub-sectors that do not provide a common competitive advantage to all of them as a group.

In the example of technological services given above, and in most other sub-sectors, competitive advantage may be classified according to three components: cultural/strategic/geographic specificity, knowledge intensiveness, and labour intensiveness. In some instances, however, two or three of these factor components may be interlinked (e.g. certain historic factors contributing to infra-structure and knowledge). Some sub-sectors also require the availability of all three.

The most obvious service that thrives on geographic advantage and cultural attributes is tourism.[10] Strategic position is a similar advantage, often enjoyed by the small island economies. Some island economies are particularly suitable for providing logistics services such as staging posts, refuelling stations, and siting of communications, meteorological and paramilitary functions, and even educa-tional facilities and the sale of shipping services (Maldives).[11] Singapore could exploit its time zone as a vital link for twenty-four-hour financial transactions. Hong Kong, similarly, used its geographical and political positioning to tranship services and manufactures from Taiwan and South Korea to the People's Republic of China (PRC).[12] In those services where there is a good deal of personal interaction with customers, cultures that place emphasis on maintaining good interpersonal relationships (rather than simple task efficiency) would be at an advantage. Bhagwati gives the example of consumer preference of Singapore or Japan Airlines, based on the more effusive on-board treatment there, than on Pan Am or TWA.

Not unrelated to the cultural ethos is the knowledge infrastructure of a country. A sustained institutional and cultural advantage in knowledge translates directly into professional services.[13] Professional services are usually associated with the temporary relocation of labour, though increasingly, disembodied professional services have been facilitated by telecommunication technology. Many developing countries, especially in Asia, are characterised by competitive standards of edu-cation. Despite ENTs and other barriers to the movement of professionals, espe-cially from developing to developed countries, the potential of developing countries in this sub-sector is significant.[14] For instance, Tunisia exports profes-sionals to French-speaking Africa and the Middle East. The export opportunity is founded on a domestic surplus of highly educated nationals (including a wide range of professionals, e.g. engineers, doctors, and qualified security guards), capable of speaking French and Arabic, and replacing European practitioners for one-half to one-third the cost.[15] India has the third largest pool of scientific and technological manpower in the world, and the second largest reservoir of such expertise which is English-speaking. India also has a highly competitive advertis-ing sector, which has shown the potential for developing at a faster rate in terms of facilities, resources, knowledge, and skills to service Indian and foreign clients in global markets by setting up the requisite international networks.[16]

In the case of Indian software exports, virtually 80 per cent of such exports were provided to clients overseas on site. But technological change and the emer-gence of Bangalore as a centre for software engineering as well as management have facilitated, in recent years, the development of offshore software and data-processing services in India.[17] Many leading firms such as Apple, IBM, Intel, and Oracle have also set up joint R&D and production ventures in India. Data-processing firms in Jamaica similarly work for clients in Canada, the US, and the

UK, on the strength of a comparative advantage of an English-speaking work force and competitive telecommunication prices. Niche markets have been found, such as the US market for punching services produced in the Philippines. The audio-visual industry in India and Pakistan has already found a growing market for its non-resident populations in different parts of the world. Language plays a critical role in these sub-sectors as well, with not only entertainment programmes and films in English but also a market for subtitling and smaller tasks in the industry which can be won on a franchise basis. Such knowledge-based advantage is characteristic of several economies in Asia, often being accompanied by advantages of language as a remnant of former colonial ties. But it is also present in some developing countries that had consciously tried to develop institutions promoting science, engineering, electronics, health, consultancy, and others. Latin American countries, particularly Brazil and Argentina, in their earlier phases of ISI had developed institutions in at least some of these areas.

Labour constitutes the third resource from which several developing countries derive their comparative advantage. The most direct result of the low wages in developing countries is trade in services through the movement of natural persons.[18] Private transfers[19] is one of the two sub-sectors (the other being travel) in which developing countries do not run deficits. Many service activities are labour-intensive. For instance, labour in hotel operations accounts for about 50 per cent of costs; construction and engineering services, maritime transport (wage bill of the crew is a principal element in shipping costs), and the distribution side of banking and financial services all thrive on significant labour inputs.

Some services require a combination of all three factor components or flourish best when all three are present. The Construction and Engineering Design (CED) sector is one such example wherein firms from developing countries have acquired a place in listings of top 250 industries of the world. South Korea had acquired a lead in the early 1980s and was followed by India and Brazil at a distant second and third. The Korean advantage in the construction industry was built on early foreign collaboration, and subsequent indigenisation with the exploitation of markets in West Asia. Underlying these strategies, however, was its reliance on low wages. Rising wage levels have been described as a primary reason for the fall in Korea's share in international construction activity from 11.2 per cent in 1982 to 2.8 per cent in 1987.[20] Most Korean construction firms that managed to retain their shares in world markets could only do so through the employment of low-cost labour from Indonesia, Pakistan, Philippines, and Thailand. Brazil, too, was unable to sustain the successful outward drive of its construction firms (whose exports were directed mainly into the Latin American region), not only because of the debt crisis that had dominated most developing countries from 1982 on. Firms that had relied on the possibility of sending cheap low-skill labour abroad soon found that the costs were higher than expected.[21]

India offers a counter-example of sustained successes in the CED sub-sector which have been based on other factors besides low-cost labour. India, in the initial stages, also relied on foreign consultancy and engineering firms and contractors in its efforts to build up a domestic capability. But the Indian process placed a different emphasis on self-reliance and indigenisation of the design and construction services that were learnt initially with foreign collaboration. The installation of collaborative steel plants was accompanied by the establishment of institutes of engineering (such as the five Indian Institutes of Technology). The development of the Indian construction industry was matched by a small but important engineering component. Engineering design services may absorb only a small fraction of the project costs, but they yield substantive positive externalities through the influence that they exercise over the selection of contractors, the sourcing of machinery and equipment as well as other manufactured goods and raw materials. The Indian comparative advantage in CED has hence proved longer lasting than the Korean and Brazilian examples.

Already, the analysis of the different sources of comparative advantage of developing countries and their differing levels of competitiveness have some serious implications for coalition formation. The most immediate implication is that interests in the services sector are more divided and messier than the bloc of developing countries had conjured them up to be.

At the simplest level, we can expect countries with similar sources of comparative advantage to coalesce together. Such coalitions were indeed evident. Countries sharing a comparative advantage based in cheap labour were particularly active. A coalition of like-minded countries (Argentina, Colombia, Cuba, Egypt, India, Mexico, Pakistan, and Peru) was responsible for the initiative and subsequent inclusion of the Annex on Movement of Natural Persons in the GATS.[22] Similarly, all the smaller tourism-oriented economies were privy to the deliberations of the Jaramillo track and continued to work in the Hotel de la Paix and Friends of Services group. The emergence of these coalitions, however, cut across alternative alignments that some developing countries were already a part of and resulted in a very complex pattern of overlapping coalitions working at cross-purposes. Equally interesting, there were several other obvious groupings that could have emerged with a focus on sub-sectors based on the source of competitive advantage. Some of these might-have-beens are explored below.

One obvious coalition in which developing countries would have enjoyed considerable bargaining power as weighty exporters, and yet has not emerged, is the potential coalition on professional services. The competitive advantage in professional services enjoyed by countries of Asia as well as some in Latin America was described earlier in this sub-section. This competitive advantage was threatened as a result of exclusionary regional agreements within the North such as the EU, and selective North–South agreements like the North American Free Trade Agreement (NAFTA). Exclusion of the greater majority of developing countries from such arrangements further necessitated the creation of a common platform against quota restrictions and non-tariff barriers (like non-recognition of qualification requirements) to the supply of professional services through the movement of natural persons. But no coalition along these lines has emerged.[23]

Another coalition with some potential among developing countries has been one with a focus on the construction industry. It is true that there is considerable divergence in the nature and extent of competitiveness of CED services in the developing world. While India and Brazil continue to dominate in disembodied technical and consultancy exports,[24] no coalition on the issue is in the offing. In part, the absence of such a coalition is a product of the diverging sources of the comparative advantage in CED of different developing countries. The labour component of CED gives India an incentive to continue with former coalitions such as the group of like-minded countries on the inclusion of the mode of supply through the movement of natural persons. Brazil is a noteworthy absentee from this eight-member coalition on the labour mode. The different sources of competitive advantage, hence, induce divergence even at the sub-sector level among countries with a competitive advantage.

The bargaining strength of at least some developing countries in sub-sectors of services lies not only in their role as suppliers of services but also as markets for services imports. Irrespective of the differences in current figures of the growth of the CED sector in developing countries, the largest potential market for these services exists in the developing world. This dependence on CED services could be transmogrified into a bargaining strength, not unlike the attempt to use their severe indebtedness by some developing countries to form a debtors' cartel. In this case, however, developing countries get caught up in their dual roles as exporters and importers of CED services, rendering coalition formation on the basis of either interest difficult.

Shipping is another sector based on a similar combination of advantages in labour costs and skills, and suggested a common position among several developing countries. It is noteworthy that Korea, China, Brazil, and Singapore ranked among the top ten exporters of shipping services in the world, even early on in the Uruguay Round.[25] Some Asian countries have negotiated cargo-sharing agreements. Malaysia, for instance, signed an agreement with Bangladesh, Turkey, and Indonesia. Indonesia, in turn, negotiated bilateral agreements with Japan, Korea, and Taiwan for carriage of logs, and with Taiwan for the carriage of general cargo.[26] In spite of the conscious efforts made by developing countries to have an active involvement in shipping, the global deficit of developing countries' sea transport balance was estimated at $21 billion in 1987.[27] Even the aforementioned Asian countries, like other developing countries, continue to generate losses from cargo reservation schemes. The relative sizes of these losses, however, divide developing countries into distinct categories. The vast majority of developing countries incur huge outflows of foreign exchange for shipping costs. Countries such as Bangladesh, Benin, Cameroon, Haiti, Mauritania, Morocco, Niger, and Togo lose 25–35 per cent of their export earnings as payments to foreign carriers. For Burkina Faso, Chad, Jordan, Mali, and Somalia, the payments were 33–60 per cent of total export earnings.[28] While it may be possible for the Asian countries running smaller deficits on shipping costs to yield to demands for an inclusion of maritime transport, most developing countries have been reluctant to surrender the few gains that they have obtained through the United

Nations Code for Liner Conferences. Once again, an obvious sub-sector coalition failed to materialise.

The reluctance of developing countries to seek obvious allies on the basis of sub-sector advantages based on a common resource endowment has a simple explanation. Divisions within the developing world and affinities among countries, even at the sub-sector level, had other sources besides the origins of comparative advantage. These sources are explored below.

### 5.2.2   *Realised versus potential advantage*

A common resource base provided only one basis to the convergence of interests at the level of the sub-sector. Fissures within the developing world and the search for other allies were, and still can be, located in the level of potential versus advantage realised in the particular issue area. This level of advantage has to be considered in the context of the development level of the economy. In the case of services, three groups may thus be noted. The first group comprised a small number of developing countries that had acquired a well-developed material advantage in the particular sub-sector. Most such countries found it easiest to build alignments with each other and also form linkages with the North. The East Asian NICs featured most frequently in this category and continue to do so, though memberships vary according to sub-sector. The second group comprised countries that had a developing advantage in the sub-sector concerned. These economies had already invested a form of 'fixed costs' in the particular sub-sector and expected returns from them to materialise within the short or medium run. For these countries, the opportunity costs of yielding domestic markets to foreign competition were the highest. The third group included some of the smallest and poorest of the developing countries. These countries had frequently already been brought under bilateral pressure to open their services markets. The high proportion of their services imports also allowed these countries to buy arguments of efficiency gains from liberalisation; their resource base and level of development offered them little opportunity of building their competitive advantage in the area. Trade-offs and linkages with the North offered cheaper access to services imports, as well as possible trade-offs on other issues. Many of the smaller resource-based African economies formed a part of this category. Their willingness to yield concessions on services was evident first and foremost in the G-48 and subsequently at the level of the sub-sector. Countries of Group I and III are still more likely to form coalitions with the North, depending on the position of each sub-sector; the possibility of forming a blocking or agenda-setting coalition was, and continues to be, much higher with Group II countries.

Development levels in varying combinations can have a cementing or disintegrative effect on coalition formation. The telecommunications negotiations provide one example. Except for the coordinated positions of the ASEAN group, the general stance of developing countries was that of resistance. Market power wielded by the developing countries provided the basis for this common position.

It contrasted with the developed countries, which had the dominant telecommunications industry in search of international markets. Smaller coalitions also emerged among developing countries. The attempt in the Telecom annex to strike a balance between the needs of users for fair terms of access and needs of the regulators and public telecommunications operators to maintain a system that fulfils trade needs but also public policy objectives was a result of the two submissions made by India, Egypt, Cameroon, and Nigeria. But the bigger coalition of developing countries that attempted to block the telecom negotiations (e.g. at the December 1996 Ministerial on Information Technology) exercised scarce influence. A landmark agreement on Basic Telecommunications was reached on 15 February 1997.

The failure of the developing country-led/UNCTAD-supported attempt to slow the telecom liberalisation lay partly in the G-10-type blocking strategies that it adopted. But more important, the attempt was a divided one. The thrust of the attempt came from the old stalwarts of the Informal Group – India and Brazil – which had already invested considerable resources into building their indigenous telecommunications industry. In relation to these investments, their telecom industry still bore a promise of success but was not competitive enough to withstand immediate world competition. Many of the smaller countries had had their telecom sector already, at least partially, penetrated by the industrialised countries. The possibility of their building an indigenous industry was small. The opportunity costs of yielding the remainder of their market to foreign competition were smaller for these countries than for India and Brazil. It is not surprising that the influence of their attempt was minimal, given that member countries of the coalition experiment were at cross-purposes.

Similar levels of comparative advantage also yielded strange bedfellows. India and the US, traditionally at loggerheads for ideological as well as economic reasons (based on structural differences of resource endowment), found common interests in the liberalisation of their advanced audio-visual services. In the context of the Annex on Air Transport Services, Malaysia and Singapore combined forces with Australia, New Zealand, and the Nordic countries. The group urged caution, stressing the use of reviews that were to be held every five years. The ASEAN countries and Australia embarked on a joint research project.[29] On the basis of similar levels of development in the sub-sector, there were alliances between state and domestic actors. The push for services by the US had derived considerably from internal business interests. The Financial Services Annex was significantly influenced by a proposal submitted by Malaysia on behalf of the South East Asian Central Banks (SEACEN) and Monetary Authorities, that is the SEACEN group of countries comprising Indonesia, Korea, Malaysia, Myanmar, Nepal, Philippines, Singapore, Sri Lanka, and Thailand. As a result of this proposal, the annex did not impose liberalisation obligations. Its provisions on domestic regulation were based on the overriding importance of prudential considerations, monetary policies, and the integrity and stability of the financial system.

Depending on how 'real' or developed the competitive advantage in the sub-sector was, several examples of counter-intuitive behaviour become more explicable.

Irrespective of some resource endowments (e.g. skilled labour/professional services) that they might share with other parts of the developing world, the ASEAN countries have already realised their competitive advantage in other services sub-sectors. Their high level of development implies a productive band-wagoning with the developed countries that share similar interests, as opposed to a resource-based affiliation on the labour mode with the key developing countries. In contrast, countries like India and Brazil have still not realised their comparative advantage in some of the key producer services. However, having already expended considerable effort in the development of some of their producer services under former import-substituted industrialisation (ISI) models (even if such strategies countered their resource endowment as per neo-liberal economic theories), they see potential yields from them in the medium- to short term. Hence, for instance, the resistance of these economies to any concessions on telecommunications, or financial services (at least in the earlier stages of the negotiations). The third category is occupied by some of the smaller island economies. Even if they enjoy certain resource endowments such as educated labour, prime location, and so forth, they rely upon services imports due to inadequate economies of scale. In the absence of some revolutionary technological breakthroughs, except in the very long run, these economies see no potential of developing their competitive advantage in key services. Greater liberalisation, as per the agenda of some developed countries, at least allows them certainty of supply of the critical producer services. Again, we see their divergence from the conventional bloc-type sector position, shared resource endowments notwithstanding. The source of this divergence is, at least partly, realised versus potential competitive advantage.

### 5.2.3  The specialisation principle

The formation and survival of a coalition at the level of the sub-sector depend on a third factor, besides the resource base and consideration of the immediate versus potential advantage. This factor is the extent of diversification of the economy and the importance of the particular sector therein. Specialisation of the economy allows a greater concentration of diplomatic effort and commitment in selective coalitions, dissuading conflicting loyalties and cross-cutting linkages. Such a specialisation is characteristic of several LDCs, reflecting a tendency to obtain the greater part of their services export receipts from a single sub-sector in services.[30] This means that the inclusion of the particular sub-sector on the agenda of the MTN would make trade-offs worthwhile on other sub-sectors.

The implications of this specialisation principle are simple. For economies enjoying such specialisation, dilemmas about loyalty to particular coalitions are easily resolved. This is especially true of the small developing island economies. These countries have higher than average export intensities in all three service categories, but are clearly most specialised in tourism, as shown in Table 5.2. The relative importance of tourism receipts was about twice the world average in 1980, rising to over three times the average in 1992. The categorical export advantage in the tourism sub-sector is complemented by an absence of national

*Table 5.2* Share in global service exports and revealed comparative advantage,[a] 1980 and 1992

|  | Tourism | | Transport | | All other | |
|---|---|---|---|---|---|---|
|  | *1980* | *1992* | *1980* | *1992* | *1980* | *1992* |
| *Share in global trade (percentage)* | | | | | | |
| Developing countries | 25.0 | 20.9 | 20.2 | 19.5 | 18.6 | 14.8 |
| OECD member countries | 75.0 | 79.1 | 79.8 | 80.5 | 81.4 | 85.2 |
| *RCA* | | | | | | |
| Small developing countries (1 million people or less) | 2.19 | 3.45 | 1.19 | 1.85 | 0.39 | 1.11 |
| Developing countries | 0.93 | 1.12 | 0.65 | 0.82 | 0.65 | 0.74 |
| OECD member countries | 1.01 | 0.96 | 1.10 | 1.02 | 1.13 | 1.06 |

Source: Hoekman (1996), p. 92.

Note

a RCA is defined as the ratio of exports of a given product to a country's total exports of goods and services, divided by the same ratio for the rest of the world. If the index is greater than one, it implies that the country is relatively specialised in that product, see fn 5 in Hoekman (1996).

economies of scale in the production of several essential services such as telecommunications. These countries must devote a larger share of their resource base for the provision of basic infrastructure services than larger countries.[31] For small countries very close to the continent or to each other, the costs of this provision may be reduced through scale economies of trade. This involvement in international trade could be conducted unilaterally to the benefit of the country concerned, but the case of services and its inclusion in the MTN provided these small economies with a bargaining chip. They could extract concessions, better terms, and inclusion on the agenda of areas such as tourism, and also gain from any inclusion of other services within the multilateral agenda as was desired by the developed countries. Most countries of the Caribbean fell into this pattern of behaviour, and Jamaica's leading role in the G-20 may be traced to these imperatives. Many of the small countries of the Caribbean found that that multilateral measures that promote travel services far outweigh any gains they make by extending their activity to other sub-sectoral coalitions or compensatory arrangements (hypothetically, for example in shipping, with other developing countries). Similarly, gains in professional services for selective countries would be far greater than the costs of liberalisation of even critical sectors such as telecommunications.

Many developing countries, however, do not have such unambiguously defined interests. This is especially the case for the bigger and more advanced of the developing economies (with large markets which allow for the possibility of exploiting economies of scale). Here, interests in a range of sub-sectors prevent concentrated loyalty and attention to one coalition. Brazil and India provide classic examples of countries faced with such a conflict of loyalties. Brazil was an active player in the Latin American group, first as a member of the SELA, and then with other Latin American groupings. Most of these groupings shared the proposal for preferential treatment of developing countries.[32] Yet, Brazil, along with India, had also expressed dissatisfaction with S&D treatment.[33] The Indo-Brazil partnership, in presenting a common front to the MTN, was endangered by the multi-directional pulls exercised by alternative coalition memberships. India and Argentina joined forces over the inclusion of labour as a mode of supply, in which Brazil had little interest. In doing so, India liased with Argentina and Colombia, countries that had defected from the 'hard line' in return for concessions on other sectors. India's former alliance with Brazil continued on telecom. Unprecedented de facto commonality of interest emerged with the US over audio-visual services.

That leadership in sub-sectoral coalition formation has been largely unforthcoming in the case of the bigger developing countries is hence, on closer inspection, unsurprising. The diversified interests of these economies produce a conflict of loyalties and memberships. Resulting linkages and concessions adversely affect the efficacy of most sub-sector coalitions involving these countries. A weak and diversified interest in the services sector is the burden of the richer developing countries. Note that this diversification works differently in the developed economies where, irrespective of diversified production and trade in different subsectors, the primacy of the services sector (i.e. a strong and expansive interest) as a whole renders broad sector coalitions and sub-sector linkages possible. The interplay of interests among developed countries and the bandwagons and balances that they produced with developing countries are examined in the next section.

## 5.3   External conditions: divisions within the developed world

The previous sections have emphasised the role of intra-coalition cohesion in the maintenance and influence of the group, but external conditions are also important. The cohesiveness or otherwise of the opposing coalition affects the strategies that developing countries can adopt. Divisions outside can be exploited in two ways. First, the weaker coalition can bandwagon with a sub-group in the opposing coalition. Second, the weaker party may choose to offer an alternative way and play off their differences against each other from the outside. The choice of strategy, however, is dependent upon the potential fissures within the opposing coalition. Both the Cairns Group and Friends of Services Group attempted the second strategy. However, as opposed to the sumo-style transatlantic confrontation over agriculture, differences between the EC and the US over services were on a smaller scale. The achievements of the Friends of Services Group are examined in Chapter 6. This section examines the first strategy, that is bandwagoning by developing countries with some industrialised countries individually and with the Quad as a coalition.

The pre-negotiation phase of the Uruguay Round had been marked by differences within the Quad at the sector level. The plan to exploit these differences, particularly between the US and the EC, had been fairly explicit in the case of the G-10. The Jaramillo track too had sought a niche in the differences between the

EC and the US that it tried to occupy through its research initiative. Both attempts were described in Chapters 3 and 4. However, the initial reluctance of the EC to allow an inclusion of services in the new GATT round was converted into enthusiasm by the time the Uruguay Round was launched. This enthusiasm derived from several national studies (some of which were conducted in the Jaramillo track and others outside it in organisations like the OECD), which indicated that the EC was a service 'superpower'.[34] Any subsequent differences between the EC and the US were more of approach than substance, at least at the sector level. At the level of the sub-sector, however, there were still some differences that offered a greater bargaining potential to developing countries.

Sub-sectoral differences played themselves out in different priorities for the developed countries. In accordance with the expectation that countries would be more willing to discuss NTBs in areas where they are exporting less volume than expected, the US attached greater importance to other services (including finance, telematics, and professional consultation). The EC gave greater priority to tourism issues. Similarly, countries would be most willing to make concessions regarding imports in areas where they are importing less than might be expected. In conformity with this, the US emphasised financial and communications-related services, while the EC was less protective about transportation.[35] For most countries of the North and the world as a whole, exports of services were larger than sales, but the opposite holds for the US. In 1980, its services exports were about $30 billion, compared with $150–200 billion in foreign sales.[36] This difference was important in establishing definitions of trade in services and the eventual inclusion of the four modes of supply to incorporate the US demand that services provided through FDI be included within GATS.

Three sets of interests dividing the developed world may be discerned. Some countries had a favourable balance in 'other services' that offset a weak position in merchandise trade. However, even within this group, there were differences. In the UK, the main sources of revenue were finance-related services (with additional revenues from consultancy and technical cooperation), while in Belgium, processing services dominated. France had a strong position in 'other services' as well as tourism. Technical cooperation and CED were dominant in the 'other services' category. The second group comprised countries from Southern Europe. These countries resembled some developing countries, with tourism and labour remittances providing net revenues to offset merchandise trade deficits. The third group included the Nordics and Japan, with a positive balance in merchandise trade but a negative balance in trade in services. Germany similarly revealed a very strong position in exports of goods, supported by investment earnings but a relatively negative position on labour payments and tourism. Canada, Australia, and New Zealand too demonstrated a strong position on the export of goods, which compensated for deficits in services, interest, and property payments.[37]

The differing priorities of developed countries had significant implications for developing countries. The importance of labour remittances for the Southern European countries, tourism for France and other countries in Southern Europe, and uncertainty regarding competitive advantage in key producer services contributed to the European preference for a 'soft agreement'. In the EC's initial negotiating position, trade was to be so defined as to include all types of transactions necessary in a sector to 'allow' effective market access. But despite a broad agreement, any binding commitments were to apply on a sector-specific level.[38] In this, the EC and developing countries found common ground that the G-10 had hoped to exploit. Some of the advanced developing countries found new allies in the middle powers, particularly Australia, New Zealand, and the Nordics (hence the coalition of Air Transport combining Australia, New Zealand, the Nordics, Malaysia, and Singapore, and the alliance between Australia and the ASEAN).

The translation of differing priorities within the developed world into liaisons with some developing countries, however, has not been a simple one. There are two reasons for this. First, as with developing countries, pre-existing alignments and cross-cutting loyalties disallowed a simple translation of common interests into coalition formation. Canada, for instance, despite its similarity of profile on services with some developing countries, maintained a pro-US position due to the large services component of the Canada–US Free Trade Area and NAFTA. Similarly, irrespective of the divergent views of France on audio-visual services, or the Southern Europeans on labour mode, their membership of the EC curtailed alliance possibilities with developing countries. In other words, developed countries were enmeshed in other institutions and alliances, which developing countries found difficult to penetrate despite some common interests at the sub-sector level. Second, it was easy for developed countries to logroll priorities in sub-sectors, as long as they fitted within the bigger, common agenda of liberalisation of services. Through the greater part of the negotiations, a divided developing world faced a developed world that was united on the sector question and only in minimal conflict at the sub-sector level.

## 5.4    Constraints and conditions for successes: sub-sector coalitions

It is noteworthy that of the many possible coalitions with a sub-sector focus, only a few have actually emerged or had any lasting duration or achievements. The few successful cases suggest that the sub-sector coalition would work well but within a set of constraints and only for a sub-set of developing countries. This section identifies the problems and limitations that afflict this coalition type and demarcates how countries can overcome or utilise them further to their advantage. In doing so, it enables us to define the conditions in which the sub-sector coalition type works in services, and why.

The first problem of cross-cutting sub-sector interests is that of distracted and ambiguous commitment to particular coalitions. The solution lies in building sub-sector coalitions, wherein the diverse sources of fissure match with each other. This is possible for the more specialised economies, with similar levels of competitive advantage in the sub-sector. The small island economies with similar geographic/strategic endowments, concentrated interests in tourism exports, and travel imports present one such example. It has been much easier for such economies to concentrate diplomatic initiative in the relevant sub-sector, and further form linkages through concessions in other sectors. The ASEAN countries reveal a similar overlap and similarity of interests that they utilised in the telecom negotiations.

The identification of a coincidence of narrower interests by the more specialised economies, however, generates the second problem affecting sub-sector coalitions. Most of the more specialised economies are also small in economic size. This has meant that even their combined market influence would still be limited (e.g. the Caribbean interests in tourism export and cheaper transport imports).

Bandwagons provide a solution to the problem. But bandwagons with the bigger developing countries yielded few successes and were even detrimental to the maintenance of the coalition. This is because the bigger developing economies were also the more diversified ones. Including them increased the combined economic size of the coalition, but it also adulterated the sub-sector agenda and expanded it to cross-cutting issues, reinforcing the first problem described above. Bandwagons with the developed countries, however, provide a more promising alternative. This is because, in spite of diversification, the developed countries offer two advantages as coalition partners over the bigger developing countries. First, the sub-sector shares of the developed countries in the particular issue area are likely to be substantial enough to allow greater bargaining weight to the coalition. Second, as was pointed out in the previous section, in spite of differing sub-sector priorities, the interests of the developed economies in the services sector are enormous. These interests present a contrast with the larger developing economies, where interests in particular sub-sectors are often at greater cross-purposes with each other. The initiative of the smaller developing countries with higher stakes in the sub-sector concerned would provide diplomatic momentum to the coalition, while the presence of developed countries would lend greater market shares. This coalition type could also combine exporters and importers (e.g. transport exporters like the EC combining with the very small economies with no expectation of developing a comparative advantage in the area) with the aim of trade liberalisation in the sub-sector. Linkages with other sectors would lend greater political feasibility to such a coalition.

Developed–developing country coalitions, in which much of the diplomatic initiative comes from the weaker countries due to their concentrated interest in the sub-sector, offer a solution to the third problem that has affected coalitions of this type. This problem may be identified as a leadership problem that was rooted in the fact that the former leaders of the developing countries continued to take the leadership in most coalitions. Owing to their diversified economies and varied levels of competitive advantage that had been translated across sub-sectors, their leadership and commitment to each sub-sector coalition were divided and confused. Smaller, more specialised economies are able to overcome this problem, while an alliance with the developed countries allows them the economic weight that they lack due to their small markets and world trade shares. The leadership niche that smaller countries may have found for themselves in the sub-sector coalitions marks, in some ways, the culmination of the initiative taken by the 'less important' developing countries in the Jaramillo track.

Coalitions focusing on the relevant sub-sector provide a viable policy option for the smaller developing countries, particularly when they are formed with the developed countries. The importance of bandwagoning with the developed countries, however, greatly circumscribes the negotiating leeway that such coalitions might enjoy, particularly when differences within the developed world are minimal. This chapter has highlighted situations in which there is a coincidence (or at least compatibility) of interests between the smaller developing and several developed countries. In such situations, North–South subsector coalitions are an effective bargaining platform for the weak. It has also been indicated that such a compatibility is likely between these two sets of countries, as far as the services issue is concerned. However, if faced with a conflict of interests between the developed and specialised developing economies, along with a persistence of diversified interests of the larger developing countries, the formula will have to be revised.

There remains a large group of developing countries for which coalitions with a sub-sector focus do not provide the answer. The question of coalition strategies for the group of countries that were classified as Group II, particularly when overlapping with the diversified developing economies, is not an easy one. The problem here is not of a lack of awareness of interests, nor an ideological reluctance of politicians to acknowledge them. This group of countries, which includes the former leaders of the Informal Group and the G-10, represents interests that are indeed sub-sectorally too diversified to allow the concentration of diplomatic effort or loyalty to a sub-sector coalition. Their large markets and potential in services are too great to be unilaterally surrendered or bartered away for concessions in some issue area with lesser growth potential or one in which lesser fixed costs have been invested. The services sector, as a whole, is also not dominant enough to allow these countries a broad sector focus with a Southern base, especially as it involves the differing priorities of the smaller developing countries. Clearly, one size does not fit all.

## 5.5   Theoretical implications and conclusion

The aftermath of the collapse of the G-10 and the rise of the Café au Lait closed one coalition possibility but also opened up a new universe of alternatives. One of the immediate follow-ups by developing countries involved their attempt to combine the strategies of the G-10 and the G-20 to construct a new coalition type. Despite the sound rationale underlying the attempt, the first section of this chapter illustrated that it suffered from several weaknesses. But even false starts can be important if they facilitate the elimination of unviable strategies and suggest alternatives. The South-sector attempt pointed to alternative coalitions on the basis of the fissures at the regional and sub-sector levels that had impeded its workability. This chapter focused on the latter type of fissures and examined the alternatives to which they pointed. It is worth recalling that the failure of the massive bloc-type coalition with its services focus is not only important for the alternatives that emerge from it.[39] Rather, it reinforces a lesson that the Informal Group and G-10 had already demonstrated, namely that a coalition is difficult to sustain if it brings together too many diverse interests. The services bloc of developing countries further adds to that lesson by indicating that, at least in services, interests of developing countries as one group are hugely diversified, and hence smaller and counter groups likely to form at the sub-sector level.

The combination sub-sector diplomacy in services has a very mixed record. Only a few have actually emerged among the many potential ones, and even fewer among them have had any lasting duration or achievements. The few successful cases suggest that the sub-sector coalition would work well, but within a set of constraints and only for a sub-set of developing countries. Two theoretical issues stand out. First, many sub-sector coalitions, due to their very narrow scope, have found their membership limited to small members in small numbers. This translates into a problem of inadequate collective bargaining weight. A coalition, no matter how internally coherent, must have a substantial external presence if it is to exercise any bargaining influence. However, second, additional partners to add to this collective weight must be selected with extreme care. If not, then coalitions of substantial weight but distracted loyalties result. Various ways of identifying the different interests that operate at the sub-sector level are elaborated below. Arbitrating between these various considerations is crucial for deciding whom to include or exclude.

Three considerations influence the pattern of coalition alignment at the level of the sub-sector. The first source of division is resource-based (resulting in the dominance of labour-intensive services in some countries, technology-intensive in others, and so forth). Factor proportions, however, are not the sole determinant of the competitive advantage and resulting coalition loyalties of developing countries. The second factor determining the interest and diplomatic effort that a developing country is willing to invest in a particular sub-sector is the actual or medium-/long-term potential advantage that it enjoys in the sector. Advantage considered in these terms is only partially dependent on resource endowments and might even ignore them. Rather, it is a product of other factors such as the size and nature of the domestic market, fixed costs already invested in services production, and the infrastructural context. The third determinant of coalition membership and loyalty at the sub-sector level is the extent of specialisation in the sub-sector (disallowing a concentration of diplomatic resources in one sub-sector category for the more diversified economies).

Based on the simultaneous operation of all three constraints, some economies would find the opportunity costs of yielding to pressures to open their markets particularly high. Diversified economies with a medium-term potential competitive advantage across sub-sectors, exemplified by Brazil and India, fall in this category. Not surprisingly, even after having surrendered their bloc-based strategies, they have frequently participated in coalitions that attempt to slow down the liberalisation process. However, the widespread and diverse levels of the sub-sector interests of these diversified economies have also led to their multiple memberships and conflict of loyalties regarding coalitions with a narrower focus. For smaller economies with a greater dependence on services imports, or the dominance of a particular sub-sector in exports, the choice has been simpler. Once interests in the particular sub-sector are met, their loyalties to other coalitions become superfluous. The interests in the particular sub-sector, however, could be met only through bandwagons formed through linkages. Bandwagoning possibilities and their limitations were examined in the previous section.

The evidence demonstrates that the bloc-type sectoral coalition is rendered difficult due to the lack of shared interests. The coalition type with a sub-sector focus has been a mixed blessing. For the smaller developing economies, it has offered a viable coalition strategy, admittedly amidst a set of constraints. The participation of the bigger developing countries in the same coalition type, however, has actually reduced the efficacy of this sub-sector coalition. The precarious world of shifting coalitions and its dangers (discussed in Chapter 2) has been dotted with coalitions of the sub-sector type. Their makeshift character is, in good measure, a product of the participation of the larger developing countries, with their conflicting priorities (across sub-sectors) and divided aims. It is only by keeping the more diversified developing economies with a medium-term interest in the particular sub-sector out, and by bringing the developed economies with more consistent interests across sub-sectors in, that the sub-sector coalition will provide a stable policy alternative for the smaller developing countries. Viable policy options for the bigger, more diversified, developing economies are explored in the next two chapters.

# 6 Evolved alliances

## The Cairns Group and Friends of Services Group

128 Evolved al
Importers' C
ditions th
to anoth
focuse
to t
is

Cause drives both friendship and enmity.
(*Panchatantra*, Book II, Verse 34)

In the mayhem of coalition experiments that followed the collapse of the G-10, the Cairns Group of Fair Traders in Agriculture is usually held up as a shining milestone. Its relevance for the argument in this book, in spite of the agricultural focus of the group, derives from three reasons. First, the Cairns Group was based on the blueprint of the Café au Lait. With the formation and achievements of the Cairns Group, the Café au Lait type of diplomacy came of age: the Cairns Group represented proof of the cross-sector reproducibility of the Café au Lait design and strategies. But second, the Cairns Group also surpassed the Café au Lait in its aims and actual exercise of influence. It transformed itself from an agenda-setting coalition into a negotiating one. In this and several other features, it represented alliance diplomacy at its most evolved. Third, and as a result of the first two points, the Cairns Group reinstated faith in the Café au Lait model, and its various avatars and extensions. The Friends of Services Group was one example of coalitions in services, which had straggled along since the launch of the Uruguay Round with scarce visibility or achievement to their credit. The achievements of the Cairns Group brought renewed hope for the Friends' Group, and others modelled along similar lines. Together, they constituted the second stream of coalitions that was mentioned in the previous chapter, that is coalitions that sought the strategies of the G-20 with minimal change.

This chapter examines the evolved Café au Lait/Cairns Group type of diplomacy as a viable alternative for developing countries in the Uruguay Round. Section 6.1 investigates the conditions that precipitated the rise of the Cairns Group. It also examines the agenda and achievements of the group, and illustrates why the Cairns Group came to be seen as an exemplar of the new Café au Lait type of diplomacy. Section 6.2 studies the conditions that were critical to the maintenance of the group. Both external conditions, as well as strategies adopted by the group, are identified and ranked with respect to each other. Section 6.3 identifies and analyses the limitations and constraints within which the Cairns Group operated. Section 6.4 compares the Cairns Group with the Food

Group (FIG). The comparison highlights some critical and unique con-
facilitated the successes of the Cairns Group and proved irreproducible
er group working even within the same issue area. The subsequent section
s on the Friends' Group and offers an explanation as to why strategies similar
e Cairns Group have not yielded the same record of achievements. Section 6.6
the concluding section. Underlying the study is the question: What does the
Cairns Group (i.e. the Café au Lait diplomacy epitomised) tell us about the conditions and strategies necessary for successful coalition formation? By answering this
question, it is also possible to determine the extent to which the Cairns Group can
be seen as a viable 'model' for subsequent coalition experiments.

## 6.1 The rise of the Cairns Group: origins and evolving agenda

The new issues, that is services, intellectual property, and investment measures,
were not the only ones in which stakes were high for both developed and
developing countries. In itself and in providing some critical linkages with the
new issues, agriculture was another area over which daggers were drawn. For
example, the EC's progressive willingness to discuss services has been linked to its
hope of deflecting attention from agriculture and its possible inclusion in the new
round. Argentine defection from the G-10, as soon as agriculture was considered
as an issue to be brought to the negotiating table, provides another example.
With the advent of the 1980s, agriculture had become an especially potent issue
with repercussions on GATT negotiations in general and services in particular.
The Cairns Group utilised the internationally politicised issue of agriculture to
carve a niche for itself. This section explains why agriculture became such a critical issue before the launch of the Uruguay Round and how it provided fertile
ground for the rise of the Cairns Group. A brief account of the rise of the Cairns
Group, its evolving agenda, and its achievements is also provided. The record is
important as it helps us understand why the group came to be seen as a 'model
coalition' for developing countries.

The first reason that lent unprecedented urgency to the agricultural issue was
the agricultural crisis of the 1980s. The downswing in world agricultural prices
had some relation to the two booms in commodity prices in the 1970s.[1] But the
fall in prices, which was the worst since the 1930s (e.g. 50 per cent in the case of
cereals by 1982)[2] had other causes besides simple cyclical upswings and down-
swings. The two booms in commodity prices of the 1970s as well as other exogenous shocks had greatly sharpened national concerns with food autonomy and
self-sufficiency. The most obvious manifestation of this concern was the increase
in protection against agricultural imports as well as new internal and export support policies. The result was oversupply as traditional net importers were transformed into net-surplus exporters. By 1983, for instance, the degree of EC
self-sufficiency in percentage terms was higher than 100 in sugar (144), wheat
(125), butter (123), poultry (110), cheese (108), beef (104), veal (104), and port
(101).[3] In response to the same exogenous shocks and the rising surplus of the EC,

the US response was to adopt similar protectionist and aggressive methods. They included the *ad hoc* decision of the US in January 1983 to openly subsidise the sale of one million tonnes of surplus wheat flour to Egypt, which had traditionally been supplied through European exports. The European Common Agricultural Policy (CAP) was globalised, as was the US policy through the Export Enhancement Program (EEP).[4] In the institutionalisation of subsidies and their globalisation by both the EC and the US lay a common effect: the targeting of traditional markets of other agricultural exporters. The competition between the US and the EC had turned into 'an open subsidy war',[5] and world prices in agriculture continued to plummet dramatically. For all exporters of agricultural commodities, the situation amounted to a crisis.

Second, the collapse in agricultural prices that had been precipitated by competitive undercutting of prices by the two giants had repercussions. For the US and the EC alike, the ploughshare war had high costs. By the early 1980s, the traditional US surplus in farm trade had turned into deficit, while two-thirds of the EC's budget was spent on supporting the CAP.[6] The costs were even higher for the 'natural exporters' of agricultural commodities, who found their traditional comparative advantage eroded due to US–EC subsidisation. These traditional exporters, from both the developed and developing worlds, further saw little hope of recovering their advantage through a similar price-cutting derived from matching subsidies. It was these traditional exporters that came together under the shared banner of the Cairns Group of Fair Trading Nations. The emergence of the Cairns Group and its solutions further offered the EC and the US a way out of their budgetary problems through a face-saving climbdown. The EC, US, and traditional exporters comprising developed and developing countries were all in need of a truce to alleviate the farm wars. The Cairns Group emerged to fulfil that need.

The first meeting among non-subsidising agricultural exporters took place in April 1986, in Montevideo, Uruguay, among Argentina, Australia, Brazil, New Zealand, and Uruguay. The similarity of the effort with the Jaramillo track, as a bridge-building exercise between two extreme positions, was marked. The objective of the five countries was a response to the immediate crisis and limited itself to a coordination of their positions to defuse the subsidy war between the US and the EC. The GATT multilateral system offered the most reliable way of achieving this aim through an inclusion of agriculture in the new round. A second meeting was held in Pattaya, Thailand, in July, with a larger group of countries.[7]

The preliminary, exploratory meetings were not formalised as a coalition until the EC attempt to block the preparatory draft. At the final meeting of the prepcom, the French blocked endorsement by EC member states of the draft ministerial declaration. This draft had in fact been prepared with the active participation of the EC. The last-minute refusal by the French to allow the Community to endorse the text derived from their fear that even this negotiating text committed the EC to negotiations on agricultural liberalisation. It was at this point that under Australian initiative in Cairns and building on the two previous meetings, ministers from the agriculture exporting nations agreed to work collectively at Punta del Este, three weeks thence.[8]

The Cairns Group comprised fourteen agricultural exporters, which met at Cairns under Australian initiative. Members of the group included Argentina, Australia, Brazil, Canada, Chile, Colombia, Fiji, Hungary, Indonesia, Malaysia, New Zealand, Philippines, Thailand, and Uruguay. Like the Café au Lait, the Cairns combined developed and developing countries. It was further similar to the Café au Lait as an issue-based coalition working at the sector level (as opposed to the narrower levels of the sub-sector or the broad bloc level). Formed in the context of the subsidies war between the US and the EC and a history of implacable disputes over the position of agriculture in the GATT system, the main concern of the group was to engineer an inclusion of agriculture into the Round. Punta del Este sealed that inclusion, thereby also establishing the credibility of the Cairns as an effective grouping. The importance of this procedural victory was clear even at the time, particularly when located against the backdrop of the exclusionary provisions that had dominated agriculture and the several failed attempts by various parties in the past to include agriculture within the regular GATT jurisdiction.

Rather than dissipate after this initial procedural victory, the Cairns Group evolved from an agenda-setting coalition into a negotiating one. Rigorous studies were carried out to build internal group consensus and also to devise formulae for agricultural liberalisation. On the basis of these studies and information exchange, the first detailed proposal of the group was put forth in October 1987 to the Negotiating Group on Agriculture. The proposal contrasted with the zero option of the US (advocating a complete removal of distortionary policies over a short phase-out period) and offered potential meeting ground between the two agricultural superpowers. While supporting the US objective of a complete removal of distortionary policies, it suggested early relief (in the form of a freeze on market access restrictions) for exporters hurt by the phase-out of support policies. Longer phase-out periods were provided for with a focus on export subsidies and quantitative import barriers for immediate address.

Most of the proposals of the Cairns Group were adopted as the basis for discussion at the Montreal mid-term review in December 1988. Continued deadlock between the US and the EC precipitated the Latin American members of the Cairns Group to stage a walkout with the announcement that without an agreement on agriculture, they would veto results in other areas.

As a result of this threat, the mid-term review was postponed. At Geneva, in April 1989, at a meeting between the EC, the US, and the Cairns Group, a freeze on levels of protection and support was agreed on, with the long-term objective of 'substantial progressive reductions'. It is true that other factors besides the reasoned voice of the Cairns Group were influential in the agricultural rapprochement. These included the willingness of the US and the EC to climb down from their extreme positions in the face of budgetary pressures, the implicit support of US hegemony for the Cairns Group, splits within the Cairns Group resulting in the threat of the Latin American walkout, and so forth. All these factors are examined in detail and ranked in the subsequent sections, but the result was big enough to set an example for developing countries. The successful operation of the Latin American members within the Cairns Group reinforced the model. The effective threat of the Latin American walkout reaffirmed the important role that developing countries could play, even when they worked in alliance with the developed countries. Tussie writes, 'Although the exact pace and extent of reduction remained to be seen, the Latin members of Cairns, especially Argentina, were vindicated; without their principled stance, the Group would have lost its calling and credibility. Moreover, they became aware of their collective importance.'[9]

Another deadlock emerged at Brussels in 1990, when the EC refused to accept the compromise text that was proposed by the Chairman of the Negotiating Group (which would have averaged a cut of about 25 per cent in protection levels). The Latin American members once again used the threat of blocking negotiations in all other areas, unless visible progress on agriculture was made.

An agreement was finally reached between the EC and the US in the Blair House Accord in November 1992. While several other factors contributed to this agreement, the Cairns Group had ensured that the momentum on the negotiations be maintained.

Even after the agreement had been reached, the Cairns Group continues to reinvent itself and evolve its agenda. Its membership has expanded, and the group advocates a decoupling of non-trade and agricultural policies through programmes of rural community development and expanded technology applications, direct government assistance to address problems of soil erosion, land degradation, and so forth. The programme attempts to curtail the tendency in many developed countries (particularly Japan, the Nordic countries, Korea, Switzerland, and Austria) to address non-trade issues such as food security, preservation of land and environment, and maintenance of local communities, through agricultural support policies.[10] Some of its more recent positions are highlighted in Chapter 8.

Since its inception as an agenda-setting coalition that successfully placed agriculture on the negotiating table at Punta del Este and subsequently through its evolving reputation as a negotiating coalition, the Cairns Group acquired a weighty diplomatic presence in the GATT/WTO circuit. It became one of the first coalitions that was publicly recognised by the WTO, providing evidence enough of the mark it had made. At a time when the EC and the US had taken their farm wars well outside the GATT purview, the Cairns Group demanded and successfully established the GATT's mandate in the issue area. The fact that the group has survived for over fifteen years has added to its attractiveness as a model coalition.

The Cairns Group demonstrated the importance of middle-power leadership for the developed countries through the role played by Australia and Canada.[11] For developing countries the Cairns Group had equally important, though different, lessons. Bandwagoning for developing countries is seldom an optimal strategy (unless the country is so small that it has no hope of making any difference at all in any coalition type, and may then prefer to free ride with the powerful). The Cairns Group, however, illustrated how developing countries could work in liaison with the developed ones and still maintain their own ground and even find a louder voice. The Latin American members presented themselves as such a sub-set of developing countries that successfully expressed their own interests and wielded considerable influence within the group. The reasons why these countries agreed to work on a platform with the more developed countries is explained in terms of their shares in world agricultural trade in the next section. The very fact of this convergence of the developed and the developing countries and the retention of influence in group activities by the latter as the negotiations progressed is worthy of note. It was indeed noted by developing countries in parallel attempts at coalition building.

Attempts to replicate the Cairns model in agriculture, services and other issue areas are not entirely surprising, given the record of achievements of the group. But it is important to remember that the successes of all coalitions are a product of a specific set of circumstances as well strategies, and the Cairns Group was no exception. The generalisability of the model depends on how specific or universal the circumstances and strategies are. The next section explores the conditions and strategies that facilitated the survival and successes of the Cairns Group. It is crucial to understanding the logic and viability (or lack thereof) of subsequent coalitions that tried to imitate the Cairns.

## 6.2 Conditions conducive to successes

While the Cairns Group exploited the agricultural crisis to its own advantage, the attention accorded to the group was far from inevitable. The EC–US confrontation and the resulting price undercutting only provided the background. Certain conditions and strategies provided the impetus to the smaller agricultural exporters to dispense effort in the creation and maintenance of the Cairns Group and further rendered that effort successful. The first factor that imparted greater sustainability to the coalition was the configuration of interests of members. These interests were aligned to allow intra-coalition cohesion as well as sufficient collective weight to exercise international influence. The second factor was an external condition, that is the fact that the liberalising agenda of the group conformed to the agenda proposed by the US, thereby ensuring de facto American support for the group. The third factor responsible for the successes of the group was strategy. Certain strategies employed by the coalition were key to its internal sustainability and external legitimacy. Each of these factors is investigated in the following three sub-sections.

### 6.2.1 *Membership of the Cairns and interest configuration*

The marked and durable presence of the Cairns Group derived in significant measure from the convergence of members' interests within sector-based perimeters. As such, the Cairns Group overcame the limitations of the G-10 and the Informal Group, that is coalitions with such a diverse membership that cross-sector logrolling had to substitute for a convergence of interests. It also avoided the problem of very narrow sub-sector coalitions, which was discussed in Chapter 5.

This happy balance between the two extremes lay partly in structural features of the agricultural sector. Despite the divergent sub-sector interests within agriculture, it was possible for the members of the Cairns Group to coalesce at the sector level. This was because it is difficult to take a narrow product-specific view of agricultural production and trade, as commodities are often substitutes for each other. Further, unlike trade in goods where participants generally have balanced interests in that they are often both importers and exporters, this is not the case for agricultural commodities.[12] Hence, as soon as agricultural reform came up for discussion onto the GATT agenda, the commodity-specific approach was abandoned in favour of a sector-wide one. Such an approach allowed producer countries of different types (e.g. tropical and temperate commodities, food and cash crops, those undercut by the US–EC subsidies' war versus those affected by the lack of market access to the EC due to the Lomé-based preferential arrangements, and from different regions) to all come together on a common platform of 'fair trading' exporters.

The Cairns members capitalised on this advantage to engineer intra-coalition deals within the broad sector of agriculture. Herein lay one of the greatest strengths of the Cairns Group, which gave it intra-coalition sustainability as well as external collective weight. These deals were engineered so as to allow the inclusion of one or more sub-sectors that more than compensated for losses incurred by the inclusion of sub-sectors that benefited other members. Both gains and losses were expected as a result of the rise in prices as per the liberalisation agenda; aggregate gains would be determined by the import–export composition of the production profiles of members. Limiting the deals within the sector meant that trade-offs and spillovers would not be expansive enough to prompt defection. Compare this with the machinations of the Informal Group and the G-10, and one explanation to the successes of the Cairns Group becomes obvious. The Informal Group and the G-10 were preserved in a similar mixed-motive situation, but their cross-sector scope meant (1) that intra-group trade-offs and linkages extended into several contradictory areas and (2) that this wide scope led developing countries to bargain in areas where they had no collective comparative advantage. The Cairns Group, in contrast, struck a balance between a sub-sector focus that allowed intra-coalition deals and sector boundaries that prevented contradictory logrolling, and also allowed the retention of the negotiations in an area where members had a comparative advantage. For all the members, agriculture (in one or several encompassing sub-sectors) occupied a large portion of the export earnings and production base. The absence of any such sub-sectors in services had some important consequences for the Friends of Services Group.

At the collective sector level, the biggest source of strength for the Cairns Group was its combined weight. The group accounted for 26 per cent of global trade in agriculture. The combined shares of the group were substantive across commodities, as illustrated in Table 6.1.

While the group started with a collective bargaining strength, which is illustrated in the figures, the biggest rationale for its formation and survival lay in the

Table 6.1 The Cairns Group in world agricultural commodity exports

Share of world (%) due to

| | Cairns Group | | EC-12 | | Japan | | United States | |
|---|---|---|---|---|---|---|---|---|
| | 1980–1982 | 1987–1989 | 1980–1982 | 1987–1989 | 1980–1982 | 1987–1989 | 1980–1982 | 1987–1989 |
| Cereals | 26 | 21 | 11 | 14 | 0.7 | 0.5 | 41 | 32 |
| Meats | 30 | 24 | 10 | 11 | — | — | 7 | 9 |
| Sugar | 29 | 20 | 19 | 19 | 0.2 | 0.4 | 3 | 3 |
| Oilseeds and nuts | 17 | 21 | 0.3 | 0.6 | — | — | 67 | 47 |
| Dairy products | 12 | 10 | 31 | 21 | — | — | 2 | 2 |
| Textile fibres | 22 | 28 | 7 | 8 | 4 | 3 | 20 | 13 |
| Vegetable oils | 46 | 41 | 12 | 14 | 0.3 | 0.2 | 13 | 9 |
| Rubber | 43 | 44 | 7 | 9 | 4 | 5 | 8 | 9 |
| Beverages | 7 | 5 | 42 | 39 | 1 | 0.5 | 2 | 3 |
| Other agriculture | 23 | 24 | 8 | 7 | 1 | 1 | 13 | 13 |

Source: Rod Tyers (1993).

shared interests of members. The first and most obvious was the large share of agriculture in the exports of members. The fact that a significant proportion of export earnings of these countries came from agriculture gave them high stakes in an amelioration of the US–EC subsidies war. For Argentina (62 per cent), Fiji (82 per cent), New Zealand (69 per cent), and Uruguay (55 per cent), agriculture provides the dominant of export earnings.[13] It is true that within the group, the stakes of members varied across sectors. For instance, the developed country members of the Cairns Group (particularly Australia and Canada) had a high agricultural content in their exports, which gave them the bargaining power of suppliers. The developing-country members shared similar or even higher values of export percentages, though they were frequently smaller in absolute terms. But even when total figures of the agricultural exports of some developing countries were small, high export and GDP shares brought a high level of individual commitment to the group. The resulting similarities of commitment in a context of differences within the group are illustrated in Table 6.2.

The second common interest that brought the heterogeneous countries of the Cairns Group together was their self-identification as a group of 'fair-trading nations'. The only exception was Canada, which offered high rates of assistance to its dairy and livestock sectors, though even here, protection took the form of import quotas rather than export subsidies. As most of the countries of the Cairns were middle powers or small states, they were in no position to match the subsidies given by the rich trading powers. To prevent further erosion of their markets

*Table 6.2* The Cairns Group, 1987–1989

| | GDP | | Exports (merchandise only) | |
|---|---|---|---|---|
| | Total (1987 US$ bn) | Share of agriculture (%) | Total (1987 US$ bn) | Share of agriculture (%) |
| Argentina | 78 | 13 | 8 | 62 |
| Australia | 192 | 4 | 28 | 37 |
| Brazil | 307 | 8 | 29 | 35 |
| Canada | 433 | 4 | 102 | 20 |
| Chile | 22 | 8 | 6 | 35 |
| Colombia | 38 | 18 | 5 | 45 |
| Fiji | 1.3 | 23 | 0.24 | 82 |
| Hungary | 26 | 16 | 9 | 23 |
| Indonesia | 81 | 23 | 19 | 22 |
| Malaysia | 32 | 20 | 21 | 36 |
| New Zealand | 16 | 10 | 8 | 69 |
| Philippines | 37 | 24 | 7 | 29 |
| Thailand | 55 | 15 | 14 | 41 |
| Uruguay | 8 | 10 | 1 | 55 |
| Total | 1,324 | 9 | 257 | 30 |
| Global averages | | 5 | | 13 |

Source: Rod Tyers, The Cairns Group Perspective, in eds, K. A. Ingersent, A. J. Rayner, and R. C. Hine, Agriculture in the Uruguay Round, London: Macmillan, 1994, p. 91.

as a result of declining prices through the export of US–EC subsidy policies, these countries found a common interest in a liberal agricultural regime. Their cohesion stemmed from the reduction in their net agricultural export earnings by more than half due to protective policies in industrial countries.[14]

The two sets of shared interests among all members were balanced by actual and potential heterogeneity within the group. The heterogeneity had two sources. First, beyond the sector level, differences in economic size, levels of development and importance of particular sectors were high and resulted in very different positions adopted by members in other issue areas. This was overcome precisely through the creation of an issue-based coalition. Attempts by some members to link agriculture with services and intellectual property were consciously resisted as far as possible (though such threat of linkage was used as the basis of the successful walkout by the Latin Americans at the Montreal mid-term review). The influence of the Cairns Group lay in this issue-area focus, which allowed it a greater flexibility of agenda, in contrast to the awkwardly built and rigidly maintained consensus of the Informal Group and the G-10.

The second source of heterogeneity was more of a double-edged sword. It lay within the agricultural sector, in the sub-sectoral differences and the relative importance of particular sub-sectors in the imports and exports balances of each member country. Devolution of bargaining at the sub-sector level could have delivered a deathblow to the coalition. Some of the short-lived sub-sector coalitions in services, discussed in Chapter 5, provide an example of such ephemeral coalitions. But a clever utilisation of specific sub-sector interests would allow a wider membership to the group and ensure a deeper entrenchment of their loyalties. This possibility of constructively utilising the sub-sector level was employed by the group to its great advantage. At the purely sector level, the dominance of the EC, Japan, and the US in agricultural trade was evident; consideration and aggregation of the sub-sector level allowed members to draw attention to areas where their comparative advantage lay. Except for cereals and oilseeds (where the US enjoyed a dominant position) and dairy products (EC dominance), the prominence of the group in the aggregate was found in almost all agricultural commodity groups.

Sub-sectoral fault lines within the Cairns found different expressions: developed versus developing country, exporters of temperate products versus exporters of tropical products, exporters of grains versus rice and sugar, and those demanding free and fair trade in agriculture versus Canada demanding the continuation of legality of import quotas. The implications of these rifts will be examined in greater detail in the next section. Nevertheless, at this point, it is important to note that most of these potential rifts were contained through the agenda, which incorporated the dominant interests of each of the member countries, all of which shared a broad common interest in agriculture.

Within the developed country members of the group, and occasionally Argentina, there was some convergence.[15] All were major exporters of temperate products. Argentina, Australia, and Canada export 35 per cent of the wheat traded. Argentina, Australia, and New Zealand account for 25 per cent of world dairy trade. The same trio accounts for 80 per cent of mutton and lamb global exports. In various permutations, a group constituted by these four countries would have had at least one producer (and usually two, and sometimes even three of the four) ranking among the world's top ten in animal feedstuffs, barley, cereal, oilseeds, vegetable oils, wheat, wool, and sugar.[16] Nevertheless, in a world where the EC commanded 31 per cent of the world's agricultural exports, and the US 14 per cent, the total share of the four in world agricultural trade would have been small. For an issue like agriculture, which had evaded the reach of 'normal' GATT rules for decades, more bargaining leeway would be required. The leeway came in the form of the Cairns Group, whose strengths derived as much from its significant market shares as its diversity. Its resulting bargaining power was both political and economic.

The political commitment behind the Cairns Group reflected widespread interests, or a huge share in one particular product that dominated agricultural and overall exports. For many, gains deriving from liberalisation in certain sectors were unqualified. Argentina, for instance, had agricultural exports constituting 60 per cent of total exports, with a wide spread across commodities. While the greatest proportion of exports came from cake soya bean (20 per cent share of total agricultural, fishery, and forest production in 1988 and 18.8 per cent in 1989), wheat exports too were not insignificant (6 per cent in 1988 and 11.8 per cent in 1989). In beef production, Argentina was a dominant world producer, with beef shares constituting significant proportions of domestic agricultural production for exports (8.5 per cent and 10.4 per cent in 1988 and 1989, respectively).[17] In such a production and export pattern of temperate products, Argentina shared common interests with Australia and New Zealand (the three accounted for 80 per cent of mutton and lamb global exports, and 25 per cent of world dairy trade); in the production of beef and veal, its interests converged with Australia, Brazil, Canada, and Uruguay (50–60 per cent of global exports). With such a significant proportion of its export income deriving from temperate products, it is not surprising that Argentina was a particularly enthusiastic member of the group.

Nevertheless, it is important to remember that even for one of the most enthusiastic developing country members of the Cairns, several losses were imminent as a result of agricultural liberalisation. Losses stemmed from the higher prices of imports that would result, and in such imports tropical products were significant. Green coffee, rubber, cocoa paste, and bananas were some. But the agricultural content of total Argentine imports was small, while the export content was huge, and hence Argentina showed a willingness to include products which constituted its imports (and which were important to other members, such as Colombia's interests in tropical products).

Brazil's membership of the group was less determined by such an obvious production profile. While a huge exporter in absolute terms, it was less dependent than its Latin American neighbours on agricultural exports. Brazil's exports were not dominated by agriculture to the same extent as they were in the case of Argentina. Brazil risked political costs of membership. Through participation in a coalition that was formed along lines of the defectors' services coalition, the

Café au Lait, Brazil risked opprobrium from the other hard-liners of the former G-10 as well as a questioning of its own international identity. There were other divisive issues that isolated Brazil such as its support of S&D treatment, which initially found backing with few of the members of the Cairns Group.

Brazil was finally won over to the formal collaboration with developed countries that underlay the Cairns Group through both economic and ideological compromise. On the economic front, the inclusion of tropical products onto the agenda of Cairns-led agricultural liberalisation gave Brazil overwhelming material interests in towing the collective line. Significant Brazilian agricultural exports included not only soya bean, but also several tropical products such as green coffee (19.9 per cent of total agriculture, fishery and food exports in 1987) and tobacco (rising importance in total export component from 1.6 per cent in 1969–1971 to 7.2 per cent by 1991).[18] Ideologically, Brazil's insistence on S&D was respected through an inclusion of a phased-out S&D proposal for the LDCs in the Cairns agenda. The political consideration of participating in a group of which five other Latin American countries were already members also came into play. Even after this, some losses were inevitable. Both Argentina and Brazil for instance were to be the biggest beneficiaries of liberalisation in beef (besides Australia and Uruguay) but were also expected to undergo offsetting losses in feed grain exports.

The inclusion of tropical products into the Cairns Group agenda was responsible for introducing a serious source of divisions within the group and for creating ambiguities within the agenda (as will be illustrated in the next section). Nevertheless, the fact that the agenda included agricultural liberalisation of both temperate and tropical products allowed a more expansive membership. The inclusion ensured that losses borne by importers of temperate products like grains would be balanced by gains in sectors which constituted a greater share of the export content of some countries. The only net exporters of temperate products were Australia, Argentina, Canada, Hungary, New Zealand, and Uruguay. The inclusion of tropicals meant that Brazil, Australia, and Canada became the major exporters of the group, followed by Malaysia, Argentina, Thailand, Colombia, Indonesia, and New Zealand.[19] Together, these countries accounted for 70 per cent of the group's exports, and the participation of a diversity of countries with significant shares in world trade in agriculture greatly enhanced the bargaining power of the group in terms of legitimacy as well as coercive strength.

The inclusion of certain sub-sectors was critical to the smaller members. Such was the case with the Philippines, whose interests in sugar exports would not have received the same attention as they did by virtue of participation in the Cairns Group. Gains would also accrue to Brazil and Australia if the sugar programmes in the US and EC were ended. Likewise, Indonesia had a keen interest in an opening of international rice markets. Irrespective of large-scale wheat imports (17.3 per cent in 1987 of total imports of agriculture, fishery, and food), soya beans (4.5 per cent in 1987, 8.4 per cent in 1988), and so forth, the attention accorded to rice (which occupied over 70 per cent of the population) made the agenda of the group worth supporting. Thailand too, as one of the world's largest rice exporters, became one of the founding members of the group.[20]

The case of Chile is more difficult to explain. Chile was clearly an exporter of food and other agricultural products, but the largest component of its exports came from horticulture and fishmeal (and fish, minerals, and forest products had to be negotiated separately in the natural resources group). It has been suggested that Chile then joined the Cairns Group as a matter of principle.[21]

These intra-coalition deals conducted across sub-sectors imparted a sectoral strength to the group and its individual members which was unprecedented. The most obvious was that the group came to constitute a collective third force. Excluding Paraguay and South Africa (which only joined the group in 1997 and 1998, respectively), and including Hungary, the thirteen countries of the Cairns Group that were WTO members contributed to 26 per cent of world agricultural exports. The wide coverage of sub-sectors meant that the group provided 21.4–91.8 per cent of the world market in thirteen different commodities.[22]

Bargaining leeway on account of the large trade shares by members in agriculture was enhanced by other structural sources. The population of the Cairns Group collectively was almost as large as that of the US, EC, and Japan combined. Already, it comprised one-tenth of the global GDP. In international trade, too, the Group had a large share. Table 6.3 illustrates the shares of exports from the EC, Japan, and the US that went to the markets of the Cairns Group's members. The figure for collective imports roughly equals the amount of manufactured goods exported by Japan. This has led some analysts to advocate cross-sectoral bargaining strategies for the group.[23] This predominance of the Group in non-agricultural areas may be seen as a structural form of power that need not be actively exercised to influence the behaviour of other players. Even without its overt display, market power may have formed a part of the reason behind the group's considerable influence in agriculture.

Influence derived from market shares was enhanced by the diversity of the group. The group epitomised the Café au Lait in transcending the North–South divide. By including Hungary, it overcame East–West divisions. It included regional powers and middle powers but also small countries. Its cross-regional, multi-continental membership imparted legitimacy to its demands that groups dominated by a bloc ideology had lacked. This diversity further allowed a role

*Table 6.3* The Cairns Group as destination for exports from the 'big three'

| Share (%) of exports of | USA | EC-12 | Japan |
|---|---|---|---|
| *All merchandise* | | | |
| 1980–1982 | 25 | 9 | 15 |
| 1987–1989 | 30 | 9 | 12 |
| *Manufactures* | | | |
| 1980–1982 | 30 | 10 | 15 |
| 1987–1989 | 34 | 8 | 11 |

Source: Rod Tyers (1994), p. 94.

differentiation and division of labour within the group. Canada as a G-7 and Quad member provided links with the developed world. Australia brought with it 'a long-established tradition of mutuality of interest and purpose with several like-minded countries on agricultural issues'; it could also capitalise on the goodwill of LDCs for championing their causes in the past.[24] Brazil as a G-10 Core member was trusted by other developing countries and could build bridges between the Cairns Group and the developing world. 'Argentina was a useful enfant terrible; Canada a bridge with G7; Brazil a bridge with developing countries; Australia the mentor, leader, and conciliator.'[25] These structural advantages of common interests, collective weight, and membership diversity were accompanied by an important external advantage.

### 6.2.2   Conformity to US agenda

Interest configuration and strategies, while critical to the internal stability of the group and external legitimacy, were not sufficient conditions to ensure the achievements of the group. It is true that the interests described in Section 6.2.1 gave the group considerable bargaining power. However, the group at best represented a 'third force' in the negotiations. Critical to the achievements of the Cairns and its bargaining efficacy was the support of the US. Getting agriculture aboard the GATT had long been on the wish list of developing countries. It is no mere coincidence that the time when this wish was taken seriously coincided perfectly with the time when the US too turned in favour of including at least certain aspects of agriculture within multilateral rules. This backing of American hegemony, while a strength of the group, was also a limitation. Precisely how this limitation constrained and tilted the agenda of the group is explored in the next section.

### 6.2.3   Strategies reinforcing intra-group cohesion and external influence

The Cairns Group adopted a careful choice of strategies to enhance its influence. These strategies built on and reinforced the strengths of the group that were described in the previous sub-sections. Key strategies employed by the group to its advantage are highlighted below.

The hallmark strategy of the Cairns Group may be traced back to the Café au Lait coalition. The group attempted to find a middle ground and presented itself as a bridge-building coalition to reconcile extreme positions outside. The extent to which the eventual compromise between the US and the EC was actually a product of the pressures of the Cairns Group, or rather the willingness of the two giants to reach such a compromise is explored in the next section. But the availability of the proposals of the Cairns Group made a comedown for both the US and the EC logistically and politically possible. In any case, the group had never sought to challenge the great powers but had restricted its agenda to 'restraining and modifying' the behaviour of larger actors. Its role as a mediating coalition was perfectly suited to this end. The role of the Cairns Group as bridge-builder won it a legitimacy that surpassed any international recognition that the Informal Group or the G-10 had ever enjoyed.

The fact that the positive, pro-liberalisation agenda of the Cairns conformed with the GATT agenda further enhanced the legitimacy of the group. Compared with the blocking extremes adopted by other coalitions (such as the FIG of LDCs in agriculture, discussed in Section 6.4), the contrast is telling. Even later, when the Latin American members of the Cairns staged walkouts or threats thereof, the long history of the Group's bridge-building activities gave the threats a veneer of legitimacy. The fact that the Latin American step was taken in the cause of free trade further enhanced this veneer.[26]

The Cairns Group founded its mediating role and pro-liberalisation agenda on the groundwork of research and analysis, rather than rhetoric or demands for unilateral concessions. The Australian research initiative was especially important in this context and was utilised explicitly as a bargaining tool in bilateral and multilateral negotiations. Australia's Bureau of Agricultural Economics took the lead in analysing the technical details pertaining to the costs of protection, as well as publicising this information to substantiate the diplomatic stance of the Cairns Group.[27] A foundation in research allowed the Cairns Group a flexibility of negotiating agenda that bloc-type coalitions find difficult to entertain. It is noteworthy that this strategy bore considerable similarity to the Jaramillo process. The Australian lead in the Cairns Group, however, took the Jaramillo example by serving as group hegemon that was able and willing to bear the costs of the research initiative. Even today, the Australian minister for trade chairs the annual ministerial meetings of the group.

The ministerial meetings too formed a part of the Cairns Group strategy. The fact that intra-coalition bargaining and the international position of the coalition have always been represented at the ministerial level helped politicise the agricultural issue in an unprecedented way. This high profile made withdrawal from commitments difficult and created higher stakes for governments for the success of the Cairns.

On the strength of its interest alignments and reinforced by its strategies, the Cairns Group was able to preserve its internal coherence as well as establish legitimacy and presence among other protagonists. By attempting to act as a mediating coalition and constantly adapting its constructive and pro-liberalisation agenda, the Cairns emerged as a negotiating coalition rather than a purely agenda-setting one. Hence, group activism continued well beyond the Punta del Este declaration.

## 6.3   Limitations and constraints

The Cairns Group had several achievements to be proud of, as illustrated in Section 6.1. Conditions and strategies that made the coalition effective were examined in Section 6.2. But in adopting the coalition as a model for other coalitions, either in other issue areas or within the issue area of agriculture, some caution is necessary. This section presents a flip side to the previous discussion. It first identifies some of the limitations of the group, and some of the potential or actual divisions within it. The second half of the section traces the sources of these limitations.

### 6.3.1   *Qualifying successes of the Cairns Group*

A closer scrutiny of the agenda and achievements of the Cairns Group reveals the need for some qualifications for the successes that are traditionally attributed to it. From its inception, the agenda of the Cairns Group was limited. Even this limited agenda was progressively narrowed. After the EC and the US had been prodded by the Cairns Group into negotiating the agricultural issue, the coalition became very much a sidelined third party operating in the face of great power bilateralism. Among the 'successes' in its list, those directly relevant to developing countries were few. The Cairns Group resembled other coalitions in that as the diminishing influence of the group became obvious, so did potential rifts. A closer inspection of these qualifications follows.

The goal of the Cairns Group from the very beginning was that of bridge-building. The middle ground that the Cairns Group claimed to represent, and its associated strategies, by definition limited the agenda of the group to 'restraining and modifying' the behaviour of larger actors in the negotiations.[28] The Cairns model thus differed from coalitions that have tried to adopt a stance that clearly diverges from the Quad position. The bridge that the Cairns built was located in the political niche created by the EC–US rift, with a tilt towards the liberalising agenda of the US that became more evident as the negotiations progressed. In presenting itself as a negotiating coalition, the Cairns Group redefined and reformulated its agenda. Flexibility, however, also translates into a scaling down of demands in response to pressures from stronger parties. Such a scaling down did occur in the case of the Cairns Group. It is noteworthy that the eventual agreement that resulted fell far short of even the revised objectives of the group.

The Blair House Accord was cited as a victory by both the US and the EC. Even this accord deviated significantly from the initial Cairns Group proposal of 10 per cent down payment, increasing import access, lowering administered prices, and initiating stock disposal of disciplines. It was reached only after the EC had addressed some of its internal concerns first and then chosen to negotiate, and focused on the key concerns of the EC and the US. EC compensation and payment policies (under which farmers were paid to take land out of production) were accepted, and a sectoral approach abandoned. The two critical commitments of the Blair House Accord concerned export subsidies, and access to the EC market for oilseeds. The Dunkel draft had incorporated the US objective of a 24 per cent reduction of export subsidies over six years. The EC had offered 18 per cent, and the final agreement specified 21 per cent. The use of an extended base period of 1986–1990 brought about an effective subsidy reduction from the 1991–1992 level to 24 per cent. The second critical provision in the Blair House Accord related to oilseeds, again an area that was of primary concern to the US and the EC.[29] The US had consistently insisted on a reduced quantitative production limit on EC domestic production of 8–9 million tonnes, compared with 12.8 million tonnes of production in 1991. Insisting that such a quantitative production limit went beyond the mandate for internal EC agricultural reform, which was limited to reduction in acreage, the EC offered a 10–15 per cent acreage reduction (calculated by the Americans at a reduction in 8.5–9.7 million tonnes, though it would be compensated by higher yields as a result of intensive farming). Note that oilseeds production is an issue area where developing countries bear little interest as exporters.

Initially, only developing country members of the group found their interests sidelined. The oilseeds focus is only one among several examples. Progressively, however, increasing bilateralism came to dominate the negotiations, in which the Cairns Group as a whole had little say.

The Blair House Accord was largely bilaterally engineered to suit bilateral needs. Subsequent negotiations did not turn more multilateral through the participation of the Cairns Group. US officials, despite the public denials of reopening the Blair House Accord, had been considering internally possible adjustments to appease the EU, particularly the French.[30] A more even phase-out was allowed for the six-year period of 21 per cent tariff reduction. The base period from which to measure the reduction was moved from 1986–1990 to 1991–1992, which allowed a higher level of subsidised exports throughout. The French wheat farmers gained in the order of 8 million tonnes over six years. The US also extended the period of the so-called peace accord, in which the US agreed not to challenge the EU farm policy in the GATT. In turn, the US received market access commitments for almonds, citrus and other fresh fruits, pork and turkey products. Further, this EU–US agreement was not made public while intensive review and approval within the EU went forward.[31] The Cairns Group, despite its claims to continued activism, had not had much say in the story.

As this sidelining of the Cairns Group became clear, potential rifts within the group developed into actual fissures. With the emergence of these fissures, the Cairns Group lost one of the chief characteristics that had sparked off imitative attempts, that is the coherence of the group in spite of its heterogeneous membership. The initial ability of the Cairns to overcome these potential differences had borne special relevance for the developing world affected by differentiation into the third, fourth, and fifth worlds. If the Cairns Group could survive and thrive on its heterogeneity, so could those who followed its example. The Cairns Group had shown a new path to developing countries, such that they would be valued partners with some developed countries.[32] But closer examination reveals latent as well as well-expressed differences among members. These differences are important for two reasons. First, they reveal the importance of another factor (identified in the next section as American hegemony, both a strength and a constraint in the operation of the Cairns) in plastering over real and potential rifts. Second, the differences suggest alternative lines along which other coalitions might emerge.

The first source of division in the Cairns Group was between producers of tropical and temperate products. The importance of including tropical products for winning the allegiance of certain critical members was discussed in Section 6.2.1. The resulting broadening of membership imparted greater weight and legitimacy to the coalition, but it also induced cracks in the base. Producers of tropical products had not been directly affected by the trade war between the US and the EC.

Their motivation for joining the group (e.g. Colombia, Malaysia, and Indonesia) was to bridge the gap that separated them from the ACP countries due to preferential access to EC markets.[33] The tension between the two producer types was exploited at different times by the two giants. The US, even initially, had tied progress on tropical products to progress on their proposal on agricultural liberalisation. The EC, similarly, chose to exploit the potential rift during the Brussels meeting by offering special concessions to tropical producers.

The second visible division was a regional one. Led by Argentina, the Latin American members of the group staged walkouts when their middle-power counterparts suggested compromise.

The regional fissure sometimes formed a part of the developed versus developing country rift. Canada and Australia were reluctant to use agriculture for cross-sectoral bargaining because of their interests in allying with other bargaining groups as well. Canadian interests, for example, along with Japan, Sweden, and Switzerland, wanted no linkages in the drafting of the financial services agreement, and Australia maintained a keen interest in the subsidies group. The Australian trade negotiations minister, Neil Blewett, indicated Australian willingness to negotiate with the EC before the Brussels meeting; Canada too did not want to force a crisis. The situation contrasted with the position maintained by the Latin Americans, that is consensus would be withheld on all other areas if positive results on agriculture were not obtained.[34] This difference between developed countries and Australia and Canada can be explained by the fact that agriculture formed a smaller part of the GDP of the developed countries. These differences were illustrated in Table 6.2, where New Zealand forms more the exception than the rule among the developed countries and the dominance of agriculture therein. The stakes of the developing countries were much higher, both in terms of the agricultural component of GDP and in terms of exports. The difference in negotiating strategy, manifested in the Latin American refusal to negotiate further until agriculture was included versus the Australian–Canadian willingness to compromise, derived directly from these structural differences.

As the influence of the Cairns Group waned, linkages with other coalitions and issues appeared, further dividing the Cairns Group. Brazil, for instance, as a leading member of the Informal Group, advocated S&D treatment in agriculture and was supported by Colombia; Argentina strongly resisted.

As the inadequacies of the Cairns Group and its progressive marginalisation in the face of increasing bilateralism became apparent, former strengths of the group became liabilities. Even the middle-power leadership, which had been hailed as a hallmark of the group and its attendant successes, produced divisions. Australia was, and continues to be, seen as the leader of the group for several reasons. Its economic profile, regional location in the southern hemisphere, and good record in North–South issues over the last decade made it an acceptable leader for developing-country members of the Cairns Group. Its membership of the western alliance in general and Australia, New Zealand, and the US (ANZUS) in particular, as well as its close relationship with Japan, made it an acceptable leader for the industrialised countries. Australia also took on the task of research and organisational leadership of the group. However, unlike hegemonic leadership, middle power leadership is one that is more open to challenges, and such a challenge did emerge from Canada.

The rift between Canada and Australia owed a good deal to the varying levels of protection that the two countries allow their producers. Canadian membership had always been doubtfully viewed by other members of the group. Canada was a net importer with an extensive supply management system through which it has sheltered its farmers from market forces. In March 1990, Canada submitted a proposal for the clarification of Article XI, though a formal separation had still not occurred. Political factors were critical in exacerbating the economic differences, and making them overt with the independent submission of a draft proposal by Canada in October 1990. The Cairns Group had submitted an offer (which Canada did not initial) requiring the elimination of Article XI; Canada's submission called for the retention of Article XI and the tariffication of only those QRs which were inconsistent with revised GATT rules. The contest between Australia and Canada for leadership status was the source of this political conflict, with Canada desirous of that status on account of its membership of the Quad, the G-7, and tradition of middle-power leadership.[35] Differing patterns of diplomacy between the two countries, and different domestic and international imperatives, exacerbated this conflict further.[36]

The Cairns Group was successful in exploiting the US–EC rift and thereby ensured that agriculture was not swept away under the carpet. As a third party to the negotiations on agriculture, however, it is important to remember that it did not drag the EC or the US screaming to the negotiating table. The Cairns Group provided the two agricultural superpowers with a modus vivendi, but the US in particular and also the EC to some extent (due to the high costs of the subsidies war) had desired such a truce. The Blair House Accord was, first and foremost, an accord between the two giants to suit their interests; any benefits that the Cairns Group derived from the accord were fortunate but incidental. The Cairns Group worked in exceptional circumstances (of the rupture within the Quad and the hegemonic support that the group enjoyed). Further, increasing marginalisation of the group exacerbated the differences that had always been latent in its functioning. Particularly in the light of the conditions favourable to the operation of the Cairns Group that were analysed in Section 6.2, the eventual results and limitations of its efforts demand a detailed explanation.

### 6.3.2   *Explaining limitations*

The qualifications to the achievements of the Cairns Group were a product of the same set of conditions that had contributed to its strengths. The Cairns Group had successfully harnessed the common interests of members to forge intra-group coherence and external presence and mobilised strategies to that purpose. But it was still constrained by the external conditions that facilitated the building of the group agenda in the first place. The most decisive of these external conditions in making and breaking the group was the American support that the Cairns had relied on.

In some ways, the Cairns Group arose in conditions that were uniquely propitious to its functioning. The most important of these conditions was the volte face of the US from its formerly restrictive practices in agriculture to the push for a GATT-based liberalisation. In the liberalising agenda of the US, and the urgency of such a liberalisation for both the US and the EC due to the subsidies war, the smaller agriculture exporting nations found a negotiating niche. The broad conformity of the agenda of the Cairns Group, with the liberalising agenda of the US, increased the possibility of its successes.

While conforming to the US ideological position and long-term goals on liberalisation of agriculture, the Cairns Group had initially attempted to present itself as a mediating coalition between the EC and the US. By the end of 1989, the group's had acquired an explicit tilt towards the American position. The tilt was a reaction to the EC's intransigence on using 1986 as a base year and not reforming its dual pricing system. The EC had further not been satisfied by the Cairns Group's concession on a ten-year phase-out of export subsidies. Instead, it had demanded the continuation of export subsidies (though with tighter disciplines) for the disposal of surpluses. The Cairns Group, at this point, accepted the US's suggestion that NTBs on agriculture be converted into *ad valorem* tariffs and then reduced to low or zero levels within ten years. The group also adopted the traffic-light approach of the US with a red, amber, and green categorisation of domestic support measures. The traffic-light approach eventually became a part of the GATT and WTO disciplines on agriculture. In fact, it has been alleged in some quarters that the US incited the Cairns Group to stage a walkout at Brussels.[37] While there is some controversy on this, the support of the US played an important role in leading the Latin American countries to walk out at Montreal and use a similar threat at Brussels.

The shared long-term objectives between the US and the Cairns Group, and increasing conformity about means to achieve them, gave the Cairns Group a powerful ally outside. However, the alliance also limited the negotiating space that the group could enjoy. Hence, Tussie writes, 'Even though the US first placed agriculture on the agenda and retained control over the overall dynamics, Cairns was able at certain points to catalyze change by bridging the gap in the extreme positions of the United States and the EC ... As the final stages of the round drew in, Cairns threw its weight to confront European intransigence over farm reform. The objective then was to add power to the US side and apply unremitting pressure on the EC so as to isolate its farm lobby and force the pace of the negotiations.'[38] For its creation, survival, 'flexible' agenda, and eventual achievements, the Cairns Group worked in close liaison with American objectives. That the successes of the group were constrained and shaped by its powerful ally is not surprising.

Accompanying the paradoxically strengthening and debilitating constraint of American hegemony were several others that limited the objectives of the group and forced it continually to scale down its demands. Leadership skirmishes within the group, and other sources of division, deprived the group of its most important internal source of strength, namely intra-group coherence. Negotiating strategies of flexibility were reliant on, and responsive to, the changing American agenda, and resulted in further scaling down of the agenda of the Cairns. Such scaling down in turn reinforced intra-group differences, such as the refusal of the Latin Americans to compromise at a time when the developed country members of the group were more willing to do so. Some of these limitations were recognised both by the Cairns Group and by the giants outside.

Paradoxically, the mere survival of the group in the face of the odds described above rendered the achievements of the group even more legendary. The Cairns became an example for developing countries as well as middle powers to aspire to. Several features were emphasised by coalitions that tried to model themselves along the lines of the Cairns Group. First, the coalition was to have an issue-based focus and operate at the sector level. Second, it was to be a crossover coalition which combined developed and developing countries with similar interests in the sector. Third, the new coalition type would emphasise its role in bridge-building. Fourth, the group had demonstrated the importance of having a positive, pro-liberalising agenda in contributing to the legitimacy of the group. The next two sections examine the fruits of the evolved alliance diplomacy that was attempted along the path shown by the Cairns.

## 6.4 The Food Importers' Group: a comparison with the Cairns

The previous section demonstrated the limitations of the Cairns Group, which leads to some caution in adopting the coalition type as a model coalition. This section investigates the extent to which other groups have replicated the successes of the Cairns. It compares the Cairns Group with another coalition that attempted to follow the Cairns example – the Food Importers' Group (FIG). The first part of the section highlights reasons why the FIG bore much promise of success and points to the similarities of the FIG with the Cairns. The failure of the attempt, however, is explained as a result of the inability of the group to reproduce the conditions that had facilitated the achievements of the Cairns. The absence of the same conditions also precipitated difficulties in applying the strategies of the Cairns Group. Once it has been demonstrated why the Cairns 'model' proved unsuitable within the same sector, agriculture, its applicability in other issue areas becomes even more suspect.

To counter the push for liberalisation that had emerged from the Cairns coalition and the US, some developing countries organised themselves into the FIG. The group was also called the W-74 group, in reference to the joint proposal submitted by it. Fundamental differences between agricultural exporters and food importers provided the rationale for its formation.[39] There were several reasons to anticipate why a group of food-importing LDCs would not have been a paper tiger. First, LDC consumers have a higher propensity to spend on agricultural and food items (Engel's law), that is 40–60 per cent of any income increase compared with 12–16 per cent in OECD states. Even in current trade terms, LDCs account for over half of the world's annual food imports.[40] Excluding the LDC agricultural exporting countries in the Cairns Group, their combined GDP was still more than $2.4 trillion. Though this was less than the GNP of the US or the EC, it still indicated the large LDC market. The food importers could be a substantive third force, much like the Cairns Group, with considerable external weight. Second, stakes for the food importers were high, and their demand for compensation urgent, if food prices did rise as expected. The food imports of some FIG members are presented in Table 6.4. Given such figures, there was reason to expect both bargaining strength and commitment in such a group. Third, the food importers were located in the same international context of the subsidies war and the US–EC rift, which the Cairns had utilised so effectively. There was much potential in this context for another negotiating niche. For instance, the food importers could align themselves with the EC and balance against the Cairns Group–US liaison. Alternatively, they could have added further bargaining power to the Cairns–US pole, in return for compensations resulting from a price increase. Fourth, the food importers could utilise similar strategies as walkouts, or threats thereof, as had been employed by some Cairns members. Cross-issue bargaining offered a credible source of strength, especially with such issues as services, TRIMs, and TRIPS, on which the Quad was keen to obtain an agreement. Additionally, the liberalisation agenda of the US and its more moderate version in the Cairns Group provided the food-importers with a readymade agenda of 'otherness' on which they could have built. A group of food importers rooted in the issue-based focus akin to the Café au Lait and the Cairns Group was not a shot in the dark.

Irrespective of all these potential advantages for the operation of food-importing LDCs as a collectivity, the attempted coalition provided no match to the Cairns. The W-74 was organised by Jamaica and included Egypt, Mexico, Morocco, and

*Table 6.4* Food imports by FIG members

| Country | Commodity | Values of imports as a percentage of total market economy in 1984 |
| --- | --- | --- |
| Egypt | Wheat unmilled | 4.5 |
| | Wheat meal or flour | 30.7 |
| | Live animals | 3.9 |
| | Butter | 2.1 |
| | Milk dry, less than 1.5% fat | 4.0 |
| | Processed animal vegetable oil | 3.6 |
| Mexico | Maize unmilled | 4.4 |
| | Cereals unmilled | 18.2 |
| | Milk, cream preserved | 2.2 |
| | Animal oils and fats | 2.8 |
| Morocco | Other wheat unmilled | 5.8 |
| Nigeria | Rice | 2.7 |
| | Milk, cream preserved | 2.9 |
| | Milk (extra dry) preserved, sweet | 10.6 |
| | Malt including flour | 9.7 |
| | Sugar | 2.5 |
| Peru | Durum wheat unmilled | 12.0 |

Source: Cooper (1990), p. 16.

Peru. It had the backing of some other countries like India, Nigeria, and Korea, although they did not co-sponsor the proposal. The group remained a weak player throughout its lifetime. Its inability to achieve much tangible success is important, particularly as the group operated in the same issue area as its model coalition, the Cairns. Obviously, even operation within the same context of the special area of agriculture and an EC–US showdown had not sufficed.

The failure of the FIG to emerge as a serious contender in the agricultural negotiations has been attributed to several reasons. They include problems of uncertainty that afflict LDCs and thereby make it difficult for them to determine their interests. Some of these difficulties were consciously overcome in the Cairns Group under the research initiative that was begun under Australia.[41] But there were indeed developing countries for which the impact of liberalisation à la Cairns would have been unambiguously detrimental. There were others, such as the ACP countries that had benefited from the preferential treatment received for their tropical agricultural produce under the Lomé conventions. They risked losing those benefits if the second part of the Cairns agenda were implemented. This critical second part pertained to equal market access for agricultural produce, especially as pushed for by tropical producers in the group, the first part of the agenda being an amelioration of the subsidies war in temperate commodities.

More than the politics of domestic groups and uncertainty of national interest, two simpler explanations provide us an insight into the failure of the attempted coalition. First, the structural interests that had driven the operation of the Cairns Group were very different in the case of the FIG. Some, such as Jamaica, did have significant food imports and hence losses from the Cairns initiative. Food imports constituted 19 per cent of all its merchandise imports, for which a price increase would entail significant consumer losses;[42] further losses were expected directly through the questioning of the preferential Lomé arrangements and indirectly through the expected decline in prices in the high-priced, hitherto protected EC markets. Jamaican leadership in the FIG, however, was unmatched by a committed following.

For many other potential losers from agricultural liberalisation, agriculture was only one of the many issues of interest to their diversified production profile. Egypt belonged to this category. Egypt further desired to appear in favour of liberalisation, in part to boost the domestic reform process, and in part to allow it concessions in other areas (and which was especially important after its association with the recalcitrant stance of the G-10). In the case of Mexico, although the value of agricultural exports was the largest in the group, agricultural trade was less important relative to the rest of the Mexican economy. While food imports constituted 7 per cent of Jamaica's GDP and 15 per cent of Egypt's, Mexican food imports consisted only 1.6 per cent of its GDP. Issues such as food aid that were critical to other members did not interest Mexico, and this would have been ineligible anyway. India, whose support for the group stemmed from its traditional G-10 stance, was caught in a similar net of competing interests wherein agriculture was only one important, but not the predominant, interest. Within agriculture, India's interest in lower world food prices fostered by protectionism derived from its position of net food importer, even though less than 1 per cent of its GDP was in agricultural imports. However, 16 per cent of all its exports were agricultural and gave it an interest in market access. India's support for the FIG was therefore weak. It never became a member of the group, its indifference to any particular outcome in agriculture being offset by its much greater interest in other sectors such as services (as the negotiations progressed), intellectual property, textiles, and others.

Nigeria belonged to yet another category of LDCs whose natural advantage in agriculture had been curbed due to several factors. Until the onset of a Dutch disease phenomenon that afflicted agriculture since the oil boom of the 1970s, Nigeria had been an agricultural exporter. Rather than a country with a persistent disadvantage in food production, Nigeria was one which might have curtailed its comparative advantage in agriculture, in part due to the depressed prices of agriculture. Its commitment to the FIG was hence also equivocal.

Effectively, there were three sets, even within the small attempted group of food-importing countries. The first set was critical to the success of the coalition (and had a sole member Jamaica), for whom expected losses from agricultural liberalisation were enormous enough and their individual leeway too small, to necessitate group action. The second included countries with a wider production set and lesser dependence on agricultural imports – such as India, Mexico, Egypt – and whose participation in the group was balanced by diplomatic investment in other issue areas. The third comprised countries which had enjoyed a translated or potential comparative advantage in agriculture in the past, and which had been curtailed in recent years; liberalisation and greater stability of prices offered a possibility of gains if they were able to recover that advantage. With the latter two types of countries in dominance, the structure of joint interests precluded an anti-liberalisation commitment that could match the pro-liberalisation zeal of the Cairns.

The inability of the FIG, however, to somehow engineer intra-group deals was also related to the absence of a second factor that had been critical in plastering the divisions of the Cairns Group together. This second factor was that of American support. As was illustrated in the previous section, the informal support of the US to the Cairns Group offered initial promise of success; the swing of the group to the US position became more overt as the negotiations progressed. The FIG, however, did not command similar support of a strong ally. In some ways, the failure of the FIG to utilise the transatlantic divide effectively is not surprising, for the FIG represented more of a third way than the Cairns Group ever had. The agenda of the FIG, with its demand for compensation in case food prices rose, was neither economically attractive as a harness for support for either the EC or the US, nor was it politically as correct as the Cairns Group's agenda of liberalisation. It is perhaps possible to develop a case that had the FIG emerged as a serious contender in the negotiations, the EC might have employed it to balance the US–Cairns *de facto* alliance. The structural configuration of interests within the FIG, analysed in the previous paragraphs, however, prevented it from emerging as this serious player. As a result, the EC concentrated its attention on the Cairns Group and attempted to split the group through individual or mini-group trade-offs.[43] The FIG did not even become a pawn in the games of the great powers.

Unable to find the same set of conditions conducive to its working, the FIG also bungled its strategies. Lacking the support of either of the strong allies, it adopted a blocking strategy that differed markedly from the positive liberalisation agenda of the Cairns. Rather than present even an appearance of building bridges, the FIG stood apart demanding concessions, thereby reverting to the former tactics of developing countries in the Informal Group. It did not even try to mediate between the EC and the US by framing its LDC-directed agenda in terms of the international debate. Occasionally, it engaged with the Cairns Group, but only when the two were at cross-purposes, for example, by stating that the Cairns Group proposal on a phased-out S&D programme was inadequate for the LDCs. Not only did the FIG lack the intra-group structural conditions that had assisted the Cairns Group, but it was also more ambitious than the Cairns. Rather than merely restraining and modifying the agenda of the two agricultural superpowers, the FIG was a coalition of resistance. There was little initiative at leadership compared with Australia in the Cairns Group, and scarce emphasis on research. In many ways, these adverse strategies were a product of, and exacerbated the effects of, the lack of conducive conditions resembling those of the Cairns Group. The group was never able to command the legitimacy that the Cairns Group had enjoyed through its research, bridge-building and agenda of liberalisation.

## 6.5   Adapting the Cairns model: Friends of Services Group

The previous section argued that the principal reason for the inability of the FIG to replicate the successes of the Cairns even within the same issue area was the absence of two initial conditions, one internal to the group and the other external. To arbitrate conclusively between the absence of similar conditions versus bad implementation of the strategies of the Cairns Group as a central cause for the limitations of the FIG, this section examines the Friends of Services Group. Depending on the successes of the Friends' Group, it will be possible to determine the ranking of factors – structural conditions and strategies – that are key to the successes of evolved alliance diplomacy.

The Friends of Services Group was based on the Café au Lait of the pre-launch phase of the Uruguay Round. The successes of the Cairns were seen as a reaffirmation of the methods demonstrated by the Café au Lait, that is mediation between extremes, developed–developing country memberships, and issue-area focus. After the launch of the Round, the G-20 and Café au Lait took various avatars. The Friends' Group was one of these avatars, with an undefined and changing membership and a limited agenda of facilitating a liberalisation in services. It is noteworthy that the Friends' Group employed exactly the same strategies as the Cairns and the Café au Lait. It combined developed and developing countries and worked at the sector level. It had a positive agenda of keeping the services issue rolling in GATT-led liberalisation. There were some rewards of following such strategies, the most important being longevity. However, though the group continued into the late 1990s, it never became more than a 'chat group' for an exchange of views. No coordinated positions emerged, nor did the forum give rise to offshoots that operated as functional coalitions in services. The few sub-sectoral coalitions that emerged seldom owed parentage to the Friends' Group and took the independent paths described in Chapter 5. The Friends' Group had minimal influence in the GATT/WTO, in spite of a replication of the strategies of the Cairns.

A plausible explanation for the minimal influence of the Friends' Group may be found in the configuration of individual state interests in the services sector. These economic conditions were accompanied by an international political scenario markedly different from that dominated by the trans-atlantic polarisation which had provided the prelude to the Cairns Group activity. Internal and external conditions that rendered the coalition very different from the Cairns and its successes are described below.

The services sector differs from agriculture in rendering sector level negotiations difficult due to the immense diversification within the sector. Reasons for this disaggregation were elaborated in Chapter 5. The disaggregation, in turn, opened up a Pandora's box of conflicting interests, generating opposing loyalties and allowing few constructive intra-sectoral linkages or trade-offs. The different levels of conflicting allegiances and their various sources were described in detail in Chapter 5. They require a brief recapitulation here.

Two lines of disaggregation were noted. First, and yet to be discussed in Chapter 7, was a more disaggregated vision of common interests in services with a regional bias. The second fracture appeared along sub-sectoral lines. Three sources of disaggregation were found. The first of these was resource-based, resulting, for instance, in coalitions among countries with a similar competitive advantage in labour-intensive services. The second and third lines of interest fell across the importance of the particular sub-sector with respect to the rest of the economy. The importance was rated according to the dependence of the economy on the sub-sector, and its actual and potential strength in it. Chile, for instance, like the East Asian NICs, was deeply integrated into the world financial system and saw clear benefits from the liberalisation of financial services. But in the case of the East Asians, interests were sufficiently diversified to produce cross-cutting loyalties, and hence their liaison with India, Egypt, Argentina, and others on promoting the labour mode as well as opening of markets to professional services. The ASEAN countries also found a common cause with the EC and Norway over the liberalisation of maritime transport.[44]

Underlying these conflicting loyalties in the case of the ASEAN, and more so in the case of the larger developing countries, was the fact that none of the sub-sectors were sufficiently dominant to allow trade-offs over other sub-sectors and thereby build lasting coalitions of mixed and shared interests. Particular interests were sufficiently dominant to allow lasting loyalties only for certain types of economies. Only in the case of a few countries such as Singapore which had evolved into service economies, for a very few small economies where just a few sub-sectors were dominant (such as island economies and their reliance on tourism), and for those which saw little development potential of an indigenous services sector (and therefore preferred easier and more stable access to an international market in services, such as Jamaica on transport services) were particular interests sufficiently dominant to allow any lasting loyalties to coalitions.

Given the sub-sectoral disaggregation of the services sector, the attempt of the Friends' Group to construct an agenda at the sector level was doomed to failure. Admittedly, smaller economies such as Jamaica with a clearly expressed interest in services liberalisation, largely in conformity to the US position, were natural members of the group. But the larger part of the varying and fluid membership of the coalition lacked this clarity of interest, and the agenda of the group remains, to this day, unspecified and vague.

Besides the absence of internal coherence within the Friends' Group, conducive external conditions were also lacking. Chapter 5 also explored the divisions within the developed world. The transatlantic rift in services had never been on the same scale as in agriculture. It was further bridged through increasing recognition (partly through the deliberations of the Jaramillo track) of a conformity of interests between the two powers. In spite of differences over sub-sectors, most developed countries had realised by the launch of the Uruguay Round that their overall interests in the sector as a whole were similar. Hence, the Friends' Group was unable to split the Quad coalition and garner the support of a Great Power. The two conditions critical to the successes of the Cairns, intra-coalition coherence and external, Great Power backing, were absent. Not all the research initiatives, developed–developing country liaisons, and issue-area focus could overcome that structural reality.

## 6.6  Conclusion

In the light of the euphoria that surrounded the rise and maintenance of the Cairns Group, the conclusions of this chapter are somewhat sobering. This chapter has argued that while attempts to emulate the Cairns Group, within and outside agriculture were understandable, there are two reasons why the group does not serve as a 'model' coalition for developing countries. First, the successes of the Cairns Group were qualified, its agenda was limited, and the group was ridden with active and latent fissures. Second, the group was a product of two unique circumstances, one internal to the coalition and economic and the other external and political. The critical economic condition was the unique character of agriculture that allowed a sector-level approach that facilitated lasting intra-coalition trade-offs (as opposed to disaggregation at the sub-sector level) and the subsidy wars of the time. The political condition was the EC–US rift and the conformity of the Cairns with the US agenda. The political condition, in particular, facilitated the adoption of the strategies of bridge-building and positive agenda of liberalisation based on an institutionalised research initiative. In the absence of these two conditions, the successes of the 'model' have been difficult to replicate.

The problems of replicating the Cairns Group were examined with the examples of the FIG and the Friends of Services Group. The FIG emerged in the same international context as the Cairns Group. Its failure, in spite of the same starting point as the Cairns, was attributed to the absence of the two critical conditions mentioned above. The FIG was unsuccessful in building intra-group cohesion due to different structural interests among members; it also failed to utilise the US–EC rift by not allying with either of the two powers. The Friends of Services group had even fewer achievements to its credit than the FIG. This was partly because the Friends' Group started out with more obvious disadvantages, the most important being the absence of a transatlantic divide. The external supportive condition of hegemonic support for the agenda of the group was also absent, given the limited divisions within the Quad in the issue area. Further, the services sector differed markedly from the agrarian sector by proving especially prone to disaggregation, and thereby rendering sector-level coalition initiatives futile from the beginning. The Friends' Group is important in reinforcing the lessons of the first two cases: in the absence of the conducive structural conditions, a replication of the strategies of the Cairns does not ensure replication of the successes of the 'model'.

Besides the internal and external structural conditions that facilitated the successes of the Cairns, Section 6.2 highlighted a third source of the achievements of the group, that is carefully devised strategies. The contrasting strategies of the FIG and attendant limitations reinforced the importance of a pro-liberalisation stance, extensive research initiative, and mediating role. But the FIG had a very different set of economic interests underlying it, which were found to bear chief responsibility for the failures of the group. The Friends' Group is important in arbitrating between the various conditions and strategies that are critical to the successes of alliance diplomacy. It takes the caveats of the FIG further by showing that even an exact reproduction of the strategies of the Cairns does not produce a comparable presence or influence of the coalition. The Cairns model works in so far as the aims of the coalition are limited, and in conformity with at least one of the great powers. But in the absence of conducive structural conditions, a replication of the strategies of the Cairns does not ensure replication of the successes of the 'model'.

As demonstrated here, the applicability of the Cairns model to other situations remains limited. The model works only in the context of the two conditions described above, and only when the aims of the group are limited to mediation. In the absence of the unusual condition of extreme bipolarity in trade agendas, a Cairns type coalition will have only limited influence. For developing countries which may seek to swim against a Quad-led tide of liberalisation, or others which represent a viewpoint opposite (rather than mediatory) to the dominant one, alternative models have to be found.

There were some significant qualifications to the achievements of the Cairns Group, and fissures underlay the unity that has traditionally been ascribed to the coalition. But it is important to note that even the fissures of the Cairns suggest alternative pathways to coalition formation. The most 'natural' and decisive of the fissures affecting the coherence of the Cairns was regional. The regional option as a springboard to bargaining is discussed in the next chapter.

# 7 Regionalism

## A springboard for bargaining?

'Very true', said the Duchess: 'flamingoes and mustard both bite. And the moral
of that is – Birds of a feather flock together'.

(Lewis Carroll, *Alice's Adventures in Wonderland*)

The idea of bargaining jointly on the basis of regional affiliations is not a new one.
It has found mention in recommendations from diverse sources and has a history
of coalition attempts behind it. The 'non-tradable' character of services in particular lends itself to a compatibility with various trends in regionalisation: 'the non-
storability and intangibility of services create strong incentives to go regional'.[1] In
the light of the findings of previous chapters on coalition alternatives, this chapter
addresses the question: Have coalitions with a regional base proved to be a more
practical and effective way forwards for developing countries? And if so, under
what conditions and for which countries have such coalitions emerged as the most
viable alignment option?

The first section of this chapter investigates why the regional option has
attracted so much attention among developing countries. It reverts back to a point
that was raised in Chapter 5. Interests in services not only disaggregate into sub-
sectors but also tend to re-group into regions at the sector level. In some ways,
coalitions that utilise regionalism as a springboard for bargaining may be seen as
'natural coalitions'. The section also highlights coalitions attempted by developing countries along these lines to find a louder voice in trade negotiations in services. Section 7.2 investigates the puzzle as to why regional coalitions have yielded
only limited successes, in spite of the initial promise of regionalism. It examines
the cases of the Latin American coalitions in detail. Several cross-cutting and
overlapping loyalties are found. The section discovers that the principal limitation
of these coalitions is that they have been founded on the strength of prior or
simultaneous efforts at regional integration (e.g. 'CUs which maintain common
external barriers must act jointly, behaving essentially as a single entity'[2]). As such,
regional coalitions have inherited the flawed legacy of regional integration (RI)
schemes on which they were based. The limitations of Regional Trade
Arrangements (RTAs) as they apply to developing countries and their implications for bargaining coalitions are discussed in the same section. It is argued that
the same limitations apply as much to the 'new regionalism' as the old, and to the

services sector as much as manufacturing. It is important to remember, however, that regional integration is not the only springboard to regional bargaining coalitions. Section 7.3 explores an alternative route with the help of the ASEAN success story. It also addresses the issue of the applicability of this model to other situations. Section 7.4 concludes.

## 7.1   Regions: 'natural' bargaining coalitions?

The aims and methods of regional cooperation among developing countries have varied considerably over time. The first wave of regionalism (1960s–1970s) was characterised by an emphasis on collective self-reliance and South–South trade accompanying strategies of import-substituted industrialisation (ISI). The second wave of regionalism has been dubbed the 'new regionalism'.[3] Beginning in the mid-1980s, the most distinctive feature of the second wave is the disappearance of its former emphasis on regional self-sufficiency. This has also allowed regional groupings involving developing countries to be more eclectic in their membership. However, even within the new regionalism, paradoxical aims can be discerned among developing countries. The second wave is often presented as only a step towards greater multilateral liberalisation through more effective export promotion at the level and strength of the region. But at the same time, it is often a reaction to the economic bloc formation of the developed world, that is a product of the 'domino effect'. There are two noteworthy points common to all these mixed aims and member-ships. First, irrespective of the phase and methods used to achieve them, all regional arrangements have a primary or secondary aim of joint bargaining. This remains true of regional arrangements today as much as the South–South trade initiatives of the first phase.[4] The second noteworthy feature is the recurrence and wide spread of the phenomenon. Regional cooperation 'remains an article of faith among developing countries, an instinctive collective response to changing international circumstances'.[5] The fact that over 100 preferential trading agreements have been notified by the contracting parties to the GATT is one indication of this pervasive faith.

A simple and intuitive reasoning underlies regional initiatives among developing countries, in spite of the diversity of their stated policy aims. Shared histories, geographies, and institutions facilitate cooperation among regional allies. To frequent critiques of the concept of the Third World and its coalition manifestations,[6] regionalism provides a ready answer. Different histories of decolonisation and development divide the Third World bloc, but also unite South Asia, East Asia, Africa, and Latin America into regions and sub-regions. Some authors have emphasised the importance of geographical proximity within a region. It has been shown that South–South trade mainly takes place among countries belonging to the same geographical area. Of Latin America's total manufactured exports to other LDCs, more than 90 per cent go to other Latin American countries. Other regions show similar trends (73 per cent in Africa, 56 per cent in the Middle East, and 67 per cent in Asia).[7] Shared histories, similar levels of development, similar cultures, and similar external threats are most likely among neighbours. Regional groupings attempt to exploit these commonalties.[8]

Propitious conditions notwithstanding, cooperative action emerges only when particular and shared interests of potential members are met. At least in the realm of services, it is possible to find a convergence of interests among developing countries that aligns according to regions. Chapter 5 investigated the difficulties in building a South-sector coalition and found that a disaggregation occurred along two lines. Only one line of disaggregation, along sub-sectors, was discussed in detail. This section explores the second line along which interests at the broad South-sector level splintered and regrouped.

Even as developing countries attempted to resurrect a bloc-type position on services, it was becoming clear that not all developing countries recorded a deficit in trade in services. In a study for 1979–1981, thirty-nine of the 120 countries reviewed were found to have a surplus in their traded services. Of these thirty-nine, twenty-one were developing countries.[9] Besides the expected developed market economies which ran surpluses in services (UK, France, Spain, Italy, and the US), developing countries with positive trade figures included the Bahamas, Barbados, Colombia, Egypt, Jamaica, Kenya, Lesotho, Mexico, Nicaragua, Panama, Paraguay, Philippines, Singapore, South Korea, and Tunisia. A closer inspection reveals further differences within the developing world.

A threefold classification has been suggested on the basis of current account profiles.[10] It is particularly interesting to the note the regional bias to this categorisation. To the first category belong countries which are major exporters of minerals and commodities, that is countries with a surplus in merchandise and a deficit in trade in services. Even with the exclusion of the vast deficits accumulated through interest payments, services make a negative contribution in this category. Examples include Brazil, countries of the Andean Group,[11] a few in Asia such as Indonesia, and most of the African commodity exporters. In Africa, except for Nigeria, all the countries recording a heavy deficit in their services trade balance devoted more than 45 per cent of their foreign exchange to imports of services. These imports were, and often continue to be, strategically linked to satisfactory performance in primary product exports. A regional concentration of these countries is discernible in Latin America and most of Africa.

The second category includes countries whose earnings from labour and travel compensate for their negative positions on trade in goods and other services categories. Sometimes, then, these countries record a surplus in the general category of trade in services. Sri Lanka is characteristic of this category and, to some extent, India (although India also has a strong position in some sub-sectors that fall within the other services category). Most of the Non-Oil Producing Exporting Countries (NOPEC) of North Africa and West Asia are also a part of this category on account of their earnings through labour remittances. Regionally, this translates into South Asia, as well as West Asia and North Africa. The small island economies of the Caribbean reveal a similar surplus in services, although its source is different from the sub-set comprising South Asia and others. The Caribbean economies generate a huge surplus in tourism but have a considerable dependence on merchandise and services imports.

The third and much smaller category includes countries whose characteristic surplus in services has historically offset merchandise deficits. Recent years, however, have witnessed their growing competitive advantage in exports of manufactured goods. The East Asian NICs comprise this set and are characterised by a very high degree of flexibility in their adaptation to developments in the world economy. South Korea, for instance, has been able to export construction services to the OPEC countries and manufactured goods to the developed countries.

That a regional concentration of interests could be effectively utilised for joint bargaining was demonstrated to developing countries by some powerful precedents at region-based bargaining by the developed countries. Members of the EC have bargained together from a joint platform with one spokesperson since the 1960s in the GATT. Bargaining power derived from this joint position has not gone unnoticed. EC members have maintained their legal status as individual GATT Contracting Parties, but in most GATT bodies since the Dillon Round (1960–1961), the EC/EU Commission participates as a GATT Contracting Party *sui generis*.[12] Ernest Preeg comments on the European bloc of over forty votes in the WTO (EU members and associates) with some alarm.[13] This 'bloc'-based power has an external component in terms of the large market that the EC constitutes and its recognition of its comparative advantage in services. But it also has a strong internal component, intra-group coherence (admittedly arrived at after much protracted negotiations and stalemates in most issues), which allows it the bargaining strength that comes from certainty of allies, certainty of regional markets, and legitimacy of large numbers. The lessons of regional power, however, climaxed in the pre-launch phase of the Uruguay Round with the resort to regional arrangements or threats thereof by the US.[14] The US repeatedly threatened to turn to 'like-minded' countries if the services negotiations stalled in the GATT. It signed its first international agreement with Israel, which explicitly included services in 1984. Preceding the Canada–United States Free Trade Agreement was the US–Canada discussion on barriers in banking and computer services in 1983. Fears of a complete sidelining of multilateralism in favour of bilateralism and regionalism were important in bringing sceptical developing countries to the negotiating table with the services issue in hand. The regional concentration of similar interests in services, and the regional precedent established in the context of services by developed countries, precipitated several efforts at joint bargaining on the basis of regional affinities among developing countries. These efforts are described below.

Among the developing countries in the pre-negotiation phase of the Uruguay Round, the most concerted attempts to ground themselves into a regional coalition came from the Latin Americans, particularly through the SELA (while also drawing on other regional institutions), and the ASEAN. The SELA, for instance, convened a coordination meeting in 1982, expressing doubts about the desirability of initiating negotiations in services and questioning the legal competence of the GATT in the field.[15] By the time the Uruguay Round was launched, rifts within the Latin American position had become obvious, with Brazil as a leader of the G-10, versus the Colombian leadership of the Café au Lait. But efforts to preserve a joint Latin American front continued. One prominent result of these efforts was the proposal put forth by eleven Latin American countries (Brazil,

Chile, Colombia, Cuba, Honduras, Jamaica, Nicaragua, Mexico, Peru, Trinidad and Tobago, and Uruguay) in February 1990 to the Group of Negotiations on Services (GNS).[16] Another text was presented by a group of seven Afro-Asian countries (Cameroon, China, Egypt, India, Kenya, Nigeria, and Tanzania).[17] Both exercised a significant impact on the negotiation process, allowing the inclusion of provisions that incorporated developing country concerns. The Afro-Asian draft made a clear distinction between the general mandatory character of certain obligations and commitments versus market access and national treatment principles incorporated through a positive list approach. The draft similarly stressed that the Part IV approach of the GATT be avoided, and instead, the development objective be incorporated as a running theme in the GATS. The ASEAN also operated as a joint platform for its members in the GATT in the pre-launch phase. Since then, it has come to resemble the EU in the WTO, in the fact that its individual members speak with one negotiator. The ASEAN is also one of the few coalitions comprising developing countries, which was accorded recognition in the GATT. Similar attempts at policy coordination in the WTO have been made by some of the African countries, discussed in Chapter 8.

The fact that regional bargaining was attempted in the GATT is unsurprising. Regional arrangements in the developing world are of various types, are large in number, have long histories, and have an explicit bargaining component in smaller or greater measure. Really surprising is the fact that relatively few long-lasting bargaining coalitions with a regional basis have actually materialised in the GATT. The list in the paragraph given above is indicative, and it is not a long one.

The limited success of regional bargaining coalitions is expressed not only in the small numbers of such coalitions. The positions adopted by these numbered coalitions were often chimerical. Under the SELA, for instance, the Latin American countries had adopted a traditional Informal Group type position. But the joint draft by eleven Latin American countries, presented in 1990, differed considerably from the conventional hard line's opposition to services. Now the Latin Americans recognised 'the need for a multilateral framework of principles and rules for trade in services and negotiations thereof, aimed at expansion of such trade under conditions of transparency and progressive liberalisation as means of promoting economic growth of all trading partners and the development of developing countries ...'[18] In other respects, however, the text conformed with traditional bloc-type positions of developing countries. It stressed the development of developing countries and increasing their participation in international trade in services as a purpose of the multilateral framework on services. From this aim emerged the principle of relative reciprocity for developing countries,[19] a priority to the liberalisation of sectors and modes of delivery of interest to developing countries,[20] commitment of financial resources by developed countries to facilitate the development of infrastructure for the services sector,[21] special clauses of technical cooperation to assist developing countries,[22] and so forth.[23]

Not only did the coalitions show vacillations that are usually detrimental to both internal and external credibility, but individual members found their allegiance diffuse across coalitions. The case of Brazil provides an instance of these divided loyalties. As a leader of the Economic Commission for Latin America and the Caribbean (ECLAC)/LAFTA/SELA-type RTAs and coalitions, Brazil was at the forefront of regionalism in various forms. Its allegiance to regional bodies continued even after the dramatic break between the G-10 and the G-20, hence its sponsorship of the 1990 Latin American draft to the GNS. The draft had stressed the importance of preferential treatment for developing countries. But Brazil, nonetheless, had joined India in expressing dissatisfaction with S&D type treatment.[24] Argentina, Colombia, Cuba, Mexico, and Peru had jointly sponsored the proposal on movement of personnel as a mode of supply, along with Egypt, India, and Pakistan – an area in which Brazil had no interest. While Brazil and India attempted to retain their hard-line position in issues such as telecommunications (where both countries laid similar stress on self-sufficiency), Brazil was building alternative friendships with very different and liberalising aims through the Cairns Group. The FIG had Jamaica as its leader and included Mexico and Peru. Irrespective of the many regional arrangements and long histories to bolster it, Latin America was a divided house. The African example yielded even fewer successes at an independent common platform based on the common interests in services that were identified above. The Afro-Asian draft and the common position on telecommunications that were discussed in Chapter 5 provide more the exception than the rule. Inefficiencies of regional groupings as bargaining platforms for developing countries have persisted in recent years. For instance, while several regional organisations participated as observers in the second ministerial conference of the WTO, May 1998, few have had histories of a joint bargaining position in general or particular issues.[25] Their member countries would, often irrespective of the 'common' regional position, present their independent stance that bore little relation to the collective stance. Reasons as to why elaborate regional networks and common interests produced only the occasional joint draft and few consistent, long-lasting coalitions are explored in the next section.

## 7.2  The relationship between regional integration and effective bargaining

To most efforts by developing countries at building regional coalitions and their attendant limitations in the GATT/WTO, there is one common feature. All the regional coalitions with their short lives and *ad hoc* influence have their roots in RTAs of various types.[26] This section finds a causal link behind this 'coincidence'. The first sub-section finds that multiple RTAs have provided the base for bargaining coalitions of developing countries in the GATT. This multiplicity has diffused loyalty through cross-cutting aims and memberships. But the multiplicity of coalitions and the diffusion of loyalties are more the symptom than the malady itself. The very fact that countries have sought so may divergent regional alliances is an indication that no one RTA has successfully provided a reliable springboard for joint bargaining in the GATT/WTO. Section 7.2.2 searches for an explanation to the paradox of established institutions of regional integration and their failure to translate into effective bargaining coalitions in multilateral trade.

### 7.2.1   Bargaining coalitions, RTAs and a conflict of loyalties: the Latin American example

While attempts at regional coalitions and derivative bargaining coalitions have not been limited to any one continent, there are two reasons for the focus on Latin America here. First, attempts by Latin America to present a joint front in multi-lateral negotiations date back to the first wave of regionalism. The tenacity of these attempts and the number of regional organisations on which they draw have also been especially high. The weak GATT presence of Latin American coalitions requires some explaining against this background. In other words, Latin America presents a particularly difficult case. If the Latin American case can be explained, failures of less tenacious/less well-institutionalised attempts of similar regional/sub-regional coalitions will also become more explicable. Second, the region continues to be regarded as an extremely promising base for bargaining coalitions, in spite of a history of limitations. By identifying the problems in the previous wave and the ongoing one, it is possible to ascertain the justifiability of the optimism and explore alternative pathways along which it may be redirected.

Most Latin American initiatives at joint bargaining in multilateral forums have been based in regional integration projects. The strongest ideological version of the Latin American bargaining purpose came with the United Nations' Economic Commission for Latin America and the Caribbean (ECLAC), which was established in 1949. Subsequent regional efforts were based on the founda-tions provided by the ECLAC. Regional integration was seen as a way of secur-ing access to larger markets for industry, and thereby allowing economies of scale to facilitate industrialisation. The ECLAC position resulted in several joint posi-tions that were adopted by the Latin Americans in different international forums. For instance, Brazil and Chile lobbied together at Havana for the Latin American right to grant each other preferential concessions as well as special concessions for developing countries. A few ECLAC prescriptions were institutionalised with the formation of the LAFTA in 1960.[27]

Successes of the LAFTA, in terms of a regional trade arrangement and bar-gaining spin-offs, proved limited. The LAFTA's trade liberalisation programme did not cover more than 10 per cent of the total tariff schedule. Tariff reductions for more competitive goods could not be negotiated. The share of negotiated trade in intra-regional trade decreased continuously after 1966, and Latin America's participation in world exports fell.[28] Already, the flawed base of RTAs among developing countries was becoming evident. The flaws were especially marked in a region where the desire to boost regional trade preceded similar attempts else-where and where regionalism had a base in a history of political independence, mutual trade, and comparatively greater industrialisation on which to draw. The failures of the LAFTA in spite of these conducive conditions can be explained in terms of classic arguments of intra- versus inter-industry, international payments, and fluctuating margins of preference deriving from an absence of common external tariff for the LAFTA.[29] The next sub-section examines why regional arrangements in Latin America were unable to overcome these difficulties.

Obvious failures of LAFTA did not dampen the fervour for regionalism. Two alternative pathways were taken up. First, in 1969, the Andean pact was created, with more ambitious plans of deeper integration at the sub-regional level.[30] The Pact introduced a faster trade liberalisation programme, agreed to harmonise social and economic policies and facilitate a joint strengthening of the industrialisation process. Second, in 1980, the LAFTA was replaced by the Latin American Integration Association (LAIA), with fewer ambitions than its predecessor. The aim of creating a free trade zone was replaced by the more pragmatic procedure of advancing towards a zone of regional preferences and fostering trade, economic complementarity, and activities that contributed to market expansion.

The split in the LAFTA process into the LAIA and the Andean Pact set a precedent for overlapping loyalties, which would increase manifold as a result of proliferating regional institutionalisation in Latin America in the 1980s. Some of these organisations had a specific issue focus, such as the Latin American Energy Organisation (Organización Latinoamericano de Energía, OLADE) formed in 1973, the River Plate Basin treaty and sub-regional cooperation in the Amazon region. The accession of the Andean Pact countries to the Amazon Co-operation Treaty created the first institutional instance of 'double affiliation' to sub-regional cooperation. Political collaboration was attempted with the Contadora Group, which sought a peaceful solution to the Central American conflict. The Cartagena group embodied the attempted debtors' cartel. Each of these regional alternatives allowed a particular joint international stance to the participating countries, which conflicted with the common platform adopted by other members.

The SELA was created in 1975, partly as a response to the potential and actual conflict between the various Latin American regional institutions. The system was a regional organisation to facilitate coordination between the multiple regional arrangements in Latin America. It also sought to include countries within the region that did not belong to any regional scheme. Greater coordination was to be achieved through the pursuit of two aims: first, by reinforcing economic cooperation, and second, by presenting a united Latin American front in the North–South dialogue of the 1970s. The SELA continued to represent the hardline position of the Informal Group in the GATT until late into the mid-1980s. Yet, from the beginning, the joint position of the SELA conflicted with joint positions at the sub-regional level. The emergence of the G-10 and the Café au Lait finally destroyed any façade of unity preserved by the SELA in the GATT.

The advent of the second wave of regionalism further exacerbated the conflict of loyalties. Most RTAs of the second wave accorded much importance to a liberalisation of intra-regional trade in services. Two approaches to services liberalisation at the regional level have been noted.[31] The first approach is a negative list approach, similar to the NAFTA, that is trade in services is to be free of restraint for all sectors unless specified otherwise. The second approach is a positive list approach similar to the GATS. Neither approach, however, has generated stability of coalition partners for bargaining in multilateral negotiations. Despite the proliferation of RTAs that include a liberalisation of services, and then bargain on the strength of common tariffs and a larger market, joint bargaining positions have been remarkably small.

Among the leading regional agreements of the second wave, the Southern Cone Common Market (Mercado Común del Sur, MERCOSUR) is prominent. The agreement has its origins in the integration process between Argentina and Brazil, and was established in 1991 to include Argentina, Brazil, Paraguay, and Uruguay. The attempt to use it as a common platform over the services issue has been founded in the MERCOSUR's services liberalisation process. The MER-COSUR calls for the mobility of all factors of production; negotiations on labour and capital mobility are ongoing. A protocol on services with a positive list approach was signed in December 1997. MERCOSUR members have committed to achieving complete liberalisation of all traded services within a ten-year period. The MERCOSUR was seen as a promising base for a new coalition in the WTO. But at least until the run-up to the Seattle Ministerial, the record of the proposals by the MERCOSUR as a bargaining group was minimal. The MERCOSUR left a very poor trail (through written records in the form of joint proposals or anecdotes related by officials or diplomats in interviews) of working even as a 'chat group' in Geneva. Some marginal improvements were made in the build-up to Doha (discussed in Chapter 8), but even now, the promise of the MERCOSUR remains, at best, latent rather than active.

Several explanations may be advanced to explain why the MERCOSUR has not provided a springboard for bargaining in the WTO. One such explanation lies in the diversion of diplomatic efforts of the MERCOSUR to negotiations on the Free Trade Area of the Americas (FTAA). The exact reason as to why the MERCOSUR may have chosen to invest its joint bargaining potential in the FTAA rather than the WTO would form the subject of an independent study in itself. In this context, however, it is important to note that the MERCOSUR has not emerged as a base for joint bargaining in multilateral forums. Other regional alignments also detract loyalties of members away from the MERCOSUR. Chile, while an associate MERCOSUR member, has been blunt in revealing its preference for the FTAA. In this, and in its hope of bandwagoning with the NAFTA, Chile is only one among several Latin American participants. In accordance with these aspirations, Chile has struck bilateral accords with Mexico and with members of the MERCOSUR. The Chile–Mexico bilateral agreement signed in 1991 encompasses harmonisation of investment regulations, an accord on double taxation to encourage joint ventures and the liberalisation of transport between the two countries. The two have adopted an open-skies and open-seas policy to further their services liberalisation.

Further balancing against the potential threat of a Brazil–Argentina accord is the Group of Three (G-3). The G-3 was launched in 1990 seeking greater integration between Mexico, Colombia, and Venezuela. Formalised into the Treaty on Free Trade Between the Republic of Colombia, the Republic of Venezuela, and the United Mexican States, it is a sub-region of considerable proportions. While MERCOSUR accounts for 45 per cent of Latin America's population, almost half the region's GDP, and 1.2 per cent of world trade, the G-3 encompasses a further third of the region's inhabitants, 40 per cent of Latin American output and some 1.5 per cent of global commerce.[32] The negative-list approach to services renders it far-reaching in scope. It remains to be seen whether the G-3 will be utilised by its members to seek closer cooperation with NAFTA or to build a common front with the Andean Pact or MERCOSUR to produce a Southern-hemisphere alliance to balance NAFTA's market power internationally.

Older regional agreements, despite their limitations, have been expanded to include services. For instance, the Andean member countries, after having transformed the Andean Group into the Andean Community in June 1997 through the Trujillo Protocol, adopted a general Framework of Rules and Principles for the Liberalisation of Trade in Services (Decision 439, which came into effect on 11 June 1998).[33]

Cross-cutting loyalties are not only a product of the various regional agreements at the sector level, described in the previous paragraphs. Rather, development of commitment to the international position resulting from any of these regional accords is further deterred by sub-regional arrangements. These include air and land transport agreements between members of the Andean Community and between countries of Central America, the treaty on telecommunications between Nicaragua, El Salvador, Guatemala, and Honduras, and treaties between MERCOSUR members and Bolivia and Chile on air services. Thirty-four such agreements have been identified at the sub-regional level. Most of these involve a statement of intention for cooperation between signatories but do not contain any binding commitments.[34]

As a result of the presence of diverse schemes of regional integration, several contradictory positions involving the Latin American countries have resulted. The attempt by the SELA to reconcile these contradictions has not worked. Common SELA-led positions have been changing and inconsistent, countered and matched by diverging interests at the sub-sector and sector level to detract commitment further to the joint stance.[35] Usually, these shifting positions are related to the proliferating RTAs in Latin America.

### 7.2.2   *Explaining the conflict of loyalties: limitations of RTAs*

A simple explanation underlies the network of cross-cutting loyalties and vacillating positions adopted by regional coalitions, in Latin America, as well as outside it in other developing country regions. In most instances, regional bargaining has been based on RTAs and other levels of regional integration. However, fundamental structural features unique to the developing world have imposed huge constraints on processes of regional integration. By rooting themselves in integrative processes, regional bargaining coalitions import the same limitations and further distort and exacerbate them to the disadvantage of any attempts at collective bargaining. The problems of regional integration in the developing world are discussed briefly, before examining their implications for bargaining coalitions. It is found that the structural deterrents to the successes of the first wave of regionalism are just as operative in the second, and their influence extends to both goods and services.

The most important reason as to why regional integration arrangements have had only limited success among developing countries can be found in pre-existing trade relations. In the case of developed market economies, regional institutionalisation represented coordination attempts at refining and regulating economic processes and interchanges that were already established by the evolution of free market forces. In regions of developing countries, however, geographical proximity did not imply more trade. Africa and South Asia, for instance, export 95 per cent of their goods outside the region. Similarly, roughly 55 per cent of most Latin American exports (excluding Mexico) go outside the Western hemisphere. In Africa and Latin America, only five of the many regional groupings pass the test of a share of intra-regional exports in total exports above 4 per cent. Regionalism in the developed world provides a striking contrast, where all the groupings qualify for an inclusion.[36] Even if it were argued that greater regional coordination would generate economic interaction among countries to make regionalism work, the historical and material basis for such neo-liberal processes was absent. One still surviving legacy of colonialism is that North–South trade linkages have predominated in the developing world. Apart from historical reasons and consumer preferences, similarity in resource endowments, skills, and comparative advantage contributed to limited trade within the South.[37] In such conditions of scarce economic interaction within the region, regional integration attempts at their best had little impact. More often, they proved trade diversionary.

The nature of trade among developing countries explains why they were unable to overcome their debilitating colonial legacies to create thriving regional markets. For regional integration to be launched and sustained successfully, there must be a demand for each country's goods by the partner country. For developed countries, such a complementarity of demand is greatest when countries are similar, that is at high levels of income, differentiated products are in greater demand. This demand forms the basis of intra-industry trade, where 'each country is both an exporter and importer of the same broad range of products'.[38] Such trade in manufactures necessitates a partial specialisation and exchange of goods within, rather than between, industries and 'is both the cause and consequence of the 'structural convergence' of developed countries.[39] Regional integration among such advanced economies is a *de jure* institutionalisation of well-entrenched, de facto trade patterns. Intra-industry trade (as contrasted with trade based on traditional comparative advantage theory) implies that exchange between countries does not result in substitution of domestic by foreign production. Trade in BMW and Renault cars is based on advantages other than purely costs; preferences for either company are likely to be based on product differentiation rather than a simple substitution of the expensive product by the cheaper one. Regional exchange is therefore less prone to acrimonious competition based on competitive price-undercutting among partners.

In contrast, the trade of LDCs is concentrated in raw materials, semi-manufactures, agriculture, and so forth, which provides little opportunity for product differentiation. Particularly in the case of primary commodities and standardised products of traditional industries like steel and textiles, lack of product differentiation means that competition is mainly price-based. The result is that free trade within an RTA leads to expansion of the industry in one country at the cost of con-traction elsewhere. While in intra-industry trade trade facilitates an increase in output and may grow faster than production, there are no such links in the case of inter-industry trade. In the absence of intra-industry trade, production exceeds trade, resulting in trade diversion from regionalism, surplus capacity, and trade conflicts.

The similarity of comparative advantage and production profile, and inter-industry trade, would suggest an obvious alternative. The problems of inter-industry trade are evident in mutually competitive developing economies, but what if the economies are complementary to each other? In other words, the alternative line of argument could be that regionalism thrives if it involves developing economies at different levels of development. But integration among countries at different levels of development generates even harder problems. Industries in the less advanced member countries migrate to their more advanced counterparts. Sub-Saharan Africa provides an example of such difficulties with regional trade arrangements. In 1990, for instance, Cameroon came to account for 90 per cent of intra-UDEAC (Union des Etats d'Afrique Centrale) exports, but only 4 per cent of imports. Some attempts were made to deal with the problem of distribution of gains. The Communauté des Etats de l'Afrique de l'Ouest (CEAO) and UDEAC provided different preferential duties to suit the 'protection needs' of the less developed partners. Duties on products originating in the least advanced members were low, while duties on entering these countries were high. Members of the Andean Pact divided industries among themselves. To facilitate this division, differential tariff cuts were imposed, with the biggest cuts on products of the member that had been assigned their production.[40] These elaborate schemes had minimal positive effects and often resulted in trade diversions and market distortions. Adverse regional conditions in turn rendered policy coordination with regional partners even more difficult. Several authors have argued that it was distortions such as these that doomed the first phase of regionalism to failure.

The most effective way of dealing with the costs of integrating complementary economies at different levels of development is through a well-established compensatory mechanism. But such compensatory mechanisms are difficult to institutionalise, as they involve an integration that goes well beyond Free Trade Agreements (FTA) and Customs Unions (CUs) and enters into an EU-like phase. It is true that compensation was crucial for the enlargement of the EC. The European regional integration, however, was a product of a very unique set of conditions (the experience of the Second World War and the development of the Cold War, American support, geopolitical concerns about a resurgent Germany, and the Soviet threat next door), which would be difficult to emulate in any other region or time. Alternatively, developing countries at very different levels of development could pursue economic integration with developed country members of the region, provided the regional hegemon were willing to bear the costs of compensation.

The role of regional hegemons in facilitating or deterring regional integration takes us into the geo-strategic component of regionalism. Hegemony can exercise an influence on regional integration in two ways. First, within the region, an actual or potential hegemon may be present, such as India, Egypt, Argentina/Brazil. Neighbours of these potential hegemons, however, are often reluctant to take advantage of the possibility of free-riding. In part, this reluctance may be attributed to a point raised in Chapter 2, that is developing countries are particularly jealous guardians of their newly acquired sovereignty. Additionally, most regions of developing countries are afflicted by problems of fluid boundaries and territorial disputes. Such antagonisms make the smaller countries of the region even more cautious in allowing any hegemonic status to a dominant regional power. Potential regional hegemony often translates into a 'Big Brother' syndrome, evident, for example, in the case of India and the limitations of South Asian Association for Regional Co-operation (SAARC). Hence, a hegemon may be necessary to bear the economic costs of compensation, but regional cooperation with the hegemon will be rejected for fears of domination. The Mexican participation in the NAFTA presents an interesting contrast with the hypothesis offered here. It may be explained in terms of power differentials as well as direction of trade flows. The facts that the US is not merely the regional hegemon but (arguably) the world hegemon and that Mexico is dependent on the US market for its exports create a somewhat exceptional geopolitical situation. Second, a dominant power may be present externally. Note, however, that such a condition differs from hegemony. The presence of such an external power and fear of its expansionary intentions (geopolitical or economic) may have an effect opposite to that of the first type. Regions or sub-regions may seek to balance against this external power, even if it involves the artificial exclusion of the power that may form a part of the region. The creation of the ASEAN, with geopolitical balancing against China, and economic balancing against South Korea and Japan, presents one example. The integration of smaller powers against an external threat, however, is dependent on the geopolitical conditions of the region (e.g. the fact that all the members of the SAARC have borders with India and very limited trade among each other, has rendered balancing against the regional power purely hypothetical) and the threat perception. The latter factor determines whether the smaller powers will bandwagon (NAFTA), balance (ASEAN), or simply be unable to achieve regional policy coordination (SAARC, Latin America to a large extent until Argentina and Brazil were able to resolve some of their differences). Depending on the strength of the individual economies as well as historical experience, diverse pulls in the direction of and away from the hegemon may also be exercised. Brazil, in keeping with its traditional role as leader of the Third World, for instance, sees a balancing role for the MERCOSUR. Other members of the MERCOSUR such as Argentina, and aspirants to MERCOSUR membership like Chile, see Brazil as the threat and hope eventually to integrate fully into the FTAA. From these varying considerations, it is difficult to devise a formula for developing countries wishing to achieve regional integration. Developing countries have hence concentrated on the economic content of regional integration, in the hope that it will be relatively more open to negotiation than the geopolitical concerns have proved to be.

The renewed faith in the economics of regionalism is founded in the new regionalism, which is no longer based on traditional doctrines of self-sufficiency and import-substituted industrialisation. It is argued that as a result, the new regionalism will prove less trade diversionary. However, the old problems of intra-industry trade and the competitive character of developing economies remain, and difficulties of institutionalising compensatory mechanisms persist. There is, hence, scarce reason to believe that the new regionalism will not founder for the same causes as its predecessor. But there is another notable feature of the second wave: its attempt to incorporate services within its agenda. The extent to which this second feature might allow regionalism a more successful record among developing countries than the first is explored below.

The importance of the services sector was recognised in the old variants of regionalism, and hence former regional efforts included projects of joint construction of roads, facilitation of transportation and communication, and so forth. But the effort to promote 'trade in services' within the region, as well as through the region for export purposes, is qualitatively new. The basis for such regional alignments was described in Section 7.1. That few of the efforts at regional liberalisation in services have yielded fruit at the level of joint bargaining in the GATT/WTO requires explanation.

While interests of developing countries in services may be grouped according to regional proximity, a regional/sub-regional integration of services has dubious utility. 'From an economic point of view, sub-regional liberalisation of services may make little sense, if the members of an integration grouping are all developing economies at roughly the same level of development, and all net service importers for services (with the exception of tourism). In such situations, these countries would benefit the most from an opening of their service market on a wider basis, in order to attract needed foreign direct investment from the most efficient services suppliers (most often based in developed economies). Also, the trade-offs needed for a real liberalisation to take place in the services area are less obvious at the sub-regional level among more similar economies than at a broader level among more diversified economies.'[41]

Accepting that most theories of goods are applicable to the services sector, developing countries continue to suffer from the problems of inter-industry rather than intra-industry trade, which deters regional integration in services.[42] The problem is in fact especially potent in the services sector, where geographical relocation and displacement of critical services sub-sector heighten intra-regional antagonism. The expansion of Indian telecommunications services into Pakistan, under a hypothetical SAARC liberalisation, would not be welcomed by Pakistan, irrespective of efficiency arguments and returns through export of labour services into India. While this is a hypothetical and extreme case, it gives us an important insight into the intra-regional trade in services. Developing countries in services face not only the usual problems of distribution of gains as a result of inter-sector/inter-industry trade but also additional problems that derive from the sensitive and strategic character of some services. The critical infrastructural role of services in national economies makes the countries even more resistant to its displacement intra-regional. The economic resistance to a displacement of critical services production with imports from neighbours is further reinforced by the geopolitical suspicions that pervade regions of developing countries. Promotion of services trade within the region through regional trade arrangements is likely then to heighten antagonism and render the development of a common bargaining platform even more difficult.

Efforts at regional integration in services are often launched on pre-existing institutions of regional integration or ones which employ a similar liberalisation in other sectors. Even if it were found that the services sector is less susceptible to the problems of intra-industry versus inter-industry trade described earlier in this section, the regional antagonisms resulting from the goods sectors would be carried over into services. If the assumption of the applicability of the argument to the services sector is correct, these initial antagonisms would be multiplied by extension into the services sector.

Regional integration schemes of developing countries have a rather dubious record. Given that most bargaining coalitions attempted along regional lines by developing countries draw on the institutional base of these integration efforts, they inherit the same flaws. Regional integration, however, is not the only platform for constructing a coalition that exploits common regional interests. The alternative route is explored below.

## 7.3 An alternative route to regional coalitions: the ASEAN example

To all the empirical and theoretical difficulties with regional coalitions that have been discussed in the previous sections, the ASEAN presents a notable exception. The ASEAN Geneva Committee (AGC) was formed in 1973 to coordinate the position of members in the GATT. The ASEAN Geneva Committee meets formally at least twice a year, and holds informal weekly meetings at the ambassador level in the WTO. *Ad hoc* coordination meetings with respect to particular issues are also conducted. Members divide up assignments for coordinating WTO issues among themselves. One or two countries are assigned to deal with each issue for a minimum duration of one year. Responsibility for coordinating work on the General Council is rotated every six months.[43] Particularly since the 1980s with the pre-negotiation phase of the Uruguay Round, the ASEAN has presented a coordinated stance in multilateral trade negotiations.[44] The ASEAN coalition also maintained its membership and agenda with an explicit dissociation from other coalition alternatives. The minimal scope for divided loyalties can be found in various statements, such as 'In the area of services and other "new" issues, it is not in the interest of Thailand to support the Brazilian or Indian stand. Both Brazil and India are big countries, while Thailand is small and it will not pay Thailand to be seen as a bad boy of the world community.'[45] This section examines the roots of the ASEAN as the most successful bargaining coalition among developing countries with a regional basis. It finds that the ability of the ASEAN to sustain itself as a bargaining bloc that is seriously taken by its own members, and by the powers with which it negotiates,[46] lies in the nature of its arrangement and the structure of its member economies. The previous two sections demonstrated how attempts at integration among developing countries exacerbate regional antagonisms due to the absence of supportive conditions of intra-industry trade or a complementarity of production patterns. In contrast, the ASEAN had few pretensions to regional integration – economic or otherwise – and herein lay its greatest strengths. The fact that the some of the fastest growing economies of the world formed a part of the ASEAN region only enhanced its bargaining leverage.

At least in terms of its lacklustre performance as a scheme in economic integration, the ASEAN resembles other regional initiatives in the developing world. Despite well-entrenched norms and practices of regional cooperation that go back to the establishment of the ASEAN in 1967, economic integration within the region has been limited. The ASEAN preferential trading arrangements have liberalised trade within ASEAN of thousands of 'non-sensitive' items.[47] Grandiose industrial projects have also achieved limited successes. Intra-ASEAN trade has traditionally been remarkably small. Except for the advancement of the Singapore economy to near-developed-country production patterns, there is little reason to believe that the ASEAN has overcome problems of intra-industry trade that afflict other developing country regions. The similarity of the ASEAN with other regional arrangements among developing countries is borne out in the limited intra-ASEAN trade illustrated in Table 7.1. The relative trade shares of individual ASEAN members, within the region and outside it are illustrated in Table 7.2.

ASEAN economies have been heavily dependent on the markets of developed countries for export. The USA and Japan accounted for 40 per cent of ASEAN's total trade in 1987; contrast this with the 16.7 per cent that was intra-ASEAN. The limited intra-ASEAN trade is particularly striking, when considered in the context of the long-standing preferential trading agreement. One reason attributed to this low level of trade within the region is the fact that most of the ASEAN economies produce more or less the same commodities in the primary as well as secondary sectors (Singapore, particularly in recent years, being the principal exception). This makes them more competitive than complementary.[48] This competition extends to most of the traditional sectors of the economies of member countries, which, until very recently, were at similar levels of development. 'Increased competition and price undercutting problems have emerged between the ASEAN trio.'[49]

*Table 7.1* ASEAN trade

| Export destination | Share 1990 (%) | Annual growth 1985–1990 (%) |
| --- | --- | --- |
| Intra-ASEAN | 17.7 | 14.8 |
| East Asia | 34.4 | 17.7 |
| EC | 14.8 | 23.4 |
| NAFTA | 18.2 | 16.7 |
| Other | 15.0 | 15.5 |
| Total | 100.0 | 17.3 |

Source: Stephenson (1994), p. 443.

Table 7.2 ASEAN: intra-regional and extra-regional trade patterns, 1987

| Country | Partner | Imports (US$ million) | % | Exports (US$ million) | %[a] | Total trade (US$ million) | % |
|---|---|---|---|---|---|---|---|
| Brunei | World | 1,296.9 | 100.0 | 1,796.2 | 100.0 | 3,093.1 | 100 |
| | USA | 101.8 | 7.8 | 15.0 | 0.8 | 116.8 | 3.8 |
| | Japan | 45.1 | 3.5 | 1,084.4 | 60.4 | 1,129.5 | 36.5 |
| | ASEAN | 495.2 | 38.2 (4.0) | 390.3 | 21.7 (2.8)[b] | 885.5 | 28.6 (3.3) |
| Indonesia | World | 10,234 | 100.0 | 16,546 | 100.0 | 26,782 | 100.0 |
| | USA | 966 | 9.4 | 3,335 | 20.2 | 4,301 | 16.1 |
| | Japan | 3,423 | 33.4 | 7,242 | 43.8 | 10,665 | 39.8 |
| | ASEAN | 704 | 6.9 (5.7) | 1,296 | 7.8 (9.2) | 2,000 | 7.5 (7.6) |
| Malaysia | World | 12,701 | 100.0 | 17,934 | 100.0 | 30,635 | 100.0 |
| | USA | 2,376 | 18.7 | 2,972 | 16.6 | 5,348 | 17.5 |
| | Japan | 2,750 | 21.7 | 3,504 | 19.5 | 6,254 | 20.4 |
| | ASEAN | 2,642 | 20.8 (21.4) | 4,337 | 24.1 (30.7) | 6,979 | 22.8 (26.4) |
| Philippines | World | 6,936.8 | 100.0 | 5,696.0 | 100.0 | 12,632.8 | 100 |
| | USA | 1,539.4 | 22.2 | 2,060.4 | 36.2 | 3,599.8 | 28.5 |
| | Japan | 1,148.5 | 16.6 | 980.4 | 17.2 | 2,128.9 | 16.9 |
| | ASEAN | 659.7 | 9.5 (5.3) | 505.4 | 8.9 (3.6) | 1,165.1 | 9.3 (4.4) |
| Singapore | World | 32,498 | 100.0 | 28,596 | 100.0 | 61,094 | 100.0 |
| | USA | 4,778 | 14.7 | 7,000 | 24.5 | 11,778 | 19.3 |
| | Japan | 6,662 | 20.5 | 2,597 | 9.1 | 9,259 | 15.1 |
| | ASEAN[c] | 5,826 | 17.9 (47.1) | 6,043 | 21.1 (42.8) | 11,869 | 19.2 (44.8) |
| Thailand | World | 13,002.6 | 100.0 | 11,301.5 | 100.0 | 24,304.1 | 100.0 |
| | USA | 1,619.7 | 12.5 | 2,119.5 | 18.8 | 3,739.2 | 15.4 |
| | Japan | 3,376.3 | 26.0 | 1,666.0 | 14.7 | 5,042.3 | 20.7 |
| | ASEAN | 2,029.5 | 15.6 (16.4) | 1,540.2 | 13.6 (10.9) | 3,569.7 | 14.7 (13.5) |
| ASEAN | World | 76,669.3 | 100.0 | 81,871.7 | 100.0 | 158,541.1 | 100.0 |
| | USA | 11,380.9 | 14.8 | 17,501.9 | 21.4 | 28,882.8 | 18.2 |
| | Japan | 17,404.9 | 22.7 | 17,073.8 | 20.9 | 34,478.7 | 21.7 |
| | ASEAN | 12,356.4 | 16.1 | 14,111.9 | 17.2 | 26,486.3 | 16.7 |

Source: Tyabji (1990), pp. 48–49.

Notes
a Percentages are computed from corresponding world figures.
b Percentage in parentheses are computed from total ASEAN trade and reflect intra-ASEAN trade.
c Singapore data exclude trade with Indonesia.

The lack of complementarity in the traditional sectors of the ASEAN economies is accompanied by an inter-industry (or inter-subsectoral) pattern of services trade, which further diminishes the possibility of intra-regional trade. Evolving development hierarchies in the ASEAN (Singapore, Malaysia–Thailand–Indonesia, Philippines, Vietnam, and oil-exporting Brunei forming an independent category in itself) have produced minor but sufficiently rankling differences to produce differential priorities without allowing the complementarities of intra-industry trade. Labour services provide one example of such differing priorities. Malaysia, Indonesia, Thailand, and the Philippines share an advantage in the export of labour services. In this, their interests are in direct conflict with Singapore, which is already highly dependent on the import of skilled and unskilled labour and is keen to reduce this dependence, for political and cultural, as well as economic reasons. Irrespective of the competitiveness of Singapore's telecommunications or professional services and resulting complementarities, the lesser developed ASEAN members will be resistant to the replacement of their domestic services sectors by regional imports.

There are other deterrents to intra-regional trade. Priorities accorded to the services sector and sub-sectors differ, resulting in differing levels of openness and trade-offs that countries are willing to engage in.[50] Among all the ASEAN economies, Singapore has the most developed interest in freeing trade in services. Singapore's position conforms in this area with the typical Northern position. Services contribute to over 60 per cent of Singapore's GDP, and a liberalisation of this highly diversified sector is likely to yield significant gains for it. The interests of Indonesia, Malaysia, and the Philippines differ significantly, with their substantial deficits in the services account. Banking, insurance, transportation, and telecommunication represent the most important segments of the highly protected services industries in these countries.[51]

In terms of competitiveness of exports, low level of regional trade, even lower level of intra-industry trade, and differing priorities on services, the ASEAN is a region similar to most other regions of developing countries that encounter difficulties in comprehensive regional integration and a joint bargaining position resulting therefrom. These difficulties are even more manifest in the services sector, where national interests and priorities differ. In spite of these problems, the ASEAN was able to sustain its joint position in the GATT, since the pre-launch phase of the Uruguay Round as it began to strike independent ground from the Informal Group. In the realm of services, the common platform was even more firmly cemented. The survival of the ASEAN when other initiatives, within the region and outside it, have had a long history of failure, can be best explained by the fact that the ASEAN began as an arrangement with very limited aims. It bypassed the route of regional integration and built a bargaining coalition on the strength of common interests in similar sectors that had rendered a traditional RTA unsuccessful.

The ASEAN incorporated its inter-industry trade and differing priorities in services and its sub-sectors into a common bargaining position through logrolling. Note, however, that this logrolling differed from the kind that had sustained and eventually destroyed the Informal Group/G-10. First, the number of members of the ASEAN was much smaller than the multiple members of the South, and hence comprised a smaller number of bilateral deals. Often, even these bilateral deals could be coordinated in consultation with other ASEAN members. Second, ASEAN logrolling on services was placed within the broader context of competitive economies, that is a great similarity of interests for bargaining internationally such as export orientation and the need for open markets, opening of commodity markets, similar approaches to IPR, and so forth. The ASEAN was able to come up with a well-coordinated stance not only in the pre-launch phase on an inclusion of services but subsequently too in critical sub-sectors. The most marked of these efforts was in telecommunications and financial services. In both instances, the ASEAN pushed for greater liberalisation. In large measure, this ASEAN position has been influenced significantly by Singapore. In part, it is a result of shared smallness of the ASEAN economies, precipitating a common search for markets and cheaper imports when a comparative advantage is absent. Their international involvement has heightened vulnerabilities (e.g. reliance on financial flows), resulting in a classic, Krasnerian search for greater stability in international economic relations. Thailand, for instance, despite its deficits in services, has supported the liberalisation because of its interest in tourism and labour-intensive services, particularly construction services.

The collective bargaining by the ASEAN based on similar interests is accompanied by a geostrategic base to the coalition. China at close quarters, particularly through Vietnam, and the danger of Communist insurgencies gave the Southeast Asian nations reason to join together. The process of dealing with the Southeast Asian security complex gave the ASEAN its agenda of economic growth, cultural development, social progress, and regional peace and security (based on the assumption of 'positive spillover effects or synergistic interactions').[52] Of particular relevance to the argument here is the resemblance of the strategic alliance of the ASEAN with its bargaining component in trade. Just as the bargaining coalition of the ASEAN bypassed the more fractious path of regional integration, its strategic alliance carefully avoided political aspirations and maintained a uniquely 'opaque style'. The foundation charter stipulates that member countries are also 'determined to ensure their stability and security from external interference' as well as to 'promote peace and stability through abiding respect for peace and the rule of law in the relationship among countries of the region'. As a strategic alliance, the ASEAN represents status quo and has evolved a tradition of *musjawarah* and *mufakat*, that is consultation and consensual decision-making, respectively. On both economic and geostrategic fronts, the ASEAN has chosen a second-best of sorts rather than an evolved RTA or military alliance.[53] In this solution lies the key to its internal cohesion and longevity in both arenas.

Debates over whether or not trade follows the flag have focused on the interaction between the economic and geostrategic dimensions of regional integration. It is possible to divide the debate, somewhat simplistically, into Realists, who argue that allies trade among themselves, and Neo-liberals, who use arguments of the Complex Interdependence variety to postulate that trade and other patterns of interdependence necessitate a peaceful security relationship with trade partners.

The Realist approach suggests that regional arrangements will conform to security alliances.[54] Between the two extremes of the argument, the ASEAN offers a midway theoretical and practical alternative. The ASEAN was directed as much at restraining members as curbing geopolitical hegemonies outside. These geostrategic 'allies' did not trade among each other, in recognition of the mutually competitive character of their economies. Instead, they utilised their competitive interests to build a joint bargaining platform, and utilised regional institutions not for greater integration but for the common pursuit of similar interests.

Recent years have seen attempts by the ASEAN to deepen and broaden regional integration. At the fourth ASEAN summit in 1992, member governments decided to liberalise intra-regional trade through the establishment of an ASEAN Free Trade Area (AFTA). In 1994, services were included in the group's liberalising effort. The ASEAN Framework Agreement on Services was signed on 15 December 1995, which initiated negotiations on specific commitments. A Protocol on Services Liberalisation was signed in 1997 as a culmination of the first round of such negotiations. The Protocol is binding on all ASEAN members (increased to ten), with commitments in maritime transport, telecommunications, tourism, and business. Will this attempt at regional integration generate cracks in the cement of competing and common interests that sustained the bargaining coalition? Already, and as Chapter 8 highlights, many countries have begun to point to the new difficulties that the ASEAN encounters in coordinating joint negotiating positions today, even though it continues as a forum for information exchange. Broadening of the coalition may produce further rifts, as broadening implies an inclusion of countries at very different levels of development.[55]

The successes of the first phase of the ASEAN at joint bargaining and limited results in the second phase when regional integration was attempted suggest an alternative route to regional bargaining coalitions that may be adopted by developing countries. The route involves few claims or ambitions of regional integration. Instead, it attempts to use the region as a launch for the same competing interests that members share to develop a common bargaining coalition. Depending on the efficacy of this bargaining coalition and domestic strategies of development, regional integration might be adopted in subsequent years.

## 7.4   Theoretical implications and conclusion

This chapter has demonstrated that there are two routes to forming bargaining coalitions with a regional base. First, and as has been traditionally and unsuccessfully attempted by most developing countries, coalitions can utilise the platform of an RTA. Without intra-industry trade to promote regional commonalties and complementarites, however, regional integration is likely to generate more antagonism than cooperation. Hence, this coalition pathway is limited mainly to developed countries. Proliferating RTAs are both a symbol of the inadequacies of these schemes for developing countries and a further cause of the confused and shifting negotiating positions that have resulted. The second route involves a bypassing of the regional integration route. Instead, countries can harness the similar and mutually competitive interests that have rendered regional integration difficult to build a joint bargaining platform. The only coalition to adopt the latter strategy in the Uruguay Round was the ASEAN. It is somewhat ironic but quite explicable in the light of this analysis that as a regional integration scheme, the ASEAN has been regarded as a failure. But as a trade coalition in the GATT/WTO, particularly since its active participation since the mid-1980s, the ASEAN maintained a visible and effective presence. The successes of the ASEAN when other, more institutionalised, RTAs have failed can be attributed mainly to the alternative strategy that it has adopted at coalition formation. The same version of the strategy was adopted in the geo-strategic component of the group.

The ASEAN example illustrates how bargaining strength need not necessarily derive from integrated market size that allows both demand and supply power. Higher levels of integration and institutionalisation have often not enhanced intra-regional trade and cooperation; in fact, integration has frequently exacerbated intra-regional conflict. Contrast this with the minimal levels of regional integration in the ASEAN, especially in the 1980s, where collective clout has been built through logrolling and aggregation of similar and competing interests. The negotiating platform of the ASEAN by avoiding the tensions that affect regional integration attempts imparted greater intra-coalition coherence to the group. It is also noteworthy that the ASEAN has been successful at logrolling where other coalitions have failed (e.g. the Informal Group and the G-10). This is because, unlike a random and large collection of developing countries, the ASEAN has been constituted by neighbours with similar interests. In other words, the regional base of the ASEAN has been critical to its successes.

While the ASEAN's particular route to regionalism has given it a bargaining efficacy that has evaded other regional groupings, other factors have reinforced its strengths. A high level of involvement in the world economy by members gives the aggregated agenda of the ASEAN an enhanced bargaining clout. The agenda of the ASEAN further enjoys a unique legitimacy. ASEAN members have established reputations of their outward orientation, which contrasted particularly with the ISI type strategies that had been followed in much of the developing world. In its effort to avoid bilateral pressures, the group has further been an avid supporter of multilateralism. As such, the ASEAN coalition has resembled the Cairns in putting forth a positive agenda that conforms to the general liberalising stance of the GATT. It is, however, important to recall that the new regionalism adopts a similar rejection of old ISI strategies and an export orientation. And yet it has not displayed (until recently, with the case of the African Group discussed in Chapter 8) a negotiating presence comparable to the ASEAN. The liberalising agenda of the ASEAN is a secondary factor that has contributed to the legitimacy it enjoys, while the key factor remains its alternative pathway to regionalism.

To what extent can regional bargaining coalitions formed via the second (ASEAN) route be seen as a viable coalition alternative for developing countries? The longevity of the ASEAN coalition, the recognition that it has been accorded in the WTO, and its ability to effectively place the concerns of its members on the negotiating agenda stand in testimony to its successes. The effective persistence of the coalition has further won for its members a stability of allies, something that has been much coveted among developing countries seeking greater bargaining leeway in the GATT. The advantage of adopting the alternative regional route is that it allows members to exploit structural similarities and common interests to build a collective agenda. The importance of having a collective agenda as opposed to a randomly logrolled one or purely an ideational one has already been illustrated in the context of the G-10 and the G-20. Members of coalitions based on regional affinities can further exploit their shared history and culture to lend internal coherence to the coalition as well as identify it against other coalitions. The greatest advantage of adopting a joint regional platform is that it avoids the uncertainty that accompanies issue-based coalitions. Regional coalitions thus allow members a stability of allies that is usually found in bloc-type coalitions but simultaneously also cater to a small number of members without producing the indiscriminate and incompatible logrolling that had sustained the Informal Group.

Regional coalitions, while certainly an important alternative for developing countries, are not unlimited and universal in their application. Their first limitation derives from the flip side of the advantages of the bloc-type approach. As was discussed in Chapter 5, particularly for the small and very specialised economies, an issue-based approach is superior. For countries with diversified interests, incentives to go regional while bargaining are strong. But the possibility of this option also effectively increases the bargaining power of the smaller countries. Should the larger members of the region wish to incorporate smaller members to maintain the cohesive identity of the regional coalition, they would have to win the smaller members away from the issue-based coalitions through sufficiently tempting carrots. The first limitation may hence be seen more as a mixed blessing. The long history of unsuccessful regional arrangements and its concrete manifestations in the form of regional institutions imposes the second constraint. It has been argued here that the successful regional coalition needs to avoid the institutions of regional integration. The burden of history makes coalitions along the alternative way difficult to construct, as regional animosities may already have been triggered owing to unviable regional integration efforts. In most instances, therefore, it would be useful to wipe the slate clean and construct regional bargaining coalitions anew, along the second (ASEAN-type) route. Given the high level of regional institutionalisation that already exists in the developing world, this task is unlikely to be easy.

# 8 Coalitions of the new round

## Developing countries at Seattle and Doha

> I am the daughter of Earth and Water
> And the nursling of the Sky
> I pass through the pores of the ocean and shores
> I change, but I cannot die.
> (Percy B. Shelley, *The Cloud*)

Contrary to the belief that inter-state coalitions would lose their relevance as individual states were increasingly enlightened by the intrinsic logic of economic liberalisation in the WTO, recent years have only seen a rise in the number and institutionalisation of coalitions of developing countries. New coalitions emerged, and old ones were rejuvenated in the early years of the WTO through the first two ministerials at Singapore (1996) and Geneva (1998). Some of these, particularly with reference to services, have already been mentioned. But the activity and importance of coalitions involving developing countries rose to new heights in the run-up to the Seattle and Doha ministerials. This was undoubtedly a product of the expanding reach of the WTO and the recognition by developing countries of the very high stakes involved, as explained in Chapter 2. In addition to this, however, was the fact that a new round was in the offing, both in the mooted attempt at Seattle (1999) and in the successful launch of the Doha Development Agenda at Doha (2001). This chapter presents an analysis of the coalitions in the preparatory process leading up to the launch of the new round associated with the last two ministerials.

Changing institutional context (from GATT to WTO and from Uruguay Round to Doha Development Agenda) notwithstanding, many of the coalitions involving developing countries today are often still permutations of the coalition types of the Uruguay Round that were discussed in Chapters 3–7. Problems of parallel, overlapping, and contradictory loyalties, that is a spaghetti bowl of coalition activity, which had been identified in Chapter 2, persist. There is still very limited rationalisation of what coalitions yield better results, especially as the range of coalitions that developing countries can potentially join increases. Desperate to deal with the juggernaut of expanding WTO regulation, meet their existing obligations, identify their interests in the forthcoming negotiations, and effectively express them, many developing countries often join several coalitions simultaneously (whether they be blocs, alliances, balances, or bandwagons). This further stretches the limited resources available to developing countries. It also undermines the efficacy of the coalitions, which end up having members with extreme differences of interests and commitment. However, not all the lessons of the Uruguay Round coalitions have gone unlearnt, especially in matters of strategy.

In the coalition diplomacy involving developing countries in recent years, three features stand out. First, despite the battering that the concept of blocs received due to the experience of the G-10 and the hope that was placed in the late 1980s in crossover, issue-based alliances, bloc-type diplomacy still flourishes. But the new blocs are often based on new principles and adopt strategies that are quite different from their former incarnations. Second, there is a greater exchange of information and even coordination between coalitions, especially if they fit within the former grouping of the developing world and are not at overt cross-purposes. Hence, even if the costs of proliferating coalitions continue, at least some attempt is now made to promote some communication and understanding between them. Third, partly in keeping with the increasing reach of the WTO and the rising public interest in its workings, coalitions too have begun to change from the secret societies of GATT days to more publicly prominent ones. This prominence manifests itself in public declarations by coalitions of erstwhile low-profile developing countries, meetings at the ministerial level, and at least some interaction with non-state actors. This chapter discusses the recent coalitions of Seattle and Doha. In keeping with the classification used in this book, the first section analyses the persistence and evolution of blocs. The second section examines the rise and influence of issue-based alliances, at both the sector and sub-sector levels. The record of groupings with a regional base is investigated in the third section. The concluding section compares and contrasts the recent coalitions from the coalitions of the Uruguay Round.[1]

## 8.1    The persistence and evolution of blocs

Despite the severe bashing that the concept of blocs received in the mid-1980s (recall the experience of the G-10 and subsequent efforts by diplomats to associate themselves with issue-based diplomacy that would combine developed and developing countries), bloc-type coalitions continue to thrive. But the blocs of today have acquired several new structural features as well as strategies, many of which are a product of the lessons of history. Some of the key blocs that have been active in the run-up to the Seattle and Doha Ministerials are discussed below.

### 8.1.1    *Informal Group of Developing Countries*

As may be recalled from Chapters 3 and 4, the first casualty of the emergence of the Café au Lait diplomacy was the Informal Group of Developing Countries (IGDC). The formal rift within the group in 1985 was unprecedented. Interestingly, however, the group did not die. Today, it once again comprises the entire developing country membership of the WTO. It meets about once a month to identify and exchange views on important issues. But the IGDC of today is very different from the Informal Group of pre-Uruguay Round phase. It is now more a forum for information exchange rather than a strict bargaining coalition attempting to arrive at a common position among members. This is scarcely surprising, given the very large membership of the group and very divergent interests within its membership. Further, some participants in the group point out that, unlike its former version, meetings seldom take place at the ambassadorial level, and usually barely 20–30 country representatives are present. But as a group with usually minimal ambitions of information exchange, it has actually yielded some successes.

Perhaps one of the most visible successes of the group, and a rare one in that it did result in a common position among the vast majority of developing countries, was that of the exclusion of labour standards from the WTO at the Singapore Ministerial. As a result, the Singapore Ministerial Declaration confirms its commitment to the observance of internationally recognised core labour standards but identifies the International Labour Organisation as the 'competent body to set and deal with these standards'. The Declaration also explicitly rejects the use of labour standards for protectionist purposes and emphasises that the comparative advantage of low-wage developing countries 'must in no way be put into question'.[2] Among the other successes of the group that are cited is the issue of the Iranian accession to the WTO that is now back on the agenda of the General Council as a result of the pressures of the IGDC. Finally, the controversy and eventual decision by the General Council that the Appellate Body cannot solicit amicus curiae briefs is also attributed to the active role played by the IGDC in resisting the former Dispute Settlement Understanding (DSU) ruling.[3]

Members agree that, while the IGDC may have allowed very few concrete joint positions and has only limited often procedural rather than substantial successes to its credit, it is often crucial in providing the venue for a preliminary exchange of views and positions. Such a venue is especially important for countries with small and overtaxed delegations in Geneva. But the IGDC may also have an indirect but important role in facilitating coalition-building among smaller groups of countries after the preliminary exchange of views. The fact that many of the new issue-based and cross-issue blocs confined to developing country memberships may not be entirely incidental to the existence of the IGDC. All in all, the IGDC may yet have a relevant role to play as a grouping that facilitates an information exchange process and one that draws on the notion of some shared identity within the developing world as the base that unites it. Further, as the joint position of almost all developing countries on the labour issue has illustrated, the group can provide a common bargaining position in certain types of issues involving blocking. However, in their agenda-setting and negotiating activities, developing countries have begun to rely on smaller blocs. Some of these blocs are discussed below.

### 8.1.2 *Like-Minded Group*

The Like-Minded Group (LMG) began its life as a classic issue-based bloc with an agenda of blocking the new issues (i.e. the Singapore issues of competition policy, government procurement, trade facilitation, and trade and investment). Its origins go back to October 1996, when eight countries (Cuba, Egypt, India, Indonesia, Malaysia, Pakistan, Tanzania, and Uganda) issued a joint statement against the inclusion of the new issues in the WTO. The group achieved some limited success in that the new issues were included only as part of a study program rather than actual negotiations in paragraphs 20–21 of the Singapore Ministerial Declaration.[4] But learning from the lessons of previous blocs and in an attempt to identify the reasons for their limited successes at Singapore, members recognised the importance of having a positive agenda rather than simply a blocking one. Hence, soon after Singapore, the LMG embarked on its agenda of getting the WTO to recognise the problems of implementing the agreements that developing countries faced. Two types of implementation issues were identified: the high costs of implementing the commitments taken on in the Uruguay Round, and the unfulfilled promises and unrealised benefits from the agreements. As a result of the activity of the LMG, the Geneva Ministerial Declaration of May 1998 accorded some attention to these issues in paragraph 9(a)(i).[5] When the preparations began for the possible launch of a new Round in the run-up to the Seattle Ministerial, the LMG became significantly more organised. The original eight were joined by the Dominican Republic, Honduras, and Zimbabwe. The agenda of the group now crystallised into one of resistance to the new round unless the concerns of developing countries with implementation were substantially incorporated. Often in slightly varied combinations of membership, the LMG put forth several drafts in the preparatory process leading up to the Seattle Ministerial.[6] The resistance of the LMG to a new round until the implementation issues were addressed contributed significantly to the impasse at Seattle and also demonstrated that the LMG could not be ignored in future negotiations.

In the preparatory process leading up to the Doha Ministerial, the LMG continued to meet and was expanded to include Sri Lanka. Jamaica joined in as a permanent observer and Kenya also began to attend LMG meetings. While retaining its focus on implementation before any new issues could be considered, the group had evolved further to now propose several issues that they were willing to discuss. It emphasised the removal of tariff peaks and tariff escalations in market access negotiations. It submitted proposals on S&D treatment, technology transfer, and the relationship between trade, finance, and debt. Many members of the group were associated with proposals for a Development Box or Food Security concerns in agriculture. The LMG also expressed concerns with the TRIPS agreement, particularly with respect to public health, and later linked up with several other developing countries including the African Group on this issue. As a result, even while retaining what may be seen as a blocking strategy through its focus on implementation, the LMG also brought several new proposals to the negotiating table.[7] According to various diplomatic accounts, the LMG held out until the eve of the signing of the Doha Declaration, thereby illustrating the cohesion that had bound the group.[8]

The LMG has had several successes to its credit. Especially relevant, particularly in the light of the chequered history of coalitions involving developing countries, is that the LMG has made its presence felt through four ministerials and maintained a cohesive front over a sustained period of time. The group has been very active and has submitted proposals, according to its delegates, to almost every body of the WTO. As one of its founding members put it, 'The LMG has now become a recognised acronym world-wide.'[9]

In terms of outcomes, the successes of the group are perhaps less dramatic, and there have been some visible failures. Perhaps the biggest failure is that the Doha Declaration arguably opens up the four Singapore issues for negotiation, albeit after the fifth ministerial (paragraphs 20, 23, 26, and 27).[10] But the demands of the LMG have not gone entirely unheeded, at least at the procedural level. Hence, for instance, the main Declaration accords considerable attention to implementation-related issues and concerns (paragraph 12), and is accompanied by a separate Decision Implementation-Related Issues and Concerns.[11] Paragraph 13 of the main declaration on agriculture affirms S&D treatment as well as the food security and rural development concerns of developing countries. Paragraph 16 directs attention to market access and specifies the reduction/elimination of tariff peaks, high tariffs, tariff escalations, and NTBs in particular on products of export interest to developing countries. The declaration on TRIPS and public health cannot be attributed solely to the influence of the LMG, but the issue did form a part of the agenda of the group in alliance with other developing country groupings. Similarly, concerns relating to debt and finance, or technology transfer, were not solely the concern of the LMG. But the LMG may have had a part to play in the establishment of working groups on both issue areas under paragraphs 36 and 37. If and how these promises will translate into substance still remains to be seen. But it is to the credit of the LMG that it has not only survived the Doha compromise but also successfully placed some of its main concerns on the Doha Development Agenda.

The survival and successes of the LMG may appear surprising at first glance, especially as the blocking strategies that it has used are reminiscent of the failed agenda and strategies of the G-10. Structurally, it resembles the G-10 in comprising the large and prominent developing countries. Not unlike the G-10 that had resisted the new issues of the Uruguay Round and insisted on Standstill and Rollback, the LMG too resisted the new issues of the Doha Round and insisted on implementation of the existing agreements. The LMG, like the G-10 and the old Informal Group, also engages in considerable logrolling in an attempt to maintain a common position.[12] In spite of these similarities, the LMG has survived, commands considerable legitimacy in diplomatic circles, and has also achieved some gains at Seattle and Doha. How may we explain these differing records and outcomes, despite the obvious similarities between the structures and strategies of the G-10 and the LMG?

Undoubtedly, the differing outcomes are in good measure a product of their times. The WTO can scarcely afford to operate as the GATT-style Rich Man's Club, especially after the failure at Seattle and the fact that the organisation has come under fire from diverse quarters for its democratic deficit. It would be extremely difficult today to simply steamroll developing countries into a ministerial consensus without at least a few olive branches, purely perfunctory though they still may turn out to be. The fact that the agenda of the LMG has found some voice in the Doha Declaration is not entirely surprising. More interesting is the fact that the LMG has managed to retain its internal coherence, in spite of the fact that it brings together countries from very different regions with interests that are bound to diverge across issue areas.

The strength, coherence, and sustainability of the group derive partly from the fact that it has evolved into a bloc that covers several issue areas and thereby allows considerable logrolling. In addition, the LMG has employed several strategies that reinforce its cohesion. First, meetings are convened on a weekly basis, allowing for institutionalisation. Second, the group meets at the expert, ambassador, and even ministerial levels, thereby reinforcing the commitment of members. Third, the fact that meetings are convened by members in an alphabetical order promotes a sense of ownership among members. Fourth, the group enjoys considerable flexibility, and it is particularly here that its contrast with the G-10 is stark. This flexibility is both internal and external. Internally, an effort is made to accommodate the divergent positions of members through logrolling. But individual members are allowed to stand out if they cannot support a particular joint position. The fact that there are many documents proposed by a core of the LMG but with some additional members shows that the coalition is willing to take non-members aboard. External flexibility of the group is illustrated through its willingness to allow observer status to some members. Jamaica and Mauritius enjoy such observer status, and even China has begun to attend some meetings of the group at the expert level. The group is also not shy of external coordination with other coalitions as the initiative on TRIPS and public health by the African Group and the LMG revealed. Fifth, one reason why the group displays such internal and external flexibility is that it lays a great deal of emphasis on research and information-sharing. As a result, its members engage not only with each other and observers, non-member developing countries, but also with non-state actors.[13] Finally, even while pursuing a blocking agenda, the coalition has taken care to have at least some positive proposals for the negotiating table and thereby commands greater legitimacy than the G-10 ever did.

### 8.1.3  *Small and vulnerable economies*

If the LMG has built on a common identity of developing countries that were denied the fruits promised in the Uruguay Round, the Group of Small and Vulnerable Economies has used a different source to cultivate its shared identity. The idea of the group came up around 1996. By the time of the run-up to Seattle, the group had an active presence with its own specific agenda.[14] In the preparatory process leading up to the Doha Ministerial, the membership of the group expanded. It continued to meet and highlight the problems unique to this sub-set of developing economies.[15]

The assumption underlying the formation of the group was that the small economies face problems that are quite different from those affecting other developing countries. One member of the group, for instance, pointed out that even the successful small economies owe their performance to preferential treatment of some sort. If these preferences are removed as per WTO regulation, the success

of these economies would be severely jeopardised. A good example is that of special incentives that certain economies offer foreign investors; were these special
incentives ruled to be illegal by the WTO, capital flight would be the obvious result.
As the reach of the WTO has expanded, the small economies have recognised that
their stakes in the organisation are huge and have begun active participation.[16]

The successes of the group are exemplified by the establishment of a work
program devoted to examining the issues of concern to the small, vulnerable
economies under paragraph 35 of the main Doha Declaration. Paragraph 38 on
technical assistance accords priority to the small, vulnerable, and transition
economies. The fact that the Committee on Trade and Development has had special sessions devoted exclusively to addressing the problems of these economies
after the Doha Ministerial indicates that the influence of the group has generated
some concrete action besides promises in the declaration.

Note that at least on the surface, the group of small economies is not very different from the possible coalitions, discussed in Chapter 5, involving small and
specialised economies. It was argued there that such coalitions of specialised
economies are unlikely to have much external weight and thereby have only minimal bargaining power. A closer inspection of the group of small and vulnerable
economies, however, reveals that it differs from the coalitions of Chapter 5 in two
ways. First, rather than focus on one particular issue and thereby work as an
alliance, the group works across issue areas and reveals a shared identity deriving
from their similar problems that is unique to blocs. As a result, the group has an
additional factor that binds it together, which issue-based alliances of specialised
economies lack. Second, the group recognises its resource limitations and hence
tries to coordinate its research with several other coalitions. For instance, it relies
extensively on the Commonwealth Representative in Geneva, which provides
material resources for its meetings as well as research contributions. Mauritius, a
leading member of the group of small economies, is also an observer in the LMG.
Even though Mauritius cannot adhere to all the positions of the LMG (or vice
versa), it derives considerable benefits from its observer status in the form of a better understanding of the current issues through the exchange of information and
research. Frequent meetings of the group (or some of its members), in tandem
with other groupings and institutions such as the LMG and the Commonwealth,
and also some interactions with NGOs, equip the group to set a positive and well-
researched agenda. As has been highlighted in earlier cases as well (e.g. Café au
Lait), a positive agenda is often key to success in the WTO and can help overcome
the limitations of the small size of member countries.

### *8.1.4  LDCs*

Of the forty-nine countries designated as LDCs, thirty are members of the WTO.[17]
While LDCs had brought some of their problems to the fore in other forums in
the past such as the UNCTAD,[18] they emerged as a coalition in the GATT/WTO
only in the run-up to the Seattle Ministerial. A coordinating workshop of Senior
Advisers to the Ministers of Trade in LDCs was convened under the joint sponsorship of the South African Government, UNCTAD, and the United Nations

Development Programme (UNDP) in Sun City, South Africa from 21 to 25 June 1999. At this meeting, the LDCs discussed their experiences and problems in implementing the Uruguay Round agreements and directly addressed the problems they encountered in participating in the WTO. In the resulting draft communication, 'The Challenge of the Integrating LDCs into the Multilateral Trading System,'[19] several solutions were proposed for implementation at different levels. Among these, a notable conclusion (Part B, paragraph 15) was: 'After considering the forthcoming WTO negotiations themselves, in particular their modalities, scope, duration and structure, the Meeting concluded that the LDCs should have a common negotiating position and as a means of improving their position, coalitions should be built with other developing countries.'[20] If the meeting itself was unprecedented in signalling the proactive engagement of LDCs with the multilateral trading system, the draft communication was equally remarkable. It outlined, in considerable detail (in Part C), the proposals that the LDCs would submit in the run-up to the Third Ministerial Conference. The extensive research that had gone into the framing of these proposals showed that LDCs had come a long way from simply a rhetorical call for distributive justice. The Zanzibar Declaration – the result of the LDC Trade Ministers' Meeting, 22–24 July 2001 – provided a similar indication of the commitment of LDCs to be prepared for Doha and also outlined some of their broad positions. The Zanzibar Declaration institutionalised the LDC Trade Ministers' Meeting to take place at least once every two years to precede the WTO Ministerial Conference. Further, the LDCs continued to meet across institutions and in Geneva to come up with several formal and informal proposals for the trade negotiations.

Especially at Doha, the LDC coalition found allies in the African Group and the ACP (due to both similarity of agenda and considerable overlap of membership). In its very clear stance on the importance of implementation issues, the LDC group further found some initial commonalty with the LMG. Many LDCs were involved in submissions on public health and TRIPS in the preparatory process for the Doha Ministerial. Note, however, that despite evidence and use of common interests and possible alliances with other developing countries, the LDC grouping retained a focus on interests and problems unique to its own members. Examples of these issues include the accession problems of LDCs, problems of representation and research, need for technical assistance and capacity-building, importance of technology transfer, and the need to consider possible negative effects of implementation of the agreements for food-importing countries and LDCs. This focus lent cohesion to the group and also allowed prioritisation in the end game at Doha. For instance, though both the LMG and LDC groupings had initially resisted the Singapore issues, the reaction of the LDC grouping to their inclusion was far milder. Ambassador Mchumo pointed out in an interview that at least these issues will not come up immediately for negotiation, whereas the development issues of concern to the LDCs will be addressed first in sequenced negotiations.[21]

The gains of the LDCs, especially since their proactive involvement with the WTO began, have been noteworthy. Procedurally, the WTO has begun to pay greater attention to technical assistance and for holding special sessions for delegations with no representation in Geneva (most of which are LDCs). The Integrated Framework (IF) for Trade-Related Technical Assistance was designed to meet the needs of the LDCs. The fact that the new round is called the 'Doha Development Agenda', as opposed to the Doha Round, has been claimed by some LDC members to be a product of their insistence on this.[22] The Ministerial Declaration acknowledges the seriousness of the concerns of LDCs in the Zanzibar Declaration and devotes paragraphs 42 and 43 exclusively to them. Admittedly, some of the provisions are mainly those of good intentions rather than bound commitments (e.g. 'We urge development partners to significant increase contributions to the IF Trust Fund…We urge the core agencies, in coordination with development partners, to explore the enhancement of the IF with a view to addressing the supply-side constraints of LDCs and the extension of the model to all LDCs…'). But even the inclusion of some of these statements suggests that the LDCs can no longer be easily ignored in the WTO. And in their promised 'commitments' as on duty-free, quota-free market access to products originating in LDCs, there is at least the promise of results, even though no time frames are given. The needs of LDCs also find attention in other paragraphs, such as on technical cooperation and capacity-building (paragraph 38) and S&D treatment (paragraph 44).

The achievements just cited are laudable in themselves but are all the more so as they accrue to some of the weakest countries in the world. They derive at least partly from simply the hard work and research undertaken by the LDCs before they come to the negotiating table. Additionally, like the group of small and vulnerable economies, the LDCs share some very similar problems and demands. The LDC group has also shown the ability to forge alliances with other coalitions. Finally, and perhaps key to the successes of the group, is the fact that internal coherence allows the group to prioritise its preferences with minimal logrolling and also make trade-offs in areas where its preferences rank lower.

## 8.2 The record of alliances

While the previous section illustrates a surprisingly positive record of blocs, at least some of the alliances that were so warmly anticipated in the late 1980s have not entirely faded away. However, it is noteworthy that many of the sustained alliance-type coalitions in the WTO have been those limited to the developing world, thereby indicating some remnants of bloc identity. The first part of this section examines sector and sub-sector alliances with a developing country membership. The second part investigates the record of the crossover alliances that transcend North–South boundaries.

### 8.2.1 Alliances with a developing-country membership

This sub-section covers three alliances that fall within the category of issue-specific coalitions with a membership of specifically developing countries: Friends of the Development Box, G-24 on Services, and Friends of Geographical Indications.

One of the most sustained and institutionalised alliances involving developing countries is the 'Friends of the Development Box'. The coalition brings together developing countries that emphasise that the concerns of the developing world about agricultural production and trade are quite different from those of the developed countries. This is because agriculture in the developing world is characterised by the following distinguishing characteristics: (1) different from the market-oriented and commercial agriculture practised in developed countries, (2) accounts for a large share of GDP, (3) employs a very large proportion of the labour force, (4) often represents a major source of foreign exchange earnings, (5) supplies the bulk of basic food and provides subsistence and income for rural populations, and (6) directly affects the problems of rural development and poverty alleviation. To enable developing countries to deal with some of these characteristics, the coalition has argued that the Agreement on Agriculture must have a 'Development Box' exclusively for developing countries. In fact, the group explicitly recognises that while agriculture is undoubtedly multifaceted, the Development Box would focus only on the problems of the rural poor of developing countries.[23] The Development Box would have provisions to allow developing countries to further their food security concerns and to take appropriate steps to alleviate rural poverty by helping their small and resource poor farmers to improve their productivity and production.

The roots of the coalition of the Friends of the Development Box go back to at least the preparatory process for Seattle. As part of the problems of implementation, some developing countries, especially those associated with the LMG, raised the demand for S&D treatment for developing countries, LDCs, and net food-importing countries through a 'development box'.[24] The members of the Friends of the Development Box Group today are Cuba, Dominican Republic, El Salvador, Haiti, Honduras, Kenya, Nicaragua, Nigeria, Pakistan, Peru, Senegal, Sri Lanka, Uganda, and Zimbabwe. Of course, not all the proposals always have the joint sponsorship of all the members. Especially when more specific proposals are made, such as market access for agricultural products, non-members may sometimes join in making the proposal.[25] But the group reached a new level of institutionalisation when it met at the ministerial level at the Doha and issued a press statement.[26]

In terms of obtaining an actual commitment to the Development Box, the group had very limited successes in Doha.[27] The Development Box was not included, whereas the non-trade concerns that had been emphasised by many developed countries were. But at least paragraph 13 of the declaration acknowledged that 'special and differential treatment for developing countries shall be an integral part of all elements of the negotiations and shall be embodied in the Schedules of concessions and commitments and as appropriate in the rules and disciplines to be negotiated, so as to be operationally effective and to enable developing countries to effectively take account of their development needs, including food security and rural development'. But in comparison with what the Development Box would have entailed, this commitment is weak. In many ways, the Friends of the Development Box, in terms of both structure and overall negotiating strategy, provides some similarities with the FIG discussed in Chapter 6.

Minimal successes of the Friends of the Development Box so far, notwith-standing, it is to the credit of the coalition that it survives today, even after Doha. It continues to conduct research and present informed proposals on the subject, drawing not only on an exchange of information among themselves but also interaction with other International Organisation (IOs) like the FAO, UNCTAD, and the South Centre as well as NGOs like the Catholic Fund for Overseas Development (CAFOD). The resilience of the group in spite of its limited achievements at Doha suggests that it still has considerable potential. Chapter 9 will suggest strategies that the coalition could adopt to improve outcomes in the future.

The second prominent alliance with a developing country membership is the G-24 on Services. The group arose formally around the issue of Guidelines and Procedures for the Services Negotiations. Under the initiative taken by India late 1998–early 1999, a group of about nine countries met to explore the possibility of cooperation among developing countries on some services issues.[28] The group came to include about twenty-four countries, with a leading role played by Brazil, India, the Philippines, and Thailand. Argentina, Bolivia, Brazil, Colombia, Cuba, Dominican Republic, Ecuador, El Salvador, Honduras, India, Indonesia, Malaysia, Mexico, Nicaragua, Pakistan, Panama, Paraguay, Peru, Philippines, Sri Lanka, Thailand, Uruguay, and Venezuela put forth a joint proposal in November 2000.[29] It emphasised that no services sector or mode of supply would be excluded from the negotiations a priori and that liberalisation would focus on sectors and modes of supply of export interest to developing countries. Credit would be given to members for autonomous liberalisation. On modalities, it stressed that negotiations must be transparent and that Request and Offer would be the principal method of negotiating specific commitments. The draft also proposed flexibility for individual developing country members in terms of open-ing fewer sectors, liberalising fewer types of transactions, and only progressively extending market access in line with their development situation. This draft came to command the support of the African Group as well as the Caribbean, thereby garnering the informal support of almost seventy-four countries.[30] The Guidelines and Procedures for the Negotiations that were eventually adopted on 28 March 2001 were based largely on the G-24 draft. The Doha Declaration reaffirmed the Guidelines as the basis for continuing the negotiations in paragraph 15.

Having achieved considerable success as a coalition on the Guidelines, the G-24 continues to meet today. The G-24 is an exemplar of how a coalition of develop-ing countries can indeed contribute significantly to the rule-making process. The coalition was distinctive in its very specific focus on Negotiating Guidelines in Services, and the fact that it comprised a group of many large developing coun-tries that shared a common interest on the issue. As such, it combined both exter-nal weight and internal coherence. The document itself was detailed rather than rhetorical and also came to enjoy considerable legitimacy by the support that it received from other developing-country coalitions.

Another example of a developing country alliance (with a sub-sector focus) at the Seattle and Doha Ministerials is the Friends of Geographical Indications.

At Seattle, this group of countries proposed that the protection of geographical indications be extended to additional products besides wines and spirits.[31] By the time the preparatory process for Doha began, the group included Sri Lanka as a leading member, besides India, Pakistan, Egypt, Kenya, Jamaica, Honduras, Dominican Republic, and Thailand. Some of the transition economies adopted similar positions, such as Bulgaria, Czech Republic, Romania, Slovakia, and Slovenia. The issue proved to be a highly divisive one, and swords were drawn between the Friends of Geographical Indications (which enjoyed the backing of the EU) and those who were sceptical of, or opposed to, the new negotiations on Geographical Indications (e.g. Paraguay, Colombia, Guatemala, Ecuador, South Korea, with the support of the US, Australia, and Canada). This translated into a division between the Old World and the New World that could have worked well in favour of the Friends of Geographical Indications, which sought an expansion of TRIPS regulation. Chapter 6 on the Cairns Group in particular illustrated how external divisions can work to the advantage of coalitions of small countries, and the Friends of Geographical Indications seemed to be operating in a similar situation. But the agenda of the coalition was not included in the Doha Declaration.

What resulted in the Doha Declaration was a compromise. Paragraph 18 of the Declaration noted, 'We note that issues related to the extension of the protection of geographical indications provided for in Article 23 to products other than wines and spirits will be addressed in the Council for TRIPS pursuant to paragraph 12 of this Declaration.'

One reason for the relatively minimal achievements for the Friends of Geographical Indications can be located in the external situation. The US, in this instance, did not play a role active enough to compare with the role that it played when the Cairns Group was formed. The rift, though extant, did not compare with the EU–US showdown in the late 1980s on agriculture. Second, the group focused on a small sub-sector issue at a time when there were several other key issues in which stakes of even the members of the group were higher. Third, the support that it received outside the coalition was large, but not large enough to establish the legitimacy of its agenda (in contrast to the seventy-four countries that eventually came to support the G-24 agenda), hence the weak compromise that resulted at Doha; whether the group will be able to establish its cause any further still remains to be seen.

### 8.2.2   *Crossover alliances*

While crossover alliances combining developed and developing countries do not overwhelm the coalition scene, they have not faded away either. The most lasting of these has been the Cairns Group. Another case covered here is the Friends of Fish Group.

The case study of the Cairns Group and its role in the Uruguay Round was presented in Chapter 6. The group has continued to be active in the negotiations that began under the Built In Agenda in 2000, with its membership now equalling eighteen members.[32] But it went a step further than its position in the Uruguay Round by demanding that the agricultural negotiations 'must result in real and substantial increases in market access for all agricultural and agrifood products covered by the Agriculture Agreement... A comprehensive, practical and ambitious approach is required in order to provide tangible improvements in access and fulfil the objective of substantial progressive reductions in agricultural support and protection, resulting in correcting and preventing distortions in world agricultural markets'.[33]

The far-reaching agenda of the Cairns Group is illustrated most clearly in the Group's Communiqué at its 22nd Ministerial Meeting, 3–5 September 2001, Punta del Este. The ministers emphasised that the Doha Conference must provide: (1) 'A clear commitment to end discrimination against agriculture and fully integrate into the WTO', (2) a clear commitment to achieve fundamental reform of agricultural trade through eliminating export subsidies, substantial improvement in market access, and the elimination of trade- and production-distorting forms of support, (3) a reaffirmation that non-trade aspects of the agreement will be taken into account in non-trade distorting ways, (4) a confirmation that enhanced and concrete S&D treatment provisions to developing countries should be an integral part of the outcome of the negotiations, and (5) a clear understanding of the time tables and benchmarks for concluding the agriculture negotiations.[34] This negotiating position of the Cairns Group was consistent with its proposals to the Committee on Agriculture in the WTO. For instance, in a proposal on export competition, the group proposed that 'WTO Members agree to the elimination and prohibition of all forms of export subsidies for all agricultural products.'[35] Similarly, in the proposal on domestic support, the group stated that 'The Cairns Group seeks major reductions in domestic support leading to the elimination of all forms of trade and production-distorting support.'[36] But in adopting such a far-reaching agenda, the Cairns Group had altered its character from a mediating coalition between the US and the EU into one that was threatening a blocking strategy.

One reason why it was difficult for the Cairns Group to sustain the mediating strategy that it had employed in the past was the different external context. The US, it is true, continued to support its agenda. A member of the US delegation is quoted as saying 'The United States and the Cairns Group are long standing allies for agricultural trade reform.'[37] The fact that US Trade Representative Robert Zoellick participated in the ministerial meetings of the Cairns Group in 2001 and 2002 would suggest that the camaraderie between the US and the Cairns Group has continued from the Uruguay Round to the present day. But given that the US also provides massive subsidies on agriculture, it is not entirely surprising that by September 2001 it was veering towards the EU position. The EU had come to the position that while they could agree to language going beyond Article 20 of the Agreement on Agriculture, they would not go much further (on issues such as including agriculture within the same rules as goods or the complete elimination of export subsidies). The US is reputed to have pressured the Cairns Group supporters to not push for a wider mandate, or even the type of language that was on the table before Seattle.[38]

Even within the Cairns Group, differences were simmering. The official position of the group had been of expressing great caution about the Development Box.[39] But, as mentioned earlier, some of the developing country members of the group had unofficially indicated support for the Development Box proposals. The Canadian decision to have a separate proposal on market access further suggested differences. The group thus operated with internal weaknesses, an external context where it was difficult to find the niche for mediation that it had utilised successfully in the past, and effectively limited support from the US.

Working within these constraints, the results of the Doha Declaration for the Cairns were unspectacular. Export subsidies were included in paragraph 13 but in the diluted version of 'reductions of, with a view to phasing out' as opposed to elimination. The phrase 'without prejudging the outcome of the negotiations' was also thrown in before the commitments to improvements of market access, reductions of export subsidies, and reductions in trade-distorting domestic support. Further, the same paragraph confirmed that non-trade concerns would be taken into account but without the qualifications that the Cairns Group had sought due to the dangers that non-trade concerns could be used for protectionist purposes.

Another interesting crossover alliance was the 'Friends of Fish' Group. The alliance goes back to the preparatory phase of Seattle, when Australia, Iceland, New Zealand, Norway, Peru, Philippines, and the US put forth a joint proposal to the General Council on the elimination of subsidies that contribute to fisheries overcapacity.[40] The proposal argued that such subsidies seriously distort trade. Further, it pointed out that the industrialised countries are responsible for the bulk of subsidies in fisheries, but with fish-exporting developing countries bearing the greater brunt of these trade distortions. In addition to this proposal, members of the group came up with several individual proposals, laying different emphases on the reasons for the elimination of fisheries subsidies (e.g. environment or trade) but all directed towards the same common end. The group sustained its efforts in the run-up to the Doha Ministerial.

The group recorded a resounding success at Doha. Until Doha, discussions on fisheries were conducted in the Committee on Trade and Environment, which had (until Doha) a very limited mandate and was not a negotiating forum in any way. The Doha Declaration, in paragraph 28, stipulated that in the context of negotiations on WTO rules, 'participants shall also aim to clarify and improve WTO disciplines on fisheries subsidies, taking into account the importance of this sector to developing countries'. Fisheries subsidies are also mentioned in paragraph 31.

The achievements of the Friends of Fish alliance are laudable, especially given the strong opposition that they encountered from the EU, Japan, and South Korea. But they are also unsurprising, as the alliance enjoyed several advantages of structure and strategy. It combined countries that were brought together by a single common interest. It also enjoyed external weight as its members had high stakes in the issue and even had the US aboard. Additionally, the group used 'value-creating' strategies.[41] For instance, it pointed out in its joint statement to the General Council that removal of fisheries subsidies would create a win–win situation in the areas of trade, environment, and sustainable development. Its emphasis on the benefits that the proposal would have for developing countries and sustainable development won it several other supporters from the outside as well as greater legitimacy. Finally, as pointed out in earlier chapters, a positive agenda, especially one with a content of trade liberalisation, is likely to gain greater legitimacy in the GATT/WTO context. The Friends of Fish had just such an agenda that appealed not only to members but also to several non-members, and also fitted into the institutional context.

## 8.3   Region-based coalitions

As may be recalled, Chapter 7 had argued that bargaining coalitions with a regional basis have much potential for developing countries, especially if they involve weak levels of actual or attempted integration. Seattle and Doha certainly saw several such coalitions emerge and flourish. Note, however, that not all such coalitions were successful or even sustainable. The Paradisus Group provides us with one example of a group that arose in the intervening years of Seattle and Doha but fizzled out even before the Doha Ministerial. This was the group of Central American countries (Dominican Republic, El Salvador, Guatemala, Honduras, Nicaragua, and Panama), which maintained mainly an issue-based focus on decision-making procedures, internal transparency and exchange of information,[42] but several other coalitions with a broader agenda than the Paradisus showed greater promise and success. Without reiterating the theoretical argument that was made in Chapter 7, this section presents a brief account of three region-based coalitions that arose fully in response to the preparation demanded by the possible new round, namely the African Group, the ACP, and the CARICOM. It also touches upon the role of the MERCOSUR and the ASEAN today.

One of the most striking examples of a sustained and active coalition with a regional base is the African Group. The African Group has its roots in the Organisation of African Unity/African Economic Community (OAU/AEC). The treaty establishing the AEC was signed in 1991 by members of the OAU and came into force on 12 May 1994. Trade ministers of the OAU/AEC, meeting at Harare in April 1998, took a key decision on the need for coordination in the formulation of a positive agenda for the forthcoming WTO negotiations and also the negotiations for a successor agreement for the fourth Lomé successor agreement.[43] The African Group even established a Permanent Delegation of the OAU in Geneva. As a result of frequent meetings and extensive research, African participation in the preparatory process leading up to Seattle was unprecedented. Proposals on behalf of the group were submitted across issue areas including technical assistance, competition policy, customs valuation, TRIPS, and so forth.[44] Greater access of the African countries to the Green Room in the preparatory process was one of the important results of this active, informed, and united engagement.

That the African Group had become a force to reckon with became fully evident towards the end of the Seattle Ministerial. After finding themselves repeatedly excluded from Green Room meetings and private consultations at the Seattle Ministerial, the African countries issued a joint statement on their marginalisation from the decision-making processes. The statement, made on 2 December 1999, the third day of the Seattle Ministerial, noted that 'There is no transparency in the proceedings and African countries are being marginalised and generally excluded on issues of vital importance to our peoples and their future. We are particularly concerned over the stated intentions to produce a ministerial text at any cost including the cost of procedures designed to secure participation and consensus.... We will not be able to join the consensus required to meet the objectives of the Ministerial conference.' To use a counterfactual, even if consensus had been reached among the other countries at Seattle, it is highly possible that the African Group would have actually blocked it on account of their marginalisation from the proceedings.

With respect to the Doha preparatory process, the African Group stated its objectives clearly in the Abuja Ministerial Declaration. The declaration was a product of the Fourth Ordinary Session of the OAU/AEC Ministers of Trade Committee on Trade, Customs and Immigration, held in Abuja from 22 to 23 September 2001. The declaration laid great emphasis on issues of implementation, in keeping with the positions that the OAU/AEC had already taken at the Second Ordinary Session of the OAU/AEC Ministers of Trade in Algiers in 1999 and subsequently at the Third Session in Cairo in 2000. It confirmed its support for the Development Agenda adopted by the LDCs at the Zanzibar Ministerial and subsequent LDC meetings. On the Singapore issues, it stated that 'African countries are not "demandeurs" of multilateral agreements on the issues concerned.... African countries recall that various working groups have been established to commence studies on the respective subjects are yet to complete their work. This study process should continue.' The Declaration was presented as a communication to the WTO.[45]

One of the most visible successes of the African Group was the Declaration on TRIPS and Public Health. In a de facto alliance with several other countries (many of them members of the LMG), the African Group had taken a leading role in presenting proposals on the issue.[46] The African Group also stood out in its ability to pursue a blocking strategy, which was operational until the last day of the Doha Ministerial. The eventual agreement of the group with the Doha Declaration was a result of the carrot that they were finally offered in the form of the waiver for the ACP/EU Partnership Agreement.

The waiver issue is related to the trade preferences that the ACP countries receive from the EU under the Cotonou Agreement (successor of the Lomé Conventions). As such preferences violate the MFN rule, a waiver of the WTO is necessary. The granting of the waiver may have led the African Group to back down from its fairly hard-line position (e.g. on implementation), but it was certainly a testimony to the success of the ACP group of countries. The ACP countries acted as a group but had also worked in liaison with other coalitions like the African Group. Hence, the Abuja Declaration included granting of the waiver request in its negotiating objectives. Given the links between the two groups, there was quite a significant overlap in the agenda of the ACP with that of the African Group. The ACP Declaration on the Fourth Ministerial Conference at Brussels on

5–6 November 2001, which was also submitted to the WTO, took a common position across issues.[47] For instance, the group stressed the importance of implementation issues, S&D treatment, technical assistance, technology transfer, debt and finance, concerns of LDCs, and opposition to the inclusion of the Singapore issues or labour and environment. But the main concern of the ACP and also the source of its group identity was the importance of obtaining the waiver. The group would be willing to make trade-offs to achieve this central aim, and indeed did so.

The existence of the ACP group and the high premium that it attached on obtaining the waiver in effect proved conducive to reaching agreement. It meant that the ACP had the EU, its long-standing partner in the preferential agreement, on its side. While it is true that there had been considerable opposition to the renewal of the waiver, particularly by the Latin American countries, it was easier for the EU to buy off this opposition (e.g. through the assurance of consultations with the Latin Americans on the new tariff structure that is due to emerge after 2006) than to grant the demands of the African Group. But while beneficial to the progress of the negotiations, the ACP agenda also effectively diluted the agenda of the African Group and further divided the support of the ACP for the positions other developing country coalitions like the LMG.

The third region-based coalition, again quite new to the WTO like the African Group, is the CARICOM. CARICOM governments established the Caribbean Regional Negotiating Machinery (CRNM) on 1 April 1997. The primary mandate of the CRNM is to develop and execute the region's trade negotiations across the three main theatres of the FTAA, Cotonou Agreement, and WTO.

The CARICOM's agenda in the WTO, since it began operating as a coalition, has had four components. First, it has pushed for S&D treatment such that it would accommodate continuing preferential treatment of the region's traditional exports with transitional protection for certain imports. Second, it has sought greater market access for non-traditional exports of goods and services that may be important regional exports in the medium/long term. Third, it has general trade liberalisation to ensure multilateral sources for needed imports. Fourth, it has pursued the goal of S&D treatment for small economies. In order to achieve these goals, CARICOM member states have supported the implementation agenda pursued by other developing countries.[48]

Relative to the African Group and the ACP, the CARICOM is perhaps less vocal as an independent coalition in the WTO, even though it has made some joint proposals to the WTO.[49] One of its own representatives attributes some of the difficulties to the fact that many CARICOM member states do not have offices in Geneva. Further, 'CARICOM as a unit has no locus standi in the WTO negotiations. In the WTO negotiations officials of the Regional Negotiating Machinery have to be included in the delegations of Member States.'[50] But these constraints notwithstanding, the CARICOM has successfully dovetailed its agenda with the agenda of other coalitions such as the ACP, the LMG, and the Group of Small and Vulnerable Economies. It also relies considerably on the assistance provided by the Commonwealth Office in Geneva as well as other sources such as the WTO Secretariat.

Two other coalitions that were discussed in Chapter 7 are worth mentioning here. The MERCOSUR has made several proposals,[51] but interviews with diplomats reveal that, so far, the promise of MERCOSUR as a bargaining coalition has fallen short in the WTO. The bargaining position of the MERCOSUR has in fact worsened in recent years due to the financial crises in the region,[52] and it is almost to be expected that members are unlikely to rely on it as a bargaining base. The ASEAN has played a more prominent role, especially in the controversy that surrounded the choice of the new Director General. The eventual compromise that resulted (a three-year, non-renewable term for Mike Moore to be followed by a three-year, non-renewable term for Supachai Panitchpakdi) may be attributed at least partially to the ASEAN's active role. It also submitted several proposals in the preparatory process leading up to Seattle. But most diplomats agree that, despite its well-institutionalised negotiating machinery, the ASEAN has increasingly found it difficult to arrive at common negotiating positions. There were fewer proposals in the run-up to the Doha Ministerial, while individual members of the ASEAN showed a greater initiative in other coalitions such as the LMG and the Cairns Group. The main benefits of belonging to the ASEAN now seem to be limited to burden-sharing and research exchange rather than the construction of a joint bargaining platform.

## 8.4   Conclusion

As the participation of developing countries in the WTO has increased, so have their coalition options proliferated. But, as this chapter has indicated, many of the old patterns of coalition-building deriving from the Uruguay Round still survive in the WTO. There is still very limited recognition of which coalition type works best, for whom, and under what circumstances. Consequently, developing countries continue to seek membership of coalitions, coalitions within coalitions, overlapping coalitions, and parallel coalitions.

While the costs of proliferating, overlapping coalitions were highlighted in Chapter 2 and have been illustrated through examples throughout the book, the new coalitions have adopted an important new strategy to minimise some of these costs. Many of these coalitions, especially when they involve mainly developing countries, allow exchanges with members of other coalitions. Hence, for example, even though many members of the LMG have expressed their concerns about coalitions that demand separate concessions for themselves (due to the divisive impact that they have on the developing world and its bargaining power), they still allow observer status to Mauritius, which is a part of several other groupings. This relative openness to members of other coalitions presents a stark contrast with the 'Us versus Them' approaches of coalitions of the Uruguay Round. There may be two reasons for this transformation. First, developing countries have recognised the crucial importance that information and research play in effective participation and are hence willing to engage in information exchanges and discussions with other coalitions. Second, there still remains an element of a broad developing world bloc identity that members acknowledge even when speaking in terms of functional, issue-based coalitions.

The fact that bloc-style diplomacy continues may appear somewhat surprising if one recalls the euphoria that had surrounded the issue-based coalition diplomacy in the late 1980s to early 1990s. But continue it does, both in the form of the coalitions that were discussed in Section 8.1 and in some coordinated, inter-coalition activity. The Declaration on TRIPS and Public Health provides a good example of such coordination between members of the LMG, the African Group, and several other developing countries. Many developing country delegates point out that, even though their positions may differ across issue areas, there are still important systemic issues that allow them to maintain some bonds of loyalty.

Both the blocs and alliances of today have learnt something from the experience of the Uruguay Round. Coalitions of all forms today lay considerable emphasis on founding their proposals in research rather than the rhetoric of distributive justice. The positive agenda emphasised by many coalitions is one example. But recent coalitions actually go further than those of the Uruguay Round in seeking information and technical expertise. Many, especially the LDCs, rely greatly on the technical assistance of the Secretariat. Recognising, however, the limitations of the WTO's technical assistance, they also use other sources, such as the Commonwealth, the UNCTAD, the UNDP, regional UN initiatives, and the South Centre. Additionally, through broader forums such as the IGDC, they draw on each other's expertise and share information across (some) coalitions. Finally, particularly after Seattle, developing countries have begun to turn to certain NGOs like the Oxford Committee for Famine Relief (Oxfam), Catholic Fund for Overseas Development (CAFOD), and the Third World Network for their support. Support of these NGOs takes the form of original research that coalitions and countries can cite to back up their proposals. But it also allows their agenda greater public dissemination and legitimacy.

All the innovations in strategy and approach are largely a product of the Uruguay Round experience and stand to the immense credit of developing countries. But inter-coalition information exchange and coordination cannot overcome the costs that these multiple loyalties involve. Having sub-coalitions and linked coalitions can also make it easier for the outside party to buy off the smaller group and dismantle the bigger coalition. Having a positive agenda can assist in gaining legitimacy within the WTO and also facilitate give and take, but it cannot guard against internal collapse of the coalition or limited external bargaining power. Chapter 9 draws out the implications of the experience of developing countries with coalition formation to date to suggest how coalition formations and strategies may be better rationalised.

# 9 Conclusion

These promises are fair, the parties sure
And our induction full of prosperous hope.
(William Shakespeare, *Henry IV*,
Part I, Act 3, Scene 1)

The record of coalitions involving developing countries in the GATT/WTO is intriguing and complex. The expensive trials and errors at effective coalition formation lead to a broad theoretical lesson that most scholars and practitioners of international trade diplomacy seem to have neglected, namely that only certain types of coalitions work for corresponding sets of countries (and often only under some specific circumstances). This concluding chapter draws on the case studies conducted in the previous chapters to arrive at a theory of inter-state bargaining coalitions. Directed specifically towards the developing world, the theory explains what kinds of coalitions work, for which groups of developing countries, and why. In reaching towards such a theory, Section 9.1 highlights the conditions that coalitions, irrespective of the type they may be, must fulfil before they can launch into the business of bargaining. With reference to these conditions and taking concrete examples from the book, Section 9.2 develops a classification of coalitions and further offers a blueprint as to which types might work for whom. Section 9.3 provides a list of strategies that can be usefully employed, once the initial conditions are met. The resulting theory is a theory of coalition formation with special respect to developing countries. It identifies the conditions that a coalition must immediately meet to ensure its survival and effectiveness, suggests ways in which states can choose between the various methods of coalition building to their optimal advantage, indicates when states will be better off joining bandwagons or balances, and discusses the utility of different strategies with respect to the phase of the negotiation and the states concerned.

## 9.1 Necessary conditions for effective coalition formation

Chapter 1 explained that it is almost irrelevant to speak of the optimal methods and types of coalition formation unless it is specified what these methods seek to achieve. In the light of the case studies that were conducted subsequently, it is now possible to specify two structural imperatives that any coalition must meet to ensure sustainability and effectiveness. Before coalitions can even begin to consider issues of strategy and adaptation, they must ensure that the coalition enjoys internal coherence and constitutes a substantial external weight. The importance of spelling out these conditions is illustrated by the minimal successes of many of the coalition experiments by developing countries, in spite of the fact that these coalitions have been founded in a learning process that draws on parallel and past lessons. This is because diplomats, while vigilant in borrowing the strategies of the more successful coalitions, have often forgotten that these strategies are directed towards the building of certain types of structures that fulfil the key conditions. Only after these structures are achieved and the coalition has some surety of survival can it get down to the actual business of bargaining and employ relevant strategies to facilitate this. The two conditions are elaborated below.

### 9.1.1   *Internal coherence*

The first general rule of coalition formation that emerges from the comparative case studies is that sustainability of the coalition hinges crucially on a shared, internally consistent agenda. This condition precedes all other considerations: a coalition that lacks internal coherence would find it extremely difficult to reach the stage of exercising its collective influence externally. At one level, this condition seems tautological to the original definition of a coalition, where the pursuit of a 'common end' was taken as fundamental. However, coalitions have been known to found themselves on elaborate processes of logrolling that result in a mutually inconsistent, badly aggregated 'collective' end. Various means can be used to paper over these inconsistencies, such as intra-coalition hierarchies that allow smaller members a free ride and incorporate their demands into the collective agenda. Similarly, a collective ideology can serve as the wickerwork for the basket of individual aspirations that constitute the group. However, these elaborate ways of preserving the coalition engender significant costs.

The costs of maintaining coalitions that lack a coherence of interests among members go beyond those of monitoring a large-n factor as conceptualised by neo-liberal institutionalism or the problem of distribution of gains as conceptualised by theories of collective action and club goods. Rather, if a coalition with a large membership is based on individual aspirations of members, its greatest costs are those of regimented hierarchies and ideology that induce inflexibility of agenda. In other words, the coalition finds that the risks of internal collapse are so great that it becomes unable to respond to the opportunities and constraints provided by the context outside. While leviathan coalitions are more likely to suffer from contradictory aims, even small coalitions can be badly constituted if they bring together a diverse set of countries with divergent interests so that there is no collective agenda to speak of. This also illustrates that it is not enough to speak of the size of the coalition (which is what most formal theories of coalitions concentrate on); rather, the nature of the agenda and interests underlying it are crucial for determining how expensive coalition maintenance will be.

The best example of the dangers of basing a coalition in aggregated and logrolled interests come from the Informal Group and the G-10. As shown in Chapter 3, a combination of multiple deals, intra-group hierarchies, and ideology was useful in plastering over differences when the Informal Group was engaged mainly in proposal-making diplomacy. But these methods proved inadequate when they were employed by the G-10 to deal with the specifics of the services issue in the pre-negotiation phase of the Uruguay Round. Note that though the Informal Group continues to meet even today (as elaborated in Chapter 8), it is no longer much of a bargaining coalition that seeks to submit joint positions and wield collective weight. Rather, it usually acts as little more than a forum for information exchange, occasionally coming up with a common position on very general issues but usually not. Institutionalised monthly meetings notwithstanding, these remain poorly attended, and it is not surprising that most countries choose to invest their diplomatic resources elsewhere.

The example of the G-10 is also useful in arbitrating between the three methods of coalition formation that were discussed in Chapter 2. The case reveals that cooperative, non-liberal processes (e.g. logrolling, creation of hierarchies) and even the introduction of ideas and identity can prove inadequate in cementing bargaining coalitions. The G-20/Café au Lait provides an obvious, if somewhat simplistic, method of avoiding the problems of contradictory interests within the coalition, that is to build issue-based coalitions that bring together collective material interests. The coalition also reveals the importance that process can have, once the initial structural needs of members are met. For instance, the G-20 laid great emphasis on an exchange of information and extensive research and was careful in presenting itself as a mediating, negotiating coalition that sought to overcome the impasse on services. One of the distinctive features of the G-20 was that it used neo-liberal cooperative processes, not as the primary basis to coalition formation but to reinforce intra-group coherence and a commonalty of interests that the Jaramillo process had already identified.

It is not surprising that subsequent coalitions sought to emulate the narrower, issue-based focus of the G-20 with great enthusiasm. However, as we have seen in Chapter 5, most of these coalitions had a very rapid turnover. Irrespective of whether they brought together mainly developing countries or combined developed and developing countries with a shared sector or sub-sector focus, most of these coalitions revealed short lives and minimal impact. Just as interesting are issue-specific coalitions that would have allowed greatly concentrated diplomatic effort and well-coordinated interests, but which did not emerge. For instance, there was no attempt by the small developing island economies to form a coalition on tourism services, in spite of the fact that these were tourism-dominated economies. Instead, these economies became enthusiastic members of the Café au Lait and, subsequently, Friends of Services Group. The short lives of focused coalitions that did emerge, and the many potential coalitions along these lines that did not, suggest that internal coherence may be a necessary condition for effective coalition formation, but it is not a sufficient one.

## 9.1.2   *External weight*

The second condition necessary for the construction of successful negotiating coalitions is critical weight that the coalition exercises externally. Well-coordinated positions of a small group of weak states with a shared and focused commitment to a particular issue at sector or sub-sector level do not overcome the bargaining weaknesses that afflict them as marginal producers or demanders in international markets. One remedy hence translates into large numbers: not maximum possible numbers[1] but numbers large enough to allow the coalition this collective weight. Many diverse variables determine the weight that a particular member will occupy in the coalition and also the collective weight that the coalition itself will wield. Examples of these variables include political presence, regional prestige, alternative alliances at bilateral and multilateral levels, the importance of the sub-sector/sector to the individual economy, and the latter's place in the world economy.[2] While this concept of sufficient collective weight is not easy to quantify, it is often inversely proportional to the risk of defection involved. Risk of defection, in turn, is closely related to the extent to which the issues of interest to the members are incorporated into the agenda of the coalition. For instance, it is not surprising that Argentina defected from the traditional G-10 hard line to the mediatory diplomacy of the Cairns Group, because of the high priority that it attached to the inclusion of agriculture in the new round. The exact point at which the coalition occupies sufficient collective weight (as opposed to the minimum necessary weight) depends on the country and coalition type involved.

Notwithstanding difficulties in quantification, even an imprecise formulation of the second condition reveals why small economies find that assets of focused and well-matched interests and concentrated diplomatic effort are not enough. The limited impact of many small, sub-sector coalitions was explained in these terms in Chapter 5. The Cairns Group case study in Chapter 6 provides the contrasting example of an issue-focused coalition whose longevity and strength derived, in some measure, from its collective weight. The group accounted for 26 per cent of global trade in agriculture. The combined shares of the Cairns Group were also substantially large across commodities (see Table 6.2). In addition, members of the Cairns Group independently had high stakes in the agricultural negotiations owing to the importance of agriculture in their export and GDP figures. As such, the coalition was successful in avoiding the problem of divided loyalties and fulfilling the condition of internal coherence.[3] A similar case can be made for the Friends of Fish Group.

Sometimes, very large numbers of countries with similar interests can also translate into critical external weight, even if the group does not collectively contribute to substantial world trade shares. For example, 30 of the 49 listed LDCs are members of the WTO, while 13 more have observer status. When such a large group of countries constitutes a coalition and makes joint demands, it cannot be easily ignored without seriously jeopardising the legitimacy of WTO decision-making procedures. Similarly, the OAU/AEC comprises 52 members, of which 38 are members of the WTO, while six have observer status.

A joint front by almost one-third of the WTO's membership presents a force to be reckoned with, even if the combined trade shares of such economies are small.

As a result, it should be borne in mind that what constitutes external weight is often context-dependent. For instance, immediately after Seattle when the WTO faced a barrage of criticism for its 'democratic deficit' and precipitated several proposals for institutional reform, countries that had traditionally been excluded from the Green Room now came to command much greater attention. The group of small and vulnerable economies (irrespective of its internal coherence), for instance, may not have been able to play the role that it did in the Doha preparatory process in the days of the GATT or even pre-Seattle WTO.

Both the conditions just identified – internal coherence and even external weight – ensure survival of the coalition and at least some visible effect, although there may be several other facilitating external conditions. Examples include a rift within the Quad that smaller countries can utilise to their advantage and present themselves as a bridge-building, mediating coalition. The Cairns Group utilised the rift within the US–EC with great skill. Similarly, having the support of one of the Quad members, and particularly major players like the EC or the US, can greatly enhance the prominence of the group. For instance, the support of the US was crucial to the achievements of the Cairns Group. The fact that the FIG did not seek similar support from the EC or exploit the US–EC rift considerably reduced its chances of achieving a prominence comparable with the Cairns. Some coalitions, which include developing countries, have been able to carve out a niche in research, especially when the issue under consideration is a new one on which an epistemic consensus is lacking. The Café au Lait and the Cairns Group were pioneers in illustrating how this external condition could be exploited. The Friends of Fish used a similar strategy of having the US on its side and further appealing to the environmental, development, and trade concerns of members and opponents. But favourable external conditions notwithstanding, coalitions have a greater chance of survival and possible influence if the two internal conditions of coherence and collective weight are met. Keeping in mind the two necessary conditions provides us with a guideline for choosing the optimal method of coalition formation. Clearly, only those methods and coalition types work, which, at the very least, fulfil the above two conditions.

## 9.2   Classification and blueprint: what works, when, and for whom?

Subject to the conditions discussed in Section 9.1, only certain kinds of coalitions work for certain country types. This book has studied several coalition attempts of developing countries over trade in services, not all of which have been successful. Some failed because the coalition type and country type were mismatched, while others floundered because the coalition type itself was fatally flawed. In both their successes and failures, these coalitions have left behind a trail of clues as to which coalition type works for whom, such that the necessary structural conditions are met.

In the madness of the coalitions of the mid-1980s that was described in Chapter 2, it is possible to find some analytical method by grouping the various experiments into categories. The flow diagram overleaf groups all the cases that have been presented in this book into four categories. All four draw lessons from the experiences of the G-10 and the G-20 and owe their origins to the cataclysmic events of the pre-negotiation phase of the Uruguay Round. Coalition type I, the issue-based bloc, had its sources in a combination of the positive lessons of the G-10 debacle and the strategies of the G-20. In services, this was represented by a bloc-type coalition that restricted its membership to the greater majority of developing countries as per the Informal Group and the G-10 but simultaneously maintained a focus on services that was founded in research rather than rhetoric. However, the disaggregation of interests of developing countries in the services sector limited the viability of this alignment. Coalition type II, the sub-sector alliance, draws on the limitations of the first and is closer to the Café au Lait in being more issue-focused and bringing together countries irrespective of North–South allegiance. Resulting coalitions focus on a sub-sector and involve small groups of either developed and developing countries or just developing countries. The third coalition type, the crossover alliance, is a direct derivative of the Café au Lait and draws inspiration from the Cairns Group on agriculture. Finally, the type IV alternative utilises regionalism as a springboard for bargaining. The learning process that underlies these coalitions is indicated using the lines in Figure 9.1, with the broken lines representing indirect borrowing.

While all the four types combine strategies of issue-based/sub-sectoral alliances and cross-issue blocs in varying proportions, their emergence and evolution provide a rich commentary on the dynamic process of coalition-building. It is noteworthy that each of the variety of end-products provides a striking contrast from the expectations in the mid-1980s that the way forward lay in issue-based, crossover coalitions which reproduced the strategies of the G-20/Café au Lait. In fact, the comparative studies conducted in this book demonstrate that if the path of traditional bloc diplomacy of the Informal Group is inappropriate for the actual give-and-take that goes beyond the rhetorical diplomacy of former years, the issue-based diplomacy of the Cairns Group has an equal set of limitations. Variations of all these types to suggest the appropriate coalition models for the corresponding sets of countries are discussed below.

As illustrated in Chapter 5, coalition type I, by bringing together the greater bloc of developing countries around one issue area, did not work very well for services as the group soon disaggregated on the basis of sub-sector interests. However, it had been pointed out that the type may prove to be more promising if it could be brought together onto an area that is less prone to disaggregation or if smaller numbers were involved. This preliminary hypothesis was borne out in Chapter 8, for Seattle and Doha have indeed yielded some prominent bloc-type coalitions. These new coalitions are confined to smaller groups of developing countries. Rather than attempt to restrict themselves to a single issue, as was attempted by the services bloc, these blocs evolve common positions in different issue areas. They also differ significantly from the old G-10 bloc-type as they tend to have detailed positive proposals as opposed to simply an agenda of resistance and blocking.

The best example of the new bloc-type coalition is the 14-member LMG. The LMG began as an issue-based bloc with a focus on resistance to the new issues at

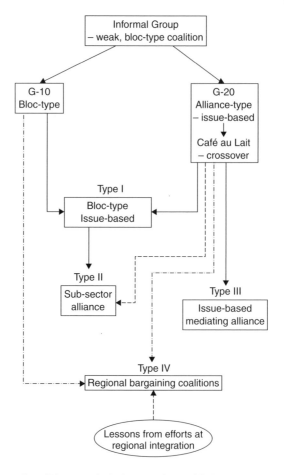

*Figure 9.1* Types of coalitions: analytical categories and linkages.

the Singapore Ministerial but soon evolved its agenda on implementation. At Seattle and Doha, it continued with its emphasis on the need to address implementation issues before any new issues could be addressed. The LDC group is another bloc-type coalition, whose identity and agenda are both situated in the issues that affect the LDCs. The Group of Small and Vulnerable Economies is similarly restricted to a sub-set of developing countries with a focus on the problems deriving from small size.

The advantage of coalition type I is that it binds its members together with the help of a shared identity, which also lends greater longevity to the group. Rather than focusing on any one issue area, the coalition shares an interest across issue areas and is even willing to take on some logrolling. But this logrolling is not indiscriminate and thereby relatively sustainable, as the membership of the group is limited to a sub-set of developing countries sharing common problems or interests. As a result, the group enjoys internal coherence. Certain variants of coalition type I can also enjoy external weight, such as the LMG with its large proportion of trans-regional, large, developing countries. Others may not enjoy collective weight based on collective trade shares, but by appealing to the problems of being small or weak (as opposed to seeking concessions in one area of interest), they can command considerable external presence through legitimacy and coordination. Further, learning from the Café au Lait, most of the new blocs meet frequently and base their proposals on considerable research, as opposed to simply the rhetoric of the old blocs.

Coalition type I presents a useful policy option for the more diversified economies that find it difficult to assign priority to any one sector. The new blocs allow these economies to bring together a range of issues, sometimes by logrolling. When the large diversified developing economies are involved (e.g. in the LMG), the bloc in turn enjoys considerable bargaining power and is able to trade concessions across issue areas that can help in facilitating agreement. Under certain circumstances, they can also work if a similar set of economies is involved, such as the LDCs or the Small and Vulnerable Economies. These economies share similar problems and interests across several issue areas. Having an institutionalised forum to discuss these different issues saves them the transaction costs of finding new allies for each issue and each negotiation. These transaction costs are not insignificant, especially when many of these small economies have small or no delegations in Geneva. But coalition type I also comes with certain associated risks, as explained below.

Blocs, even in their new incarnation and especially when they include the large developing countries, show a tendency to err on the side of blocking than mediating or negotiating. If such a strategy is pursued right up to the endgame, two costs may result. First, such hard line tactics can prevent agreement and thereby may have possible adverse effects at the systemic level. Second, the group itself flounders, as happened fatally in the case of the G-10 at Punta del Este (when most of its members defected) and the LMG at Doha (when, on the last day of the Ministerial, India stood alone opposing consensus). The reason why blocs may adopt inflexible positions is related partly to the fact that as they address a large number of issues according to the different priorities of members, which involves some measure of logrolling. Amending and updating such an agenda continuously can be a time-consuming and expensive process. This problem was classically illustrated by the Informal Group and the G-10 before 1986, and is present (though to a lesser extent because of its different history and structure) in the LMG. At least a significant part of this problem may be overcome through a greater attention to strategy choice and process of negotiation, both within the group and with outside parties. Some of these strategies are discussed in Section 9.3. The other possibility for the large developing countries is to build blocs that include a more similar set of countries. Coalition type IV exemplifies this possibility, as does a variation on type III, both of which are discussed later in this section.

The LDC coalition and the Group of Small and Vulnerable Economies do not suffer from the problem of inflexible positions because they combine countries with some very similar priorities. But both these blocs, because they combine some of the smaller economies, are at least partly dependent on the post-Seattle institutional context. Their gains are less a product of bargaining weight and more a result of their appeal to ethics at a time when the developed countries and the WTO must listen, or at least pretend to. It is also worth bearing in mind that most of the achievements of these coalitions so far have been on areas where other parties proved willing to make concessions, such as technical assistance for LDCs. In areas where these coalitions have acted as coalitions of resistance, on implementation for example, they have had few successes. If the external and institutional environment were to change drastically through a reversal of the WTO to a Rich-Man's Club (admittedly an unlikely event in the foreseeable future), these economies would have to resort to issue-based bandwagoning with stronger economies, that is coalition type II.

Coalition type II, that is the sub-sectoral alliance, bears particular relevance for small economies with high levels of specialisation.[4] As argued in the latter part of Chapter 5, specialisation allows small economies to concentrate their diplomatic effort to the sub-sectoral coalition and avoid contradictory sub-sectoral loyalties. In other words, the first structural condition of internal coherence is fulfilled. However, as specialised economies in the developing world often have only limited bargaining power individually or even jointly, balancing coalitions of such economies have often proved fleeting. In order to ensure that the second condition of sufficient external weight is met, small, specialised economies are best off bandwagoning with the developed countries that share interests in the particular issue area. Two types of developing economies can benefit from such a bandwagoning. First, if the economy has an advanced competitive advantage in the sub-sector, it can gain by allying with other developing and developed country exporters. The East Asian economies with their competitive advantage in infrastructural services, and the Caribbean economies with a highly developed tourism sector, form a part of this category. Second, economies which see no short- to medium-term advantage in the particular sub-sector can also bandwagon with the developed world and the first type of economies. 'Concessions' by these less developed economies can be offered in return for trade-offs in some other key areas. Countries included in this category are those that are dependent principally on commodity exports and generate their greatest deficits through services imports. These small economies have nothing to lose and much to gain by bandwagoning with others that have a core exporting advantage in the sub-sector. Sub-sectoral alliances require little consideration for 'like-mindedness' among members, as the primary method of cementing this coalition relies on a similarity of interests in the relevant sub-sector.

The reason why only a few such coalitions have had a visible efficacy as bargaining groups lies in the fact that they have usually been tried with the larger, more diversified countries. In view of the fact that specialised economies are often the smaller ones, this is not altogether surprising; if the coalition is to have any weight, it would need to include larger economies from either the developed or developing world. However, coalitions with a sub-sectoral focus are the bane of large, diversified, developing economies. From diversified economies emerges an inability to assign priority to any one sub-sector, and crosscutting, conflicting loyalties to contradictory sub-sectoral coalitions result. These conflicting loyalties were described in Chapter 5. The interests of the middle-range developing countries are especially different from those of the very advanced or least developed countries discussed in the preceding paragraph. Bandwagoning with the developed countries is not a preferred option for such middle-range economies as India and Brazil. This is because their markets and levels of development allow them a potential export advantage in services. Hence, these countries can neither compete in the league of their more advanced counterparts, nor easily make concessions in this area like the LDCs. When the more diversified developing countries with a potential advantage in services make common cause with the more specialised economies, sub-sectoral coalitions come tumbling down like a house of cards. Successful sub-sectoral coalitions are usually those that have kept the diversified giants of the developing world out. For the latter, another, more viable alternative is available.

Coalition type III, a direct descendant of the Café au Lait, comprises crossover alliance diplomacy that is epitomised in the Cairns Group. However, as Chapter 6 illustrated, coalitions combining developed and developing countries and at the vanguard of mediation are effective only under exceptional circumstances. Among these, key is a fundamental rift within the Quad and an ability to exploit this rift by the alliance by winning the support of some of the powerful developed countries. The only other coalition that has had such a scenario to operate in and utilised it successfully is the Friends of Fish Group discussed in Chapter 8. But the unfulfilled promise of crossover alliances notwithstanding, a permutation of these in the form of issue-based alliances among the larger developing countries has proved more successful. The G-24 on services epitomised this formation, beginning at first as a coalition among the twenty-four but then developing the support of many other developing countries.

Coalition type IV involves coalitions that utilise regionalism as a base for joint bargaining. The advantage of the regional route is that it can allow members to exploit structural similarities and common interests to build a common agenda while restricting membership to smaller numbers. This similarity of interests ensures that the coalition is internally coherent, while the inclusion of large, diversified economies within the region into the alliance assures the coalition of substantial collective weight. Interestingly, the same similarity of interests impedes intra-regional trade and regional integration, hence the argument, in Chapter 7, that regional bargaining coalitions have been most effective and durable when they have avoided the pathway of regional integration and chosen instead to utilise their similar and competing interests. The ASEAN in the Uruguay Round provided an example of a successful bargaining coalition based on such lines, while recent years have seen some very effective participation by the African Group, the ACP, and the CARICOM to a lesser degree. In addition, regionalism often comes with the paraphernalia of other cementing/coalition-reinforcing factors such as shared ideas, culture, identity, and so forth. These factors facilitate the preservation of coalitions that incline towards the bloc type and strengthen cross-issue collective positions that are important for the more diversified economies. Regional institutional machinery is especially useful for the smaller countries with minimal resources at both capital and Geneva levels. The unprecedented involvement of the African countries in the preparatory processes at Seattle and Doha suggests the far-reaching utility of the regional option.

## 9.3   Strategies

Once a coalition is constructed along the lines suggested in Sections 9.1 and 9.2, certain strategies can be utilised to enhance the legitimacy and effectiveness of the coalition. First, and perhaps most important, is the significance of a sustained process that allows coalition members to meet frequently and further develop and revise their agenda. In fact, the importance of such institutionalisation explains, in good measure, the persistence of bloc diplomacy, even in the face of several setbacks. One key negotiator, for instance, pointed out that for both psychological and practical reasons, the coalition must be an active process with members meeting on a fairly regular basis and sometimes with the assumption that the issues will raise themselves. On the same principle, he further argued that issue-based coalitions, as they arise only to meet a particular interest and do not have a history of process and negotiation behind them, often tend to have shorter lives and lesser impact.[5]

Second, even if the issue-based coalitions of the 1980s do not provide us with model coalitions, they offer us a crucial lesson in strategy. The examples of the G-20/Café au Lait in services and the Cairns Group in agriculture drive home the importance of having a positive agenda as opposed to a purely blocking one.[6] A positive agenda is important in the institutional recognition and support that it wins from the GATT/WTO. Institutionalised coalitions, in turn, are easier to sustain than those that operate like secret societies. But the successes of a positive agenda do not point to the complete rejection of blocking strategies.

Blocking can be effective in two situations. Some influence can be exercised by using blocking strategies in the pre-negotiation phase, if the purpose of blocking is to build in brakes in the bargaining process. For instance, even though it was the G-20 agenda that was eventually adopted as the basis of the Punta del Este declaration, the G-10 had some important achievements to its credit. It catapulted the concerns and doubts of developing countries to unprecedented institutional and public attention. Not only did the G-10 slow down the pre-negotiation phase, but it was also successful in building some 'safeguards' in the GATS that eventually emerged. Blocking strategies have also had notable successes in a second situation, namely in the negotiation phase when a group with a positive agenda uses the occasional blocking tactic. The threat of the six Latin American members of the Cairns Group at the Montreal Mid-Term Review of the Round was effective because the six dissenters had already proven themselves to be enthusiastic members of a bridge-building mediating coalition. The walkout staged by such members was taken more seriously, especially because it differed from the first situation, that is the persistent blocking tactics that the G-10 had adopted.

Third, a research-based agenda formulation is an important coalition asset. This is especially the case in the pre-negotiation phase if new issues are involved. The investigative forum under Jaramillo's leadership stood out dramatically against the almost ideological blocking by the hard-liners and provided a secure and legitimate base for the Café au Lait Group. The effect of research, moreover, is not limited to areas where there is conceptual ambiguity. The Cairns Group, while operating in the traditional area of agriculture, founded its mediating role on the groundwork of research and analysis. Australia's Bureau of Agricultural Economics took the lead in analysing the technical details about the costs of protection as well as publicising this information to substantiate the claims of the Cairns Group.[7] This research component of the activity of the group gave substance and legitimacy to its demands.

Fourth, flexibility of agenda – that is often a product of simple coalition structure – facilitates negotiating manoeuvre, as the examples of the G-20 versus the G-10 demonstrated. A simple coalition that pursues the collective interests of its members has greater negotiating space, in comparison with a complicated coalition that rests precariously on internal logrolling and contradictory interests of the members. This flexibility of agenda also imparts greater legitimacy to the coalition by presenting it in terms of a negotiating coalition rather than a blocking one. If some of the existing blocs are able to incorporate such flexibility into their agenda, even if this may involve reducing numbers or increasing the frequency of group meetings, their effectiveness and legitimacy will both be enhanced.

Fifth, all the coalition experiments of the 1980s have, through both successes and failures, taught developing countries an important lesson in realpolitik. They have illustrated the importance of framing demands in the language of liberalisation rather than protectionism or unilateral concessions. The walkouts by the Latin American members of the Cairns Group acquired a veneer of legitimacy as they were staged in the cause of free trade. Even the LMG, while towing a relatively hard line, presents its agenda in terms of recruiting the gains of liberalisation by addressing implementation issues rather than as a challenge to the liberal orthodoxy.

Sixth, even while the number of coalitions involving developing countries has proliferated, many of these coalitions actually engage with each other in at least information exchange and sometimes even position coordination. This is a very welcome development that has arisen only in recent years and is a response to the recognition that the fragmentations and rifts within the developing world in the 1980s contributed to the adverse bargaining outcomes of the Uruguay Round. Hence, in contrast to the G-10 versus Café au Lait stand-off, we now have the LMG allowing observer status to members who do not share its position, the African Group and the LDCs back each other, and the ACP and the African Group have overlapping and coordinated agendas.

Seventh, coalitions of developing countries are already outward-looking in a way that coalitions of the Uruguay Round seldom were. This trend is only to be encouraged. Hence, coalitions now not only interact more with each other but also engage with NGOs and several other IOs besides the WTO and the UNCTAD to facilitate their information gathering and further legitimise some of their positions.

At least some answers are now clear. Coalitions must, first and foremost, fulfil the two conditions of internal coherence and external weight before they can reach the stage of bargaining. Given the very different sizes and nature of interests of developing countries, countries will need to find the appropriate coalition type, such that the two conditions are met. It has been demonstrated that the potential of bloc diplomacy is still far from over, even though it is accompanied by some risks. Sub-sector coalitions offer a viable option for small, specialised economies. Their greatest advantage lies in that they bring together countries sharing the particular interest and hence easily meet the first condition of internal coherence. But it is important that only economies that share focused interests constitute such coalitions, as opposed to diversified developing economies with some interest in the particular issue but with simultaneous loyalties to other coalitions in other sub-sectors. Bandwagoning ensures that the second condition, collective weight, is also met. Issue-based coalitions working at the sector level have only limited value when they combine developed and developing countries. But they have shown much promise when built with the larger developing countries. Regionalism as a springboard for bargaining might provide one way of bringing together countries with similar interest but also sharing a 'like-mindedness' deriving from shared regional security complexes, cultures, and identities. Having established what kinds of coalitions work best for whom and the causation that underlies these links, certain strategies that coalitions can usefully employ have also been traced.

The availability and use of so many diverse coalition options might lead to the impression that there exists little by way of a developing world identity today. However, even while acknowledging the importance of working in smaller and more relevant coalitions, many developing countries agree that there are still certain systemic concerns that bring them together. It is also the same set of concerns that allows coalitions of developing countries to exchange information with each other and contributes to the greater longevity and effectiveness of issue-based coalitions that are restricted to developing countries. The old North–South diplomacy may be dead, but the media-savvy, outward-looking, research-reliant coalitions of today borrow at least as much from the bloc diplomacy of yester year as they do from the issue-based, shifting coalitions of the 1980s.

# Notes

## Introduction

1 Reasons as to why the GATT proved unconducive to coalition activity by developing countries are analysed in Chapter 2.

## 1 Bargaining together: why and how?

1 Waltz (1979) defines 'internal balancing' as balancing behaviour based on own capabilities rather than on the capabilities of allies, p. 168.
2 Martin (1992), p. 4.
3 Strange (1994) and Baldwin (1979).
4 Schelling (1966), p. 2.
5 Jackson (1990).
6 Ayoob (1995).
7 Buzan (1983), Neuman (1998).
8 Ayoob (1998), p. 43.
9 Clapham (1985).
10 Ibid.
11 Jackson (1990).
12 For conceptualisation of power in terms of will and skill, see Baldwin (1989).
13 Ayoob (1989).
14 Snyder and Diesing, 'The military inferiority of one party may be compensated by its greater interests engaged, thus making the parties equally skilled' (p. 190).
15 This point is drawn from Helleiner (1976).
16 Narlikar (2001).
17 WTO document, WT/L/31, 7 February 1995.
18 Ibid.
19 For example, see Claude (1964).
20 Decision-making procedures of the GATT and the WTO are discussed in Chapter 2.
21 For example, Nehru 'used foreign policy as an instrument to develop and safeguard India's national interests and to develop the self-reliance, self-confidence and pride of the Indian people, even while serving the cause of peace and anti-colonialism. The policy of non-alignment was formulated in order to assert India's will for national independence and to strengthen its independence'. See Chandra (1993), p. 122.
22 Chapter 3 studies the successes and limitations of one manifestation of the South in the GATT context.
23 Neuman (1998).
24 Gamson (1964), p. 86.
25 See Hinkley (1979).

26  Sandler and Tschirhart (1980).
27  Similar to the distinction between club goods and public goods, Olson (1965) draws a distinction between 'exclusive' collective goods and 'inclusive' collective goods. Also see Buchanan (1965).
28  Riker (1962), p. 32.
29  Gamson (1964).
30  Frohlich *et al.* (1971).
31  Browne (1973).
32  Ricupero (1998), p. 15.
33  'A point worth mentioning is the absence of protectionist lobbies in Geneva… Somehow the comings and goings of their country's delegates to and from Geneva seem to have escaped their influence. Perhaps because they deemed the Geneva negotiations to be of little importance, there has on the whole been little evidence of lobbying pressure on negotiators in Geneva… It has been said that this geographical separation of the negotiations from the places of political manoeuvring and lobbying has considerably helped the climate in GATT negotiations and deliberations.' See Curzon (1965), p. 53.
34  McDonald (2000), p. 202.
35  Rogowski (1989).
36  Frieden (1991).
37  Alt *et al.* (1996), p. 692.
38  For an explanation of intra-industry trade, refer to Krugman and Obstfeld (1997), pp. 121–158. On the implications of intra-industry trade for coalition formation at the national level. See Alt *et al.* (1996).
39  Tussie (1987).
40  Walt (1979) quoting Palmerston, p. 33.
41  Grieco (1988).
42  Kenneth Waltz (1979), p. 117. Also, Walt (1987), p. 28.
43  Waltz (1979).
44  Ibid., p. 127.
45  Liska (1968).
46  Schweller (1994), p. 81. Walt (1987) distinguishes between the two strategies as follows: 'Balancing is defined as allying with others against the prevailing threat; bandwagoning refers to alignment with the source of danger', p. 17. Waltz (1979) also uses the terms and credits the usage to Stephen Van Evera.
47  Walt (1987), p. 29.
48  Schweller (1994).
49  Alt *et al.* (1996).
50  Ricupero (1998), citing Ambassador Paul Tran, p. 15.
51  Axelrod (1984). For debates on Cooperation Under Anarchy and other types of neo-liberal institutionalism, see also World Politics (1985).
52  Axelrod and Keohane (1985), p. 226.
53  However, it has been argued elsewhere that if one is concerned with the problem of relative gains, besides cheating, large numbers may improve cooperation as 'relative losses can be attenuated in a multilateral setting'. See Milner (1992) for a summary of the numbers debate.
54  Mearsheimer (1995).
55  Axelrod (1984), p. 176.
56  Risse-Kappen (1995). In contrast to a reflectivist interpretation, Walt (1997) offers a Realist one – '…a sense of common identity may slow the process of dissolution for quite some time, but the level of solidarity and mutual identification is not strong enough to prevent states from pursuing an independent course once their interests begin to conflict', p. 170.
57  Goldstein and Keohane (1993), Hall (1995), and Woods (1995).

58 Wendt (1988), Katzenstein (1996), and Lapid and Kratochwil (1996).
59 Walt (1987).
60 Walt (1987), p. 38.
61 Woods (1995), pp. 174–175.
62 Wendt (1994), p. 391.
63 Sen (1986), p. 351.
64 Dingman (1979), p. 245.
65 Hamilton and Whalley (1989), p. 547.
66 Niou and Ordershook (1994).
67 Walt (1997), p. 157.
68 Wendt (1994), p. 386.
69 Hamilton and Whalley (1989) classify coalitions as proposal-making, agenda-setting, blocking, and negotiating.
70 Samuelson and Nordhaus (1989), p. 968.

## 2 Coalitions in the GATT and the entry of services

1 Wilkinson (2000), Ostry (1997), and Hoekman (2001).
2 For example, Hansen (1979), Rothstein (1979), Brandt Commission Report (1980), Mortimer (1984), and Aggarwal (1996).
3 The Quad group combined Canada, EC, Japan, and the USA.
4 Hoekman and Kostecki (2001).
5 Krasner (1985).
6 Ricupero (1998).
7 For details on this negotiating procedure as well as others that were introduced in later years, see Hoekman and Kostecki (2001).
8 A GATT official, in a brief interview, completely denied any existence of coalition activity in the GATT or the WTO, August 1997, Geneva.
9 Evans (1968) makes the point that the GATT was the first multilateral instrument arising out of the US Trade Agreements Program with emphasis on reciprocal bargaining. As such, it was assumed that any benefits to be obtained under the GATT must be paid for, and the underdeveloped countries were convinced that their own bargaining power was inadequate to extract concessions of value from others.
10 Whalley (1987).
11 UNCTAD (1990).
12 Krugman and Obstfeld (1997).
13 Although the bulk of NTMs in developed countries were imposed on exports from other developed countries, developing countries were affected more than proportionately, with two-thirds of their major manufactures facing NTMs, whereas for the same products from the developed countries, the share was one-fifth. If agriculture is included, over a third of the developing countries faced some form of volume restraining measures and other bilateral pressures, see Weston (1987).
14 See Dobson and Jacquet (1998).
15 'Basically one has to draw a distinction between services as embodied in the supplier of the services and requiring their physical presence where the user happens to be and services which can be disembodied from the supplier and provided without a physical presence being necessary.' Bhagwati (1984), p. 101. On the tradability of services, Medhora (http://www.idrc.ca/tec.emerging.html) writes, 'They are directly and indirectly traded in large and growing numbers. As such, and despite the fact that they do not hurt if dropped on your foot, they can be analysed in much the same manner as goods trade.'
16 Sapir (1982), p. 79.
17 Sapir (1985). Also Hindley (1988).

18 For the initial debates and positions of developed and developing countries, see Hoekman (1992 and 1993).
19 The term has been borrowed from Medhora, http://www.idrc.ca/tec.emerging.html
20 Medhora (http://www.idrc.ca/tec.emerging.html).
21 See Hurrell (1998) for an excellent interpretation that challenges both the liberal enlightenment view that is put forth by economists and the hegemonic oppression view that is presented by the Left.
22 Michalopoulos (1998).
23 Woods and Narlikar (2001).

## 3 Bloc diplomacy: the Informal Group and the G-10

1 Indian representative at the GATT, quoted by Kock (1969).
2 Quoted by Williams (1994), p. 165.
3 Quoted by Williams (1991), p. 24.
4 See Hansen (1979) on NIEO.
5 For a critical view of the GATT and its impact on developing countries, see Watkins (1992), and Raghavan (1990).
6 Hansen (1979).
7 Coalitions, as commonly understood, are groups of negotiators who agree to act in concert to achieve *a common end*; See Chapter 1 for a full definition and typology.
8 Krueger and Michalopoulos (1985).
9 Wolf (1984).
10 Krueger and Michalopoulos (1985).
11 Chishti (1991).
12 Hoekman and Kostecki (1995).
13 Krasner (1985), p. 5.
14 Wolf (1984).
15 Rothstein (1982).
16 Williams (1991), p. 11.
17 Kumar (1995b), p. 166.
18 Burnell (1986) notes the operation of such quid pro quo in the context of other groupings representing the Third World.
19 Gosovic (1972), p. 279, identifies Brazil, Chile, Nigeria, Ghana, Algeria, United Arab Republic, India, Pakistan, the Philippines, and the former Yugoslavia as the leading members of the South.
20 Jackson (1990).
21 Gosovic (1972), p. 278.
22 Abreu and Fritsch (1989), p. 183.
23 Ibid.
24 Abreu (1995).
25 Abreu and Fritsch (1989), p. 185.
26 Rothstein (1979).
27 Rothstein (1982), p. 162.
28 The idea of distinguishing between two levels of ideational factors – core/constitutive and strategic/instrumental – draws upon Goldstein and Keohane (1993) who distinguish between principled and causal beliefs. But 'principled beliefs' may be unprincipled and might exercise an influence as causative as the 'causal' beliefs. Hence, this book uses the terms '*core*'/'*constitutive*' beliefs to refer to the broad normative framework of Goldstein's and Keohane's principled beliefs; the term 'causal beliefs' is replaced by '*instrumental*'/'*strategic*' beliefs, that is beliefs that implement the core beliefs.
29 Toye (1987), p. 8.
30 Raghavan (1990), p. 70.
31 Ricupero (1998), p. 14.

32 Shukla (1994).

33 Mendoza (1989).

34 Hart (1995), pp. 186–187.

35 Interview with a high-level EC delegate who was a key player at the time, 27 January 1998. Also reported in SUNS and Riddle (1986).

36 Interview with a high-level developing country delegate who played a crucial role in the G-10, 6 January 2000, and EC delegate, 27 January 1998. Also Shukla (1994).

37 The 'Dirty Dozen' are discussed in Chapter 4.

38 'Third World Ministers come out against US moves in GATT', SUNS, no. 626, 14 October 1982.

39 This Latin American coordination meeting was held from 4 to 6 October 1982, in Geneva. References found in Mendoza (1989), p. 59. Also, 'SELA Joint Position for November GATT meeting,' SUNS, 632, 22 October 1982.

40 The move was foiled, see 'US move on services and investment misfires', SUNS, 636, 22 October 1982.

41 UNCTAD (1994).

42 Raghavan (1990), p. 73.

43 'Third World Cool to US moves for new trade negotiations', SUNS, no. 889, 12 November 1982.

44 'Little progress on GATT consultations on services', SUNS, no. 962, 7 March 1984.

45 'Third World "no" to new round', SUNS, no. 987, 11 April 1984.

46 'Little evidence of implementation of undertakings', SUNS, no. 1011, 17 May 1984.

47 A tactic that Hampson and Hart (1995), refer to in another context, as agenda-packing, that is 'deliberate proliferation of issues … to consume time and energy', p. 353. A leading EC representative in the GATT explained the change in the EC position in terms of evolving compromise within the EC. He pointed out how possible linkages with agriculture induced French acceptance of the issue, and thereby overcome the initial divergence within the EC on the inclusion of services (Interview with EC representative, 27 January 1998). Hart (1995) has also noted the importance of intra-EC deals and compromises.

48 'New global trade talks', SUNS, no. 1180, 8 January 1985.

49 Japan's eventual support for the US derived in good measure from an attempt to resist American bilateralism and the multilateral focus on NTBs.

50 'Third World group rules out trade negotiations', SUNS, no. 1142, 4 December 1984.

51 'Third World countries expect more US pressures', SUNS, no. 1198, 6 March 1985.

52 'US frowns on any Third World grouping in GATT', SUNS, no. 1245, 14 May 1985.

53 Hart (1995), p. 207.

54 'US for managed trade in services', SUNS, no. 1494, 7 June 1986.

55 'Prepcom discusses possible recommendations on new round', SUNS, no. 1500, 17 June 1986.

56 GATT document, PREP.COM(86)/W/41, 23 June 1986.

57 Interview with a high-level EC delegate, 27 January 1998.

58 The smaller developing countries working along the Jaramillo track were referred to pejoratively as the 'Enthusiasts' by the G-10. A detailed discussion on the Enthusiasts follows in Chapter 4.

59 'No New Round through Illegitimate Means – Brazil', SUNS, no. 1519, 12 July 1986.

60 GATT document, PREP.COM (86)/W/41/Rev.1, 16 July 1986.

61 Kumar (1995a), p. 208.

62 In conversation with WTO and UNCTAD officials, summer 1997.

63 Kumar (1995a), p. 211.

64 Hoekman (1993), p. 12.

65 Ibid., p. 12.

66 Sauvé (1995).

67 Interview with a leading member of the G-10, 6 January 2000.

68  Chapter 8.
69  Shukla (1994).
70  Interview with a senior official in UNCTAD, August 1997.
71  Chapter 6.
72  Ricupero (1998) likens the North–South dimension in the GATT to sex in Victorian England – 'ostensibly ignored, but nevertheless present everywhere' (p. 15).

## 4  Alliance diplomacy: the issue-based, crossover coalitions of G-20 and Café au Lait

1   Economist (1986), p. 54.
2   Kumar (1995).
3   'New round and services still an open question', SUNS, no. 1332, 3 October 1985.
4   Kihwan and Soo (1980).
5   Ibid.
6   A high-level delegate at the Jamaican mission pointed out that the first proposal for an international code on services was made by his country well before the US had begun lobbying for the new issues and the new round, Interview, 15 September 1997.
7   An account of some of these interests may be found in Ricupero (1998).
8   Hamilton and Whalley (1987).
9   'Standstill and rollback, a must for launching new round', SUNS, no. 1461, 18 April 1986.
10  Jamaican delegate, Interview, 15 September 1997, Geneva. Also, 'GATT Committee to hear views on new issues for trade round', SUNS, no. 1429, 1 March 1986.
11  GATT document, MIN (86)/4, 15 September 1986.
12  GATT document, MDF/6, para. 13, Minutes of 24 January 1985.
13  GATT document, MDF/15, para. 8, Minutes of 7 June 1985.
14  GATT document, MDF/10, para. 16, Minutes of 1–2 April 1985.
15  On increasing structural differentiation within the developing world before the Uruguay Round, see Chishti (1990), pp. 73–77.
16  Bhagwati and Patrick (1990) and Brock (1985).
17  Drake and Nikolaidis (1992).
18  Kumar (1995a).
19  Ibid., p. 221.
20  Oxley (1990), p. 136.
21  Drake and Nikolaidis (1992).
22  Ibid.
23  GATT document, PREP.COM (86)W/47, 17 July 1986.
24  For example, Preeg (1995).
25  Economist (1986).
26  GATT, PREP.COM W/47 Rev. 2, 30 July 1986, II (e) General Principles Governing Negotiations, p. 3.
27  GATT, PREP.COM W/47 Rev. 2, 30 July 1986, II (f), General Principles Governing Negotiations, p. 3.
28  GATT, PREP.COM W/47 Rev. 2, 30 July 1986, IV, Subjects for Negotiations, p. 8.
29  Contemporary reporting of the two groups, even before the final draft was formulated, noted the achievements of the Café au Lait, such as, Economist (1986), pp. 54–55.
30  For a categorisation of coalitions as agenda-moving, proposal-making, blocking, and negotiating, see Hamilton and Whalley (1989).
31  Drake and Nikolaidis (1992).
32  For an argument stressing the role of this epistemic consensus, ibid.
33  Interviews with ambassadors from the G-10, some UNCTAD officials, and officials of the Third World Network.
34  Examples of writings emphasising this new approach include, Habeeb (1988), Finlayson and Weston (1990), Pratt (1990), Cooper (1997).

## 5 Combination diplomacy: issue-based blocs and sub-sectoral crossover alliances

1 Gibbs (1985).
2 Trade in factor services refers to transactions involving the movement of factors of production.
3 UNCTAD (1988), p. 139.
4 Ibid., p. 194.
5 For example, Mendoza (1989), pp. 61–63.
6 Gibbs and Mashayekhi (1989), pp. 98–105.
7 Ibid.
8 Lall (1986).
9 Ibid., p. 131.
10 Even tourism, which is so conditional upon geographic factors, displays the importance of other factors in promoting it; see OECD (1989), p. 23.
11 UNCTAD (1985).
12 Riddle (1987).
13 Feketekuty defines professional services as the application of knowledge and skills by experts to meet clients' needs, quoted by Mallampally (1990).
14 For details on barriers to trade in professional services, see Gibbs and Mashayekhi (1996).
15 OECD (1989).
16 Sengupta (1989).
17 Srivastava (1989).
18 Trade in services for GATS purposes is defined as the supply of a service through four modes of supply, namely cross-border supply, consumption abroad, commercial presence, and provision of services through the temporary movement of natural persons.
19 Private transfers refers to labour remittances, such as remittances to their home country by Indian labour employed in the Gulf countries.
20 Heydon (1990).
21 Braga (1990).
22 GATT document, MTN.GNS/W/106, 18 June 1990.
23 Should such a coalition emerge, it would divide the developing world into importers and exporters of professional services (with large parts of Africa and West Asia importing services).
24 Lall (1984).
25 Annex table 4 of UNCTAD (1988).
26 Lee (1990).
27 Faust (1989), p. 124, drawing on IMF Balance of Payments Statistics Yearbook, 1988.
28 Yeats (1990), p. 85.
29 UNCTAD (1985).
30 Hoekman (1988).
31 UNCTAD (1985).
32 Latin American groupings are examined in detail in Chapter 7.
33 'We believe that we should not base our approach on the assumptions borrowed from [the] familiar area of trade in goods supplemented by carving out exceptions in terms of special and differential treatment for developing countries.' – delegation of India to the Group of Negotiations on Services, 'Statement of India at the GNS meeting on 23 February 1987' – quoted by Mark and Helleiner (1988), p. 26.
34 The term service 'superpower' is used by Kakabadse (1987).
35 Riddle (1986).
36 Sapir (1985).
37 UNCTAD (1988).
38 Hoekman (1993).
39 Note, however, this does not preclude the viability of smaller blocs of developing countries, examples of which are illustrated in Chapter 8.

## 6  Evolved alliances: the Cairns Group and Friends of Services Group

1  For an account of the events leading up to the subsidies war of the 1980s, see Higgott and Cooper (1990), Josling (1996).
2  Tussie (1995), p. 182.
3  Johnson (1985), cited by Higgott and Cooper (1990), p. 597.
4  Higgott and Cooper (1990).
5  Tussie (1995), p. 182.
6  Ibid.
7  Hamilton and Whalley (1989).
8  Oxley (1990).
9  Tussie (1995), p. 197.
10  Department of Foreign Affairs and Trade, Australia (1998b). Also, UNCTAD (1991), p. 167.
11  Examined in detail in the context of strategies of the group in Section 6.2.
12  Hoekman (1987).
13  Tyers (1994).
14  Tyers (1993), p. 58.
15  For the sub-sectoral component of exports of individual member countries, see Tussie (1995).
16  Higgott and Cooper (1990).
17  Food and Agriculture Organisation (1993). Similar profiles continue into the 1990s – in 1998, agriculture accounted for nearly 7 per cent of Argentina's GDP, nearly a third of goods production, almost 53 per cent of export revenues, and directly employed 16 per cent of the workforce, http://www.dfat.gov.au/trade/negotiations/cairns_group/members/argentina.html.
18  Food and Agriculture Organisation (1993).
19  Tussie (1995), pp. 188–189.
20  Data from Food and Agriculture Organisation (1993).
21  Tussie (1995), p. 189.
22  Higgott and Cooper (1990), pp. 604–605.
23  Anderson and Tyers (1987), also discussed by Finlayson and Weston (1990).
24  Higgott and Cooper (1990), p. 610.
25  Tussie (1995), p. 199.
26  '…the Latin American decision was legitimated by its perfect consonance with the culture of an organization founded on the belief in free trade in all goods as far as possible. This makes a veto based on the demand for the integration: it places the onus of justifying opposition to liberalisation squarely on the shoulders of the other parties.' Ricupero (1998), p. 19.
27  Higgott and Cooper (1990).
28  Ibid.
29  On the role that oilseeds in disputes involving the US, see Preeg (1995).
30  For a detailed account of the negotiations, ibid.
31  At least some diplomats from non-Cairns group developing countries commented in interviews that the intra-Quad collusion that had led developing countries to resentfully dub the GATT a 'Rich Man's Club' was operative once again, this time between the two giants.
32  Members of the Cairns Group 'have been aided in this' (i.e. 'the profound influence on the conduct of the Round') 'by the new importance of developing countries in other aspects of the Round: in the negotiations on services trade and on intellectual property rights. The Developing countries in the Cairns Group have been able to make progress in these areas conditional on progress on agriculture.' See Rod Tyers (1993), p. 58.
33  Note that such a broadening of the agenda from compensation to market access issues, by Mexico, in the case of the Food Importers' Group, jeopardised the friable coalition further.

34  Tussie (1995), pp. 198–199.
35  Interview with a representative of the Cairns Group, Geneva, September, 1998.
36  Cooper and Higgott (1993).
37  Tussie (1995), 'Brazil … became convinced of withdrawing from the round only by US prodding after a visit by Yeutter, a few weeks before the Brussels meeting', p. 199.
38  Ibid., p. 200.
39  For a discussion of this divergence of interest, see Cooper (1990).
40  Hopkins (1993), p. 145.
41  For five country case studies demonstrating the problems of uncertainty and domestic pressures as they affected LDC ability to organise themselves into an effective food importers' coalition, ibid.
42  Ibid.
43  Divisive techniques of the EC included more generous offers on tropical products. Specifically, the EC proposed to eliminate tariffs on raw materials, to reduce duties on semi-processed goods by 35 per cent and to cut duties on processed goods by 50 per cent. Products included were coffee, cocoa, tea, tropical fruits, spices, cut flowers, essential oils, rubber, and wood articles. The offer was accompanied by another to restrict its original idea of rebalancing to corn gluten feed and citrus pellets, and thereby exclude soya beans from a tariff hike. Tussie (1995), pp. 199–200.
44  Interview with a senior WTO official in Services Division, World Trade Organisation, 15 April 1999.

## 7  Regionalism: a springboard for bargaining?

 1  Hoekman and Sauvé (1994), p. 72.
 2  Winters (1998), p. 47.
 3  On the two 'waves', see de Melo and Panagariya (1993).
 4  For example, 'Above all, the regional community is becoming even more a deliberate instrument to coordinate foreign policy, to strengthen bargaining power in the international arena, and to restructure the local environment for its member-states', Byron (1994), p. 2. Similarly, Agarwal (1989) analyses South–South trade in terms of 'the two usually-mentioned rationales for encouraging SST: namely, to enlarge the size of markets and permit LDCs to take advantage of economies of scale, and to act as a bargaining chip in North–South negotiations'. While most RTAs have a joint bargaining component to their aims, regional bargaining coalitions need not necessarily be founded on RTAs. This distinction is of considerable importance and will be discussed in detail in Section 7.2.
 5  Byron (1994).
 6  Gilpin (1985).
 7  Stewart (1976), p. 101.
 8  On the various bases of regionalism and theoretical approaches to understanding them, Hurrell (1994).
 9  UNCTAD (1985).
10  UNCTAD (1988).
11  The Andean Group includes Bolivia, Colombia, Ecuador, Peru, and Venezuela. Note that the data on a trade surplus in services for Colombia, cited in the previous paragraph, refer to the study for 1979–1981.
12  Hilf *et al.* (1986).
13  Preeg (1998).
14  Bhagwati (1993) identifies the conversion of the US to regionalism as 'the main driving for regionalism today', p. 29.
15  Mendoza (1989).
16  GATT document, MTN.GNS/W/95, 26 February 1990.
17  GATT document, MTN.GNS/W/101, 4 May 1990.

18  GATT document, MTN.GNS/W/95, 26 February 1990, Preamble, p. 4. Note that the SELA position in the pre-Uruguay Round phase had been a hard-line opposition to the inclusion of services within the GATT.

19  Ibid., chapter I, 7(a).

20  Ibid., chapter I, 7(c).

21  Ibid., chapter I, 7(j).

22  Ibid., Article 9.

23  The problems of having coalitions with memberships that cut across each other is anticipated in the African context as well, for example, Blackhurst *et al.* (1999) and Chapter 8 of this book.

24  Cited by Mark and Helleiner, p. 26.

25  Regional bodies of developing countries that circulated joint statements at the WTO Ministerial in Geneva included the South Asian Association for Regional Cooperation (WT/MIN(98)ST/49), the Common Market for Eastern and Southern Africa (WT/MIN/(98)ST/74), the OAU/African Economic Community (WT/MIN(98) ST/72), and the South Centre (WT/MIN(98)ST/20). Many of the expected regional positions did not emerge for example, from the Latin Americans, though some references were made by Argentina to the MERCOSUR. The only exception to all these coalitions was the ASEAN (WT/MIN(98)ST/108), whose joint position in the WTO goes back to the days of the launch of the Uruguay Round. The case of the ASEAN is examined in detail in Section 8.3.

26  However, even the consolidated market power of developing countries through a regionally integrated market often does not match up to the consolidated or individual power of developed countries. It has, for instance, been argued that greater unity in Sub-Saharan Africa (SSA) during the Uruguay Round negotiations may not have improved the outcome for SSA, since acting as a group, SSA countries had little more clout than they have individually, see Wang and Winters (1997). The ASEAN example is discussed later in this chapter to show that the bargaining power of regional coalitions need not derive from regional integration and can have other sources.

27  The LAFTA was a regional organisation in the sense of encompassing the entire region rather than the sub-region. Membership comprised Argentina, Bolivia, Brazil, Chile, Colombia, Ecuador, Mexico, Paraguay, Uruguay, and Venezuela.

28  Instituto de Relaciones Europeo-Latinoamericanas (1993), p. 4.

29  Tussie (1987), pp. 115–128.

30  Members of the Andean Pact include Bolivia, Colombia, Ecuador, Peru, and Venezuela.

31  Catagorisation according to two approaches borrowed from Stephenson (1999).

32  Ibid.

33  Ibid.

34  Ibid.

35  Commitment to the joint stance can be measured qualitatively through memberships of other coalitions with opposing positions. Simultaneous membership of the Café au Lait and the SELA in the pre-launch phase when the SELA adhered to the hard line provides one example.

36  From the proceedings of the Conference 'New Dimensions in Regional Integration', 2–3 April, 1992, sponsored by the World Bank and the Centre for Economic Policy Research, published later, De Melo and Panagariya (1993).

37  For more on the coordination problems within regions, see Kumar (1988).

38  Tussie (1987), p. 40.

39  Ibid. p. 44.

40  Proceedings of conference, New Dimensions in Regional Integration (1992).

41  Stephenson (1999), pp. 73–74.

42  'Conventional trade theory applies not only to goods but also to services…' Sapir (1982), p. 79. Also, see Sapir and Winter (1994).

43 Blackhurst *et al.* (1999) and Stephenson (1994).

44 The initial ASEAN position in the pre-launch phase of the Uruguay Round was to support the G-10 hard-line position, 'Trade: no consensus on high level meeting for new round', Special United Nations Service, SUNS, No. 1247, 17 May 1985, p. 2. The shift to opposing the hard line and realignment with the Café au Lait by the Southeast Asian countries was also collective, under the umbrella of the ASEAN.

45 Ajanant *et al.* (1988).

46 Just how seriously the ASEAN is taken by its own members and outside, and why, is illustrated in the following statement, taken from the Report of the Group of Fourteen on ASEAN Economic Cooperation and Integration (1987): 'It is an indisputable fact that ASEAN carries far greater collective weight than individual member countries. ASEAN is for many countries a large market. In the case of Japan, for example, ASEAN was in 1985 second only to the United States (accounting for 10.3 per cent of Japan's exports) and was a larger market for Japanese goods than the EEC (which only accounted for 9.5 per cent of all Japanese exports in 1985)', p. 64.

47 Frost (1990), pp. 10–14.

48 Tyabji (1990).

49 Meyananthan, quoted in ibid., p. 33.

50 Factors contributing to these differences were discussed in Chapter 5.

51 See table V-6, in Chng Meng Kng *et al.* (1988), p. 144.

52 Khong (1997).

53 Khong (1997) notes that contrary to readings of the ASEAN as an economic organisation along the lines of the EC (a failed one at that), the ASEAN did not have regional economic integration as a goal. It was also not a military alliance like NATO, p. 326.

54 For a summary of these arguments, see Busch and Milner (1994). For a more detailed analysis, see Gowa (1994).

55 The shocks of inter-industry trade generated by the broadening may be cushioned by the presence of an internal or external hegemon willing to bear the costs, along the lines suggested in Section 7.2.2. American support and the exceptional circumstances, for instance, allowed Europe special provisions for its lesser developed countries. But the reproducibility of such conditions is doubtful, and there is little sign of their operation in the ASEAN on a similar scale. The Asia–Pacific Economic Cooperation (APEC) might have the potential of enjoying hegemonic support, but it would also go well beyond the EC in its diversity of membership.

## 8 Coalitions of the new round: developing countries at Seattle and Doha

1 The coalitions studied in this chapter are not limited to services. This is because, unlike the Uruguay Round, there were several other issues at Seattle and Doha that acquired paramount importance. Services, while still controversial, at least formed a part of the Built-In Agenda.

2 Paragraph 4, WTO document, WT/MIN(96)/DEC, 18 December 1996.

3 Interviews with members of the IGDC, November–December 2002.

4 WTO document, WT/MIN(96)/DEC, 18 December 1996.

5 WTO document, WT/MIN(98)/ DEC/1, 25 May 1998.

6 For example, see WTO document, WT/GC/W/354, Communication from Cuba, Dominican Republic, Egypt, El Salvador, Honduras, India, Indonesia, Malaysia, Nigeria, Pakistan, Sri Lanka, Uganda, 11 October 1999. Also WTO document, WT/GC/W/355, 11 October 1999. For reports on LMG activities, see also www.twnside.org.sg

7 For example, see WTO document, WT/GC/W/442, Communication from Cuba, Dominican Republic, Honduras, India, Indonesia, Kenya, Malaysia, Pakistan, Sri Lanka, Tanzania, Uganda, and Zimbabwe, 19 September 2001. Also, WTO documents WT/GC/W/443, 19 September 2001; WT/GC/W/444, 18 September 2001; WT/GC/W/445, 18 September 2001.

8  Exactly what bilateral or multilateral deals were struck to win over the members of the LMG to consensus is work in progress, Narlikar and Odell (2003).
9  Interview with LMG member, 20 December 2002.
10  WTO document, WT/MIN(01)/DEC/1, 20 November 2001.
11  WTO document, WT/MIN(01)/17, 20 November 2001.
12  Interview with a founding member of the LMG, 12 November 2002.
13  For example, the ambassadors of the LMG had an interactive dialogue with NGOs and journalists on 5 July 2001 to inform them of the state of play four months before the Doha Ministerial, South Bulletin 16.
14  For example, WTO document, WT/GC/W/361, Communication from Barbados, Dominica, Fiji, Grenada, Jamaica, Lesotho, Mauritius, Papua New Guinea, Solomon Islands, St Lucia, Trinidad, and Tobago, 12 October 1998.
15  For example, WTO document, WT/GC/W/441, 6 August 2001.
16  Interview with a leading member of the group, 13 November 2002.
17  See Table 2.2 for a list of the full membership of the group.
18  Khor, http://www.twnside.org.sg/title/pli-cn.htm, May 1997.
19  WTO document, WT/GC/W/251, 13 July 1999.
20  Ibid.
21  South Bulletin, 24–25, 30 November 2001.
22  Ibid.
23  WTO document, Special Session of the Committee on Agriculture, Informal Meeting, 4–6 February 2002, The Development Box, Non-paper by Cuba, Dominican Republic, El Salvador, Honduras, Kenya, Nigeria, Pakistan, Sri Lanka, and Zimbabwe. See also WTO document, G/AG/NG/W/13, 23 June 2000.
24  Chakravarthi Raghavan, New Revised Draft Text for Seattle, www.twnside.org.sg/title/chairman-cn.htm, 20 October 1999.
25  India, for instance, though not a part of the group, has actually made joint statements with the same group of countries formally (e.g. WTO document, G/AG/NG/W/37, 28 September 2000) and informally supported some proposals of the group. Similarly, it is alleged that the Friends of the Development Box enjoyed the cautious support of certain Cairns Group members including Indonesia and the Latin Americans in the Cairns Group.
26  Press Statement by the Friends of the Development Box, 10 November 2001, Doha, http://www.focusweb.org/publications/2001/friends-of-the-development-box-press-statement.html
27  Weston (2001).
28  Interview with a leading member of the group, 8 January 2003.
29  WTO document, S/CSS/W/13, 'Elements for Negotiating Guidelines and Procedures', 24 November 2000.
30  Raghavan, WTO's revised draft guidelines for GATS talks, http://www.twnside.org.sg/title/secretariat.htm, 20 March 2001.
31  WTO document, WT/GC/W/208, 17 June 1999.
32  Argentina, Australia, Bolivia, Brazil, Canada, Chile, Colombia, Costa Rica, Fiji, Guatemala, Indonesia, Malaysia, New Zealand, Paraguay, Philippines, South Africa, Thailand, and Uruguay.
33  WTO document, G/AG/NG/W54, Cairns Group Negotiating Proposal, Market Access, 10 November 2000. Canada was the notable absentee member in this proposal and instead had an independent proposal in G/AG/NG/W/12, 19 June 2000.
34  Cairns Group Communiqué, 22nd Ministerial Meeting, Punta del Este, 21–23 September 2001, available at www.cairnsgroup.org/meetings/min22_communique.html
35  WTO document, G/AG/NG/W/11, 16 June 2000.
36  WTO document, G/AG/NG/W/35, 22 September 2000.
37  USTR Press Release, 16 October 2002.

38 Chakravarthi Raghavan, Agricultural Compromise is fig leaf for Cairns, http://www.twnside.org.sg/title/leaf.htm, 5 October 2001.

39 Daily Doha Update, BRIDGES, http://www.ictsd.org/ministerial/doha/wto_daily/englishissue3.htm, Issue 3, 12 November 2001.

40 WTO document, WT/GC/W/303, Fisheries Subsidies, 6 August 1999.

41 For definition of value-creating strategy, Odell (2000).

42 Interview with a member of the Paradisus Group, 12 December 2002.

43 Luke (2000).

44 For example, WTO documents WT/GC/W/137, 26 January 1999; WT/GC/W/299, 6 August 1999; WT/GC/W/300, 6 August 1999; WT/GC/W/301, Customs Valuation Agreement, 6 August 1999; WT/GC/W/302, 6 August 1999.

45 WTO document, WT/L/423, 18 October 2001.

46 WTO document, IP/C/W/296, 29 June 2001.

47 WTO document, WT/L/430, November 2001.

48 McIntyre (2000).

49 For example, WTO document, G/AG/NG/W/100, 15 July 2001.

50 Weston (2002).

51 WTO documents, WT/GC/W/334, 23 September 1999; WT/GC/W/335, 23 September 1999; WT/GC/W/336, 23 September 1999; WT/GC/W/337, 23 September 1999; S/CSS/W/2, 14 April 2000; G/AG/NG/W/139 (proposal by MERCOSUR plus other developing countries) 21 March 2001.

52 Americas Quarterly Spotlight, www.bocm.com/bocmrs/Research_FX/americasquarterly/americasquarterly_2001-09.pdf, September 1999.

## 9 Conclusion

1 Recall the problem of large-n that was discussed in Chapter 1.

2 India provides a good example of a country that has always enough weight to be invited to Green Room consultations, in spite of its limited involvement in world trade in the past. Similarly, Bangladesh and Tanzania have, in recent years, exercised considerable influence owing to their role in the LDC group in the WTO.

3 Note, however, that external conditions were key to the reputed successes of the group.

4 Type II coalitions are to be distinguished from Type III in terms of the level on which they operate.

5 20 December 2002, interview with a high-level developing country negotiator.

6 One instance of attempts by developing countries to internalise this lesson can be found on the UNCTAD website, where 'Positive Agenda' is listed and detailed as an independent project; see http://www.unctad.org/en/posagen/index.htm

7 Higgott and Cooper (1990).

# Bibliography

Abreu, M. de P. (1995) Trade policies and bargaining in a heavily indebted economy: Brazil. In *The Developing Countries in World Trade*, eds D. Tussie and D. Glover. Boulder, CO: Lynne Rienner.

——and Fritsch, W. (1989) Brazilian export growth obstacles and MTNs. In *Developing Countries and the Global Trading System*, ed. J. Whalley. London: Macmillan.

Agarwal, M. (1989) South–South trade: building block or bargaining chip? In *Developing Countries and the Global Trading System, Volume 1, Thematic Studies from a Ford Foundation Project*, ed. J. Whalley. London: Macmillan.

Aggarwal, V. K. (1996) *Debt Games: Strategic Interaction in International Debt Rescheduling*. Cambridge: Cambridge University Press.

Ajanant, J., Chirathivat, S., and Iamkamala, C. (1988) Trade Policy Options for Thailand. In *ASEAN Trade Policy Options*, eds M. Ariff and T. Loong-Hoe. Singapore: ASEAN Economic Research Unit, Institute of Southeast Asian Studies.

Alt, J. E., Frieden, J., Gilligan, M. J., Rodrik, D., and Rogowski, R. (1996) The political economy of international trade: enduring puzzles and an agenda for inquiry. *Comparative Political Studies* 29, 689–717.

Ariff, M. and Loong-Hoe, T. (eds) (1988) *ASEAN Trade Policy Options*. Singapore: ASEAN Economic Research Unit, Institute of Southeast Asian Studies.

Avery, W. P. (1993) *World Agriculture and the GATT*. Boulder, CO: Lynne Rienner.

Axelrod, R. (1984) *The Evolution of Cooperation*. New York: Basic Books.

——and Keohane, R. (1985) Achieving cooperation under anarchy: strategies and institutions. *World Politics* 38(1), 226–254.

Ayoob, M. (1989) The Third World in the system of states: acute schizophrenia or growing pains. *International Studies Quarterly* 33(1), 67–79.

——(1995) *The Third World Security Predicament: State-Making, Regional Conflict and the International System*. Boulder, CO: Lynne Rienner.

——(1998) Subaltern realism, international relations theory meets the Third World. In *International Relations Theory and the Third World*, ed. S. G. Neuman. London: Macmillan.

Baldwin, D. A. (1979) Power analysis and world politics. *World Politics* 31(2), 161–194.

——(1989) *Paradoxes of Power*. Oxford: Blackwell.

Bhagwati, J. (1984) Splintering and disembodiment of services and developing nations. *The World Economy* 7(2), 133–143.

——(1993) Regionalism and multilateralism: an overview. In *New Dimensions in Regional Integration*, eds J. De Melo and A. Panagariya. Cambridge: Cambridge University Press.

——and Hirsch, M. (1998) *The Uruguay Round and Beyond: Essays in Honour of Arthur Dunkel, Studies in International Economics*. Ann Arbor, MI: University of Michigan Press.

Bhagwati, J. and Patrick, H. (1990) *Aggressive Unilateralism: America's 301, Trade Policy and the World Trading System*. Ann Arbor, MI: University of Michigan Press.

——— and Ruggie, J. (eds) (1984) *Power, Passions and Purpose: Prospects for North-South Negotiations*. Cambridge, MA: MIT Press.

Blackhurst, R., Lyakurwa, B., and Oyejode, A. (1999) *Improving African Participation in the WTO*, Paper commissioned by the World Bank for a Conference at the WTO on 20–21 September 1999.

Braga, C. A. P. (1990) Brazil. In *The Uruguay Round: Services in the World Economy*, eds P. A. Messerlin and K. P. Sauvant. Washington, DC and New York: World Bank and the United Nations Centre on Transnational Corporations.

Brandt Commission Report (1980) *North–South: A Program for Survival, Report of the Independent Commission on International Development Issues*, chaired by Willy Brandt. London: Pan.

Brock, W. E. (1985) Statement: US trade policy toward developing countries. In *Hard Bargaining Ahead: US Trade Policy and Developing Countries*, ed. E. H. Preeg. New Brunswick, NJ: Transaction Books.

Broinowski, A. (ed.) (1990) *ASEAN into the 1990s*. Basingstoke, UK: Macmillan.

Browne, E. (1973) *Coalition Theories: A Logical and Empirical Critique*, Sage Professional Papers in Comparative Politics, Serial No. 01-043. Beverly Hills, CA: Sage.

Buchanan, J. M. (1965) An economic theory of clubs. *Economica* 32(125), 1–14.

Burnell, P. J. (1986) *Economic Nationalism in the Third World*. Brighton, UK: Wheatsheaf Books.

Busch, M. L. and Milner, H. V. (1994) The future of the trading system: international firms, regionalism and domestic politics. In *Political Economy and the Changing Global Order*, eds R. Stubbs and G. R. D. Underhill. Basingstoke, UK: Macmillan.

Buzan, B. (1983) *Peoples, States and Fear: The National Security Problem in International Relations*. Brighton, UK: Wheatsheaf Books.

Byron, J. (1994) *Caricom in the Post-Cold War Era: Regional Solutions or Continued Regional Contradictions, Working Paper 178*. The Hague, The Netherlands: Institute of Social Studies.

Cairns Group documents available at www.cairnsgroup.org

Chandra, B. (1993) *Essays on Indian Nationalism*. Delhi: Har-Anand.

Chishti, S. (1991) *Restructuring of International Economic Relations*. Delhi: Sage.

Clapham, C. (1985) *Third World Politics*. London: Croom Helm.

Claude, I. L., Jr. (1964) *Swords into Plowshares: The Problems and Progress of International Organization*. London: University of London Press.

Cooper, A. F. (1990) Exporters versus importers: LDCs, agricultural trade, and the Uruguay Round. *Intereconomics* 25(1), 13–17.

———(1997) *Niche Diplomacy: Middle Powers after the Cold War*. Basingstoke, UK: Macmillan.

———and Higgott, R. (1993) Australian and Canadian approaches to the Cairns Group: two level games and the political economy of adjustment. In *World Agriculture and the GATT*, ed. W. P. Avery. Boulder, CO: Lynne Rienner.

Curzon, G. (1965) *Multilateral Commercial Diplomacy: The General Agreement on Tariffs and Trade and its impact on National Commercial Policies and Techniques*. London: Michael Joseph.

De Melo, J. and Panagariya, A. (eds) (1993) *New Dimensions in Regional Integration*. Cambridge: Cambridge University Press.

Department of Foreign Affairs and Trade (DFAT), Australia (1998a) South Africa joins the Cairns Group of Agricultural Countries, Media Release, D10, 2 February 1998.

———(1998b) Non-Trade Concerns, *Agriculture: Process of Analysis and Information Exchange*, Informal Paper: AIE/36, 4 September 1998, http://www.dfat.gov.au/trade.nego … airns_group/cairns_non_trade.html

Dingman, R. V. (1979) Theories of, and approaches to, alliance politics. In *Diplomacy: New Approaches in History, Theory and Policy*, ed. P. G. Lauren. New York: Free Press, Macmillan.

Dobson, W. and Jacquet, P. (1998) *Financial Services Liberalization in the WTO*. Washington, DC: Institute for International Economics.

Drake, W. J. and Nicolaidis, K. (1992) Ideas, interests and institutionalization: 'trade in services' and the Uruguay Round. *International Organization* 46(1), 37–100.

East, M. A. (1973) Size and foreign policy behaviour: a test of two models. *World Politics* 24(4), 556–576.

*The Economist* (1986) The café-au-lait trade round. August 2, 54–55.

Evans, J. (1968) The General Agreement on Tariffs and Trade. *International Organisation* 22(1), 72–98.

Faust, P. (1989) Shipping. In *Trade in Services: Sector Issues*. New York: United Nations.

Fawcett, L. and Hurrell, A. (eds) (1994) *Regionalism in World Politics*. Oxford: Oxford University Press.

Finlayson, J. A. and Weston, A. (1990) *The GATT, Middle Powers and the Uruguay Round*. Ottawa: North–South Institute.

Food and Agriculture Organisation (1993) *1993 Country Tables, Basic Data on the Agricultural Sector*. Rome: United Nations.

Frieden, J. (1991) Invested interests: the politics of national economic policies in a world of global finance. *International Organization* 45(4), 425–451.

Frohlich, N. Oppenheimer, J. A., and Young, O. R. (1971) *Political Leadership and Collective Goods*. Princeton, NJ: Princeton University Press.

Frost, F. (1990) Introduction: ASEAN since 1968. In *ASEAN into the 1990s*, ed. A. Broinowski. Basingstoke: Macmillan.

Gamson, W. (1964) Experimental studies of coalition formation. In *Advances in Experimental Social Psychology*, ed. L. Berkowitz. New York: Academic Press.

GATT/WTO Records, GATT Secretariat Minutes of meetings on Services and analytical summaries, 1985–1986 – MDF/6, Minutes of 24 January 1985; MDF/10, Minutes of 1–2 April, 1985; MDF/15, Minutes of 7 June 1985; MDF/17, Summary of information made available by relevant international organizations, 16 September 1985; MDF/20, Minutes of 18 September, 1985; MDF/W/58, Summary Table of Issues Raised in the Exchange of Information on Services, 26 November 1985.

——, PREP.COM (86) W/41, Draft Ministerial Declaration from the Permanent Delegation of Brazil, circulated by Argentina, Brazil, Cuba, Egypt, India, Nicaragua, Nigeria, Peru, Tanzania, Yugoslavia, 23 June 1986.

——, PREP.COM (86) W/41/Rev. 1, 16 July, 1986.

——, PREP.COM (86) W/41/Rev. 1/Add.1, 22 July 1986.

——, PREP.COM (86) W/47, Draft Ministerial Declaration from the delegations of Colombia and Switzerland, 17 July 1986.

——, PREP.COM (86) W/47/Rev.1, 28 July 1986.

——, PREP.COM (86) W/47/Rev. 2, 30 July 1986.

——, PREP.COM (86) W/49, Draft Ministerial Declaration from Argentina as a proposed amendment to PREP.COM(86)W/47/Rev.1, 30 July 1986.

——, Report of the Chairman of the Meetings on Services, H.E. Mr. Felipe Jaramillo, Ambassador of Colombia, to the Session of CONTRACTING PARTIES at Ministerial Level, MIN (86)/4, 15 September, 1986, GATT.

——, MIN(86)/W/19, Draft Ministerial Declaration on the Uruguay Round, 20 September 1986.

GATT/WTO Records, Proposal to the GNS, MTN.GNS/W/95, Communication from Brazil, Chile, Colombia, Cuba, Honduras, Jamaica, Nicaragua, Mexico, Peru, Trinidad and Tobago and Uruguay, 26 February 1990.

——, Proposal to the GNS, MTN.GNS/W/101, Communication from Cameroon, China, Egypt, India, Kenya, Nigeria and Tanzania, 4 May 1990.

——, Communication from Argentina, Colombia, Cuba, Egypt, India, Mexico, Pakistan and Peru, Annex on Temporary Movement of Services Personnel, MTN.GNS/W/106, 18 June 1990.

——, Guidelines for Appointment of Officers to WTO bodies, approved by the General Council on 31 January, 1995, WT/L/31, 7 February 1995.

——, Singapore Ministerial Declaration, WT/MIN(96)/DEC, 18 December 1996.

——, Ministerial Conference, December 1996, Statement by H. E. Mr Mah Bow Tan, Minister for Communications, 96-5251, 11 December 1996. (http://www.wto.org/wto/archives/st60.htm – for statements by other countries, http://www/wto.org/wto/archives).

——, Geneva Ministerial Declaration, WT/MIN(98)/DEC/1, 25 May 1998.

——, Organisation of African Unity/African Economic Community, Joint Statement Circulated by Ministers of Trade, WT/MIN(98)/ST/72, 18 May 1998.

——, SAARC, Statement Circulated by the Commerce Ministers, WT/MIN(98)/ST/49, 18 May 1998.

——, Statement Circulated by ASEAN (as an Observer), WT/MIN(98)ST/108, 20 May 1998.

——, South Centre, Statement Circulated by Mr Branislav Gosovic (as an Observer), WT/MIN(98)/ST/20, 18 May 1998.

——, Common Market for Eastern and Southern Africa, Statement Circulated by the Honourable Enoch Kavindele, Chairman of the Council of Ministers (as an Observer), WT/MIN(98)ST/74, 18 May 1998.

——, WT/GC/W/137, General Council Discussion on the Follow-up to the High Level Meeting on Integrated Initiatives for Least Developed Countries' Trade Development, 14 and 16 December 1998, Communication from Egypt on behalf of the African Group at the Informal Intersessional General Council Meeting, 26 January 1999.

——, WT/GC/W/299, Technical Assistance, Communication on Behalf of the African Group from Kenya, 6 August 1999.

——, WT/GC/W/300, Interaction between Trade and Competition Policy, Communication from Kenya on behalf of the African Group, 6 August 1999.

——, WT/GC/W/301, Customs Valuation Agreement, Communication from Kenya on behalf of the African Group, 6 August 1999.

——, WT/GC/W/302, The TRIPS Agreement, Communication from Kenya on behalf of the African Group, 6 August 1999.

——, WT/GC/W/354, Implementation Issues to be addressed before Seattle, Communication from Cuba, Dominican Republic, Egypt, El Salvador, Honduras, India, Indonesia, Malaysia, Nigeria, Pakistan, Sri Lanka, Uganda, 11 October 1999.

——, WT/GC/W/355, Implementation Issues to be Addressed in the first year of Negotiations, Communication from Cuba, Dominican Republic, Egypt, El Salvador, Honduras, India, Indonesia, Malaysia, Nigeria, Pakistan, Sri Lanka, and Uganda, 11 October 1999.

——, WT/GC/W/334, Transparency in Food Aid, Communication from MERCOSUL (with Chile WT/GC/W/334/Add. 1), 23 September 1999.

——, WT/GC/W/335, Tariff rate Quotas, Communication from MERCOSUL (with Chile WT/GC/W/335/Add. 1), 23 September 1999.

GATT/WTO Records, WT/GC/W/336, Special Safeguards, Communication from MERCOSUL (with Chile WT/GC/W/336/Add. 1), 23 September 1999.

——, WT/GC/W/337, State Trade Enterprises, Communication from MERCOSUL (with Chile in WT/GC/W/337/Add. 1), 23 September 1999.

——, WT/GC/W/444, Proposal for the Establishment of a Working Group for the Study of the Inter-Relationship between Trade and Finance, Communication from Cuba, Dominican Republic, Honduras, India, Indonesia, Kenya, Malaysia, Pakistan, Sri Lanka, Tanzania, Uganda and Zimbabwe, 18 September 2001.

——, WT/GC/W/445, Proposal for the establishment of a Working Group for the Study of the Inter-Relationship between Trade and Debt, Communication from Cuba, Dominican Republic, Honduras, India, Indonesia, Kenya, Malaysia, Pakistan, Sri Lanka, Tanzania, Uganda, Zimbabwe, 18 September 2001.

——, WT/L/423, Organization of African Unity/African Economic Community, Fourth Ordinary Session of the Committee on Trade, Customs and Immigration, 19–23 September 2001, Abuja, Nigeria, Communication from Zimbabwe, 18 October 2001.

——, WT/GC/W/361, Proposals for addressing the concerns on Marginalisation of Certain Small Economies 1, Communication from Barbados, Dominica, Fiji, Grenada, Jamaica, Lesotho, Mauritius, Papua New Guinea, Solomon Islands, St Lucia, Trinidad, and Tobago, 12 October 1998.

——, WT/GC/W/208, Agreement On TRIPS: Proposal Regarding Extension of Protection of Geographical Indications under paragraph 9(a)(i) of the Geneva Ministerial Declaration, Communication from Cuba, Dominican Republic, Egypt, Honduras, India, Indonesia, Nicaragua, and Pakistan, 17 June 1999.

——, WT/GC/W/251, The Challenge of Integrating LDCs into the Multilateral Trading System, Coordinating Workshop for Senior Advisers to Ministers of Trade in LDCs in Preparation for the Third WTO Ministerial Conference, Sun City, South Africa, 21–25 June 1999, 13 July 1999.

——, S/CSS/W/2, Communication from MERCOSUR members, Elements of a Proposed First Phase of the Services Negotiations Mandated Under GATS Article XIX, 14 April 2000.

——, G/AG/NG/W/12, WTO Negotiations on Agriculture: Market Access, A Negotiating Proposal by Canada, 9 June 2000.

——, G/AG/NG/W/13, Agreement on Agriculture: Special and Differential Treatment and a Development Box, Proposal to the June 2000 Special Session of the Committee on Agriculture by Cuba, Dominican Republic, Honduras, Pakistan, Haiti, Nicaragua, Kenya Uganda, Zimbabwe, Sri Lanka, and El Salvador, 23 June 2000.

——, G/AG/NG/W/37, Market Access, Submission by Cuba, Dominican Republic, El Salvador, Honduras, Kenya, India, Nigeria, Pakistan, Sri Lanka, Uganda, Zimbabwe, 28 September 2000.

——, S/CSS/W/13, Elements for Negotiating Guidelines and Procedures, 24 November 2000.

——, G/AG/NG/W54, Cairns Group Negotiating Proposal, Market Access, 10 November 2000.

——, G/AG/NG/W/11, Cairns Group Negotiating Proposal, Export Competition, 16 June 2000.

——, G/AG/NG/W/35, Cairns Group Negotiating Proposal, Domestic Support, 22 September 2000.

——, G/AG/NG/W/139, Export Credits for Agricultural Products, Proposal by MERCOSUR, Bolivia, Chile, Costa Rica, Guatemala, India, and Malaysia, 21 March 2001.

GATT/WTO Records, IP/C/W/296, TRIPS and Public Health, Submission by the African Group, Barbados, Bolivia, Brazil, Cuba, Dominican Republic, Ecuador, Honduras, India, Indonesia, Jamaica, Pakistan, Paraguay, Philippines, Peru, Sri Lanka, Thailand, and Venezuela, 29 June 2001.

——, G/AG/NG/W/100, WTO Negotiations on Agriculture – Market Access, Negotiating Proposal on behalf of the CARICOM, 15 July 2001.

——, WT/GC/W/441, Issues of Concern to Small Economies, Communication from Antigua and Barbuda, Barbados, Dominica, Dominican Republic, Fiji Islands, Grenada, Haiti, Jamaica, Maldives, Mauritius, Papua New Guinea, St Kitts and Nevis, St Lucia, St Vincent and the Grenadines, Solomon Islands, Trinidad and Tobago, 6 August 2001.

——, WT/GC/W/442, Proposal for a Framework Agreement on Special and Differential Treatment, Communication from Cuba, Dominican Republic, Honduras, India, Indonesia, Kenya, Malaysia, Pakistan, Sri Lanka, Tanzania, Uganda, and Zimbabwe, 19 September 2001.

——, WT/GC/W/443, Proposal for the Establishment of a Working Group for the Study of the Inter-Relationship between Trade and Transfer of Technology, Communication from Cuba, Dominican Republic, Honduras, India, Indonesia, Kenya, Malaysia, Pakistan, Sri Lanka, Tanzania, Uganda and Zimbabwe, 19 September 2001.

——, WT/L/430, ACP Declaration on the Fourth Ministerial Conference, Brussels, 5–6 November, Communication from Kenya, 9 November 2001.

——, WT/MIN(01)/DEC/1, Doha Ministerial Declaration, 20 November 2001.

——, WT/MIN(01)/17, Implementation-Related Issues and Concerns, 20 November 2001.

——, Special Session of the Committee on Agriculture, Informal Meeting, 4–6 February 2002, The Development Box, Non-paper by Cuba, Dominican Republic, El Salvador, Honduras, Kenya, Nigeria, Pakistan, Sri Lanka, and Zimbabwe.

Giarini, O. (1987) *The Emerging Service Economy*. Oxford: Pergamon, for the World Services Forum.

Gibbs, M. (1985) Continuing the international debate on services. *Journal of World Trade Law* 19(3), 199–218.

——and Mashayekhi, M. (1989) Elements of a multilateral framework of principles and rules for trade in services. In *Uruguay Round: Papers on Selected Issues*. New York: United Nations.

——and Mashayekhi, M. (1996) *Services: Unfinished Business and Built-In Future Agenda*, Third World Network, Seminar on the WTO and Developing Countries, Geneva, 10–11 September.

Gilpin, R. (1985) *The Political Economy of International Relations*. Princeton, NJ: Princeton University Press.

Goldstein, J. and Keohane, R. O. (eds) (1993) *Ideas and Foreign Policy*. Ithaca, NY: Cornell University Press.

Gosovic, B. (1972) *UNCTAD: Conflict and Compromise: The Third World's Quest for an Equitable World Economic Order through the United Nations*. Leiden, The Netherlands: A. W. Sijthoff.

Gowa, J. (1994) *Allies, Adversaries and International Trade*. Princeton, NJ: Princeton University Press.

Greenaway, D. and Winters, L. A. (1994) *Surveys in International Trade*. Oxford: Blackwell.

Grieco, J. (1988) Anarchy and the limits of cooperation: a realist critique of the newest liberal institutionalism. *International Organization* 42(3), 487–507.

Habeeb, W. M. (1988) *Power and Tactics in International Negotiations: How weak nations Bargain with Strong Nations*. Baltimore, MD: John Hopkins University Press.

Hall, P. A. (1989) *The Political Power of Economic Ideas: Keynsianism across Nations.* Princeton: Princeton University Press.

Hamilton, C. and Whalley, J. (1987) A view from the developed world. In *Dealing with the North: Developing Countries and the Global Trading System*, ed. J. Whalley. CSIER Research Monograph, Centre for the Study of International Economic Relations, London, Ontario: University of Western Ontario.

——(1989) Coalitions in the Uruguay Round. *Weltwirtschaftliches Archiv* 125(3), 547–556.

Hampson, F. O. and Hart, M. *Multilateral Negotiations: Lessons from Arms Control, Trade and the Environment.* Baltimore, MD: John Hopkins University Press.

Hansen, R. D. (1979) *The North–South Stalemate.* New York: McGraw Hill.

Hart, M. (1995) The GATT Uruguay Round, 1986–1993: the setting and the players. *Multilateral Negotiations: Lessons from Arms Control, Trade and the Environment*, eds F. O. Hampson and M. Hart. Baltimore, MD: John Hopkins University Press.

Hartcher, P. (1997) Why Soros may be Mahathir's red herring. *Australian Financial Review*, August 26.

Helleiner, G. K. (ed.) (1976) *A World Divided: The Less Developed Countries in the International Economy.* Cambridge: Cambridge University Press.

Heydon, K. (1990) Developing country perspectives. In *The Uruguay Round: Services in the World Economy*, eds P. A. Messerlin and K. P. Sauvant. Washington, DC and New York: World Bank and the United Nations Centre on Transnational Corporations.

Higgott, R. A. and Cooper, A. F. (1990) Middle power leadership and coalition building: Australia, the Cairns Group and the Uruguay Round of trade negotiations. *International Organization* 44(4), 589–632.

Hilf, M., Jacobs, F. G., and Peterson, E.-U. (1986) *The European Community and the GATT, Studies in Transnational Economic Law.* Deventer, The Netherlands: Kluwer.

Hinckley, B. (1979) Twenty-one variables beyond the size of the winning coalitions. *Journal of Politics* 41(1), 192–212.

——(1981) *Coalitions and Politics.* New York: Harcourt Brace Jovanovich.

Hindley, B. (1988) Service sector protection: considerations for developing countries. *World Bank Economic Review* 2, 205–223.

Hoekman, B. M. (1988) *The Uruguay Round Negotiations: Investigating the Scope for Agreement on Safeguards, Services and Agriculture*, Unpublished PhD thesis, University of Michigan Ann Arbor, MI.

——(1992) *Conceptual and Political Economy Issues in Liberalizing International Transactions in Services, Discussion Paper No. 666*, June. London: Centre for Economic Policy Research.

——(1993) *Developing Countries and the Uruguay Round Negotiations on Services, Discussion Paper No. 822*, October. London: Centre for Economic Policy Research.

——(1996) Assessing the General Agreemment on Trade in Services. In *The Uruguay Round and the Developing Countries*, eds W. Martin and A. Winters. Cambridge: Cambridge University Press.

——and Kostecki, M. (2001) *The Political Economy of the World Trading System: From GATT to WTO*, 2nd edition. Oxford: Oxford University Press.

——and Sauvé, P. *Liberalising Trade in Services, World Bank Discussion Papers 243*. Washington, DC: International Bank for Reconstruction and Development/World Bank.

Hopkins, R. F. (1990) Developing countries in the Uruguay Round: bargaining under uncertainty and inequality. In *World Agriculture and the GATT*, ed. W. P. Avery. Boulder, CO: Lynne Rienner.

Hurrell, A. (1994) Regionalism in theoretical perspective. In *Regionalism in World Politics*, eds L. Fawcett and A. Hurrell. Oxford: Oxford University Press.

Hurrell, A. (1998) *Coercive Socialization or Progressive Enmeshment? Understanding Policy Change in Brazil, 1985–95*, Unpublished paper.

——(forthcoming) Power, institutions and the production of inequality. In *Power and Global Governance*, eds M. Barnett and R. Duvall.

Ingersent, K. A., Rayner, A. J., and Hine, R. C. (eds) (1994) *Agriculture in the Uruguay Round*. New York: St Martin's Press.

Instituto de Relaciones Europeo-Latinoamericanas (1993) *Integration and Cooperation in Latin America: New Concepts, Multiple Efforts, Dossier No. 44*, March. Madrid: Instituto de Relaciones Europeo-Latinoamericanas.

Jackson, R. (1990) *Quasi-States: Sovereignty, International Relations and the Third World*. Cambridge: Cambridge University Press.

Johnson, D. G., Hemmi, K., and Lardinois, P. (1985) *Agricultural Policy and Trade: Adjusting Domestic Programs in an International Framework – A Report to the Trilateral Commission*. New York: New York University Press.

Kakabadse, M. A. (1987) *International Trade in Services: Prospects for Liberalisation in the 1990s, Atlantic Paper No. 64*. London: Crook Helm, for the Atlantic Institute for International Affairs.

Katzenstein, P. (ed.) (1996) *The Culture of National Security: Norms and Identity in World Politics*. New York: Columbia University Press.

Khong, Y. F. (1997) ASEAN and the Southeast Asian Security Complex. In *Regional Orders: Building Security in a New World*, eds D. Lake and P. Morgan. University Park, PA: Pennsylvania State University Press.

Khor, M. (1997) The WTO and the South: implications and recent developments, May, http://www.twnside.org.sg/title/pli-cn.htm

Kihwan, K. and Soo, C. H. (1980) Korea's domestic trade politics and the Uruguay Round. In *Domestic Trade Politics and the Uruguay Round*, ed. H. R. Nau. New York: Columbia University Press.

Kng, C. M., Low, L., and Heng, T. M. (1988) Trade policy options for Singapore. In *ASEAN Trade Policy Options*, eds, M. Ariff and T. Loong-Hoe. Singapore: ASEAN Economic Research Unit, Institute of Southeast Asian Studies.

Kock, K. (1969) *International Trade Policy and the GATT, 1945–47*. Stockholm: Almqvist Wiskell.

Krasner, S. D. (1985) *Structural Conflict: The Third World Against Global Liberalism*. Berkeley, CA: University of California Press.

Krueger, A. O. and Michalopoulos, C. (1985) Developing-country trade polices and the international system. In *Hard Bargaining Ahead*, ed. E. H. Preeg. New Brunswick, NJ: Transaction Books.

Krugman, P. G. and Obstfeld, M. (1997) *International Economics: Theory and Practice*. Reading, MA: Addison Wesley.

Kumar, R. (1988) The coordination problem. In *Towards Regional Cooperation in South Asia, ADB/EWC Symposium on Regional Cooperation in South Asia, 9–11 March 1987, Manila*. Manila: Asian Development Bank.

——(1995a) Developing-country coalitions in international trade negotiations. In *The Developing Countries in World Trade*, eds, D. Tussie and D. Glover. Boulder, CO: Lynne Rienner.

——(1995b) The walk away from leadership: India. In *The Developing Countries in World Trade*, eds, D. Tussie and D. Glover. Boulder, CO: Lynne Rienner.

Lake, D. and Morgan, P. (eds) (1997) *Regional Orders: Building Security in a New World*. University Park, PA: Pennsylvania State University Press.

Lall, S. (1984) Exports of technology by newly industrializing countries: an overview. *World Development* 12(5/6), 471–480.

——(1986) Comparative advantage in trade in services. In *Theory and Reality in Development: Essays in Honour of Paul Streeten*, eds S. Lall and F. Stewart. London: Macmillan.

Lapid, Y. and Kratochwil, F. (eds) (1996) *The Return of Culture and Identity in IR Theory, Critical Perspectives on World Politics*. Boulder, CO: Lynne Rienner.

Lauren, P. G. (ed.) (1979) *Diplomacy: New Approaches in History, Theory and Policy*. New York: Free Press, Macmillan.

Lee, C. H. (1990) East Asian Countries. In *The Uruguay Round: Services in the World Economy*, eds P. A. Messerlin and K. P. Sauvant. Washington, DC and New York: World Bank and the United Nations Centre on Transnational Corporations.

Liska, G. (1968) *Nations in Alliance: The Limits of Interdependence*. Baltimore, MD: John Hopkins Press.

Luke, D. F. (2000) OAU/AEC member states, the Seattle preparatory process and Seattle: a personal reflection. *Journal of World Trade* 34(3), 39–46.

McDonald, A. L. (2000) Organisation and management of a complex, international, economic negotiation, Tokyo Round: multilateral trade negotiations. *World Economy* 23(2), 199–220.

McIntyre, A. (2000) CARICOM and the WTO. *Social and Economic Studies* 49(1), 83–112.

Mallampally, P. (1990) Professional services. In *The Uruguay Round: Services in the World Economy*, eds P. A. Messerlin and K. P. Sauvant. Washington, DC and New York: World Bank and the United Nations Centre on Transnational Corporations.

Mark, J. and Helleiner, G. K. (1988) *Trade in Services: The Negotiating Concerns of the Developing Countries*. Ottawa: North–South Institute.

Martin, R. (1992) *Bargaining Power*. Oxford: Clarendon Press.

Martin, W. and Winters, A. (eds) (1996) *The Uruguay Round and the Developing Countries*. Cambridge: Cambridge University Press.

Mearsheimer, J. J. (1995) The false promise of international institutions. *International Security* 19(3), 5–49.

Medhora, R. (1997) *Emerging Issues in International Trade Relations: Some Research Directions*. IDRC: Research Programs: TEC, http://www.idrc.ca/tec.emerging.html

Mendoza, M. R. (1989) Latin America and the negotiations on trade in services. In *Uruguay Round: Papers on Selected Issues*. New York: United Nations.

Messerlin, P. A. and Sauvant, K. P. (eds) (1990) *The Uruguay Round: Services in the World Economy*. Washington, DC and New York: World Bank and the United Nations Centre on Transnational Corporations.

Michalopoulos, C. (1998) *Developing Countries' Participation in the World Trade Organisation, Policy Research Working Paper, 1906*. Washington, DC: World Bank, in collaboration with the WTO.

Milner, H. (1992) International theories of cooperation among nations: strengths and weaknesses. *World Politics* 43(3), 466–496.

Mortimer, R. A. (1984) *The Third World Coalition in International Politics*. Boulder, CO: Westview.

Narlikar, A. (2001) *WTO Decision-Making and Developing Countries, T.R.A.D.E Working Paper, No. 11*. Geneva: South Centre.

——(2002) The politics of participation: decision-making procedures and developing countries in the WTO. *The Round Table: Commonwealth Journal of International Affairs* 364, April, 171–185.

Nau, H. R. (ed.) (1980) *Domestic Trade Politics and the Uruguay Round*. New York: Columbia University Press.

Neuman, S. G. (ed.) (1998a) International relations theory and the Third World: an oxymoron? In *International Relations Theory and the Third World*. London: Macmillan.

——(ed.) (1998b) *International Relations Theory and the Third World*. London: Macmillan.

Niou, E. M. S. and Ordershook, P. C. (1994) Alliances in anarchic international systems. *International Studies Quarterly* 38(2), 167–191.

Odell, J. (2000) *Negotiating the World Economy*. Ithaca, NY: Cornell University Press.

Olson, M. (1965) *The Logic of Collective Action: Public Goods and the Theory of Groups*. Cambridge, MA: Harvard University Press.

Organisation for Economic Cooperation and Development (OECD) (1989) *Trade in Services and Developing Countries*. Paris: OECD.

Oxley, A. (1990) *The Challenge of Free Trade*. New York: Harvester Wheatsheaf.

Pratt, C. (1990) *Middle Power Internationalism – the North South Dimension*. Kingston, UK: McGill-Queen's University Press.

Preeg, E. H. (ed.) (1985) *Hard Bargaining Ahead: US Trade Policy and Developing Countries*. New Brunswick, NJ: Transaction Books.

——(1995) *Traders in a Brave New World: The Uruguay Round and the Future of the International Trading System*. Chicago: Chicago University Press.

——(1998) *From Here to Free Trade*. Chicago: Chicago University Press.

Raghavan, C. (1990) *Recolonization: GATT, the Uruguay Round and the Third World*. London: Zed.

Report of the Group of Fourteen on ASEAN Economic Cooperation and Integration (1987) *ASEAN: The Way Forward*. Kuala Lumpur, Malaysia: Institute of Strategic and International Studies.

Ricupero, R. (1998) Integration of developing countries into the multilateral trading system. In *The Uruguay Round and Beyond: Essays in Honour of Arthur Dunkel*, Studies in International Economics, eds J. Bhagwati and M. Hirsch. Ann Arbor, MI: University of Michigan Press.

Riddle, D. (1986) *Service-led Growth: The Role of the Service Sector in World Development*. New York: Praeger.

——(1987) The role of the service sector in economic development: similarites and differences by development category. In *The Emerging Service Economy*, ed. O. Gavini. Oxford: Pergamon.

Riker, W. (1962) *The Theory of Political Coalitions*. New Haven: Yale University Press.

Risse-Kappen, T. (1995) Collective identity in a democratic community: the case of NATO. In *The Culture of National Security: Norms and Identity in World Politics*, ed. P. J. Katzenstein. New York: Columbia University Press.

Rogowski, R. (1989) *Commerce and Coalitions*. Princeton, NJ: Princeton University Press.

Rothstein, R. (1979) *Global Bargaining: UNCTAD and the Quest for a New International Economic Order*. Princeton, NJ: Princeton University Press.

——(1982) The North–South dialogue: the political economy of immobility. In *The Foreign Policy Priorities of Third World States*, ed. J. J. Stremlau. Boulder, CO: Westview Special Studies in International Relations.

Samuelson, P. A. and Nordhaus, W. D. (1989) *Economics*, 13th edition. New York: McGraw Hill.

Sandler, T. and Tschirhart, J. T. (1980) The economic theory of clubs: an evaluative survey. *Journal of Economic Literature* 18(4), 1481–1521.

Sapir, A. (1982) Trade in services: polity issues for the eighties. *Colombia Journal of World Business* 17(3), 77–83.

Sapir, A. (1985) North South issues in trade in services. *World Economy* 8(1), 27–42.

—— and Winter, C. (1994) Services trade. In *Surveys in International Trade*, eds D. Greenaway and L. A. Winters. Oxford: Blackwell.

Sauvé, P. (1995) Assessing the General Agreement on Trade in Services – Half-full or half-empty. *Journal of World Trade* 29(4), 125–145.

Schelling, T. (1966) *Arms and Influence*. New Haven, CT: Yale University Press, 1966.

Schweller, R. (1994) Bandwagoning for profit: bringing the revisionist state back in. *International Security* 19(1), 72–107.

Sen, A. K. (1986) Rationality, interest and identity. In *Development, Democracy and the Art of Trespassing: Essays in Honour of Albert O. Hirschman*, eds A. Foxley, M. S. McPherson and G. O' Donnell. Notre Dame, IN: University of Notre Dame, 1986.

Sengupta, N. (1989) India's Advertising Services and International Competitiveness. In *Services and Development Potential: the Indian Context*. New York: United Nations.

Shukla, S. P. (1994) The emerging international trading order. In *World Economy in Transition: An Indian Perspective*, eds G. S. Bhalla and M. Agarwal. Delhi: Har-Anand, issued under the auspices of Indian Institute of Advanced Study, Simla.

Snyder, G. and Diesing, P. (1977) *Conflict Among Nations: Bargaining, Decision Making and System Structure in International Crises*. Princeton, NJ: Princeton University Press.

*Special United Nations Service (SUNS)* published everyday in Geneva and Rome, by the IFDA, in cooperation with IPS Third World News Agency (now called South–North Development Monitor).

Srivastava, S. (1989) Computer software and data processing: export potential. In *Services and the Development Potential: the Indian Context*. New York: United Nations.

Strange, S. (1994) *States and Markets*. London: Francis Pinter.

Stephenson, S. (1994), ASEAN and the multilateral trading system. *Law and Policy in International Business* 25(2), 439–448.

Stephenson, S. M. (1999) *Approaches to Liberalizing Services, Policy Research Working Paper, No. 2107*. Washington, DC: World Bank.

Stewart, F. (1976) The direction of international trade: gains and losses for the Third World. In *A World Divided: The Less Developed Countries in the International Economy*, ed. G. K. Helleiner. Cambridge: Cambridge University Press.

Stubbs, R. and Underhill, G. R. D. (eds) (1994) *Political Economy and the Changing Global Order*. Basingstoke, UK: Macmillan.

Toye, J. (1987) *Dilemmas of Development: Reflections on the Counter Revolution in Development Theory and Policy*. Oxford: Blackwell.

Tussie, D. (1987) *The Less Developed Countries and the World Trading System: A Challenge to the GATT, Studies in International Political Economy*. London: Francis Pinter.

——(1995) Holding the balance: the Cairns Group in the Uruguay Round. In *The Developing Countries in World Trade: Policies and Bargaining Strategies*, eds D. Tussie and D. Glover. Boulder, CO: Lynne Rienner.

—— and Glover, D. (eds) (1995) *The Developing Countries in World Trade: Policies and Bargaining Strategies*. Boulder, CO: Lynne Rienner.

Tyabji, A. (1990) The Six ASEAN economies: 1980–88. In *ASEAN into the 1990s*, ed. A. Broinowski. Basingstoke, UK: Macmillan.

Tyers, R. (1993) The Cairns Group and the Uruguay Round of International Trade Negotiations. *Australian Economic Review* 101(1), 49–60.

——(1994) The Cairns Group Perspective. In *Agriculture in the Uruguay Round*, eds K. A. Ingersent, A. J. Rayner, and R. C. Hine. New York: St Martin's Press.

Tyers, R. and Anderson, K. (1987) *Liberalising OECD agricultural policies in the Uruguay Round: Effects on Trade and Welfare, Working Paper in Trade and Development, 0816–5181, No. 87/10.* Canberra: Australian National University, Research School of Pacific Studies.

United Nations Conference on Trade and Development (UNCTAD), Geneva (1985) *Services and the Development Process,* TD/B/1008, Rev. 1. New York: United Nations.

——(1988) *Trade and Development Report, 1988,* UNCTAD. New York: United Nations.

——(1989a) *Services and Development Potential: The Indian Context,* Papers from the UNCTAD/ICRIER Seminar on the Role of Services in the Development Process: International Experience and its Relevance to India, UNCTAD/ITP/22. New York: United Nations.

——(1989b) *Trade in Services: Sector Issues,* UNCTAD/UNDP Projects of Technical Assistance to Developing Countries for Multilateral Trade Negotiations. New York: United Nations.

——(1989) *Uruguay Round: Papers on Selected Issues* UNCTAD/UNDP Projects of Technical Assistance to Developing Countries for Multilateral Trade Negotiations. New York: United Nations.

——(1990) *Handbook of International Trade and Development Statistics, 1989.* New York: United Nations.

——(1994) *The Outcome of the Uruguay Round: An Initial Assessment, Supporting Papers to the Trade and Development Report,* 1994, UNCTAD/TDR/14 – Supplement. New York: United Nations.

Walt, S. M. (1987) *The Origins of Alliances.* Ithaca, NY: Cornell University Press.

——(1997) Why alliances endure or collapse. *Survival* 39(1), 156–179.

Waltz, K. (1979) *Theory of International Politics.* New York: McGraw Hill.

Wang, Z. K. and Winters, L. A. (1997) *Africa's Role in Multilateral Trade Negotiations, World Bank Policy Research Working Paper, No. 1846.* Washington, DC: World Bank.

Watkins, K. *Fixing the Rules: North–South Issues in International Trade and the GATT Uruguay Round.* London: Catholic Institute for International Relations.

Wendt, A. (1994) collective identity formation and the international state. *American Political Science Review* 88(2), 384–396.

Weston, A. (2001) Reflections on the Doha Development Agenda, http://www.nsi-ins.ca/ensi/news_views/oped37.html, The North–South Institute, Ottawa, November.

Weston, B. A. (2002) *Implications of the Free Trade Area of the Americas,* address by Mr Bernard Anthony Weston, Director, International Trade and Economic Relations/CARICOM and Caribbean Affairs Division, American Chamber of Commerce of Trinidad and Tobago (AMCHAM), June Monthly Meeting, 13 June.

Whalley, J. (ed.) (1987) *Dealing with the North: Developing Countries in the World Trading System.* CSIER Research Monograph. London, Ontario: University of Western Ontario.

Whalley, J. (ed.) (1989) *Developing Countries and the Global Trading System: Vol. 1 and 2.* London: Macmillan.

Wilkinson, R. (2000) *Multilateralism and the World Trade Organisation: The Architecture and Extension of International Trade Regulation.* London: Routledge.

Williams, M. (1991) *Third World Cooperation: The Group of 77 in UNCTAD.* London: Francis Pinter.

——(1994) *International Economic Organisations and the Third World.* New York: Harvester Wheatsheaf.

Winham, G. (1990) GATT and the international trade regime. *International Journal* XLV(4), 796–822.

——(1998) The World Trade Organisation: institution-building in the multilateral trade system. *World Economy,* May, 21(3), 349–368.

Winters, L. A. (1998) Regionalism and the New Round. In *Launching New Global Trade Talks: An Action Agenda, Special Report 12*, ed. Jeffrey J. Schott. Washington: Institute for International Economics.

Wolf, M. (1984) Two edged sword: demands of developing countries and the trading system. In *Power, Passions and Purpose*, eds J. Bhagwati and J. Ruggie. Cambridge: MIT Press.

Woods, N. (1995) Economic ideas and international relations: beyond rational neglect. *International Studies Quarterly* 39, 161–180.

——and Narlikar, A. (2001) Governance and the limits of accountability: the WTO, the IMF and the World Bank. *International Social Science Journal* 53(170), 569–583.

*World Politics* (1985) Special Issue on International Cooperation 38(1).

Yeats, A. J. (1990), Maritime transport. In *The Uruguay Round: Services in the World Economy*, eds P. A. Messerlin and K. P. Sauvant. Washington, DC and New York: World Bank and the United Nations Centre on Transnational Corporations.

Zartman, I. W. (ed.) (1987) *Positive Sum: Improving North–South Negotiations*. New Brunswick, NJ: Transaction Books.

# Index